Psychological Trauma and Addiction Treatment

Psychological Trauma and Addiction Treatment has been co-published simultaneously as *Journal of Chemical Dependency Treatment*, Volume 8, Number 2 2006.

Psychological Trauma and Addiction Treatment

Bruce Carruth, PhD, LCSW
Editor

Psychological Trauma and Addiction Treatment has been co-published simultaneously as *Journal of Chemical Dependency Treatment*, Volume 8, Number 2 2006.

Routledge
Taylor & Francis Group
NEW YORK AND LONDON

Psychological Trauma and Addiction Treatment has been co-published simultaneously as *Journal of Chemical Dependency Treatment*™, Volume 8, Number 2 2006.

First edition published by The Haworth Press, Inc
10 Alice Street, Binghamton, NY 13904-1580 USA

This edition published 2011 by Routledge

Routledge
Taylor & Francis Group
711 Third Avenue
New York, NY 10017

Routledge
Taylor & Francis Group
27 Church Road, Hove
East Sussex BN3 2FA

Cover design by J.L. Grausgruber

Library of Congress Cataloging-in-Publication Data

Psychological Trauma and Addiction Treatment / Bruce Carruth, editor.
     p. cm
     "Co-published simultaneously as Journal of chemical dependency treatment, volume 8, number 2 2006."
     Includes bibliographical references and index.
     ISBN-10: 0-7890-3189-2 (hard cover : alk.paper)
     ISBN-13: 978-0-7890-3189-1 (hard cover : alk.paper)
     ISBN-10: 0-7890-3190-6 (soft cover : alk.paper)
     ISBN-13: 978-0-7890-3190-7 (soft cover : alk.paper)
     1. Psychic trauma. 2. Substance abuse. 3. Self-destructive behavior. I. Carruth, Bruce. II. Series.
     [DNLM: 1. Stress Disorders, Traumatic–complications. 2. Substance-Related Disorders– complications. 3. Stress Disorders, Traumatic–therapy. 4. Substance-Related Disorders–therapy. W1 JO58L v.8 no.2 2006 / WM 270 P9732 2006]
RC552.T7P759 2006
616.85′21–dc22

                                      2006010871

Psychological Trauma and Addiction Treatment

CONTENTS

ABOUT THE EDITOR

Bruce Carruth, PhD, LCSW, lives and practices in San Miguel de Allende, GTO, Mexico. For the last 25 years he has specialized in treating chemically-dependent individuals and couples, people with a variety of trauma syndromes and individuals struggling with characterological injuries. He has led over 600 workshops on these topics throughout North and Central America and Europe. He is Senior Editor, Chemical Dependency Treatment publications, for The Haworth Press, Inc. Dr. Carruth is also founding editor of *Alcoholism Treatment Quarterly* and *Journal of Chemical Dependency Treatment*. He has held faculty appointments at the University of Arkansas and Rutgers University and has received numerous awards for his work as a clinician, teacher and researcher.

About the Contributors

Patricia A. Burke, MSW, has been on the faculty of Rutgers University Summer School of Alcohol and Drug Studies since 1989 and is currently on the faculty of Brown University Center of Alcohol Studies, Addiction Technology Transfer Center. She maintains a private clinical and consulting practice in West Baldwin, Maine, where she specializes in trauma and addiction treatment.

Bruce Carruth, PhD, LCSW, lives and practices in San Miguel de Allende, GTO, Mexico. He is Senior Editor for Chemical Dependency Publications for The Haworth Press, New York and is on the faculty of Rutgers and numerous other schools of alcohol and drug studies.

Joan M. Cook, PhD, is Assistant Professor of Psychology in Psychiatry at Columbia University School of Medicine. She has numerous publications in geropsychology and traumatic stress fields including research on the effects of traumatic stress on older adults.

Barbara Davis, MFS, MSW, LCSW, is a psychotherapist in private practice in South Orange, New Jersey and a part-time faculty member of the Graduate School of Social Work, Rutgers University. She is a candidate at the Institute of Psychoanalysis and Psychotherapy in New Jersey and has served as the Executive Director of a halfway house for women with co-occurring addictive and mental health disorders.

Ronald Potter-Efron, MSW, PhD, is a clinical psychotherapist in private practice in Eau Claire, Wisconsin, and the author of the *Handbook of Anger Management* and many other books on anger, shame and addictions.

Joyce Fowler, PhD, is a clinical psychologist in private practice in Little Rock, Arkansas. She has an extensive background in addictions treatment and specialized training in Health Psychology and neuropsychology.

Lisa M. Najavits, PhD, is a research psychologist, National Center for PTSD, Woman's Health Sciences Division, VA Boston Healthcare System and is Associate Clinical Professor in Psychiatry, Harvard Medical School, Boston, Massachusetts.

Casey O'Donnell, MA, is currently finishing his doctoral internship in clinical psychology. His publications and current research interests are in the field of traumatic stress.

John Omaha, PhD, created affect centered therapy and the affect management skills protocol. He founded the Institute for Affect Centered Therapy. He is author of *Psychotherapeutic Interventions for Emotion Regulation* and has conducted workshops throughout the U.S., Europe, and Australia.

David Prichard, PhD, is Professor of Social Work in the Graduate Program of Social Work at the University of New England, Portland, Maine. He is coordinator of the school's Addictions Counseling Certificate Program and teaches advanced trauma-based practice, death and dying in psychopharmacology. He has a private psychotherapy and consulting practice in Maine.

Carol J. Ross, MA, CADAC, ICRC, is a licensed professional counselor in private practice and at Sierra Tucson, where she has been employed since 1989. She was one of the designers of Sierra Tucson's Program for Sexual and Trauma Resolution and has published articles on sexual abuse, sexual compulsivity, trauma and addictions. She is a past board member of the Society for the Advancement of Sexual Health.

John M. Schibik, PhD, LPC, LCADC, holds a Masters in Counseling Psychology, a Masters in Systematic Theology and a Doctorate in Social Work. He had a private counseling, consulting, coaching and training service in New Jersey for 20 years and now practices in Naples, Florida. He has taught at Rutgers Summer Schools of Alcohol and Drug Studies since 1989.

Steven V. Schneider, PhD, CADC III, is on the faculty of the Harold Abel School of Psychology, Capella University. He consults to area universities in the Milwaukee, Wisconsin area. His special interests are developmental disabilities, hypnosis, psychological testing and addictive/compulsive behavior.

E. Hitchcock Scott, PhD, NCC, LISAC, ATR, REAT, is a primary therapist for Sierra Tucson in the program for sexual and trauma recovery. She is a diplomat addictions therapist and a registered art therapist with 20 years of professional experience with trauma victims. Her research includes an exploration of self-mutilation by dissociative disordered patients.

Chelly Sterman, LCSW, LCADC, NLP Level II, EMDR Level II, has been in private practice in Central New Jersey for 25 years. The focus of her practice has been on trauma and addicted survivors of sexual abuse. She has written and lectured widely on these topics.

Jody Yeary, PhD, is a consultant, lecturer and psychotherapist in private practice in San Francisco who has worked in the field of substance dependence for 30 years. She uses a family of origin model integrating systems with somatic recovery.

Joan E. Zweben, PhD, is a clinical psychologist with over 35 years experience treating addiction and training treatment practitioners. She is the Executive Director of The 14th Street Clinic and East Bay Community Recovery Project, and is Clinical Professor of Psychiatry at the University of California, San Francisco.

Preface

Psychological trauma is the most common complicating factor in treatment and recovery from addictive disorders and can seriously impede personal, interpersonal and spiritual growth in recovery. People who might otherwise blossom in treatment become our treatment failures. Clients resist engaging in treatment of both disorders simultaneously because of misinformation gained in treatment and self-help settings. Perhaps most pervasively, individuals treated for addictive disorders, but not treated for their trauma reactions, reach a point in recovery and don't continue to grow. They maintain abstinence, but are never able to overcome the psychological and interpersonal effects of trauma. They become, in effect, our walking wounded.

In recent years there has been an increasing interest in co-occurring disorders in general and, more specifically, in co-occurring trauma and addictive illnesses. Clinicians who address the needs of trauma survivors seem much more open today to confronting the co-occurring problems of addiction, other compulsive behaviors, depression, anxiety disorders, sexual dysfunctions, and relational problems experienced by trauma survivors as well as the direct sequela of trauma wounds. Counselors and therapists working in addictions treatment settings likewise appear more knowledgeable and skilled in treating co-occurring disorders commonly seen in addicted clients. The "folk wisdom" that if people get sober they will see a remission of symptoms of other disorders, that concurrent treatment of co-occurring disorders will interfere with addictions recovery and that addressing symptoms of other disorders invites the client to continue to be "in denial" of their addictive illness are no longer as prevalent in clinical settings. This misinformation is being

[Haworth co-indexing entry note]: "Preface." Carruth, Bruce. Co-published simultaneously in *Journal of Chemical Dependency Treatment* (The Haworth Press, Inc.) Vol. 8, No. 2, 2006, pp. xxi-xxii; and: *Psychological Trauma and Addiction Treatment* (ed: Bruce Carruth) The Haworth Press, Inc., 2006, pp. xix-xx. Single or multiple copies of this article are available for a fee from The Haworth Document Delivery Service [1-800-HAWORTH, 9:00 a.m. - 5:00 p.m. (EST). E-mail address: docdelivery@haworthpress.com].

replaced by new knowledge, increased understanding, and perhaps most importantly, greater compassion for trauma disordered people in addiction treatment settings.

This volume synthesizes and integrates the expanding body of knowledge to specifically address the needs of clinicians working in addiction treatment environments. But the information is also cogent and applicable to those working in other human services environments where people with co-occurring addictive disorders and psychological trauma are found. The ethical considerations, underlying theoretical constructs and methodological processes discussed in the following pages are valid across treatment settings.

The first section introduces ideas about the nature and primary symptoms of psychological trauma and some of the impacts and manifestations of trauma on chemically dependent people.

Chapters two through seven are surveys of different approaches to treatment. Included are all of the primary treatment frameworks currently practiced today in trauma treatment. Chapter eight is an overview of the psychoneurology of trauma and the implications of psychoneurology in addictions and trauma treatment. Chapter nine considers the implications of trauma in intensive early recovery treatment environments and correspondingly, chapter ten addresses the implications of trauma in self-help programs. The remaining chapters consider adjunctive therapies and the needs of special populations.

Finally, this is a book of hope. Every author in this text has a firm belief that people with co-occurring trauma and addiction *can* recover, *can* maintain quality relationships, *can* confront life's challenges as they arise and *can* be happy and fulfilled. We hope that you, the reader, can embrace this hope.

Bruce Carruth, PhD, LCSW

Psychological Trauma
and Addiction Treatment

Bruce Carruth, PhD, LCSW
Patricia A. Burke, MSW

SUMMARY. The interaction of psychological trauma and addiction has been noted for years, but only in the last decade has significant attention been focused on treating the two disorders concurrently. This chapter provides an overarching conceptual framework for understanding the nature of psychological trauma and its relationship to chemical dependency disorders and an introduction to the best thinking and practice in meeting the treatment needs of psychologically traumatized, chemically addicted people. *[Article copies available for a fee from The Haworth Document Delivery Service: 1-800-HAWORTH. E-mail address: <docdelivery@haworthpress.com> Website: <http://www.HaworthPress.com> © 2006 by The Haworth Press, Inc. All rights reserved.]*

KEYWORDS. Psychological trauma, addiction treatment, co-occurring disorders

INTRODUCTION

Psychological trauma, in its broadest sense, is a wound to one's self, one's personhood. Trauma impacts how people perceive their worlds, their thoughts, judgments and intuition, what feelings they allow them-

[Haworth co-indexing entry note]: "Psychological Trauma and Addiction Treatment." Carruth, Bruce, and Patricia A. Burke. Co-published simultaneously in *Journal of Chemical Dependency Treatment* (The Haworth Press, Inc.) Vol. 8, No. 2, 2006, pp. 1-14; and: *Psychological Trauma and Addiction Treatment* (ed: Bruce Carruth) The Haworth Press, Inc., 2006, pp. 1-14. Single or multiple copies of this article are available for a fee from The Haworth Document Delivery Service [1-800-HAWORTH, 9:00 a.m. - 5:00 p.m. (EST). E-mail address: docdelivery@haworthpress.com].

selves to have and what feelings they can't stop themselves from having. Perhaps most importantly, trauma impacts people's sense of who they are as unique individuals and their sense of soul–one's connection to something greater than the self. Trauma simultaneously causes hyper-arousal and emotional constriction. The strategies people develop to contain and manage these trauma reactions can ultimately develop into a disorder of control–being out of control and trying to be in control.

The interaction of psychological trauma and addiction has been noted for years, but only in the last decade has significant attention been focused on treating the two disorders concurrently. This chapter provides an overarching conceptual framework for understanding the nature of psychological trauma and its relationship to chemical dependency disorders and an introduction to the best thinking and practice in meeting the treatment needs of psychologically traumatized, chemically addicted people.

THE NATURE OF PSYCHOLOGICAL TRAUMA

Traumatic events injure a person's dignity and sense of integrity. People often feel damaged, incomplete, and less human as a result of the experience. At the same time, trauma challenges and alters people's beliefs about the world, their potency, benevolence, significance and worthiness and damages their ability to trust themselves and the environment. As a result, traumatized people are often more guarded and less willing to venture out and take risks. Trauma also distorts people's sense of time and timing. Time becomes defined by traumatic events and therefore, people's judgment about when to act is impaired, leaving them to react impulsively or hesitantly. Judith Herman (1992) has described psychological trauma as a process of withdrawal and disconnection. In withdrawing from the world, traumatized people lose connection to that which is meaningful . . . family, community, spiritual life. In addition, trauma can impair people's ability to rejuvenate and recuperate and as a result, they are more susceptible to the debilitating effects of subsequent traumatic events.

Finally, traumatic events can overwhelm people's adaptive responses and their sense of control, connection, and meaning. When overwhelmed, people tend to engage in a defensive strategy of disconnection that protects them from further threat, whether actual or perceived (Herman, 1992). Paradoxically, this process of disconnection actually limits opportunities for recovery. Reconnection to self, others, community, the environment, and a sense of that which is sacred is a key to full recovery. Recovery and treatment should focus on restoring connection in all areas where connection has been disrupted.

While psychological trauma is characterized by disruptions in a person's sense of control, addiction can also be viewed as a disorder of control, or more accurately, an inability to control. The loss of control is insidious, often unrecognized by the addict until, in Alcoholics Anonymous's terms, life becomes unmanageable. When a traumatized individual becomes addicted, or when an addicted person experiences trauma, the problem of control multiplies. People who are concurrently traumatized and addicted are particularly difficult to treat in traditional addiction settings where implicitly or explicitly clients are asked to give up control to the treatment program and other individuals. More often than not, the client ends up being blamed as uncooperative, not ready for treatment, obstructive or "in denial." Understanding the dynamic of control with people who are concurrently impacted by trauma and addiction is essential to successful treatment. The manifestations of this control dynamic along with approaches to treatment are clearly described by several authors in this text.

TRAUMATIC REACTIONS

Psychological trauma isn't the traumatic event itself. It is an experience characterized by an intense feeling of fear and helplessness. The traumatic event represents an outward manifestation of the inner experience of trauma. Trauma is sometimes described as "unspeakable," yet, traumatized people try to verbalize their inner experience by telling about the external events. The recollection of and retelling of the events become the vehicle by which traumatized people speak the unspeakable. The value of languaging one's experience, i.e., putting words to or naming it even though it cannot be fully described, is that it brings the inner experience into outward expression where it is possible to gain some perspective and place the traumatic events in the larger context of the totality of one's life.

Trauma reactions are truly individualistic. Some people may be significantly impaired by a relatively (in the eyes of others) inconsequential event, while other people move through devastating (in the eyes of others) events with little lasting impairment. As Peter Levine (1997) states, "It is important to remember that a traumatic reaction is valid regardless of how the event that induced it appears to anyone else" (pp.

49-50). Why some people are disabled by an event and others emerge relatively unscathed by the same or similar experience has to do with a person's resilience or ability to rebound, ego strengths, environmental supports, societal perceptions and timing. In diagnosis and treatment, then, it becomes important to understand the meaning of the event(s) to an individual and to address those meanings in the context of recovery.

While people can't change what has happened, the event, they can change their experience of the event. And that is what good trauma treatment does; it changes people's perception of what happened, who, if anyone, was at fault, what could have been done to prevent it, and, most important, what the experience means to that individual in the here and now.

A useful way of conceptualizing this process is to think about it from a relational perspective. We have a relationship with ourselves and a relationship with others; however, we also have a relationship to our own experiences. If I am engaged in a relationship with another person that is not satisfying or detrimental I cannot change the other person; however, I can explore the dysfunctional dynamics and work to change my own patterns of relating. The same is true regarding people's relationship to the traumatic events in their lives. We cannot change the traumatic event, but we can change our relationship to that experience. In this way it becomes possible to build mastery and enhance a felt sense of empowerment, both of which are disrupted by traumatic events, and thus mitigate some of the long-term psychological impact.

There are a number of aspects of this relational engagement with traumatic experiences that include cognitive/perceptual, sensate/physical, affective/emotional, and spiritual–that is, how we make meaning of our lives and place the meaning of trauma in the larger context of human experience. All of these aspects must be addressed in the treatment of psychological trauma.

THE IMPACT OF PSYCHOLOGICAL TRAUMA ON IDENTITY

Judith Herman (1992) also describes the multidimensional impact of trauma on identity. "Traumatic events call into question basic human relationships. They breach the attachments of family, friendship, love, and community. They shatter the construction of the self that is formed and sustained in relation to others. They undermine the belief systems that give meaning to human experience. They violate the victim's faith in a natural or divine order and cast the victim into a state of existential crisis" (p. 51).

The impact of trauma on identity depends, in part, on the age of the traumatized person, the chronicity of the events, and whether or not the trauma was of human origin. In the case of childhood trauma of human origin (e.g., sexual abuse, physical violence, or emotional abandonment or neglect) where the developing sense of self becomes organized around the breach of trust with the primary caretaker(s), there can be a terrible wounding to the child's sense of dignity and integrity. The child may struggle with a pervasive sense of shame which shapes an identity of being "damaged goods." In the case of chronic or single episodes of trauma of human origin in adulthood (e.g., domestic violence or rape), the individual's identity may become organized around a pervasive sense of powerlessness, guilt, and inadequacy. In the case of traumatic events of nonhuman origin (e.g., natural disasters) or events of human origin on a large scale (e.g., war, terrorism attacks, the holocaust), the individual's relationship to God or a sense of belonging to humanity may become altered and the impact on identity may take the shape of a spiritual crisis of faith and a disruption of worldview. The world may no longer be a safe place and faith no longer a safe harbor, where the individual can find comfort and make meaning of their suffering. Meaning and purpose may be lost and one's spiritual identity damaged. It is important to remember that while it is during childhood where identity development is most important, trauma in adulthood can also have a tremendous impact on a person's sense of integrity, trust, ade-quacy, and meaning. All of these disruptions to one's relationship to self, others, one's community, the world, and the divine must be addressed in treatment.

EXPERIENCING TRAUMATIC EVENTS

There are a number of variables which influence the way people experience traumatic events and thus, shape their relationship to those events. Some of those factors include the nature of the event itself, the reactions of others to the disclosure or witnessing of the traumatic event, the reaction of society, an individual's previous history with trauma, pre-trauma coping styles, and resilience.

With regard to the nature of the traumatic event, the element of sur-prise where people have no time to fight or flee or prepare psychologi-cally for the assault (e.g., World Trade Towers and Oklahoma City terrorist attacks and the Tsunami in Indonesia) can increase a person's vulnerability to the effects of the trauma. The blindsiding nature of traumatic events also means that it is more difficult to recover from their effects. Trauma survivors will often say: "If I had only known what was going to happen" to describe this blindsiding experience. One response to being caught unaware or unprotected is to become hypervigilant: a primary trauma syndrome symptom. This hypervigilance or hyperarousal then activates secondary effects such as misinterpretation of environmental stimuli, an inability to "let down" emotional armor, and overreaction to the perception of internal and external threats. In short, trauma exhausts the traumatized, and causes them to be unduly vigilant, suspicious and mistrustful. Research has shown that when it is possible to prepare for a stressful event, preparation increases a person's sense of control and actually helps train the autonomic system to respond more effectively to the stressor (Shalev, 1996), thus mitigating hyperarousal and hypervigilance.

In addition, the threat of death or violation of bodily integrity through violence (e.g., child sexual abuse or rape), the incomprehensible brutality of the abuser (e.g., torture), the frequency, repetition, chronicity of the events (e.g., ongoing child abuse), and a negative response toward the traumatized person by family (e.g., adults do not believe a child's disclosure of sexual abuse) or the culture (e.g., blaming the rape victim for being vulnerable to assault) all contribute to an increase in the severity of the impact on the traumatized person. You will often hear adult survivors of childhood abuse describe the reactions of family members to their disclosure as more traumatic than the events themselves. One adult survivor, a recovering alcoholic, talked about her experience of testifying in court at the age of eight against her uncle who had fondled her. She became overwhelmed with shame when the adults in the courtroom, including some family members, laughed at her child's way of describing his body. She reported that this courtroom experience was much more traumatic for her than her uncle's touch. The elements of the traumatic events described above represent risks to the individual in developing both psychological trauma symptoms and addiction problems.

In addition to the nature of the traumatic event itself, how others in the traumatized person's life and the society as a whole respond to trauma can have either a detrimental or ameliorating impact on how the traumatized person experiences the traumatic event, makes meaning of it, and negotiates the emotionally hazardous landscape of his/her relationship to the trauma. Because traumatic events create disconnections in relationships, the people closest to the traumatized person can lessen that experience of disconnection (and thereby ameliorate the influence of the traumatic events on a person's identity, meaning, and worldview) by responding in a supportive way, offering hope, comfort, a sense of safety, acceptance and compassion, and by helping the traumatized person realize that his/her reactions to the traumatic event are normal, not a personal failure. It is essential that the clinician provide a context in therapy within which the traumatized person can feel safe enough to be vulnerable, rebuild connection, and repair damage to his/her sense of self.

The hard work of rebuilding connection, unfortunately, must be done in a societal context that all too often blames victims for their vulnerability. Society also shuns victims because it does not want to believe that events like child abuse, incest, abandonment and rape happen and places too much emphasis on personal responsibility without considering the social context which shapes traumatized people's lives and identities. A recent example of this occurred in the aftermath of the devastating hurricanes on the Gulf Coast. While there were efforts to evacuate many people from the city of New Orleans, for example, and some chose to stay in their homes who could have left, there were many thousands of people living in poverty who had no means of evacuating. Some of the initial reactions to those stranded in their homes included blaming them for their own plight. "People had plenty of warning. They should have left." There was little consideration from some sectors of society for the trauma of poverty itself nor a willingness to accept some responsibility for the conditions of poverty which had a direct and negative impact on people's ability to prepare for, respond to, and recover from these natural disasters. The impact on those who are blamed for their own victimization is often a pervasive sense of being invisible and devalued.

Some of the psychological variables that impact how a person experiences and reacts or responds to traumatic events include a previous history of psychological trauma, the ability to make meaning of the events and integrate that meaning into a person's schema, the ability to negotiate emotional reactions to trauma, and pre-trauma coping skills and resilience. A previous history of unresolved trauma will make it more difficult for a person to negotiate the experience of current trauma. By nature of their developmental status, children lack the cognitive, emotional, physical, and spiritual (or meaning-making) skills necessary to cope with overwhelming experiences. This is why it is so important for children who have experienced traumatic events to receive adult help and support immediately. When this support is lacking or the adults in a child's life are the source of the trauma the child will develop his/her own strategies for coping that can include rigid ego defenses, compulsive behaviors which may be a precursor to addictive disorders, limited affective responsiveness, and a chronic sense of over-responsibility, guilt, and shame. While these strategies are essentially creative survival tools for a child, they may inhibit a child's psychological and emotional development and his/her ability later in life to have a fulfilling relational life.

Resilience is the most important psychological factor that can mitigate the negative long-term impact of traumatic events. It helps people develop and maintain a different relationship to their traumatic experiences. It differentiates people who are debilitated by traumatic events and those who are able to minimize the negative impact on their sense of self, their relationships, and their lives. Gina O'Connell Higgins (1994) defines psychological resilience as an active process of self-righting and growth that includes an ability to negotiate "emotionally hazardous experiences proactively rather than reactively" (p. 20) and an ability to make positive meanings out of experience. Higgins (1994) describes resilient people as those who demonstrate strong ego development and empathetic attunement, and possess internal resources such as creativity, imagination, an ability to envision a different future in spite of a traumatic past, and an ability to recruit and receive support from others (e.g., the abused child who seeks out "surrogate parents" in the form of a friend's parents, teachers, coaches, etc.). As noted later in this volume (Burke, 2006), resilience can act to buffer the stress reaction in traumatized people and that a strong sense of spirituality not only enhances and promotes resilience, but can prevent substance abuse and enhance long term recovery. Therefore, one of the most important aspects of the integrated treatment of psychological trauma and addictions may be to support traumatized people to explore their spirituality as a resource in recovery and help them discover and enhance those internal resources that describe resilience.

RECOGNIZING TRAUMA SYNDROMES

There is little consensus on how much trauma, how much impairment one must have before being diagnosed with a trauma syndrome. Many people with trauma syndromes are diagnosed with other psychiatric illnesses, such as depression and anxiety reactions. Often the manifestations of trauma syndromes are hidden behind substance abuse and other addictive behaviors. Finally, people with primary psychiatric disorders may assume their symptoms are a result of a trauma experience, when in fact, they are the result of another psychiatric illness. As a result, the science of trauma syndrome diagnosis is inexact and could benefit from further development.

The two most common DSM IV diagnoses used for trauma disorders are Acute Stress Reaction and Post Traumatic Stress Disorder. Both of these disorders are addressed in some detail in later chapters. But we also know that many people, severely limited by their trauma experiences, aren't necessarily a good "fit" for these diagnoses. Judith Herman (1992) used the term "Complex Post Traumatic Stress Disorder" to describe individuals for whom the trauma experience resulted in profound depersonalization. Individuals with profound and seemingly unresolvable grief become intrapsychically and interpersonally limited by their irascibility, perfectionism, obsessiveness, inappropriate interpersonal interactions and obsessiveness, but don't meet the standards for conventional psychiatric diagnoses.

Finally, many people with cumulative developmental trauma such as parental addiction, mental illness or incarceration, chronic physical illness or death of parent(s) certainly have residual impacts from the experience that limit options in adult life. Sometimes the trauma is more subtle, when a parent is consistently emotionally absent, too emotionally immature or too absorbed with their own dilemmas to experience and address the emotional needs of the child. Even when parents are emotionally attuned and available, dynamics such as pervasive poverty, a childhood physical disfigurement, an exceptionally rigid, chaotic or brutal subculture, familial or extrafamilial sexual abuse or other dynamics can cause the child to take a limiting psychoemotional adaptive life stance. Such life circumstances have a powerful impact on development of core psychological attributes such as hope, trust, competency, potency, integrity, self-soothing and empathy as well as limiting an individual's psychological development, self-esteem, attachment styles and psychosocial and interpersonal skills. While many people are significantly impacted by childhood adversities, it is the adaptive stance taken to manage the emotional and psychological response to overwhelming adversity that becomes, in adulthood, a limiting and defining part of personality. Some of the adaptations or coping strategies often seen include addiction, psychiatric symptomatology, overachieving and underachieving, lack of depth in relationships, compulsive behaviors and emotional rigidity. A hallmark of the limiting adaptive stance is that an individual can be highly successful in some arenas of life while being significantly impaired in others. This hallmark often differentiates people with limiting life resources from people with significant personality disorders.

TREATMENT APPROACHES

To the extent that psychological trauma has historically been addressed in addiction treatment settings, it has been relegated to a "wait until later" status. This approach has been congruent with a larger effort to prioritize treatment goals, beginning with preparing/mobilizing an individual for treatment, then building a foundation of abstinence and control of problem behaviors, then building strengths in sobriety and finally, working on "peripheral" issues such as marriage and other familial dynamics, psychological trauma, mental health, occupational issues and spiritual growth. Researchers and writers in the "dual diagnosis" movement of the late 1990s came to term this approach a "sequential pattern" of treatment (Mueser, Noordsy, Drake and Fox, 2003). Two findings began to challenge the assumptions underlying sequential treatment. First, particularly with the advent of interest in individuals with dual diagnoses, it became apparent that some people could not build a platform of abstinence, maintain control over problem behaviors and develop significant psychological strengths in recovery without concurrently addressing mental health and psychological trauma dynamics. Secondly, as efforts were initiated to address these issues earlier in the recovery process, it was learned that not only did clients not regress or fail in treatment, but they actually benefitted from earlier interventions. In short, researchers and clinicians began to challenge assumptions about the capabilities (or lack thereof) of clients to handle these issues earlier in recovery and concomitantly maintain sobriety.

Mueser, Noordsy, Drake and Fox (2003) cited additional problems with sequential treatment, including a recognition that the untreated disorder often worsens the treated disorder, making it impossible to stabilize one disorder without attending to the other and secondly, that it is more often than not unclear when one disorder has been successfully treated so that treatment of the other disorder can commence. As a result, one disorder goes untreated.

Still, even with the recognition that clients could benefit from earlier intervention for mental health and psychological trauma disorders, two problems appeared. First, addiction treatment has historically been provided in a distinct and separate treatment environment from mental health and psychological trauma services. As a result, clients had to enter multiple treatment programs designed to treat specific problems. Secondly, a pool of adequately trained and supervised clinicians did not exist who could treat multi-problem/dual-diagnosed people. As a result, multi-problem people had to have multiple therapists and counselors. From this dilemma grew a pattern of "parallel treatment," in effect, treating separate problems at the same time, but in different settings and/or with different counselors. There are obvious disadvantages of such an approach. Mueser, Noordsy, Drake and Fox (2003) point out: (1) that treatment providers and agencies often fail to communicate with each other; (2) that the burden of integrating treatment falls on the client; (3) that funding and eligibility barriers in accessing both treatments exist; (4) that different treatment providers and agencies may have differing and conflicting philosophies; (5) that no agency has "final accountability" for the client's progress and recovery.

An increasing recognition of the need for a treatment protocol that integrates services designed to meet specific client needs has emerged from the research. Nowhere is this need more apparent than for people with co-occurring addiction and psychological trauma disorders. As a result, two patterns have evolved. The first is an increasing recognition of the need for providers to be "cross-trained." The second is the recognition that new treatment models need to be developed that recognize and appreciate the needs of individuals with both disorders. Najavits (2002) in her "Seeking Safety" program clearly addresses both of these concerns.

Some of the other concerns in integrated treatment, addressed by Mueser, Noordsy, Drake and Fox (2003), include integration of services, a long term perspective and time unlimited services, shared decision making on the part of providers and the client, the need to offer a comprehensive range of services and assertiveness in outreach and client management. While their work is focused on the larger issue of mental health disorders and addiction, most of their concerns are equally appropriate for treating co-morbid trauma and addiction disorders.

In summary, the advantages of an integrated treatment approach greatly outweigh any disadvantages. The reasons for not implementing an integrated treatment approach are more often a function of funding, a history of segregated, "problem specific" treatment and limitations of understanding both disorders on the part of counselors and therapists.

This collection makes a reasoned and coherent argument for integrated treatment.

WHO IS QUALIFIED TO TREAT CHEMICALLY DEPENDENT TRAUMATIZED PEOPLE?

It is unreasonable to expect that all individuals who staff chemical dependency treatment environments should be proficient in treating trauma disorders. Likewise, it is unreasonable to expect that all people competent in treating trauma disorders are sufficiently well versed, trained and have the agency resources to treat chemical dependency. At a minimum, however, all counselors and therapists should have a working knowledge of the problems faced by addicted, traumatized clients and an awareness of the resources necessary to address both problems. If counselors have this working knowledge, some trauma treatments, for instance, Najavits, manualized "Seeking Safety" model, can be implemented with minimal training and ongoing clinical supervision.

What is needed in both substance abuse and mental health treatment domains is a broad base of clinicians who are able to recognize individuals with co-occurring psychological trauma and chemical dependency disorders, a somewhat smaller group of clinicians who can, with supervision, conduct basic treatment protocols and a still smaller group who are highly knowledgeable and skilled in providing advanced treatment and are sufficiently trained to supervise other staff in the provision of services to individuals with co-occurring disorders.

The ability of chemical dependency treatment clinicians to understand the impact of psychological trauma on chemically dependent people, how that impact manifests as symptoms, how trauma symptoms appear as behavioral patterns and how those patterns might be significant impediments to chemical dependency treatment should be basic knowledge for all chemical dependency counselors. Concomitantly, because of the close relationship between trauma and chemical dependency, anyone who works with traumatized people should be aware of the basic symptoms of addictive disorders, should understand how an active addictive disorder might manifest in individuals with diagnosed trauma syndromes and should appreciate that both disorders have to be treated concurrently for the affected individual to have a reasonable chance of recovery. Additionally, staff of treatment programs for both groups should have a working knowledge of diagnostic and treatment resources for both disorders and should be able to provide basic client education about both disorders.

To provide adequate concurrent or integrated treatment of individuals with co-occurring trauma and addictive disorders, there needs to be a body of clinicians who not only are *trauma and addiction disorder aware*, but are also *trained and informed* in core treatment methods. Trauma and addiction informed counselors should be prepared to help clients recognize and accept diagnoses of trauma and addiction disorders, should help clients build safety with trauma symptoms and the exposure of those symptoms, should be capable of treating, under supervision, acute stress disorders and grief reactions, and with supervision, conduct structured manualized treatment protocols for traumatized people in addiction treatment settings. Likewise, trained and informed counselors should be able to help clients recognize and accept symptoms of addictive illnesses, help those clients mobilize to enter treatment and be able to provide, under supervision, basic addiction treatment services.

A third group of clinicians necessary for quality concurrent or integrated treatment might be termed *trauma and addiction treatment competent*. This group of clinicians should have advanced training in treatment of difficult cases, should have advanced skills in specific approaches and methodologies for treatment of co-occurring trauma and addiction, and, perhaps most importantly, should have skills in team leadership and supervision to provide direction and consultation to counselors. While it might not be reasonable to expect that every addiction or trauma treatment program could have such a clinician, it seems perfectly reasonable that such a clinician can be employed part-time or in a consultant capacity. Without such an individual in the treatment team, it is doubtful a treatment program can maintain the focus, direction and success necessary for quality treatment of people with co-occurring disorders.

CONCLUSION

Significant changes have occurred in the last decade in the recognition of the co-occurrence of psychological trauma and substance abuse. There is now considerable agreement that the best treatment is to confront both disorders concurrently in early addiction recovery with an integrated treatment staff that is emotionally responsive and technically proficient to address the total needs of the client. There is also a greater appreciation for the impact of trauma on quality of life when the trauma syndrome manifests later in recovery. There is widening appreciation for the scope of trauma disorders beyond PTSD and Acute Stress Reactions and how those other trauma disorders manifest in substance abusing clients. There is an increasing armament of resources and methodologies including manualized treatment, use of EMDR, Affect Regulation Therapy and experiential therapies to complement the growing body of knowledge in the more conventional realms of psychodynamic therapy, the cognitive therapies and the 12-Step recovery movement. There is an increasing awareness of the special needs of women in treatment, of the roles of spirituality and forgiveness in recovery and the impact of psycho-neurology on the treatment process. This book represents a concerted effort to bring together current thinking, best practices, and supportive resources in furtherance of an integrated approach to the treatment of psychological trauma and addiction.

REFERENCES

Burke, P.A. (2006). Enhancing Hope and Resilience Through a Spiritually Sensitive Focus in the Treatment of Trauma and Addiction. In B. Carruth (Ed.). *Psychological Trauma and Addiction Treatment* (pp. 187-206). New York: Haworth Press.

Herman, J. L. (1992). *Trauma and Recovery*. New York: Basic Books.

Higgins, G. O. (1994). *Resilient Adults: Overcoming a Cruel Past*. San Francisco: Jossey-Bass.

Levine, P. (1997). *Waking the Tiger: Healing Trauma*. Berkeley, CA: North Atlantic Books.

Mueser, K.T., Drake, R., Noordsy, D., and Fox, L. (2003). *Integrated Treatment for Dual Disorders: A Guide for Effective Practice*. New York, NY: Guilford Press.

Najavits, L. M. (2001). *Seeking Safety: A Treatment Manual for PTSD and Substance Abuse*. New York, NY: Guilford Press.

Shalev, A. Y. (1996). Stress versus Traumatic Stress: From Acute Homeostatic Reactions to Chronic Psychopathology. In B. A. van der Kolk, A. C. McFarlane, & L. Weisaeth (Eds.), *Traumatic Stress: The Overwhelming Experience on Mind, Body, and Society* (pp. 77-101).

Cognitive-Behavioral Therapies for Psychological Trauma and Comorbid Substance Use Disorders

Casey O'Donnell, MA
Joan M. Cook, PhD

SUMMARY. In this chapter, a brief explanation of the CBT conceptualizations for PTSD and associated substance abuse are presented and several of the most prominent traditional CBT interventions are discussed. More contemporary CBT interventions such as Acceptance and Commitment Therapy (ACT; Hayes, Strosahl, & Wilson, 1999) and Dialectical Behavioral Therapy (DBT; Linehan, 1993) are discussed in the latter section of this chapter. *[Article copies available for a fee from The Haworth Document Delivery Service: 1-800-HAWORTH. E-mail address: <docdelivery@haworthpress.com> Website: <http://www.HaworthPress.com> © 2006 by The Haworth Press, Inc. All rights reserved.]*

KEYWORDS. Cognitive-behavioral therapies, psychological trauma, comorbid substance use disorders

Utilizing a cognitive-behavioral approach to the conceptualization and treatment of posttraumatic stress disorder (PTSD) and concomitant substance use disorders (SUD) is both empirically indicated and is intu-

[Haworth co-indexing entry note]: "Cognitive-Behavioral Therapies for Psychological Trauma and Comorbid Substance Use Disorders." O'Donnell, Casey, and Joan M. Cook. Co-published simultaneously in *Journal of Chemical Dependency Treatment* (The Haworth Press, Inc.) Vol. 8, No. 2, 2006, pp. 15-39; and: *Psychological Trauma and Addiction Treatment* (ed: Bruce Carruth) The Haworth Press, Inc., 2006, pp. 15-39. Single or multiple copies of this article are available for a fee from The Haworth Document Delivery Service [1-800-HAWORTH, 9:00 a.m. - 5:00 p.m. (EST). E-mail address: docdelivery@haworthpress. com].

Available online at http://www.haworthpress.com/web/JCDT
© 2006 by The Haworth Press, Inc. All rights reserved.
doi:10.1300/J034v08n02_02

itively sound in practice. Existing research indicates that various cognitive-behavioral therapies (CBT) show promise in the efficacious and effective treatment of individuals who suffer from trauma-related psychiatric disorders, including but not limited to PTSD and SUD. The CBT tradition has a long history in the intervention for fear reactions, and offers scientifically-informed conceptualizations of the etiology of PTSD and treatments for the associated fear networks, avoidance strategies, learning contingencies and maladaptive belief systems of the individuals suffering from PTSD and SUD (see Harvey, Bryant, & Tarrier, 2003 for a review of randomized clinical trials of CBT for PTSD and Irvin, Bowers, Dunn, & Wang, 1999 for a review for SUD).

Since its beginnings in the 1960s, the behavior therapy movement has pledged itself to the design of psychological interventions using empirical data and well-known behavior principles. Under the umbrella of CBT, there are a multitude of approaches; however, standard theory and practice primarily focuses on cognitions (such as, "The world is a dangerous place" and "I am incapable of managing danger"), and behaviors (such as managing physiological anxiety and systematically facing fearful situations). Over the last decade emerging developments in the CBT tradition are leading to the inclusion of dialectics, spirituality, acceptance and mindfulness-based conceptualizations and interventions (Hayes, 2004). The premises and practices of this "third-wave" of behaviorally-informed therapies may represent an evolution or a revolution against limitations of standard CBT.

In this chapter, a brief explanation of the CBT conceptualizations for PTSD and associated substance abuse are presented and several of the most prominent traditional CBT interventions are discussed. More contemporary CBT interventions such as Acceptance and Commitment Therapy (ACT; Hayes, Strosahl, & Wilson, 1999) and Dialectical Behavioral Therapy (DBT; Linehan, 1993) are discussed in the latter section of this chapter.

INTRODUCTION
TO THE COGNITIVE-BEHAVIORAL THERAPY MODEL

Understanding current cognitive-behavioral practices depends on an examination of the principles of CBT and the associated conceptualizations of PTSD and SUD. Though standard CBT includes a plethora of techniques ranging from the cognitive work of Beck and colleagues (Beck, Rush, Shaw & Emery, 1979) to the behavioral work of Lewinsohn (Lewinsohn, Biglan & Zeiss, 1976), its most common and contemporary application is a blend of both cognitive and behavioral techniques.

The foundation of CBT is based on the premise that psychopathology results from maladaptive or distorted thinking which affects both emotion and behavior. In turn, emotions and/or behaviors can reciprocally and cyclically affect thoughts which are reflective of distorted beliefs regarding self, world, and others. Patterns of behaviors are believed to be established and maintained by an individual's history of learning (both operant learning and classical conditioning). These learning patterns often result in impaired functioning later in life. Criticism of CBT has historically focused on the perceived minimizing of the role of emotion; however, on the contrary, emotions are believed to be linked directly to cognition and are thought to be part of the stimulus-response chain that drives both adaptive and maladaptive behaviors.

As depicted in Figure 1, the cognitive-behavioral model accounts for thoughts, emotions, physiological experiences, and behaviors. This model is not linear and conceivably a line could be drawn between any of these elements. That is to say each of these factors can act as a stimulus as well as serve as a response. Take for example a person who intermittently has intrusive images of a recently experienced severe motor vehicle accident. At the end of the day, this person may be at work staring at the clock on the wall. In that moment, the person may be anticipating driving home and may think "there will be a lot of traffic on the road tonight," which may lead to the intrusive image of the accident and stim-

FIGURE 1. Cognitive-Behavioral Model

Thoughts

Behaviors

Emotions

Physiology

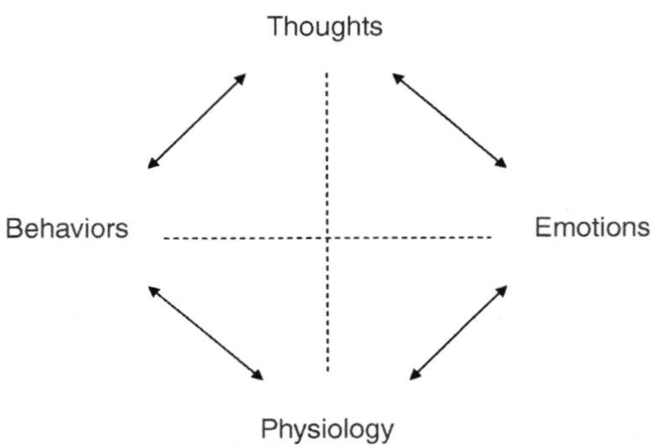

ulate feelings of anxiety, including increased heart rate. The individual's negative pattern may continue to spiral by stimulating additional thoughts of future dangerous driving conditions as well as the previous car accident (e.g., intrusive thoughts or flashbacks). These thoughts, emotions and physiological experiences might easily lead to the person waiting past rush hour to go home from work or perhaps contribute to the person having an alcoholic beverage in order to "relax" and suppress the stressful reaction (specifically physiological responses). This brief description exemplifies how negative thinking associated with previous learning negatively impacts the functioning of the client. Thus the goal of the traditional CBT therapist is to facilitate the identification, examination, and management of thoughts, associated emotions, physiological responses, and behaviors.

EXPLANATORY THEORIES
OF PTSD AND SUBSTANCE ABUSE

The various cognitive-behavioral theories that have emerged to explain the establishment and maintenance of PTSD and SUD are rooted in behavioral learning theories, specifically how the pairing of stimuli, thoughts, fear, and both emotional and experiential avoidance occurs. The following theories (operant learning, classical conditioning, two-factor theory, social cognitive theory, information processing, and duel representation theory) clearly overlap and they each continue to adequately explain at least some portion of trauma-related pathology.

Substance use among other avoidant behaviors is considered by some investigators to be an *operant behavior* learned and reinforced by contingencies that are physiological, cognitive, emotional, and environmental. Often this reinforcement is negative (the removal of painful stimuli) as the use of drugs and/or alcohol provide a means of emotional and experiential avoidance of distressing internal or external events (i.e., distressing symptoms or situations). For example, in the situation described above, drinking alcohol was used to temporarily "relax" when anxiety was provoked by thoughts of the car accident. Conversely, substance use may be positively reinforced (rewarded) as substances might facilitate a sense of control, improve perception of social interactions, or facilitate the expression of emotion such as anger related to trauma (Ruzek, Polusny, & Abueg, 1998). Avoidance of anger may also be accomplished through other maladaptive behaviors such as self-isolation. For example, if a combat veteran finds that he can avoid yelling at his wife by being alone, he might end up isolating himself constantly to ensure avoiding his negative emotions and his interpersonally destructive behaviors.

Classical conditioning in the case of PTSD describes the pairing of stimuli in the environment (either externally observed such as sounds or imagined such as thoughts and mental images) and the actual feelings associated with the traumatic event (often described as reexperiencing). In the previous example, classical conditioning could explain how thoughts of driving or perhaps the sound of tires screeching could cause a fear reaction. Sitting in his/her office, there was no actual threat in the environment, however, the thought or sound adopted the stimulus properties of the accident.

Rohsenow, Childress, Monti, Niaura, and Abrams (1990) describe substance abuse and relapse to use as a classically conditioned (rather than operantly learned) set of behaviors. Certain stimuli that become paired with use, such as having a drink of alcohol when intrusive flashbacks of a motor vehicle accident occur, become stimuli which evoke the unconditioned response of urges or heightened anxiety due to a lack of substance in the body. Therefore, a client suffering from comorbid PTSD-SUD might not only experience anxiety when he has a trauma-related intrusive thought, but he might also experience an urge or craving for alcohol which further exacerbates the experience. Existing research indicates that when individuals with PTSD-SUD are exposed to trauma-related stimuli, they experience greater levels of withdrawal symptoms (Peirce et al., 1996) than individuals with only one disorder. Those who suffer from PTSD are also thought to experience greater levels of negative emotional intensity and emotional dysregulation due to their trauma exposure (Najavits, Weiss, & Liese, 1996; Taylor, Koch, & McNally, 1992), therefore substance use may be viewed by the patient as a "relief" from a range of negative emotions. In CBT conceptualization, this is viewed as substance use becoming a powerful reinforcer (Villagomez, Meyer, Lin, & Brown, 1995).

Mowrer's two-factor theory (1960) includes both classical conditioning as the means by which fear is acquired and operant learning as the means by which it is maintained. According to this theory, the avoidance resulting from operant learning does not allow normal extinction of conditioned responses because of negative reinforcement (Resick & Calhoun, 2001). That is to say, if someone has a drink every time they have a traumatic flashback, their anxiety will not have a chance to decrease naturally. This is directly associated with the CBT exposure-based techniques which are explained later in this chapter.

Social cognitive theory explains the impact of cognitions within the social context. Although it partly focuses on information processing, it is more concerned with the individual's belief structure and how that structure was impacted by the traumatic events. Therefore interventions are structured around how to "reconcile the traumatic event with prior beliefs and expectations" (Follette, Ruzek, & Abueg, 1998, p. 63). Other social-cognitive theorists conclude that the traumatic experience shatters the individual's beliefs about the world and self. For example, Janoff-Bulman (1992) claimed that traumatic experiences can destroy positive assumptions about the world and self. Bolton and Hill (1996) described how traumatic incidents can have a significantly negative effect on self perception related to one's competence and may leave an individual feeling helpless. Therefore the task of therapy is the development or reconstruction of an adaptive/healthy belief system.

In addition to the examination of thoughts and beliefs, Resick and Schnicke (1993) proposed that the result of trauma also included primary and secondary emotions. Primary emotions are the emotions experienced during the trauma event(s) such as fear, and secondary emotions are those which result from later interpretations of the event such as guilt. Expression and resolution of these emotions is also fundamental for integration and complete processing of traumatic material. These theorists believe that secondary emotions along with intrusive thoughts dissipate as beliefs are challenged and primary emotions are experienced and understood.

Although learning theories continue to offer premises from which to base treatment, Mowrer's two-factor theory does not appear to adequately explain all intrusive recollections in conscious and sleeping states. Chemtob, Roitblat, Hamada, Carlson and Twentyman (1988) proposed that trauma-related memory is unique and is not "processed" like other memories, resulting in psychopathology. *Information processing theories* postulate that trauma-related material needs to be integrated within the wider memory system. Unlike the social-cognitive model, this inability to integrate information is due to the traumatic experience itself rather than preexisting beliefs.

Thus, Foa, Steketee, and Rothbaum (1989) proposed that a fear network is developed in memory which initiates escape and avoidance behaviors. This fear structure includes stimuli, responses and also schemata (ingrained beliefs which are a lens through which events are examined and explained). Over time this network is cued by various stimuli in the environment including events, people, places, sounds, etc., which are thought to be associated with the trauma. Therefore when the network is triggered, intrusive thoughts, beliefs and images enter into consciousness or dreams. This process is thought to result in avoidant behavior. In part this system is quite functional in that it promotes survival. For example, if an individual was attacked by a dog it would be adaptive to have a fear network that is triggered by any future potential dog attacks.

According to *information processing theory*, exposure to the content of the traumatic memories will result in habituation to the memory, therefore decreasing the experience of fear and changing the fear structure. These changes also include changes in beliefs regarding self (Resick & Calhoun, 2001). Foa et al. (1989) added that traumatic incidents are so influential that they change previously held beliefs regarding safety, and create fear networks that are adaptively stronger than other response networks resulting in PTSD symptoms. They also claimed that these networks have a lower threshold for activation. More recently, Foa and Riggs (1993) and Foa and Rothbaum (1998) have expanded this theory to "*emotional processing*" to explain what occurs during exposure-based therapies and to address how rigidity in thinking affects the etiology of PTSD.

Brewin, Dalgleish and Joseph (1996) introduced a *dual-representation theory* in an effort to integrate information processing and social-cognitive theory. Dual representation theory postulates that conscious memories can be intentionally retrieved and are called "verbally accessible memories" (VAMs). These memories include sensory information, information regarding memory and physiological experience and beliefs regarding the events. These memories are believed to be narrow in range due to the limits of attention during traumatic experiences. Memories that are less accessible are called "situationally accessed memories" (SAMs). This type of memory may be more extensive, but only come into consciousness when they are cued by trauma-related stimuli including thinking about the trauma. This type of memory is considered intrusive memory or intrusive sensory recall of the traumatic event (Brewin & Holmes, 2003).

Similar to the social cognitive model, this theory proposes that there are two categories of emotional reactions. The first type of emotion is that which is conditioned during the traumatic event and often includes fear or anger. The second type of emotion results from interpretation of the traumatic event or associated primary emotions. Like the example in social-cognitive theory this might include, for example, guilt (Rothbaum, Meadows, Resick, & Foy, 2000).

Emotional processing of these memories includes cognitive restructuring through exposure to SAMs along with the challenging of thoughts and relaxation or habituation exercises for the physiological components of anxiety. The social-cognitive portion of the intervention includes regaining a sense of control or meaning through examination and challenging of beliefs regarding the traumatic experience. This would include an effort to resolve cognitive dissonance between beliefs and expectations which existed prior to the event and meaning of the event(s) (Resick & Calhoun, 2001).

CBT TREATMENT MODELS AND TECHNIQUES

PTSD symptoms and substance abuse are often intertwined, yet their treatment is frequently separate and sequential. Often depending on severity, many clinicians require that a client obtain treatment for their substance abuse or dependence first and maintain a period of abstinence prior to entering into treatment for PTSD. This is thought to be in the best interest of the client, as the treatment of trauma-related symptoms is at times intensely fear provoking and often requires adaptive and positive coping strategies. Recently, however, treatments have begun to emerge which, in an integrative fashion, address both PTSD and substance abuse simultaneously. This section will first offer the foremost treatment methods for SUD and PTSD separately, then will address contemporary integrative models.

CBT FOR SUBSTANCE USE DISORDERS

CBT focuses on current, as opposed to historical, factors that maintain drinking. This continues to be true in the case of trauma-related stress symptoms, as these are a current problem despite the historical event. This approach reflects patterns of learning as substance use results from external antecedents due to pairing with positive or negative reinforcement or the anticipation thereof. Therefore individuals may drink to feel better or drink in the hopes of not feeling bad. Both cognition and emotion mediate the relationship between triggers (stimuli) and substance abuse (response).

McCrady (2001) lists seven considerations when treating a substance abusing client which include problem severity, concomitant life problems, client expectations and motivation, therapeutic relationship, variables maintaining the current drinking system, and maintenance of change. These factors, although relevant, are embedded in the concrete CBT approach which depends on thorough initial and ongoing assessment, motivation and relapse prevention.

Assessment in CBT treatment is an ongoing process, but initially defines targets for intervention. Assessment is a collaborative effort in that successful treatment will depend on the client's ongoing self-monitoring and honest accounting of substances used including frequency and quantity. Most salient to treatment and the structure for self-monitoring is the functional analysis. This analysis, which is used throughout treatment, including during relapse prevention, is an identification (and often recording as part of homework) of what functions the substance use has and under what conditions. This occurs by identifying the antecedent condition, thoughts, emotions, physiological responses, behaviors and outcomes. Often this process begins with the behavior and it may take time for the client to be able to identify and separate other factors. For instance, initially a client might only be able to identify, "I drank last night." With further examination and practice the client reveals, "I drank last night because I was feeling anxious," then "I drank that night because I was feeling anxious after I watched a movie that reminded me of my trauma" and so on.

McCrady (2001) described a "SORC" model for functional assessment which stands for **S**timuli, **O**rganismic factors (thoughts, emotions, physiological experiences like cravings, anxiety, negative self-evaluation), **R**esponses (drinking) and **C**onsequences of drinking that maintain behavior. This model is not specific for substance abuse and can be used in any behavioral analysis. Once this chain of events is identified the therapist and client intervene directly on the behaviors, but additionally on the thinking and the physiological responses (urges and the physiological component of anxiety). Marlatt and Gordon (1985) described the management of urges through acceptance-based approach (e.g., urge surfing) or action-oriented imagery (e.g., attacking urge with a sword; see Hester & Miller, 1995).

The cognitive component includes addressing cognitive distortions. For example, an individual may believe that drinking enables him/her to forget. Since complete removal of traumatic event from memory is near impossible, identification of reminders and triggers is essential to treatment. If a client learns to identify what triggers their use and their comorbid trauma-related symptoms, they can either not put themselves in situations which present triggers or learn to cope more effectively with triggers. This identification is a large portion of relapse prevention. Abueg and Fairbank (1992) described relapse prevention applied to substance use and PTSD, which includes psychoeducation and identification of stressors.

Because substance abuse affects an individual's ability to use sound judgment, it is essential to facilitate the use of more effective coping strategies for both substance use and PTSD symptoms. New coping strategies may include the challenging of automatic thoughts and irrational responses or finding other sources of positive reinforcement. For many substance abusers, positive reinforcement may occur in the form of social support. This support is essential to successful treatment and may be accessed through family or friend networks or often through programs such as Alcoholics Anonymous. Sober social support is essential in that one frequent trigger is interaction with other people who use. Participation in a support group may also prevent social isolation or detachment which is often a symptom of PTSD.

PTSD and SUD are often associated with interpersonal difficulties, which could pose a problem for both group and individual interaction (also in establishing a therapeutic relationship). It is also possible that a client wants help with PTSD symptoms but does not want treatment for their substance use (or vice versa). In this case, the client and therapist must assess the pros and cons of substance use and focus on motivation for treatment. Miller and Rollnick (1991) offer non-confrontational motivational techniques. These authors claimed that the elements to enhance motivation are represented by the acronym "FRAMES" which is **F**eedback, emphasis on **R**esponsibility of the client for change, clear **A**dvice about the need for change, **M**enu of client options and **E**mpathy and enhancing **S**elf-efficacy. At a minimum, motivational techniques appear to assist in the process of moving through the stages of change that are widely acknowledged in SUD treatment.

The proponents of the stage model have observed though practice and empirical study that tailoring both the intervention and the therapeutic relationship to the client's identified stage of change can enhance outcome as measured by attrition and success of treatment (Ackerman et al., 2001). Prochaska, DiClemente, and Norcross (1992) offer a six stage model to understand the processes of behavioral change for the SUD client. These six stages include precontemplation, contemplation, preparation, action, maintenance and termination. Individuals progress through each stage which includes a specific set of tasks to be achieved, although different clients proceed through each stage at different rates. Additionally, it is believed that these stages of change occur for people who are attempting to overcome their SUD behaviors on their own without professional intervention (Prochaska et al., 1992). Identification of which stage an individual is in can be accomplished through a discrete categorical measure (DiClemente et al., 1991) or a continuous measure which results in scales for each stage (McConnaughy, Prochaska, & Velicer, 1983).

The first precontemplation stage is typified by a client's refusal to admit their problematic SUD use and thus refusal to seek treatment on their own; rather he/she is most often pressured into treatment because of family, friends, or the court system (Prochaska & Norcross, 2001). Once this pressure is removed, the client typically returns to SUD use and other problematic behaviors (Prochaska et al., 1992). Contemplation, the second stage, hinges on the client's awareness that a problem exists and consideration to address the problem, yet is devoid of any effort or commitment to do so. These clients can often be classified by their stating that they intend to take action within the next six months. This stage relies mostly on consciousness raising, self-reevaluation, readiness and decision making (Prochaska & Norcross, 2001). People are known to get stuck in contemplation for a considerable length of time (Prochaska et al., 1992). The third stage is preparation. This includes not only the commitment to take action within the following month, but also the client's having made unsuccessful attempts at overcoming the problem within the past year.

Often the most difficult stage is the following, which is action. During this stage, an individual must make identifiable behavioral changes that are maintained between one day and six months. Prochaska and colleagues (1992) warn therapists not to utilize insight-based techniques during this stage because although necessary for long term maintenance, insight has been shown to be insufficient for behavioral activation or change. This stage requires management of reinforcement contingencies, stimulus control, and "counterconditioning" (Prochaska & Norcross, 2001). The maintenance stage is considered to be continuous behavioral change for greater than six months, where the focus is on relapse prevention. Termination, the last stage, is completion of the intervention with successful prevention of relapse in situations identified as high risk and the absence of SUD urges.

Cognitive techniques are most often utilized in precontemplation and contemplation stages, whereas behavioral techniques are frequently applied in the action and maintenance stages (Norcross, 1993). Prochaska and Norcross (2001) explain that only 10% to 20% of clients are pre-pared for action and advise therapists to be cautious in initiating ac-tion-oriented interventions. Thirty to forty percent of clients are thought to be in contemplation stage, while the remaining (50%-60%) are in precontemplation (Prochaska & Norcross, 2001). Therefore, therapists must be aware of reasonable treatment goals and proceed according to clients' stage. Additionally, individuals may spiral through stages, and can work through stages several times (Prochaska et al., 1992) often de-pending on the severity of use. The therapeutic relationship is viewed as essential and requires matching the stage to appropriate interpersonal approach (Norcross, 1993), especially in the case of a client who has lapsed back to use. The APA Division of Psychotherapy Task Force sup-ports this matching and makes additional recommendations regarding client therapist relationships, including tailoring the relationship to the client's diagnosis (Ackerman et al., 2001).

CBT FOR PTSD

In a wide-ranging review of the psychosocial interventions for PTSD, CBT was found to be the most efficacious treatment approach (Foa, Davidson, & Frances, 1999; Foa, Keane, & Friedman, 2000). Of these, the most extensively studied in controlled trials across trauma pop-ulations is *exposure therapy* (for review, see Rothbaum, Meadows, Resick, & Foy, 2000). Exposure therapy is a class of treatments that in-cludes imaginal and/or in vivo confrontation with the traumatic memo-ries and with avoided trauma reminders.

One exposure-based therapeutic program, *prolonged exposure* (PE), consists of four components: psychoeducation, breathing retraining, imaginal exposure and in vivo exposure (Foa & Rothbaum, 1998). PE is usually administered in 9 to 12, 90-minute sessions on a once or twice a week basis. The first session comprises presentation of the treatment ra-tionale and goals, description of procedures, and discussion about the traumatic event(s) and associated symptoms, particularly, the reex-periencing and avoidance symptoms. It is explained that PE includes two exposure procedures: imaginal exposure and in vivo exposure. In imaginal exposure clients are asked to close their eyes and give a present tense detailed descriptive account of the traumatic event for 30-60 min-utes, including accompanying thoughts and feelings. In in vivo exposure clients are asked to identify situations or objects that are trauma-related and fear-evoking, but inherently safe (e.g., for motor vehicle accident survivors, driving or riding in a car). These situations or objects are then arranged in a hierarchy according to how much psychological and physiological distress they induce. Subsequently, clients are encouraged to confront these situations or objects systematically, beginning with those that provoke moderate fear and proceeding to those more fear-evoking on the hierarchy.

The treatment rationale for imaginal exposure is that it facilitates emotional processing of trauma by allowing the patients to revisit the details of the traumatic event in a safe and supportive manner and to gain new perspectives (e.g., "The rape was not my fault"; "I did the best under the circumstances"); by sharpening the distinction between remembering and reencountering the traumatic event and thus the realization that the latter but not the former is dangerous; by helping patients create a coherent, organized narrative of the traumatic event; by demonstrating to clients that emotional engagement with the traumatic memory results in reduction rather than increase in anxiety; and by increasing patients' sense of mastery. In vivo exposure provides clients with corrective information that the avoided trauma-related situations are not dangerous. Thus, their anxiety decreases, increasing sense of mastery and broadening positive life experiences. When implementing PE or other exposure-based approaches, it is particularly important to promote emotional engagement with the traumatic memory and to select situations that will demonstrate safety (Foa & Cahill, 2002). A more detailed conceptual theory for PE's mechanism of action is presented in Foa and Kozak (1986) and further elaborated by Foa and Rothbaum (1998).

Cognitive Processing Therapy (CPT; Resick & Schnicke, 1993) is a 12-session empirically-supported intervention based on the information-processing model, which includes exposure plus cognitive therapy. CPT addresses specific thoughts and beliefs affected by the trauma and includes daily homework between sessions. Foa and colleagues (1989) described how traumatic fear structures are established and deconstructed. In order to intervene and reduce fear, it was hypothesized that this structure must be activated and then new dissonant information must be incorporated. The exposure component offers the opportunity for fears to be confronted, reevaluated and habituated to. As discussed previously, this appears to only address the emotion of fear. Other secondary emotions, such as guilt and shame, are thought to be left unaddressed and unresolved.

CPT was designed in part to additionally examine and address these secondary emotions and their associated maladaptive beliefs. The cognitive component addresses the conflict between thoughts and beliefs pertaining to the traumatic event and the beliefs held prior to the event. One example of this is the conflict between the belief that the world is a safe place versus a trauma-related belief that the world is a dangerous place. This type of conflict is described as a "stuck point" (Resick & Calhoun, 2001).

The exposure component of CPT is different from that in PE, as clients are instructed to journal the details of the traumatic event along with their responses and their experiences. During the therapeutic session, the client reads the journal entries aloud, with the therapist assisting in identification and processing of stuck points.

Anxiety Management Training offers coping skills to gain self-mastery and reduce anxiety levels. Kilpatrick and Amick (1985) proposed that mastery over fears was derived from learning coping skills. Mastery and reduced anxiety usually involved stress inoculation training, relaxation skills, and self-talk. *Stress Inoculation Training* (SIT) is based on Meichenbaum's (1985) approach (discussed further below). SIT Phase I is the preparation for treatment, which includes conceptualization of anxiety related to trauma from a social learning perspective. This includes explanations regarding physiological, behavioral, and cognitive responses. Concrete examples are provided by the therapists and clients then explain examples from their own lives. SIT Phase II involves coping skills training with identified target fears. The therapist provides a minimum of two coping strategies per response channel (i.e., physiological, behavioral and cognitive), and the relationships between channels are discussed. This phase includes the use of daily recording of maladaptive thoughts (otherwise known as "thought records") and monitoring of emotional distress (often referred to as an "emotional thermometer").

Explanations are offered by the therapist for the use of coping strategies in regards to how and why they work and demonstrations are conducted. Clients practice these skills in session as well as monitor the use and effectiveness outside of session. Associated coping strategies include Progressive Muscle Relaxation (Bernstein & Borkovec, 1973), Breathing Control or Diaphragmatic Breathing (Rapee & Barlow, 1988), Covert Modeling (Kazdin, 1978; imaginal exposure of an anxiety provoking situation and imagined confrontation), role-playing (in session and with friends or family members), and guided self-dialogue.

Constructive Narrative Perspective (CNP; Meichenbaum, 1994) is another model that focuses heavily on cognition (i.e., beliefs, assumptions and interpretations) in the form of the client's "story." In CNP treatment, the therapist collects the client's descriptive accounts of self, others, and world, because they are believed to offer meaning and organization to how clients' representations have been altered by trauma. The CNP model posits that individuals do not respond directly to events, but rather respond to their interpretation of events and what they foresee the implications of the events to be, which helps make sense of traumatic experiences.

Thus it is believed that the client becomes a narrator, and the therapist facilitates change through changing understanding of the past and restructuring cognitions. As the narrative script changes, the reactions to events and clients' roles are also thought to change. Intervention also includes gaining some level of acceptance, making favorable social comparisons, identifying positive personal attributes, deriving some possible benefit from the event (such as personal growth) and normalization of their reactions.

For example, clients with trauma-related pathology often need to make changes from a position of blaming, victimization and undoing (e.g., thoughts such as, "Why did the traumatic event happen to me?" or "What if I did something differently, would the trauma not have happened to me?"). These undoing questions thematically arise in the story line. What also appears out of the story line is the use of metaphor(s) due to an inability to adequately describe emotions and reactions. These metaphors offered by clients are used by the therapist to draw out more personalized descriptions. For example, if the client states "I am a ticking time bomb," the therapist might question "When does the bomb explode?," or perhaps "How can the time bomb be diffused?" Therapists may also choose to find a thematic thread to the metaphors offered and assist in the replacement of positive or adaptive ones such as the renovation of an existing structure.

CNP treatment occurs in five phases. The introductory Phase I involves the establishment of therapeutic alliance, facilitatation of sharing of the client's "story," establishment of treatment goals including establishment of safety, assessment of treatment needs and client's strengths, psychoeducation on PTSD, validation and instillation of hope.

CNP Phase II focuses on stabilization and symptom reduction, teaching coping skills for specific situations and assessment to determine if psychotropic medication or adjunctive treatment is warranted. Phase III involves the restructuring of the story and transforming self-perception from victim to survivor. This is accomplished through retelling the story with a sense of mastery and integration and finding meaning, and reexperiencing of memories with a sense of control. Other techniques involve exposure and guided imagery to trauma cues in a supportive manner, while addressing clients' beliefs through cognitive restructuring and journaling and addressing feelings of guilt and self-blame. Additionally, this phase of treatment includes the therapist's attempts to assist in the strengthening of social supports, a shifting of time orientation from past to present and future, provision of opportunities for improved social interactions and client development of ability to build on own experience. CNP Phase IV involves reconnecting socially and interpersonally and avoiding revictimization. And Phase V is the termination phase where the therapist attempts to bolster self-confidence, discuss relapse prevention and discuss booster sessions.

RECENT CBT INNOVATIONS IN TREATMENT OF PTSD AND/OR SUD

Innovative new advances in CBT or variants thereof continue to be developed and tested for the treatment of PTSD and/or SUD. For instance, Ehlers, Clark, Hackman, McManus and Fennell (2005) described the development of a cognitive therapy for PTSD that is based on a recent cognitive model, and presented promising findings from a small randomized controlled trial comparing this treatment to a waitlist condition. Additionally, there is a growing understanding that CBT treatments must not only be efficacious but must be accessible. Efficient methods of delivering CBT interventions to a wider range of clients (e.g., traumatized patients who live in rural areas) and those in other settings (e.g., primary care medical settings) are also underway. One novel example is a therapist-assisted, Internet-based self-help intervention to treat PTSD, which involves a modified form of stress inoculation training, promoted through daily homework assignments (Litz, Williams, Wang, Bryant, & Engel, 2004).

Client non-adherence, or partial or incomplete treatment responses can occur utilizing any theoretical orientation. In a very thoughtful book on advances in CBT treatments for PTSD, Taylor (2004) attempts to address this dilemma by suggesting that CBT therapists broadened their therapeutic repertoire to include other trauma-related psychopathology.

Treatment of individuals with SUDs and co-occurring psychiatric disorders, including PTSD, is typically delivered using one of three paradigms: parallel, sequential and integrated (Drake & Mueser, 2000). Many programs deliver parallel services where patients receive treatment for SUD in one program and treatment for psychiatric disorders (e.g., PTSD) in another. Parallel treatment can lead to fragmented care and increased barriers to treatment. Patients with PTSD-SUD may be unable to navigate the separate treatments systems or make sense of different communications about treatment and recovery.

Some treatment programs use the sequential model that focuses first on abstinence from substance use, followed by treatment for trauma-related distress or symptomatology. Consequently patients with PTSD-SUD often find themselves in a situation where important symptoms and problems are unaddressed. For example, patients in abstinence-oriented SUD treatment programs who are not equipped to manage PTSD symptoms may experience worsening as their substance abuse symptoms improve.

An integrated model of treatment involves treating both disorders simultaneously in a coordinated fashion. One integrated CBT for PTSD-SUD that has been acquiring empirical support is Seeking Safety (Najavits, 2002; for a more in-depth discussion of this noteworthy treatment, see chapter 8 of this book). Two other CBT manual-based treatments for SUD-PTSD (Back, Dansky, Carroll, Foa & Brady, 2001; Brady, Dansky, Back, Foa, & Carroll, 2001; Triffleman, Carroll, & Kellogg, 1999) exist and are in various stages of empirical investigation. Both of these contain an exposure-based component.

In a comprehensive book on the causes, consequences, and treatment of PTSD-SUD, Ouimette and Brown (2003) advocate for routine PTSD and SUD screening in all treatment programs. They highlight the importance of educating clients of the link between the two disorders and recommend that PTSD-SUD clients receive integrated treatments. Although they advocate the consideration of exposure treatment, they suggest that it be considered a second stage intervention.

THE THIRD WAVE OF CBT

The next evolutionary stage of CBT, the "third wave" (Hayes, 2004), has developed out of the existing cognitive-behavioral tradition and shares many of the same premises regarding the etiology and maintenance of symptoms, yet expands the processes and goals for behavioral, cognitive and emotional change to include acceptance and non-judgmental present-centered experience. This third wave is most widely represented by Acceptance and Commitment Therapy (ACT; Hayes, Strosahl, & Wilson, 1999) but also by Dialectical Behavioral Therapy (DBT; Linehan, 1993). Both offer interventions for PTSD symptoms and substance abuse, although DBT was initially developed for the treatment of borderline personality disorder. Becker and Zayfert (2001) describe promising means of integrating DBT practices into exposure-based therapies for PTSD. Additionally, many leading clinicians have endorsed the integration of acceptance and mindfulness techniques into already well-established CBT treatments (Hayes, Follette, & Linehan, 2004), and ACT is actively being applied as a treatment for comorbid PSTD-SUD with veteran populations (e.g., Batten & Hayes, 2005).

The ACT conceptualization of PTSD shares the existing information processing premise that normal adaptive integration of the information related to trauma does not occur. Also in this model, avoidance continues to be identified as one of the most salient problems in trauma-related distress. Similar to other behaviorally-informed therapies, avoidance is established and maintained by conditioned reinforcement contingencies.

Walser and Hayes (1998) explain that experiential avoidance encompasses cognitive, emotional and behavioral avoidance of trauma-related stimuli or symptoms. Substance abuse is the most relevant example of one of the maladaptive avoidants (Varra & Follette, 2004), along with self injury, social isolation and dissociative features. These avoidant behaviors are thought to be part of the reinforcement contingency which maintains PTSD. In the ACT model the alternative to avoidance is acceptance, which further differentiates ACT from other cognitive-behavioral therapies. Additionally, ACT and more traditional CBT approaches share the basic premise that cognitive processes (i.e., automatic thoughts, intermediate beliefs and core beliefs) are also at the foundation of maladaptive adjustment to traumatic experience (Hayes & Strosahl, 2004).

The primary function of ACT, distinguishing it from other existing CBTs, is alleviation of symptoms. Instead, ACT seeks to increase functioning despite symptoms and reduce the cognitive, emotional and behavioral impact of symptoms. Hayes and other proponents of ACT claim that all individuals, including trauma survivors, need to remain functional and lead successful lives with the cumulative positive and negative events which make up their personal histories (Hayes et al., 2004). Living a successful life and functioning effectively requires addressing and overcoming avoidance and the "fusion" which occurs with cognitions, most specifically language (Hayes, Barnes-Holmes, & Roche, 2001).

ACT specific techniques for both PTSD symptoms and substance abuse begin with the facilitation of "values clarification" to create the context for change (Varra & Follette, 2004). Values are identified in ten life domains as a means to provide a sense of direction, however, stating a value may also create intense cognitive dissonance that substance abusing clients may also attempt to avoid values identification as they had previously been pushed out of awareness (Wilson & Murrell, 2004). This first fundamental goal of creating a "valued living plan" is in a sense identifying what the client wants. One factor of ACT for SUD is agreement on client committed action based on values. Often the commitment to remain abstinent is in service of fulfilling another commitment such as "being a better father or husband." With successful values clarification, maladaptive behaviors can be examined in regards to their effect on the identified values and on daily functioning.

Additional facets of ACT treatment include creative hopelessness interventions, use of metaphor, mindfulness exercises, cognitive defusion strategies, and willingness and acceptance techniques. Creative hopelessness interventions attempt to create a contrast between the client's identified values and the client's efforts to exert control (a fundamental problem) over emotions and thoughts through their avoidant behaviors such as substance abuse. The therapist and client discuss the "unworkability" of behaviors (Wilson & Byrd, 2004), such as using substances (e.g., making explicit that the client's easy solutions to their problem have not worked thus far so they need to be open to the possibility of change). Metaphor is a fundamental tool in ACT treatment. For example, the *tug of war with a monster,* which illustrates the client letting go of the rope or relinquishing control (see Hayes, Strosahl, & Wilson, 1999 for more examples of ACT metaphors). Defusion strategies show the client how they are fused with the story and language of their trauma. These exercises include deliteralization of words, thoughts, emotions, and physiological experiences. The purpose is to take away the power of the event and the event-related information. Self-as-context exercises are a process of objectively examining self and behavior. This teaches the client that they are not what they feel and think. These exercises are looking to get the client in touch with their immediate private content and have experience without judgment. Willingness and acceptance are basically a form of exposure; however, these efforts are meant to increase psychological flexibility in responding to feared stimuli rather than habituate to it.

Dialectical Behavioral Therapy (DBT) also focuses on coping with negative affect and shares many of the techniques of ACT (such as mindfulness and acceptance) as well as some of the underlying premises, such as the negative impact of avoidant behavior. DBT is a capability deficit and motivational model, which targets emotional dysregulation, impulsive maladaptive behaviors such as substance abuse, and maladaptive cognitive strategies.

The DBT treatment model seeks to facilitate the client's use of "wise mind" which is a learned balance between the rational "reasonable mind" and "emotional mind." Wise mind thinking is thought to result in improved problem-solving, greater experiences of joy, greater capacity to withstand negative emotion, and more validating interpersonal relationships. Validation is fundamental in DBT and needs to occur throughout treatment especially when managing trauma-related information. Linehan (1993) claims that the management of trauma-related stress and substance abuse is purely a matter of sequence in treatment, and that the key to managing trauma-related stress symptoms is adequate coping.

The first phase of therapy includes the management of substance abuse, increasing behavioral skills such as mindfulness skills, interpersonal effectiveness, emotional regulation, distress tolerance and self-management. The second phase of therapy is structured to focus on decreasing posttraumatic stress. Stage three targets increasing self-respect and achieving individual goals. The treatment hopes to replace dichotomous thinking with dialectical thinking, improve the client's motivation for change, and ensures that new capabilities generalize to the natural environment (Linehan, 1993).

CONCLUSION

With the increasing recognition of the effects of traumatic stress including PTSD and SUD, it is imperative that clinicians learn how to recognize and treat these disorders. In addition to comprehensive information collection through interviewing the use of reliable and valid PTSD and SUD assessment measures may improve in the recognition, diagnosis and subsequent treatment of these disorders (for a review of PTSD assessment measures readers are directed to Frueh, Elhai, & Kaloupek, 2004).

CBT has a basic structure which involves the identification and correction of maladaptive thinking and behaviors along with the promotion of more adaptive coping strategies to manage negative emotions and psychological symptoms. CBT for PTSD-SUD typically involves education about trauma and misuse of substances and their effects, challenging unhelpful thoughts with rational more accurate responses (and meaningful and accurate beliefs), learning "triggers" and how to more effectively cope with present and future anxiety and substance use urges, use or development of social supports and exposure to traumatic material in a safe and controlled environment. Additionally, third wave behaviorally informed treatments include the premise and practice of accepting the presence of negative emotion and symptoms without allowing them to significantly negatively impact the client's functioning or emotional well-being.

The cognitive-behavioral tradition has a commitment to empirical investigation. Although it is recognized that many front-line clinicians are time-restrained and resource-limited, it is advised that they stay well-informed and empirically-minded. On-going randomized clinical trials of psychosocial interventions should provide the field with the latest evidence regarding the efficacy and parameters of interventions as well as the optimal combination and ordering of techniques.

A number of additional factors may influence CBT conceptualization and treatment including chronology and severity of trauma, acuity of symptoms, cultural, ethnic and gender considerations, motivation for and acceptability of treatment, personality, other psychiatric comorbidities and family history of psychopathology. All of these factors require consideration to structure CBT assessment and best practices for psychosocial interventions for those with co-morbid PTSD-SUD.

REFERENCES

Abueg, F. R., & Fairbank, J. A. (1992). Behavioral treatment of co-occurring PTSD and substance abuse: A multidimensional stage model. In P. A. Saigh (Ed.), *Posttraumatic stress disorder: A behavioral approach to assessment and treatment.* Boston: Allyn & Bacon.

Ackerman, S. J., Benjamin, L. S., Beutler, L. E., Gelso, C. J., Goldfried, M. R., Hill, C. et al. (2001). Empirically supported therapy relationships conclusions and recommendations of the division 29 task force. *Psychotherapy, 38*, 495-497.

Back, S. E., Dansky, B. S., Carroll, K. M., Foa, E. B., & Brady, K. T. (2001). Exposure therapy in the treatment of PTSD among cocaine-dependent individuals: Description of procedures. *Journal of Substance Abuse Treatment, 21*, 35-45.

Batten, S. V., & Hayes, S. C. (2005). Acceptance and commitment therapy in the treatment of comorbid substance abuse and posttraumatic stress disorder: A case study. *Clinical Case Studies, 4*, 246-262.

Beck, A. T., Rush, J., Shaw, B., & Emery, G. (1979). *Cognitive therapy of depression.* New York: Guilford Press.

Becker, D. B, & Zayfert, C. (2001). Integrating DBT-based techniques and concepts to facilitate exposure treatment for PTSD. *Cognitive & Behavioral Practice, 8*, 107-122.

Bernstein, D. A., & Borkovec, T. D. (1973). *Progressive relaxation training.* Champaign, IL: Research Press.

Bolton, D., & Hill, J. (1996). *Mind, Meaning and Mental Disorder.* Oxford: Oxford University Press.

Brady, K. T., Dansky, B. S., Back, S. E., Foa, E. B., & Carroll, K. M. (2001). Exposure therapy in the treatment of PTSD among cocaine-dependent individuals: Preliminary findings. *Journal of Substance Abuse Disorders, 21*, 47-54.

Brewin, C. R., Dalgleish, T., & Joseph, S. (1996). A dual representation theory of posttraumatic stress disorder. *Psychological Review, 103,* 670-686.

Brewin, C. R., & Holmes, E. A. (2003). Psychological theories of posttraumatic stress disorder. *Clinical Psychology Review, 23,* 339-376.

Chemtob, C., Roitblat, H. L., Hamada, R. S., Carlson, J. G., & Twentyman, C. T. (1988). A cognitive action theory of post-traumatic stress disorder. *Journal of Anxiety Disorders, 2,* 253-275.

DiClemente, C. C., Prochaska, J. O., Fairhurst, S. K., Velicer, W. F., Velasquez, M. M., & Rossi, J. S. (1991). The process of smoking cessation: An analysis of precontemplation, contemplation, and preparation stages of change. *Journal of Consulting and Clinical Psychology, 59,* 295-304.

Drake, R. E., & Mueser, K. T. (2000). Psychosocial approaches to dual diagnosis. *Schizophrenia Bulletin, 26,*105-118.

Ehlers, A., Clark, D. M., Hackmann, A., McManus, F., & Fennell, M. (2005). Cognitive therapy for post-traumatic stress disorder: Development and evaluation. *Behaviour Research and Therapy, 43,* 413-431.

Foa, E. B., & Cahill, S. P. (2002). Specialized treatment for PTSD: Matching survivors to the appropriate modality. In R. Yehuda (Ed.) *Treating trauma survivors with PTSD* (pp. 43-62) Washington: American Psychiatric Publishing.

Foa, E. B., Davidson, J., & Frances, A. J. (1999). Treatment of posttraumatic stress disorder (Expert consensus guideline series). *Journal of Clinical Psychiatry, 60* (supplement 10).

Foa, E. B., Keane, T. M., & Friedman, M. J. (Eds.). (2000). *Effective treatments for PTSD.* New York: Guilford Press.

Foa, E. B., & Kozak, M. J. (1986). Emotional processing of fear: Exposure to corrective information. *Psychological Bulletin, 99,* 20-35.

Foa, E. B., & Riggs, D. S. (1993). Post-traumatic stress disorder in rape victims. In J. Oldham, M. B. Riba, & A. Tasman (Eds.), *American Psychiatric Press Review of Psychiatry, vol. 12* (pp. 273-303). Washington, DC: American Psychiatric Press.

Foa, E. B., & Rothbaum, B. O. (1998). *Treating the trauma of rape: Cognitive behavioral therapy for PTSD.* New York: Guilford Press.

Foa, E. B., Stekeete, G. S., & Rothbaum, B. O. (1989). Behavioral/cognitive conceptualizations of posttraumatic stress disorder. *Behavior Therapy, 20,* 155-176.

Follette, V., Ruzek, J. I., & Abueg, F. R. (1998). A contextual analysis of trauma: Theoretical considerations. In V. Follette, J. I. Ruzek, & F. R. Abueg (Eds.), *Cognitive Behavioral Therapies for Trauma* (pp. 1-14). New York: Guilford Press.

Frueh, C. B., Elhai, J. D., & Kaloupek, D. G. (2004). Unresolved issues in the assessment of trauma exposure and posttraumatic reactions. In G. M. Rosen (Ed.), *Posttraumatic Stress Disorder: Issues and Controversies* (pp. 63-84). New York: John Wiley and Sons.

Harvey, A. G., Bryant, R. A., & Tarrier, N. (2003). Cognitive behavioral therapy for posttraumatic stress disorder. *Clinical Psychology Review, 23,* 501-522.

Hayes, S. C. (2004). Acceptance and commitment therapy, relational frame theory, and the third wave of behavioral and cognitive therapies. *Behavior Therapy,* 35, 639-665.

Hayes, S. C., Barnes-Holmes, D., & Roche, B. (Eds.). (2001). *Relational frame theory: A post-Skinnerian account of human language and cognition.* New York: Plenum Press.

Hayes, S. C., Follette, V. M., & Linehan, M. M. (Eds.). (2004). *Mindfulness and acceptance: Expanding the cognitive behavioral tradition.* New York: The Guilford Press.

Hayes, S. C., & Strosahl, K. D. (Eds.). (2004). *A practical guide to acceptance and commitment therapy.* New York: Springer Science + Business Media Inc.

Hayes, S. C., Strosahl, K. D., & Wilson, K. G. (1999). *Acceptance and commitment therapy: An experiential approach to behavior change.* New York: Guilford Press.

Hester, R. K., & Miller, W. R. (1995). *Handbook of alcoholism treatment approaches* (2nd ed.). New York: Pergamon.

Irvin, J. E., Bowers, C. A., Dunn, M. E., & Wang, M. C. (1999). Efficacy of relapse prevention: A meta-analytic review. *Journal of Consulting and Clinical Psychology, 67,* 563-570.

Janoff-Bulman, R. (1992). *Shattered assumptions: Towards a new psychology of trauma.* New York: Free Press.

Kazdin, A. E. (1978). Covert modeling: The therapeutic application of imagined rehearsal. In J. L. Singer & K. S. Pope (Eds.), *The power of human imagination: New methods in psychotherapy* (pp. 255-278). New York: Plenum.

Kilpatrick, D. G., & Amick, A. E. (1985). Rape Trauma. In M. Hersen & C. Last (Eds.), *Behavior Therapy Casebook* (pp. 86-103). New York: Springer.

Lewinsohn, P. M., Biglan, T., & Zeiss, A. (1976). Behavioral treatment of depression. In P. Davidson (Ed.), *Behavioral management of anxiety, depression and pain* (pp. 91-146). New York: Brunner/Mazel.

Linehan, M. M. (1993). *Cognitive-behavioral treatment of borderline personality disorder.* New York: Guilford Press.

Litz, B. T.,Williams, L., Wang, J. L.,Bryant, R. A., & Engel, C. C. (2004). A therapist-assisted internet self-help program for traumatic stress. *Professional Psychology: Research and Practice, 35,* 628-634.

Marlatt, G. A., & Gordon, J. R. (1985). *Relapse prevention: Maintenance strategies in the treatment of addictive behaviors.* New York: Guilford Press.

McConnaughy, E. A., Prochaska, J. P., & Velicer, W. F. (1983). Stages of change in psychotherapy: Measurement and sample profiles. *Psychotherapy, 20,* 368-375.

McCrady, B. S. (2001). Alcohol Use Disorders. In Barlow, D. H. (Ed.), *Clinical Handbook of Psychological Disorders* (pp. 376-433). New York: Guilford.

Meichenbaum, D. H. (1985). *Stress inoculation training.* New York: Pergamon Press.

Meichenbaum, D. H. (1994). *A clinical handbook/practical therapist manual for assessing and treating adults with Posttraumatic Stress Disorder (PTSD).* Clearwater, Florida: Institute Press.

Miller, W. R., & Rollnick, S. (1991). *Motivational Interviewing: Preparing people to change addictive behaviors.* New York: Guilford Press.

Mowrer, O. H. (1960). *Learning theory and behavior.* New York: Wiley.

Najavits, L. M. (2002). *Seeking Safety: Cognitive-behavioral therapy for PTSD and substance abuse.* New York: Guilford Press.

Najavits, L. M., Weiss, R. D., & Liese, B. S. (1996). Group cognitive-behavioral therapy for women with PTSD and substance use disorder. *Journal of Substance Abuse Treatment, 13,* 13-22.

Norcross, J. C. (1993). The relationship of choice: Matching the therapist's stance to the individual clients. *Psychotherapy, 30*, 402-403.

Ouimette, P., & Brown, P. J. (2003). *Trauma and Substance Abuse: Causes, consequences, and treatment of comorbid disorders.* Washington, DC: American Psychological Association.

Peirce, J. M., Brown, J. M., Long, P. J., Nixon, S. J., Borrell, G. K., & Holloway, F. A. (1996). Comorbidity and subjective reactivity to meaningful cues in female methadone maintenance patients. Paper presented at annual meeting of the Association for Advancement of Behavior Therapy, New York.

Prochaska, J. O., DiClemente, C. C., & Norcross, J. C. (1992). In search of how people change: Applications to addictive behaviors. *American Psychologist, 47*, 1102-1114.

Prochaska, J. O., & Norcross, J. C. (2001). Stages of change. *Psychotherapy, 38*, 443-448.

Rapee, R. M., & Barlow, D. H. (1988). Cognitive-behavioral treatment. *Psychiatric Annals, 18*, 473-477.

Resick, P. A., & Calhoun, K. S. (2001). Posttraumatic stress disorder. In D. H. Barlow (Ed.), *Clinical Handbook of Psychological Disorders* (Third Ed.) (pp. 60-113). New York: Guilford.

Resick, P. A., & Schnicke, M. K. (1993). *Cognitive processing therapy for rape victims: A treatment manual.* Newbury Park, CA: Sage.

Rohsenow, D. J., Childress, A. R., Monti, P. M., Niaura, R. S., & Abrams, D. B. (1990). Cue reactivity in addictive behaviors: Theoretical and treatment implications. *International Journal of the Addictions, 25*, 957-993.

Rothbaum, B. O., Meadows, E. A., Resick, P., & Foy, D. W. (2000). Cognitive behavioral therapy. In E. B. Foa, T. M. Keane, & M. J. Friedman (Eds.), *Effective treatments for PTSD* (pp. 60-83). New York: Guilford Press.

Ruzek, J. I., Polusny, M. A., & Abueg, F. R. (1998). Assessment and treatment of concurrent posttraumatic stress disorder and substance abuse. In V. Follette, J. I. Ruzek, & F. R. Abueg (Eds.), *Cognitive behavioral therapies for trauma.* New York: Guilford Press.

Taylor, S. (2004). Advances in the treatment of posttraumatic stress disorder: Cognitive-behavioral perspectives. New York: Springer.

Taylor, S., Koch, W. J., & McNally, R. J. (1992). How does anxiety sensitivity vary across the anxiety disorders? *Journal of Anxiety Disorders, 6*, 249-259.

Triffleman, E., Carroll, K., & Kellogg, S. (1999). Substance dependence posttraumatic stress disorder therapy: An integrated cognitive-behavioral approach. *Journal of Substance Abuse Treatment, 17*, 3-14.

Varra, A. A., & Follette, V. M. (2004). ACT with posttraumatic stress disorder. In S. H. Hayes & K. D. Strosahl (Eds.), *A practice guide to acceptance and commitment therapy* (pp. 133-152). New York: Springer Business + Science Media Inc.

Villagomez, R. E., Meyer, T. J., Lin, M. M., & Brown, L. S. (1995). Post-traumatic stress disorder among inner city methadone maintenance patients. *Journal of Substance Abuse Treatment, 12*, 253-257.

Walser, R. D., & Hayes, S. C. (1998). Acceptance and trauma survivors: Applied issues and problems. In V. Follette, J. I. Ruzek, & F. R. Abueg (Eds.), *Cognitive Behavioral Therapies for Trauma* (pp. 256-277). New York: Guilford Press.

Wilson, K. G., & Byrd, M. R. (2005). ACT for substance abuse and dependence. In: S. C. Hayes & K. D. Strosahl (Eds.), *A practical guide to acceptance and commitment therapy* (pp. 153-184). New York: Springer Science + Business Media Inc.

Wilson, K. G., & Murrell, A. R. (2004). Values work in acceptance and commitment therapy. In S. C. Hayes, V. M. Follette & M. M. Linehan (Eds.), *Mindfulness and acceptance: Expanding the cognitive behavioral tradition* (pp. 120-151). New York: The Guilford Press.

Psychodynamic Psychotherapies and the Treatment of Co-Occurring Psychological Trauma and Addiction

Barbara Davis, MFS, MSW, LCSW

SUMMARY. The goal of this chapter is to define some of the basic principles of psychodynamic psychotherapy and to demonstrate how these therapies are useful in helping people recover from co-occurring addictive and trauma related disorders. In distinguishing psychodynamic psychotherapies from other forms of therapy, I will highlight the importance of the context and meaning of trauma, the therapeutic relationship, and the recovery process. After defining trauma and psychodynamic psychotherapy, I will offer an alternative way to conceptualize some commonly seen ego defenses. Effective interventions for assisting clients who present with co-occurring addictive and trauma related disorders will be offered. Lastly, I will point out commonalities between traditional addictions treatment and a model of psychodynamic psychotherapy. *[Article copies available for a fee from The Haworth Document Delivery Service: 1-800-HAWORTH. E-mail address: <docdelivery@haworthpress.com> Website: <http://www.HaworthPress.com> © 2006 by The Haworth Press, Inc. All rights reserved.]*

KEYWORDS. Psychodynamic psychotherapies, co-occurring psychological trauma, addiction

Thanks to Jed Klein, LCSW, who contributed the direction for the original draft of this chapter.

[Haworth co-indexing entry note]: "Psychodynamic Psychotherapies and the Treatment of Co-Occurring Psychological Trauma and Addiction." Davis, Barbara. Co-published simultaneously in *Journal of Chemical Dependency Treatment* (The Haworth Press, Inc.) Vol. 8, No. 2, 2006, pp. 41-69; and: *Psychological Trauma and Addiction Treatment* (ed: Bruce Carruth) The Haworth Press, Inc., 2006, pp. 41-69. Single or multiple copies of this article are available for a fee from The Haworth Document Delivery Service [1-800-HAWORTH, 9:00 a.m. - 5:00 p.m. (EST). E-mail address: docdelivery@haworthpress.com].

INTRODUCTION: THE FOUNDATION

We develop psychologically in the context of our primary caregivers, generally our parents. The success of our development is in part contingent upon whether or not our innate characteristics are a "good match" for our caregivers' parenting style, their life circumstances and the larger environment of our upbringing (including but not limited to, extended family, neighborhood, school, socio-economic status, ethnicity, race, culture and level of acculturation, religious involvement, etc.) The meaning and impact of early trauma will be greatly influenced by the relationship between the primary caregivers and the trauma. For instance, are the primary caregivers the perpetrators of the trauma (parent-child abuse/neglect)? Are the primary caregivers the victims (sudden death, illness)? Are the child and parents together the victims of trauma (racism, chronic poverty)? Is the trauma acknowledged or denied? It is *within* the context of these primary relationships that the trauma is given meaning, and is processed. When trauma occurs later in life, the reactions of one's environment may or may not play a significant role.

The impact and meaning of trauma on the individual is strongly influenced by the relationship between the trauma and the environment, regardless of when the trauma occurs. For instance, if physical abuse between a husband and wife is culturally sanctioned, this will shape the meaning the woman assigns the abuse, her interest in seeking help and even her ability to name the behavior as abuse. In addition, the way in which she copes with trauma is related to her prior coping style, the coping style of her environment and the nature of the trauma. In this way, the trauma cannot be separated from the environment in which it occurs. Those who turn to substance use as a means of coping with the impact of trauma are often predisposed to substance abuse disorders by any number of possible factors: genetics and heredity, role modeling of family members who use substances to cope, availability of drugs and alcohol in the family/neighborhood, peer pressure, or pre-existing/co-occurring mental health disorder. The reader will note that all of these risk factors have to do with an individual's relation with others, either through biological, familial or social connection (with the possible exception of other pre-existing/co-occurring mental health disorders, which have their own relational components).

All of this is to say, if we "get sick" or are traumatized, in relation to others, we must also heal in the context of a relationship. Addicted, traumatized individuals have developed rigid defense mechanisms that pose particular challenges for counselors and treatment programs. This rigidity, which developed as a form of protection, can make intervention difficult. The trauma inhibits the individual's ability to trust and disrupts her sense of safety. Since trust is necessary to connect to a therapist (or group) to recover, these individuals often have difficulty engaging in the treatment process. These clients have difficulty managing the intensity of the treatment relationship and related affects. To compensate for this, traumatized individuals push others away, often through confusing and disruptive behavior.

Individuals with co-occurring addictive and trauma related disorders often feel quite hopeless. Some clients use alcohol and other drugs to numb their feelings of helplessness and hopelessness. Asking someone to stop using drugs and alcohol is equivalent to asking them to feel these overwhelming feelings. For some clients it feels as if we are trying to take away the only thing that gives them a sense of power. Counselors are called upon to help reduce despair, provide coping strategies and offer realistic hope while not promising more than they can do. These clients are afraid of hope as the slightest disappointment can trigger tremendous grief and hopelessness.

Individuals with traumatic histories have difficulty engaging in the treatment process, not because they don't want help but because they have no basis by which to trust the process. Because they are always on the lookout for further victimization, traumatized individuals often misinterpret the benign actions and statements of treatment professionals, reacting with mistrust and hostility. It is easy, even for an experienced counselor, to misunderstand the behavior of these clients and respond in such a way as to exacerbate the situation, ultimately disrupting the therapeutic alliance. The significance of therapeutic relationship cannot be overstated when working with traumatized people. Just as the trauma and the addictive disorder developed in the context of relationships, so must the healing occur *in relation* to others.

What Is Trauma?

Trauma is the wounding of the self. Traumatic experiences are about being rendered utterly powerless, in the face of an atrocity (caused by another person) or a disaster (caused by nature). Traumatic events overwhelm our ability to feel a sense of control, connection and meaning (Herman, 1992, p. 33). The horrific events of September 11, 2001, and other world atrocities have brought much attention to the impact of trauma on individuals and societies, and to the survivors of trauma. As a result there have been great advances in the treatment of trauma. It is normal for people, regardless of their psychological make-up, to respond to trauma with shock, fear, grief, hopelessness, avoidance of related stimuli and even dissociation. When individuals dissociate or disconnect, they are protecting themselves from overwhelming and extraordinarily painful stimuli. A rather common example of an acute stress reaction is when an individual "forgets" the events which lead up to a car accident caused by an icy road, in which they were injured. Somehow doctors, counselors and family all "accept" this "memory loss" as a protective, if not normal, way of coping. We do not blame the individual. We are concerned for them and grateful that they were not more seriously injured.

Most of the people we see in treatment have not been traumatized by one discreet incident, such as a terrorist attack, a rape, or car accident. Although clients may recall specific disturbing and painful events, their experience of trauma is often ongoing and life long. Trauma can be pervasive, such as in the case of chronic poverty; sometimes unrecognized by family and the community, as in the case of incest, or imprisonment; undefined, as in the case of emotional abuse; and perhaps not even "known" by the individual, in the case of repressed physical or sexual abuse. Sometimes clients in treatment will focus on one experience to represent several instances of trauma or a pervasive environment of trauma. It is important to not get caught up in the detail but to remember to focus on the meaning of and feelings associated with the trauma(s). In the most extreme cases, we see people for whom the once protective defense of dissociation has become incorporated into their character structure. These people show us their trauma, often through acting out and chaotic behaviors (the kind that reek havoc on residential treatment programs, staff and clients alike). Our first and foremost job is to help these clients keep themselves safe. Next, we can help them learn the vocabulary they need to begin to appropriately express what is going on in their internal world. The intensity and rigidity of many residential substance abuse programs can be extraordinarily difficult for these clients to manage, and sometimes even contraindicated.

While it is important for an individual to be able to tell her trauma story, we must remember that the *meaning* of the trauma to the individual is of greater importance than the specific facts. Trauma can be physical, sexual, psychological, and most often, some combination. When a group experiences a traumatic event, such as in the events of September 11, 2001, there is validation in the shared experience and knowledge of the event. However, in the cases of individual trauma, such as neglect, emotional abuse, incest, or assault, the victim is left feeling as if the trauma was directed at them, personally. This type of trauma leaves victims feeling isolated, at fault, and disconnected from oneself and from others. The reality that we are not able to prevent such horrible things from happening to us is terrifying. To defend against this terror, we all have a tendency to look for what we could have done to "invite" the trauma or what we could do in the future to "prevent" it from happening again. In other words, we take responsibility for what happened to us. The belief that we are in control, and somehow "brought this on ourselves," is less terrifying than the reality that sometimes horrible things happen that we cannot stop.

We all need to feel some sense of control over our lives. Psychodynamic psychotherapists, in addition to wanting to know how clients function in love, work and play, are interested in the extent to which their clients feel in control of their lives. This sense of personal agency is a necessary component of mental health. In addition to losing control over their substance use, people who are chemically dependent have lost control of their lives. Abstinence from substances is the first step in regaining a sense of control or agency over one's life. Traumatization often destroys an individual's sense of control. It is obvious to many that the individual feels unable to control the specific harmful events; less apparent is the fact that people who have lived in traumatic situations often feel unable to control other aspects of their lives as well. Without proper treatment, many victims struggle with the powerful emotions of grief, guilt, shame, fear and hate. Feeling emotionally out of control confirms the individual's fear that they cannot control themselves. Many trauma survivors turn to alcohol and drugs to numb these intense feelings or alter their moods, only to become chemically dependent, ultimately perpetuating the feeling of being out of control. In addition, trying to contain this level of emotionality is exhausting, leaving little energy to identify and pursue one's life goals.

What Is Psychodynamic Psychotherapy?

Psychoanalytically informed psychotherapies, also known as psychodynamic psychotherapies, fall along a continuum from uncovering psychotherapies, such as psychoanalysis, to expressive psychotherapies to supportive psychotherapy. For the purposes of this paper, I will focus my attention on expressive and supportive psychotherapeutic techniques.

Psychodynamic psychotherapy, rather than a collection of established intervention strategies, is better defined as a mindset or general framework to guide the therapist. The most fundamental aspect of psychodynamic psychotherapies is the pursuit of the truth. This ethic dates back to Sigmund Freud who stated, "We must not forget that the analytic relationship is based on a love of truth, that is, on a recognition of reality . . ." (Freud, 1937, p. 248). The psychotherapist's job is to help the client to find her own truth. To the outsider, psychodynamic psychotherapies, with a focus on the past, may appear to be about "blaming the parents" (especially the mother). It is important to understand that the focus on the past is to help understand the present and offer better options for the future. Although clients must grieve their trauma(s) and other disappointments of their upbringing, the goal is never to get stuck in the anger and resentment but to accept the past, learn from it and most importantly, move forward. Historically it may be true that some psychodynamic therapists may have been too focused on the past, and almost neglectful of present day behavior. On the other hand, addictions counselors have often been too focused on the here and now behavior without taking the time to understand the origin of the behavior. Just as the disease concept of alcoholism (Jellinek, 1968) offers a framework by which to understand the actions of an addicted person, psychodynamic theory offers a framework with which to understand underlying relational patterns, ego defenses and resistances.

Psychodynamically oriented therapists value collaboration with their clients, sometimes referred to as a working or therapeutic alliance. The psychodynamic therapist does not believe that she has the answers but rather sees her job as guiding the client to discover her own truth. By encouraging the client to identify her own beliefs and needs, the therapist assists in promoting a sense of self-efficacy. The psychodynamic therapist is highly attuned to the quality of the relationship with the client and encourages the client to talk about her experiences of the therapist and the therapy. Some therapists refer to this practice as "getting supervision from the patient" (McWilliams, 1994, p. 86).

Many people see the therapeutic relationship as a model of all others. In general, the client will demonstrate her relationship style in her relationship with the counselor (sometimes attempting to put on her best face). Her style of communication, her ability to identify and express emotion, her ability to identify and state her own needs, and her ability to deal with conflict, will all be part of her relationship with her counselor. If a client cannot state her needs to the counselor, it is likely that she cannot do this in her other relationships either. If she misinterprets the actions of the counselor, it is likely that she misinterprets the actions of others.

Difficulties in the relationship with the therapist help the psychodynamic psychotherapist to understand the kinds of difficulties the client has in relationships with others. The psychodynamic psychotherapist uses her own reactions to the client to help her understand how to intervene with the client. The psychodynamic psychotherapist tries to experience both what the client experiences and what others experience in relation to the client. By understanding the client's perspective and how others see the client, the therapist is able to help the client change. In addition, if the client can work through difficulties in relationship to the therapist, she is much more likely to be able to do this in other areas of her life. Research shows that when the client perceives a positive working alliance with the therapist, generally by experiencing the therapist as empathetic, trustworthy, and expert in her field, the client is more likely to experience the treatment as successful (Luborsky, 1993).

When a client in a psychodynamic psychotherapy has a complaint about the therapist or the therapy, the therapist carefully considers what the client has to say. Although the therapist may not agree with the client's perceptions, the therapist views this as an opportunity to learn more about the client, the therapy relationship and the client's other relationships. The therapist may decide that she has made a mistake that requires an apology, a clarification and/or a change in tactic. The therapist may conclude that the client's perceptions are distorted, offering the therapist additional diagnostic information about the client. Sometimes in traditional addictions treatment programs the staff view questions about treatment protocol or criticisms of the counselor as evidence of resistance to treatment or that the client's "disease is active." Although this may be the case, an alternate possibility is that the counselor is missing something important about how the client interacts with, and interprets, others, creating a block in the therapeutic relationship.

None of us enjoy hearing about or experiencing our imperfections. Therefore, we all defend against this awareness in some way. Psychodynamic psychotherapists want to understand *how* a client defends against the knowledge of her problems and painful affects, so that they can work with the defense (or resistance). It is easy to spot overt resistance, in statements such as, "I don't need your help," "I am not an addict," or behaviors such as not attending treatment. However, when a client participates in treatment yet rejects the counselor's interventions, it is helpful to use a psychodynamic frame and consider *why* the client is resistant. A collaborative, rather than confrontational, stance between the counselor and client can aid in treatment retention and increase the likelihood that the client will feel safe enough to explore her own resistance. Resistance may appear in the form of some common ego defenses such as denial, repression, intellectualization, rationalization, and projection. If the counselor can identify which defenses are at work, she can frame her interventions accordingly. A confrontational intervention can feel like an assault, or a re-victimization, to someone who has been traumatized. If this happens, the client may react with increased defensiveness, hostility or flight from treatment. It is important to be prepared to help the client understand her reaction in light of the intervention, the therapeutic relationship and the client's history, without also becoming defensive. Ultimately, there needs to be a balance between keeping the client safe, engaging her in a collaborative exploration, and encouraging her to take the risks necessary to address her self-destructive behavior.

Psychodynamic psychotherapists value curiosity, complexity, empathy, attunement to affect, attachment and faith (McWilliams, 2004, pp. 27-45). Psychodynamic psychotherapists are curious about their clients; they always seem to want to know more. It is common to hear a therapist ask, "Can you tell me more about that?" This curiosity is motivated by a belief in the complexity of people and relationships, and by a desire to help each client to learn more about herself. No two clients are the same (even two clients with the same symptoms). In addition, asking open-ended questions supports the psychodynamic value of promoting a sense of personal agency. This is especially valuable for people who have been victimized or controlled by others. Sometimes traumatized people look to others to tell them what they are thinking and feeling. This may be a habitual pattern of relating that developed as an (unconscious) way of protecting oneself. Resisting the urge to tell a client what to do helps her learn that she can make healthy choices for herself, helping her to move out of the role of victim.

Psychodynamic psychotherapists are empathetic. One important goal of treatment is to understand and identify with the feelings of their clients in hopes of expressing empathy, concern, and compassion. Many people who seek treatment for psychological and substance abuse disorders have not had the experience of having their feelings supported and validated by people close to them. This is especially true for people who have traumatic histories. It is not uncommon for a survivor of childhood sexual abuse to be as mad with or hurt by the adult/parent who denied the trauma when the child sought protection, as she is with the perpetrator of the abuse. The lack of support, help and validation can be an additional part of the trauma, and sometimes more confusing. This is, in part, why people who experience trauma as a group have a better prognosis. They have validation of their experience in the other survivors. Group therapy and self-help groups provide an excellent venue through which clients may reduce their isolation and feelings of shame by identifying with other survivors.

Psychodynamic psychotherapists want to help clients identify and express the specific emotions that have been historically difficult for them. Most of us have a "default" emotion, the emotion(s) that we tend to express automatically in lieu of others. Typically, we are most comfortable with the emotions that we express regularly. We tend to use these emotions to cover other emotions with which we are less comfortable. For instance, someone might present anger in lieu of sadness, or sadness in lieu of shame. A common goal of most therapies is the increased capacity to manage one's emotions appropriately. Emotional health has three components: the ability to identify emotions as we are having them, the skills to appropriately express emotions and our ability to relate to others while they are having emotions. Good treatment helps clients to better cope with all three aspects of emotional health.

Trauma survivors, especially those who are not conscious of their trauma, disconnect from their emotions because they seem too painful, even dangerous. Clients may act out their feelings in disruptive, and even self-destructive ways. When clients are not safe with their emotions, safety becomes a treatment issue. Clients in early recovery from chemical dependence are at risk of relapse in reaction to intense and overwhelming emotion. In addition, counselors must be on the look out for other self-destructive behaviors including, but not limited to, sexual acting out and treatment non-compliance, even suicide. Psychodynamic psychotherapists strive to create physical and psychological safety for their clients by educating clients about emotions, helping clients differentiate between feelings and actions, normalizing feelings and experiences, and helping clients to experience emotions in small, tolerable doses. In addition to creating emotional safety, this adds to the client's sense of personal control. When affects are excessive, labile and interfere with the client's ability to participate in treatment, psychiatric evaluation and medication monitoring may be required.

Psychodynamic psychotherapists focus on the client's relationships to significant others in the client's past and present life, including but not limited to, parents, lovers, friends, therapists. The psychodynamic psychotherapist wants to understand how the client's present relationships, including her relationship to her drug(s) of choice, reflect her childhood relationships and her relationships with those involved with her trauma. An individual's manner of forming relationships, or attaching, is often modeled, unconsciously, after the individual's early relationships, especially with the parents. Without treatment, any kind of disruption in this primary attachment will be re-enacted unconsciously throughout the course of an individual's life. This re-enactment serves to create homeostasis, or the maintenance of the status quo ("this is how all relationships work") and the hope of resolving the original trauma ("If only I can do it different this time").

A traumatic loss or abuse early on, especially within the context of one of the primary relationships, severely impacts an individual's ability to develop trusting and supportive relationships. Many trauma survivors recreate their trauma through their substance abuse, dysfunctional relationships and related behaviors and consequences. A psychodynamic psychotherapist wants to know what relationships an individual is recreating, both consciously and unconsciously, through substance use and abuse, as the grieving and healing of these losses will be the cornerstone of long-term stable recovery. In addition, these disruptive and even traumatic relationships will be re-enacted in treatment, especially in more intensive programs. These are the clients who are often "administratively discharged" from facilities for their acting out behavior and inability to "follow the rules." Since this often occurs on the unconscious level, it is inappropriate to expect even a motivated client to be able to explain to the therapist the dynamic processes at work. The goal of understanding past relationships is to help reduce the acting out behavior and prevent relapse. When a thorough assessment of past relationships and traumas has been conducted, counselors can anticipate when to expect that there will be acting out or disruptive behavior. Knowing this, the counselor can educate the client about what she might expect to happen and give the client preventative instructions about how to handle the urge to act out. This can help to lower client recidivism and improve treatment outcome. It also helps to lower staff burn-out.

Psychodynamic Psychotherapy and Integrated Recovery from Co-Occurring Substance Abuse and Trauma Related Disorders

Psychodynamic psychotherapies have several common components: the focus on affect and expression of emotion, the exploration of resistance, the identification of patterns of thought, feelings, experiences and relationships; an emphasis on the past as it relates to the present; a focus on interpersonal experiences; an empathetic therapeutic relationship and an exploration of the client's intra-psychic dynamics (McWilliams, 2004, p. 3). It is important to understand that the emphasis on the past is for the sake of understanding the present. In the case of co-occurring addiction and trauma, we seek to understand how substance abuse originated and was sustained, and the context, meaning and impact of the trauma. This knowledge guides all aspects of the counseling relationship, including the focus of the relapse prevention work. This type of therapeutic focus is quite compatible with traditional addictions and trauma treatment, and especially with 12-step recovery.

Psychodynamic psychotherapists support their clients in the identification of feelings and the appropriate expression of affect. It is commonly understood in the addictions treatment field that many individuals relapse in response to powerful emotions for which they do not have appropriate coping mechanisms. All addictions programs focus on teaching clients to cope with their feelings. People who have been victimized often believe that their feelings are wrong, inappropriate, and even a liability. For instance, some abusive partners may say things like, "No one will love you the way I do," or, tell their partners they are "too emotional" or "too weak" to be on their own. In addition, since trauma survivors often (and understandably) feel overwhelmed by their emotions, it is easy for them to believe they cannot handle them on their own. Teaching people to feel (usually in small amounts at first), express and embrace their emotions is a significant step towards recovery. Because victims of abuse have often been told that their feelings are wrong, they are particularly sensitive to how therapists respond to their emotional states. One way a therapist creates safety is by accepting emotions, by not being overwhelmed by them, and by assuring the client that together they can get through even the most turbulent emotional times. Some therapists refer to this process as "normalizing" the client's experience, or creating a "holding environment."

Psychodynamic psychotherapists work with their clients to discover patterns: patterns in the client's feelings, relationships, behaviors, and thoughts. The identification and interruption of unproductive patterned thoughts and behaviors is in fact the goal of many therapies, behavioral as well as psychodynamic. Psychodynamic therapists focus on the part of this process that involves making the "near conscious or unconscious, conscious," while cognitive behavioral therapists focus on thinking and behavior, and behaviorists focus on the conditioning, and reconditioning of behaviors. An example of an intervention designed to help an alcoholic to stop drinking/stay sober would be as follows: Identify a belief, such as, "I am bad," the feeling, such as shame; and the related behavior (drink alcohol) that stops the thought process and alleviates the painful emotion. Written this way it is hard to distinguish a cognitive-behavioral therapy from a 12-step oriented discussion of relapse prevention, from a psychodynamic view of looking at substance abuse. The difference lies primarily in the emphasis. A 12-step discussion would focus on not using substances, CBT would focus on the thoughts and behavior associated with using substances and psychodynamic psychotherapies would focus on the feelings and the "near conscious" thoughts underlying the whole process. It is important to note that skilled psychodynamic psychotherapists understand and honor the tenet, held in most addictions programs, that much of this work cannot be done while a person is still abusing substances.

Stages of Integrated Recovery

With a focus on the past, psychodynamic psychotherapists are especially well suited to help clients with traumatic histories. The goal of exploring one's past is to learn from it, to grieve it, and to be free not to repeat it. In AA this is summarized in the saying, "We will not regret the past, nor wish to shut the door on it" (Alcoholics Anonymous, 1976, p. 83). We can learn to put our past into perspective and move forward. This is the hope that is offered by the Twelve Steps and Twelve Promises of AA, and the healing sought by psychodynamic therapists. The healing lies in acknowledging, as honestly as possible, what has happened, how we feel about it and how it has affected our lives, and moving on. In AA parlance, this would be what a member does when telling her story. The suggested guideline is to tell, "What it was like (active addiction), what happened (what brought the person to AA), what it is like now (living in recovery)." AA stresses taking responsibility for one's own actions and faults. This is complicated for an individual with a history of trauma. Victims of trauma have spent much of their lives feeling responsible for the terrible thing(s) that happened to them. They often have thoughts such as this: "If only I had been (smarter, well behaved, stronger, less seductive, good), so and so would not have had to (beat, abuse, neglect, molest, abandon) me." Counselors working with individuals who are recovering from substance abuse and trauma need to tread lightly in this area, allowing the individual a lot of space and time to explore issues of responsibility and accountability in a safe environment. Although counselor neutrality is important, neutrality includes clarity that abuse is wrong (Herman, 1992, p. 135).

In her 1992 book, *Trauma and Recovery, The Aftermath of Violence– From Domestic Abuse to Political Terror*, Judith Herman, MD, describes three stages of recovery from trauma: establishing safety, remembrance and mourning, and reconnection. In addition, she devotes an entire chapter to the importance of the healing relationship (Herman, 1992). These stages of recovery from trauma parallel the stages of recovery from active addiction, and the phases of treatment generally described by psychodynamic psychotherapists as the beginning, middle and termination phases of treatment. These parallel processes lend themselves to an integrated model of treatment in which the client can receive services for multiple problems simultaneously.

Stage One

In both addictions treatment and trauma recovery the first stage of recovery is to establish personal safety. With regards to substance use, safety generally corresponds with abstinence. When a client seeks services in the midst of trauma, the priority is on physical safety. In addition, early in treatment all clients need skills training to help them deal with urges to use substances, setting limits with others and a plan to address emergency situations and lapses to substance use. Most clients do not seek treatment until long after the trauma has occurred, so that psychological, rather than physical safety, becomes the foundation for recovery and healing.

For many clients the goal of psychological safety is elusive and difficult to establish. This early work of treatment includes helping the client to feel safe with her emotions, helping her to know when and how to ask for help, helping her manage memories, nightmares or flashbacks, and helping her to feel safe with the counselor. Establishing safety in the therapeutic relationship can be one of the more difficult tasks of the treatment. Sometimes the client that appears most "treatment compliant" is the one who feels most unsafe in the relationship. Compliance can be generated out of a fear of being harmed and a desire to prevent future victimization. When a client is not aware of her past trauma, she may not even realize how much she doesn't trust the counselor (because it is unconscious). The client has learned that people with power will use it against her, giving her no reason to believe the counselor is different.

Psychodynamic psychotherapies offer a solid basis for how to establish psychological safety through the establishment of a working alliance. This happens through collaboration, emotional honesty and being authentic. Counselors need to demonstrate their trustworthiness, and not assume that the client can take it for granted. Clients with a history of trauma can be prone to misinterpreting the benign, and even helpful, suggestions and statements of their counselors and peers in recovery.

For instance, a young man who was sexually abused as a child may view an older man with long-term sobriety who invites him for coffee after an AA meeting as a potential abuser rather than a potential sponsor.

Individuals who have lived through traumatic situations are highly attuned to others. Many clients are very good at reading the emotional states and understanding the needs of their counselors. This is adaptive behavior, in light of their traumatic circumstances, that served as a form of protection. In treatment, however, these skills can cause difficulties for clients and counselors alike. Counselors can unknowingly take advantage of clients who unconsciously invite role reversal, with the client attending to the needs of the counselor, rather than the other way around. Although with many clients it can be helpful to be somewhat opaque and vague, clients with trauma histories need us to be as real and clear as possible so that they can distinguish us from those who abused them. By real I do not mean self-disclosing about our own histories but rather authentic in our responses, upfront about our rationale for certain intervention strategies and firm about our professional boundaries.

Another consequence of being focused on the needs of others is the inability to identify one's own needs and feelings. A significant component of the treatment should be focused on helping the client identify her own needs and feelings, express her emotions appropriately and to be able to feel safe in doing so (which may include learning where, when and with whom to express emotions). Treatment can be frustrating to both the client and the counselor when the client cannot identify how she feels. If the counselor can frame this as a protective defense, rather than a resistance to treatment, she can help both herself and the client have greater tolerance for the (slow) process of recovery. This will help facilitate the creation of a safe environment for the client.

It is of the utmost importance to establish safety before moving on to explore the trauma and origins of the addiction. When safety in the therapeutic relationship has not been established, there will be a disruption in the future work, sometimes in the form of relapse to substances or behavior that leads to further traumatization. As much as the client wants connection and assistance, she fears being overcome by people in authority, in this case, the counselor. She may act out this conflict in behavior that is difficult to manage: pushing boundaries about appointments and other contact with the counselor outside of treatment, payment, and re-enacting crisis, to which the counselor must respond. The counselor may set an appropriate limit but to the client it feels like a rejection. Another possibility is that the counselor may get over involved with the client, because of the intense pull to help. This could feel like a boundary violation to the client. These types of interactions may set up the client to act out by fleeing treatment, engaging in substance use, getting involved in unhealthy relationships or other behaviors that are equally self-destructive. Although most likely to occur in the beginning phases of treatment, these disruptions can occur at any time. Whenever the therapy appears to be at a standstill, the counselor should consider the issue of safety and explore the quality of the therapeutic relationship (McWilliams, 2004, p. 77).

In AA and NA, recovery begins with the first three steps: acknowledging unmanageability, a belief in the ability to change, and the decision to rely on others or a higher power (Alcoholics Anonymous, 1952). This beginning phase of the work can incorporate concepts from the "Stages of Change" model defined by Prochaska and DiClemente (Prochaska and DiClemente, 1983). Part of preparing people to change is to increase their motivation to change. As clients project their desire for approval onto counselors, and look to counselors as positive role models, the establishment of the therapeutic relationship creates motivation to change. The development of the therapeutic relationship is therefore an important component of the contemplation and preparation phases of treatment. A psychodynamic psychotherapist would refer to this beginning phase of treatment as the development of the working alliance and the transference.

From a psychodynamic point of view, healing must occur within the context of the relationship. Part of what occurs is that, to varying extents, the client's primary attachments must get reenacted with the therapist. This is what is known as the transference. Simply put, the client "transfers" her experiences of her past relationships (both good and bad) onto the therapist, and assumes that the therapist will respond in kind. The transference allows the therapist and the client to experience the client's past relationships, while the working alliance allows them to keep a foot in the present day and examine the experience together (Bromberg, 1996, p. 268). Many traumatized individuals have difficulty separating the past from the present, making the need to distinguish between the current therapeutic relationship and past relationships critical to the establishment and maintenance of the working alliance.

Stage Two

During the second stage of recovery the focus of the work is on helping the client learn about herself. The client retells her story, puts together the pieces of her past, and begins to understand the relationship between her trauma and substance abuse. By connecting her trauma and substance abuse, the client is creating her own relapse prevention plan. The client learns to identify the situations that put her at risk, and coping skills to manage her emotions, urges to use drugs and alcohol and other symptoms. Many traumatized individuals hold onto the belief that they are responsible for what happened to them. Letting go of this belief can be a long and painful process but one that can lead to an enhanced sense of self-efficacy and an increased ability to care for one's self (including one's recovery). It is during this phase that the client begins to assign appropriate responsibility for events, feelings and attitudes from her past. By redefining her history, the client changes her perspective on her current situation, freeing herself to take responsibility for the things she can change (her feelings, thoughts, attitudes). She may notice new feelings ("I don't feel stuck or hopeless anymore"), an improved self-image (no longer a victim, rather someone who happened to be abused), and a new perspective on her ability to take action on her own behalf (hope).

This is a time of great pain, known by some as "remembrance and mourning," when the client reconstructs her story and grieves (Herman, 1992, p. 175). Freud established the relationship between the inability to grieve disappointments, loss and trauma, and depression. Freud came to see the mourning process as the means to avoid, or resolve depression (Freud, 1917). Grieving therefore is a significant component of relapse prevention with as many as 30-40% of substance abusers experiencing co-occurring depression (Sadock, 2003, p. 388). In AA and NA, this is the time when people generally do the work of the fourth through ninth steps. This is a painful time and there is an understandable urge to push through this phase quickly. The counselor's role is to help the client be with the feelings (not rush past them) and normalize the experience of the grief by honoring the time and space needed to do the work.

In psychodynamic psychotherapy this is when the transference is at its height and the client is working through the issues of past relationships through the relationship with the therapist. Generally speaking, the client's emotions are in a heightened state during this phase of the work. As in any close relationship, these emotions enter into the therapeutic relationship. It is during this phase that the client may become aware of intense emotions that are directed at the therapist. Clients may feel love, hate, ambivalence, anger, sadness, disappointment or rage towards the therapist and the work of the therapy. It is not uncommon for a client to feel disappointment and annoyance that therapy is "taking too long." It is the counselor's job to invite the client to say these things directly and to process them together.

If the client and therapist have made it to this point in the work, the client has grown to trust the therapist. Feeling disappointment in someone (sometimes the only one) who has been helpful, even life saving, can be terrifying. Having grown dependent on the counselor, the client must now cope with the humanity (limitations) of the counselor. It can be startling to a counselor, as well as to the client, when an initial idealized transference suddenly becomes negative. If the client can successfully negotiate her feelings with the counselor and continue to feel safe in the relationship, she will be working through a developmental milestone. However, if the client and counselor cannot work through these emotions together, the therapy can be seriously jeopardized, stalled, and the client may even flee treatment.

Having compartmentalized the counselor as all good and those involved in her trauma (and perhaps herself) as all bad, the client has had a constricted and unrealistic outlook. Being able to accept the limitations of the therapist, the client has the opportunity to put her own limitations into perspective. As uncomfortable as it can be to experience the anger and disappointment of a client, some counselors find the love and admiration of clients even more unsettling. It is advantageous for a counselor to utilize supervision and her own therapy to feel more at ease with working with transference feelings. Lastly, if the client and counselor have not first established a solid working alliance, this phase of the work will be disrupted because there will not be a strong enough foundation on which the client can rely to help her feel safe when confronting her feelings about the relationship.

Stage Three

The last stage of recovery is maintenance or reconnection. This parallels the termination phase of psychodynamic psychotherapy. Maintenance refers to maintaining sobriety and continuing the new skills and self-care learned in the earlier phases of treatment. In addition, it is a time to reconnect to the larger community and to "give back" by offering support to others. In AA this is the time when people focus on the 10th-12th steps and often help others by sponsoring newcomers. This offers them connection, a sense of self-efficacy and a way to "keep their memory green" so that they do not return to substance use. For a client whose trauma involved known perpetrators, or others who did not protect the client, it may be during this phase that she decides to confront these individuals. Confrontation may include hope of validation of circumstances, but more realistically is the opportunity for integration of experiences. For many clients, the confrontation is not with others from their past but rather a psychological confrontation, or coming to terms with their individual histories, which occurs within the context of the therapeutic relationship. Some refer to this as the process of acceptance.

It is also the time when people feel like they are living again. Trauma specialists often refer to this part of the work as "reconnection," as it is usually during this phase of the therapy that survivors begin to feel connected to themselves and others in a new, more productive way. During this phase of the work, the client begins to explore her personal goals so as to create the life she wants for herself (Herman, 1992, p. 202). Sometimes this is the time when survivors connect or reconnect with family. Individuals should never be pushed to confront or reconnect with family prematurely because of the risk that the family will not be able to respond appropriately. Survivors need to be well grounded and have appropriate support before they take this very risky step. This phase also correlates to the termination phase of treatment when the client moves away (sometimes physically, but always emotionally) from the treatment program or therapist, to the greater community and begins to rely more heavily on friends and family, and less on the therapist. In psychodynamic terms, this is when the therapist and client work to resolve or undo the transference.

Ego Defense and Resistance

Psychodynamic theories provide a framework with which to understand psychological structure. Sigmund Freud conceived of the structural model of the mind as the Id (It), the Ego (self), and the Superego (the conscience, ego ideal). Freud was interested in how the self/ego, with both conscious and unconscious elements, coped with and found balance between drives, desires and feelings that originated from the id (seen as unconscious drives) and the constraints of the superego, conceived of as the learned values, norms, standards of the individual (Freud, 1923). For instance, clients can be seen as having too harsh of a superego (highly self-critical to the point of inhibiting their own functioning) or too defended against their id (limiting their energy to engage in productive and life-fulfilling activities). Someone with flexible and health-promoting ego defenses is able to function well in love, work and play, without being flooded by feelings (guilt, shame, fear) or symptoms (depression, anxiety, substance abuse, mania) that are the product of these unresolved conflicts. Some people's ego defenses are unable to regulate their feelings causing them to be overwhelmed, while others are considered too rigid, not allowing the person the opportunity to appropriately process and integrate their feelings and experiences. Ego defenses are an integral part of human psychological functioning, without which we could not function. The goal of psychodynamic treatment is not to do away with defenses but rather to help each client to increase her capacity to utilize a varied repertoire of ego defenses. An apt analogy is the saying, "If your only tool is a hammer, every problem looks like a nail." The goal is not to get rid of the hammer so much as to give the client additional tools she can use, saving the hammer for the rare instance when it is the most appropriate response.

In psychodynamic terms, defenses provide the mechanism by which we regulate our emotions and the flow of energy between our insides and our environment. The goal of ego defense is to provide emotional protection to the ego (self), to regulate energy and feelings and to help us feel safe. Defenses that originate as the normal developmental response of the young, preverbal, child are considered more primitive or "primary." Primitive defenses tend to be unconscious and global in their functioning. Secondary defenses have their origins in the primary defenses, utilize our verbal and intellectual capacities and are more selective in their functioning. They are considered to be "higher order" defenses. Defenses are not in and of themselves healthy or unhealthy but rather adaptive, based on developmental age, environment, and circumstances. Although some aspect, or outcome of a defense may be conscious, to be a defense, the process must be unconscious and involuntary (Greenson, R., 1967, p. 36). For example, a client may know that she has a sarcastic sense of humor but she may not be aware of how the sarcasm defends her against the possibility of vulnerability by keeping others at bay. Both primary and secondary defenses will be present in a neurotic or "healthy" person. Which defense is predominant at any given moment will depend on current and past circumstances, character structure and the individual's history.

When effective, ego defenses are activated to help protect us from uncomfortable feelings, such as intense sadness, but will give way to these feelings over time allowing us to experience and integrate them. Someone who is smart and well educated will be likely to have easy access to the defense of intellectualization, considered a higher order defense. This is one of her strengths. On the other hand, if she intellectualizes all the time, she could be missing out on some important aspects of life (intellectualizing rather than feeling, for instance). I know a bright, academic woman who initially coped with the death of her father by buying and reading several books on grief. After reading a few of these books, she "saw" how she was defending herself against her feelings, talked about it, even laughed at herself. Then she began to feel her loss. As counselors we would not worry about her as she became aware of the impact of her defense and was able to move through the feelings. However, if she had continued to intellectualize her father's death, without experiencing the range of feelings she had in relation to him and his death, we would be concerned about her and how her unresolved grief would interfere with her life. On the other hand, the person who uses splitting would have more difficulty integrating her feelings as the sadness would be "split off" or disconnected from her experiences and likely to reveal itself through symptom formation (i.e., depression, mania, anger). Being "split-off" from her awareness, the feelings of grief don't exist for her. Without some awareness of the significance of her emotions, it would take this person much longer (if ever without treatment) to integrate her sadness with her other experiences. We all know someone who has cried over the death of a pet but cannot express any emotion about the death of a family member. This person is displacing her emotions from one event to another. Many people find satisfaction and relief in watching sad movies for the same reason.

A psychodynamic understanding of ego defenses can augment the assessment process, helping to shed light on the complexities of each client, beyond Axis I diagnosis (Blanck and Blanck, 1974, p. 91) The psychodynamic orientation of viewing ego defenses in light of developmental issues and character style, rather than as either good or bad can facilitate the treatment process. The psychodynamic psychotherapist wants to know which ego defenses are dominant and how well these defenses are working. Understanding of a variety of ego defenses and defensive styles can help counselors to differentiate between the ego defense of denial and other defenses such as repression, isolation, intellectualization, rationalization and projection. The counselor can then position herself with the client in such a way as to support and encourage more flexible and adaptive defenses while loosening those ego defenses that are rigid and causing problems for the client. Lastly, gaining an appreciation for the protective function of defense mechanisms reinforces the importance of ensuring that clients have alternative means of self-regulation and coping before the counselor tries to loosen the client's ego defenses or suggest abstinence from substance use.

Someone who has been subjected to chronic stress or trauma may have unevenness in her psychological development, including a limited repertoire of more primitive and rigid defenses. She may have impairments in psychological functioning or ego defense that result in difficulty distinguishing psychological boundaries, misinterpreting the actions/statements of others, difficulty feeling safe and trusting of self and others, desperately needing and simultaneously fearing closeness. A few examples are as follows: The person who projects uncomfortable emotions and thoughts onto others, the person who "shuts down" during or withdraws from situations in which she perceives conflict, the person who gets very close to others quickly but rejects them equally fast when they disappoint her. Such a person is likely to become quickly attached to her counselor yet will be at risk of being easily hurt, disappointed, enraged when the counselor is not meeting her needs as she wants, and therefore at risk of leaving treatment prematurely. During stressful times, we all rely more heavily on primitive defenses to protect ourselves, as primitive defenses are generally more global in their ability to block out painful affect and stimuli.

Psychodynamic psychotherapists expect clients to bring their preferred ego defenses and resistance into the treatment setting. In fact, resistance is always present in the treatment setting as it "defends the status quo," and protects the individual from painful affect. From the psychodynamic point of view, treatment becomes the arena in which the resistance appears and then gets worked through (Greenson, R., 1967, p. 36). In psychodynamic psychotherapies one goal is to uncover (help both the client and counselor to see) the ego defenses and understand the resistance. The resistance must enter the treatment to be explored. The goal is "to uncover how the patient resists, what he is resisting and why he does so" (Greenson, R., 1967, p. 36). The goal of treatment is to raise the unconscious into consciousness. Once conscious, there is opportunity to work through what was previously inaccessible to the client. Even when conscious, defenses are by generally ego-syntonic, in other words, they "feel right" or in accordance with the individual's vision of herself. Successful treatment renders these processes ego-dystonic, or in conflict with one's self-image, opening them to change. Through treatment, clients develop an expanded and more flexible repertoire of ego defenses and coping skills, and adapt higher-level defenses. For instance, rather than dealing with painful affect through isolation, the client will be able to feel her anger, shame and sadness while talking about her trauma. In addition, she will utilize compartmentalization at times when it is not appropriate to be re-experiencing her trauma, so that she can go about her daily life.

In treatment, the counselor attempts to create a working alliance with the health-promoting aspect of the client's ego (self). In traditional addictions treatment settings this is accomplished by naming "the disease" (of addiction) part of the client. People in recovery learn to talk about their "disease" as if it is separate from themselves or at least a discreet part of themselves that needs help. This is consistent with the psycho-dynamic effort to connect with the healthy part of the client's ego (self) through the working alliance, in a mutual effort to explore and change the parts of the self that are wounded, dysfunctional and resist change. Therapy occurs in an "as if" setting, as if the healthy self is separate from the unhealthy self. The therapist and the healthy ego of the client work together to help the unhealthy aspects of the client's self feel safe enough to be exposed, explored and changed. The client and the psychodynamic psychotherapist each have a foot in the present, in the client's past and in the client's future through the hope that the client will feel better and live a more satisfying life in the future (Bromberg, P., 1996, p. 510). This type of working alliance requires a level of psychological stability and sense of personal safety that may not be present in someone who has unresolved traumatic injury.

When the client's ego (self) and ego defenses are not sufficiently de-veloped, the client has difficulty entering into a therapeutic alliance with the counselor. The first work of therapy then is to help the client's ego (self) develop to the place where such an alliance can be established. If the client does not have the ability to psychologically separate her dis-ease and the ego defenses that protect it from the rest of her (ego-dystonic), she will feel attacked when the counselor attempts to confront her disease. Regardless of the motivation of the client, defenses mobilize to provide protection from pain and discomfort, sometimes thwarting the efforts of the counselor. If the client's denial is confronted prema-turely, she may be flooded with emotions with which she is not prepared to cope. This may result in a treatment crisis or premature termination of the treatment. In other cases, alternate or evolved defenses will begin to function on behalf of "the disease" (the client's substance abuse and dys-functional behavior patterns), to maintain the status quo. Clients may begin to rationalize their behavior or intellectualize an understanding of their situation, without experiencing any affect. If the counselor is aware of the shift in the client's ego defenses, she can frame her interventions accordingly. In addition, when the counselor can hold on to the under-standing that these defenses are working to protect the client from what feels like unbearable affect (pain, shame, rage, fear), the counselor has the ability to help the client slowly experience the feelings that the de-fenses are trying to keep at bay. While access to this affect is necessary to facilitate growth and change, it is so painful that many people will "do anything" (leave treatment, relapse or return to abusive situations) to avoid it. Therefore, it is of the utmost importance to not push the client to experience these feelings before she is ready. During this phase of treatment, much of the work for the counselor is in helping the client to manage her feelings.

In 12-step recovery and traditional addictions treatment, any pattern of behavior, thought or affect that serves to deny, diminish or deflect awareness of one's substance use disorder is seen as denial. From a psychodynamic point of view, denial is one of several ego defenses used by all of us. Denial is a basic defense that serves a variety of functions, some helpful and some not. In times of significant crisis, denial may be activated so that an individual can take action, without feeling terror, allowing her the clarity needed to save her own, or someone else's life. The reaction, "Oh No," or "This can't be happening," when we hear of a catastrophic event or death of a loved one, is evidence of denial at work (McWilliams, 1994, p. 101). Denial also allows us to tune out irrelevant information in our environment, allowing us to function effectively (the TV in the background, the static on the phone). Individuals who are unable to tune out background noise and concentrate on the task at hand, often have difficulty in completing school and work related tasks, interfering with their ability to function. For those of us with a varied repertoire of ego defenses, our denial of bad news shifts as we begin to integrate the information. When someone does not have other defenses available to them, they "remain in denial," as if refusing to acknowledge what to others seems obvious. From a "Stages of Change" perspective, denial correlates to the pre-contemplation stage, in which from the client's perspective, there is no problem to even consider. It can feel like (and corresponds developmentally to) magical or childlike thinking (McWilliams, 1994, p. 101). When the client is unaware of the problem, one of the first tasks of treatment is to help the client become aware of it, or bring it into consciousness.

In addictions treatment, denial has traditionally been viewed as a wall that the addict and alcoholic has built up to protect her disease. Denial is seen as the enemy, the vehicle that supports active addiction and interferes with the possibility of recovery. Counselors have been taught to confront denial head on by labeling it so that the client will identify her denial, and be released from it. Being released from one's denial is synonymous with accepting that one has the disease of addiction, and accepting responsibility for getting better through behaviors such as: becoming abstinent, going to treatment, attending 12-step meetings, working with a sponsor. When a client does not take these actions, she is seen to still be "in denial." Sometimes, a client's "denial" is preserved by the adaptation of a more sophisticated defense that appears in the form of treatment compliance. Clients appear to be doing the right things, saying the right things and following treatment and self-help suggestions. However, the underlying structure that supports the addiction has not changed. Treatment compliance can be motivated by fear. When a client has experienced oppression, victimization or trauma, she may not have past experiences to support a belief in her counselor's desire to help.

Understanding a client's range of ego defenses has significant implications for substance abuse and trauma treatment. For instance, if the counselor sees that a client "denies" her addiction with rationalization, "I deserve to drink, it's the only time I can relax," and her trauma through isolation, "I can talk about my trauma but I don't have feelings," then the counselor can design interventions accordingly. The counselor can point out how the client justifies her use, provide the client with alternate relaxation techniques, the skills to cope with feelings and explore the life stressors that are impacting the client. If the ego defense of denial is at work, these interventions might not be effective and the client might feel as if the counselor didn't understand her. This client might require a more supportive psychotherapy that helps her develop more versatile defenses before confronting her addiction. With isolation, the client may report the facts of her trauma without the corresponding affect. The affect may "leak out" in inappropriate situations. The counselor's job would be to help the client feel safe with her emotions, develop skills to express emotions and then help the client connect the affect with the events.

TREATMENT CHALLENGES

Trauma survivors with substance use disorders bring unique challenges to treatment and are best served by a flexible integration of a variety of treatment philosophies and techniques. Psychodynamic theories offer a perspective with which to understand the experience of the client and a context within which to develop treatment interventions. Substance abusing trauma survivors often engage in styles of relating that strain the therapeutic relationship. Some of these patterns are as follows: blaming others, being the victim, being disconnected from oneself, one's emotions and others; being non-compliant or oppositional. These patterns are an unconscious attempt to avoid painful affect. The repetition of earlier, traumatic relationships can be an unconscious attempt to recreate the past in order to "make it right," and heal. Unconscious behavioral and affective patterns serve to protect the client from realities that she is may not be ready to confront. In addition, trauma survivors are especially sensitive to real and perceived boundary violations. A psychodynamic view of the therapeutic relationship can help the counselor to successfully manage treatment boundaries.

Projection, experiencing what is inside oneself, as coming from the outside, is a defense that can be particularly challenging to address. The client "sees" her emotions, needs, limitations and strengths as originating outside of herself and when she talks she sounds as if she is blaming others for her problems. Helping clients own what is theirs, and disown what is not, is particularly challenging when the client has been victimized. In fact, these clients often inappropriately blame themselves for their trauma, and yet cannot take appropriate responsibility for their current behaviors and feelings. An example is a client who accuses a counselor of being angry with her, when in fact, it is the client who is angry with the counselor, but unable to identify or express this emotion. Another example is when a client sees herself as a victim, and cannot let go of this self-image. From a dynamic point of view, there is a secondary gain for being a victim that must be addressed before the client is able to move out of this role. Sometimes the client fears taking responsibility for herself and fears the expectations of others. If she can convince others that she is always a victim, then she does not have to take responsibility for herself and her recovery. There is great confusion about psychic boundaries and therefore, about where responsibility lies. Another factor is that should the client become clear about the true scope of her responsibility, she would have to face overwhelming feelings (rage, fear, shame, pain) of having really been a victim at some time. From a psychodynamic point of view, projection is seen as a primitive defense that develops at a preverbal time when the child cannot differentiate from what is inside herself and what comes from the environment.

Other clients appear disconnected. They may report the "facts" of their abuse without any emotion. Or, in situations that feel stressful or emotionally overwhelming, they may "go blank" or withdraw, which can look like apathy, lack of interest in treatment or even disrespect for the counselor. This maybe an unconscious protective process that began during the trauma. Although this type of disconnection is not a normal part of development, it is a normal response to trauma. When we are exposed to life-threatening situations (rape, natural disasters, serious illness, domestic violence, terrorism) many of us have the ability to disconnect or dissociate as a way to survive the horror. Many victims of abuse report disconnecting from their bodies during the abuse, "It was as if I was watching it happen." Active confrontation of this defense can be experienced by the client as an attack resulting in a boundary violation, further disconnection or a rupture in the therapeutic relationship. Clients are helped when counselors gently probe with questions such as, "Can you tell me what's going on right now?" or "Can you tell me where you were just a moment ago?" Clients are almost always unaware of the extent of their disconnection and gentle probing like this can help bring them back into themselves. With time, patterns in the episodes of disconnection will appear. This will help both the counselor and the client begin to understand the nature of what is being defended. Some clients who have developed the knack of disconnection may find the disconnection is activated even in situations where they have some sense that is not warranted, for instance, in a therapy group.

Whether a client appears ready to address her trauma or is disconnected from it, the first step in the trauma work must be to address the issue of safety (Najavits, 2002). Connecting to the source of the original trauma can be terrifying, defended against at all costs. Many clients will not be able to do this work during their first treatment episodes. In fact, some individuals in recovery from substance dependence find they need to enter therapy several years into recovery to address the issues surrounding their trauma. If the counselor in the primary treatment setting has been able to work with the client around issues of safety, the counselor will have opened the door for the client to address her trauma sometime in the future.

Some clients test the limits, or are oppositional. They appear to go against the established guidelines just "for the sake of being difficult." This can be particularly challenging for the counselor who is in the position of having to constantly set limits, while also trying to establish a therapeutic alliance. This behavior can be interpreted as a fear of engulfment, or repeated trauma. Unconsciously, if the client gets close to and feels safe with the counselor, she will be vulnerable. The client believes (based on past experiences) that if she is vulnerable, she will be abused. The client's defenses are attempting to protect the client from any further abuse. Given the past violations, the client cannot differentiate a safe person/environment from an unsafe person/environment. The client also "pushes" the counselor away out of a belief that the counselor will never really accept her. Rather than face the inevitable rejection and humiliation, the client attempts to avoid being known. This type of acting out behavior can also be viewed as a test to determine how the counselor will react, and if she is going to be trustworthy. Clients who have been traumatized expect to have their boundaries violated. They "push the limits" as a way of testing to see if the counselor will maintain appropriate boundaries. Despite the pull to become over-involved, it is these clients who need to know that no matter what, the counselor will not violate their boundaries. The clients find this out by testing the counselor. While it is important to set firm professional boundaries, it is also important to interpret or hypothesize with the client the meaning of her behavior and her ideas and feelings about how the counselor responds.

Sometimes the counselor feels trapped. The client appears to reject the interpretations and support and yet pulls for the counselor to make concrete suggestions or get overly involved. This can be frustrating for both the counselor and the client. Naming the dilemma by pointing out the client's desire for and fear of help can assist the client in seeing some of these patterns in her current and past relationships. Generally speaking, if the counselor is feeling "trapped," this feeling is mirroring the client's experience and should be addressed directly and compassionately. Feeling trapped is a symptom of the hopelessness that many trauma survivors experience, the quintessential experience of "being caught between a rock and a hard place." A key element of treatment is a realistic hope of recovery. Treatment goals need to be attainable so that the client can experience improvement and believe in her ability to get better. Group therapy and self-help meetings offer contact and identification with other survivors that can add to one's belief in the process.

The complexity of the boundary issues that arise for substance abusing clients with a history of trauma cannot be overstated. Given the focus on the therapeutic relationship, psychodynamic psychotherapies are particularly sensitive to the issue of boundaries and can offer some guidelines for working with this population. The therapist's interest in the client's experience of the treatment helps both parties to maintain appropriate boundaries. The therapist demonstrates her concern for the client and the value she places on the client's perspective by encouraging the client to talk about her experiences of the therapist and treatment. The therapist responds in a non-judgmental and accepting manner, even when she disagrees with the client's perspective. This information educates them both about what the client needs and how the client experiences others. If the client feels heard, she will be less likely to act out what is going on in her internal world.

The psychodynamic therapist uses her experiences of the client to inform the treatment. The therapist pays attention to how she feels and the associations she has when working with a client. Rather than reacting to her feelings, she reflects on them to gain insight into the experiences of the client. For instance, if a client is speaking without affect and the counselor suddenly feels sad (and has no reason of her own to feel sad), she can hypothesize that the client's defenses have isolated (or otherwise disconnected) the feeling of sadness from the subject matter. If a working alliance has been established, and the counselor knows that the client has the ability to manage some feelings, the counselor might gently probe for a feeling. However, if the working alliance has not been established or the client is not prepared to manage intense feelings (both of which are likely given the lack of affect presented) the counselor would hold onto this information until a later, more appropriate time. In psychodynamic psychotherapy it is often the case that the therapist must go on an "emotional roller coaster ride" on behalf of the client, before the client is able to experience her own feelings. It is tempting to tell the client what she is feeling but to do so prematurely could be a boundary violation and reactivate an old wound. Countertransference and counselor self-care is addressed in Chapter 14 of this work by Patricia Burke, Bruce Carruth and David Prichard.

CONCLUSION

Psychodynamic theories can provide a useful framework with which to shape treatment for substance abusing clients with a history of trauma. The careful attention to the therapeutic relationship can assist in the formation of a therapeutic alliance, increase the client's sense of self-efficacy and can help to reduce boundary violations and recidivism. The deep appreciation for the protective function of ego defense that is emphasized by the psychodynamic literature can help counselors understand the complexity of resistance and motivation. An understanding of varied unconscious ego defenses can aid in the formulation of realistic goals and individualized interventions. Lastly, psychodynamic psychotherapies can support and enhance the client's experience of self-help and traditional 12-step model of addictions recovery.

REFERENCES

Alcoholics Anonymous World Services, Inc. (1952). *Twelve Steps and Twelve Traditions*. New York.
Alcoholics Anonymous World Services, Inc. (1976). *Alcoholics Anonymous*, Third Edition. New York.

Blanck, G. and Blanck, R. (1974*). Ego Psychology: Theory and Practice.* New York and London. Columbia University Press.

Bromberg, P. (1996), Standing in the spaces: The multiplicity of self and the psychoanalytic relationship. *Contemporary Psychoanlysis*, 32, 509-535.

Davis-Kasl, C. (1992). *Many Roads, One Journey: Moving Beyond the 12 Steps.* New York: HarperCollins.

Freud, S. (1937). Analysis Terminable and Interminable. *Standard Edition, 23,* 209-254.

Freud, S. (1912). The Dynamics of Transference. *Standard Edition, 12,* 99-108.

Freud, S. (1923). The Ego and the Id. Standard Edition, *19,* 13-59.

Freud, S. (1917). Mourning and Melancholia. *Standard Edition, 14,* 243-258.

Greenson, R. (1967). *The Technique and Practice of Psychoanalysis Volume I.* Madison, CT: International Universities Press, Inc.

Herman, J. (1992). *Trauma and Recovery.* New York: Basic Books.

Jellinek, E.M. (1968) *The disease concept of alcoholism.* New Haven: College and University Press.

Luborksy, L. (1993). The role of the therapeutic alliance in psychotherapy. *Journal of Consulting and Clinical Psychology, 61*: 4, 561-573.

McWilliams, Nancy (1999). *Psychoanalytic Case Formulation.* New York: Guilford Press.

McWilliams, Nancy (1994). *Psychoanalytic Diagnosis: Understanding Personality Structure in the Clinical Process.* New York: Guilford Press.

McWilliams, Nancy (2004). *Psychoanalytic Psychotherapy. A Practitioner's Guide.* New York: Guilford Press.

Miller, W. and Rollnick, S. (2002). *Motivational Interviewing: Preparing People to Face Change.* New York: Guilford Press.

Najavits, Lisa M. (2002). *Seeking Safety: A Treatment Manual for PTST and Substance Abuse.* New York: Guilford Press.

Prochaska, J. and DiClemente, C. (1983). Stage and Processes of Self-Change of Smoking: Toward An Integrative Model of Change. *Journal of Consulting and Clinical Psychology, 51:3,* 390-395.

Sadock, Benjamin and Sadock, Virginia (2003). *Kaplan and Sadock's Synopsis of Psychiatry,* Ninth Edition. New York: Lippincott, Williams and Wilkins.

Attachment, Trauma and Addiction

Ronald Potter-Efron, MSW, PhD

SUMMARY. The major linkages between insecure attachment, traumatic experiences and addictive processes are described in this chapter, along with distinct treatment suggestions for dismissively attached, preoccupied, and fearfully attached addicted clients. *[Article copies available for a fee from The Haworth Document Delivery Service: 1-800-HAWORTH. E-mail address: <docdelivery@haworthpress.com> Website: <http://www.HaworthPress.com> © 2006 by The Haworth Press, Inc. All rights reserved.]*

KEYWORDS. Attachment, trauma, addiction

INTRODUCTION

Three complicated, difficult concepts: attachment, trauma and addiction. The relevant question is how do these three variables interact? The answer, of course, is that they mingle, merge and diverge in countless patterns. There is no single connection between attachment, trauma and addiction but rather dozens of possible interactions amongst them. It would be virtually impossible to write meaningfully about each of them. Instead, I will focus during this chapter upon some of the more common inter-weavings of these concepts–the ones that are particularly likely to be found among clients in addiction and mental health centers.

[Haworth co-indexing entry note]: "Attachment, Trauma and Addiction." Potter-Efron, Ronald. Co-published simultaneously in *Journal of Chemical Dependency Treatment* (The Haworth Press, Inc.) Vol. 8, No. 2, 2006, pp. 71-87; and: *Psychological Trauma and Addiction Treatment* (ed: Bruce Carruth) The Haworth Press, Inc., 2006, pp. 71-87. Single or multiple copies of this article are available for a fee from The Haworth Document Delivery Service [1-800-HAWORTH, 9:00 a.m. - 5:00 p.m. (EST). E-mail address: docdelivery@haworthpress.com].

Available online at http://www.haworthpress.com/web/JCDT
© 2006 by The Haworth Press, Inc. All rights reserved.
doi:10.1300/J034v08n02_04

Here are a few examples: (a) an alcoholic mother is both neglectful and abusive of her child, who in turn develops into a dismissive adult who eschews intimate relationships as useless and boring; (b) a 20 year old woman who grew up in a loving family marries a batterer. She gradually feels less and less secure in her life and turns to drug use for relief; (c) a 50 year old man "drinks to remember" the abuse he suffered while being terribly bullied by his school mates during his youth. His distrust of all human beings emerges during these drunken bouts but so does a desperate, clingy part of himself that he normally hides from view.

First, I will describe the major concepts of attachment in the next section of this work. Then I will detail some of the specific relationships between attachment, trauma and addiction. Finally I will suggest therapeutic goals and processes to help clients in early recovery from addiction move through or around their traumatic histories to achieve greater attachment security.

ATTACHMENT THEORY: KEY CONCEPTS

Definition: Attachment is an enduring emotional bond that involves a tendency to seek and maintain proximity to a specific person, particularly when under stress . . . a mutual regulatory system that provides safety, protection and a sense of security.

Attachment is "an intense and enduring bond biologically rooted in the function of protection from danger" (Wilson, 2001, p. 38).

John Bowlby (1969, 1973, 1980) developed the concept of attachment bonding after intense observation of the ways infants and young children up to about two years old interacted with their mothers (later this information was discovered to apply to fathers and other primary caregivers as well but the original research was exclusively focused upon the mother/infant bond). Bowlby and his co-researcher Mary Ainsworth noted that the core relationship between mother and child could be observed by how they responded to a simple experiment labeled the "strange situation" in which mothers briefly left their children in an unfamiliar play room (with an attendant) and then returned a few minutes later. Four distinct patterns emerged:

- *Secure*: the child feels distressed, seeks out mother, feels relief, returns to play;
- *Anxious/Avoidant*: the child feels distressed but ignores mother when she returns;

- *Anxious/Ambivalent*: the child demonstrates high distress through a mixed approach/rejection reaction when mother returns (e.g., hugs but arches away);
- *Disorganized/Disoriented*: there is no consistent pattern or the child displays unusual behaviors upon mother's return (e.g., fall to floor, turn in circles).

Each of these patterns reflected the mother's behavior but also predicted the child's response. For example, mothers who tended to hold themselves apart from the child and who were least demonstrative upon returning to the playroom tended to have children who in turn were relatively undemonstrative or affectionate as well. The bonding relationship was in effect a mutual and reciprocal process in which each player acted upon and reinforced the other.

Parental behaviors predict children's attachment style: sensitive and consistently responsive parents tend to have secure children; parents who are unresponsive and rejecting of proximity tend to have avoidant children; inconsistent parents who alternate between unavailability and intrusiveness tend to have anxious/ambivalent children; excessively disturbed parents with very unpredictable behavior tend to produce disorganized/disoriented children.

CORE ASPECTS
OF CHILD/CAREGIVER ATTACHMENT BONDING

Several key concepts have emerged from attachment studies. These include:

- The need to develop and maintain attachment bonds is not a drive but an equally powerful independent behavioral system. It is rooted in the infant's utter dependency upon adult caregivers for protection and survival. Infants are hard-wired to move, act and make sounds that trigger the adult's hard-wired (but not inevitable) urge to respond to the infant with nurturing behaviors and bonding emotions.
- Attachment bonds primarily regulate the physical distance between infant and caregiver. Any parent who remembers how difficult it was to leave his or her young child has felt the powerful magnetism of the attachment bond. "Don't leave me" is the in-

fant's plea. "Don't worry, I could never do that," is the bonded caregiver's reply.

- Attachment bonds are organized around specific attachment figures. A unique infant forms a specific bond with a unique adult. That bond generates its own particular rhythm and patterns that will be at least slightly different than that infant's bonds with other adults or the adult's bonds with other infants. No two attachment bonds are exactly alike. Thus, the parental phrase "I love you all the same" cannot be entirely true. Rather, "I love each of you tremendously (but not the same)" is more accurate.

- The goal of the attachment bond is felt security. Physical safety is certainly the pivotal point to obtain a feeling of security. However, psychologically experienced feelings of safety and security go beyond the issue of immediate physical well-being. They involve a deeper, more long-term belief system that the world is or is not a safe place in which to reside.

- When attachment needs are well met the infant develops a sense of having a *safe haven*. The world is a safe place at the center of which are caregivers who are consistently present and protective. The familiar saying "I know that whatever happens I can always go home and there will be a place for me" reflects the felt presence of a safe haven.

- When attachment needs are well met the infant also develops a sense of having a *secure base* from which he or she can explore the environment. It is a sense of safety at the center of one's being that is critical for children and adults to find the courage to explore their environment. For infants this exploration begins with the bold adventure of toddling away from Mommy's or Daddy's safe grasp, at least for a few moments before feeling overcome by anxiety and rushing to return. Children and adults with a strong sense of attachment security can leave that connection partly because they know that they will be welcomed upon return and even more because they carry inside their minds a firm and clear sense of being loved and wanted.

- The attachment system is not always active. People are not normally attuned to their attachment needs on a moment-to-moment basis. To be so would be overwhelming and totally distracting. Rather, they tend to become aware of their attachment relationships during particularly powerful moments of exceptional closeness, when the infant's attachment figures move away from the infant, or when the child feels threatened. Note that the state of feeling threatened is based on the appearance of threat in one's mind. The incredibly jealous husband of a faithful wife can easily imagine her being erotically attracted to her neighbor, work associate, or even to any man walking down the street regardless of her actual behavior or intent. That man fears losing his attachment figure, the one in his mind as much or more than the real person beside him.

- When threatened with the loss of an attachment figure, the infant behaves in ways designed to restore adult proximity (crying, wailing, crawling after the caregiver, etc.). There is a standard sequence of infant reactions to attachment figure separation: first *Protest,* then *Despair,* and finally *Detachment (Reintegration).* All the infant knows is that the caregiver is going away. Since that child cannot yet comprehend the concept "But he or she will soon return" the protest is desperate, a fight to retrieve that which is absolutely necessary for survival. If protest fails the infant slumps into the hopeless despair of someone abandoned to die. Fortunately, this despair is usually a wasted tragedy. Mommy or Daddy do indeed come back and the infant can celebrate their renewed relationship as if they had truly returned from the dead. But sometimes caregivers fail to return. They run off, become too disabled to nurture, or die. Then the child must go to the third phase of the attachment process, namely what Bowlby called "detachment" but I prefer to label "reintegration" since "detachment" has become a term associated with codependency and has a different meaning now then when Bowlby utilized the term. The concept of reintegration refers to the need for the infant or adult who has indeed lost an attachment bond to grieve that loss and then go on to form new bonds. Fortunately, human beings at all ages appear to have this ability although one's past experience significantly affects a person's ability to create new bonds.

- Children gradually develop (age 9-18 months: Diamond and Blatt, 1994) *internal working models.* These models are based upon their early attachment experiences. Internal working models are mostly an unconscious set of expectations about whether and how well their security needs will be met by significant others. These models usually include a sense of the self as worthy or unworthy and lovable or unlovable, in other words whether the person is someone others will want to bond with. The internal working model also includes expectations about the nature, benefits, costs and consequences of attachment. This model provides a context for later social relationships (Dutton, 1998) although it can sometimes be altered by later attachment experiences. While positive internal working models prepare children for a world in which they feel welcome, attractive, loved and secure, negative working model can be devastating because children develop beliefs about themselves that hinder the creation of long-term attachment bonds. These beliefs include thoughts such as: "I am bad, unwanted, worthless, helpless, unlovable"; "Caregivers are unresponsive, insensitive, hurtful, untrustworthy"; "Life is unsafe, not worth living" (Levy and Orlans, 2000, p. 12). Clearly individuals harboring these belief patterns are quite vulnerable to the lure of addictions as a substitute for intrinsically unsatisfying human relationships.

• There are many benefits for children who develop a secure sense of attachment. These include: (a) felt sense of safety and protection; (b) basic trust in others and an expectation for positive reciprocity in significant relationships; (c) an ability to explore the world; (d) self-soothing and self-regulation of affect; (e) identity formation as competent, worthy, and lovable; (f) an achieved balance between autonomy and dependency; (g) a pro-social sense of morality; (h) a positive view of others and the world; (i) a sense of resiliency; (j) and, particularly relevant to the concerns of this paper, well-met attachment needs provide children with a defense against stress and trauma (Levy and Orlans, 2000).

ADULT ATTACHMENT MODEL

Bowlby hypothesized that adults would retain and be strongly affected by their internal working attachment models throughout adulthood. Research eventually validated that position although adults can and do change their perspective on attachments over time in tune with their actual life experiences.

Adult attachment has been defined as "The stable tendency of an individual to make substantial efforts to seek out and maintain proximity with one or a few specific individuals who provide the subjective potential for physical and/or psychological safety and security" (Berman and Sperling, 1994, p. 8).

Kim Bartholomew has developed a model of adult attachment styles. She describes individuals with four different styles as noted below.

- *Secure*: Basic trust in self and others; resilient, flexible, adaptive; able to seek and receive support when stressed; able to give support to others; positive view of self but can admit weaknesses and needs; interdependent in relationships; comfortable with both intimacy and autonomy.
- *Dismissive*: High self-worth but low worth of others; low anxiety and high avoidance; defends against attachment anxiety by lessening need for attachment; apparent self-sufficiency; however, dismissive individuals may become very anxious when attachments lost if defenses against feeling are broken through; low trust; pulls away when partner seeks intimacy; autonomy and self-reliance treasured; withdraws when others are stressed and needy; overly critical and controlling when helping partners; often perceived as cold and hostile by others; doesn't use partner as safe haven or secure base (Fraley et al., 1998); denies value of close relationships; limited and over-idealized memories of childhood.
- *Preoccupied*: Low self-worth and high worth of others; high anxiety and low avoidance; seeks acceptance, safety and validation from others; enmeshed in earlier unresolved attachment autonomy compromised because of need for security; demands emotional contact but never satisfied because of unrealistically high demands ("I scare people away. I want to be so close, all the time, and they get nervous."–Bartholomew et al., 2001, p. 47)
- *Fearful*: Low self-worth and low worth of others; high anxiety and high avoidance; desire acceptance but avoid intimacy because of fear of and anticipation of rejection ("I'm afraid I'll say something that ruins the relationship."–Bartholomew et al., 2001, p. 47); need others to validate self-worth; conscious fear of anticipated rejection; distrustful of other person's commitment level and faithfulness.

Actual people, of course, seldom fit perfectly into just one of these four cells. Most individuals report a mixture of characteristics from each type but still they tend to fit better into one cell than others. Some persons' report fit into a particular attachment style with one significant other but another style with someone else.

I suggest the following authors for good overviews of attachment theory: Berman and Sperling (1994); Karen (1994); Levy and Orlans (2000); Wilson (2001).

PRIMARY LINKAGES BETWEEN THE CONCEPTS OF ATTACHMENT, TRAUMA AND ADDICTION

1. All three variables (attachment, trauma and addiction) are ongoing, dynamic psychological events that reflect both an individual's history and current circumstances;
2. For heuristic purposes any of the three variables can be considered causal of the other two. The reality, however, is that each interacts with the others in complicated feedback loops;
3. To complicate matters further, these three variables do not constitute a closed system. Other considerations, such as genetic predisposition to anxiety or depression, may influence any or all of these variables;
4. It is not just the client but also the client's family of origin and/or current relationships that must be considered with regard to attachment, trauma and addictive processes. For example, the child of an active, violent alcoholic parent receives modeling that life is dangerous, parents can be dangerous and cannot be relied upon, and that addictive processes somehow might make life more manageable. One of my clients with this background made a conscious decision by age twelve to become alcoholic. She achieved that goal before her sixteenth birthday;
5. Secure attachment serves as a buffer against the development of addiction even in the face of traumatization: "I always knew Dad loved me even though he couldn't keep me safe from Mom after their divorce." These are the words of a young man who was beaten by his step-father from age eight to twelve when his mother finally left that man. My client's father knew his son was being harmed but could only rescue him for occasional brief week-ends. Still, the son's awareness and felt love from his father partially inoculated him from his step-father's influence. Yes, he was beaten. But even so my client maintained a belief that most people are good and trustworthy. He emerged from his adolescence with a secure attachment style and has not been tempted to seek addictive relief;
6. By contrast, insecure attachment increases someone's vulnerability to addiction, especially in combination with traumatization. Dismissive individuals, for example, might consciously or subconsciously seek the ease of a relationship with an addictive process as against the relative chaos of a real relationship. Preoccupied individuals may be attracted to addictions because

of their reliability, not having to worry about being abandoned by a drug or pornographic magazine. Fearful people, meanwhile, find addictions particularly attractive because they can trust their addictions more than they can trust human beings. As Craig Nakken writes, addiction is "an emotional relationship, through which addicts try to meet their needs for intimacy" (Nakken, 1996, p. 8);

7. Traumatization generally decreases one's ability to form and maintain secure attachment bonds and generally increases a person's vulnerability to becoming addicted to a substance or event. Traumatization at any age will tend to move people away from secure attachment and toward the other three styles, in particular toward fearful attachment. If the kind of brain damage described by Joseph LeDoux (1996) occurs, in which the brain's physical structure is altered to increase sensitivity to danger (in particular, the hippocampus diminishes in size), then trauma survivors will have great difficulty developing and maintaining long-term positive relationships. Addictive processes are certainly more probable under these conditions;

8. Early traumatization may make it almost impossible for children to form attachment bonds. Some children develop a "Reactive Attachment Disorder" which is characterized by an inability to form normal relationships and an impairment in social development and may be marked by sociopathic behaviors during childhood such as cruelty to animals, fire-setting and enuresis (Wilson, 2001);

9. Traumatization can simultaneously intensify and distort an individual's need to attach. So-called "trauma bonds" have been known to form between people being held hostage and their captors. A more common example of this phenomenon, though, occurs between batterer and batteree in situations where the batterer systematically controls his partner. Here the batterer's position of power and control as well as his use of violence and threat for aggression activate attachment bonds even though the attachment figure is the very source of the threat. Essentially the batterer establishes a position in which he both undermines his partner's sense of attachment security and attractiveness through violence, shaming and isolation ("Nobody else would ever want you") while casting himself as the batteree's only hope for sustained attachment ("You're just lucky I stay with you.") This

pattern represents one explanation for the tremendous stability of many dysfunctional relationships;

10. Addiction increases a person's vulnerability for traumatic victimization, such as getting beaten or raped while intoxicated. Thus, addiction tends to decrease someone's safety even as he or she seeks it for internal security;

11. The nature of addictive processes generally includes a falling away from secure attachment relationships as the addiction gains power and control. Addictions erode positive relationships as addicts spend more time meeting their addictive needs and less time nurturing their relationships. In addition, defensiveness, aggressiveness, impulsivity and poor judgment may all increase during intoxication or in general, thus adding to the likelihood for violence within relationships;

12. Insecurely attached individuals will generally form an attachment relationship with their addictive substance or event in a similar way to how they attach to people. Thus, dismissive clients will dismissively deny their problem ("I can quit drinking any time I want to"), preoccupied clients will act in a preoccupied manner ("I worry all the time about running out of my medicine"), and fearful persons will act fearfully ("I'm afraid. I know I'm trapped but I don't think I can ever get away from it.") towards their particular addiction;

13. It is important to view at least some addictive processes as attempts by people to heal attachment wounds that have been caused or exacerbated by trauma. They do so by substituting addictive processes for human relationships. In doing this they hope to increase their internal sense of safety and security in a far too threatening world.

HELPING ADDICTED CLIENTS WHOSE ATTACHMENT ABILITIES HAVE BEEN AFFECTED BY TRAUMA

The general goal with clients who have any of the three insecure adult attachment styles (dismissive, preoccupied, fearful) is to help these individuals develop or recover a better ability to form positive, strong and stable bonds with others. The ideal therapeutic role, then, is to help each client "contemplate and indeed re-experience his or her life story within a safe and healing context, with an emotionally available and sensitive other who gives new meaning and shape to life events and the patient's sense of self and relationship" (Slade, 1999, p. 586). To do so, therapists must attempt to help clients: (a) develop a secure base for personal exploration; (b) consider how they engage in relationships and their expectations with significant figures [their working models]; (c) examine their relationship with the therapist as that relationship reveals information about the client's models; (d) recognize how early parental expectations and experiences affect current perceptions and expectations; (e) realize that these models may or may not be appropriate in the present and future and (f) encourage the development of new, more autonomous models (Berman and Sperling, 1994; Lyons; Clulow, 2001). This is not an easy task, especially when placed within the time limits of structured inpatient or outpatient addiction treatment programs.

Here is a set of questions that are particularly helpful in identifying and addressing the client's attachment history, beliefs, and current behaviors:

Do you remember when you were growing up how you handled situations in which your parents or other important people in your life left you? Did you get angry? Feel scared? Feel hurt? Feel little or nothing at all? Can you give me a few examples?

When you were growing up, what attachment style best describes the relationship you had with your mother? With your father? Other important caregivers? Can you give me examples of why you say that?

How do you think growing up that way has affected your adult relationships? Your sense of safety and trust in relationships? Your ability to depend on others and to be dependable? Your ability to give and receive love?

In terms of parenting styles, how much are you like your mother? Your father? How do you want to be like them? How do you want to be different? Can you give some examples of how you have chosen to act differently than your mother or father in this area?

How have past adolescent or adult relationships affected your attachment style? Have they helped you become more secure? Less secure? In what ways?

How is your current relationship affecting your attachment style? Is it helping you become more secure? Less secure? In what ways?

In addition to these questions, addiction counselors with traumatized clients need to direct their clients' attention to the following questions: (1) How have your traumatic experiences affected your ability to establish and maintain intimate relationships in the past? (2) What about now? How are they still having an effect? (3) How have your traumatic experiences affected your behavior with regards to alcohol and drug use and other addictive behaviors? (4) To what extent do you rely upon your addictive experiences to provide you with feelings of safety and security? (5) To what extent do you use your addiction as a substitute for human interactions? (6) If you were to quit using addictive substances and processes how would you meet your basic needs for friendship, closeness to others, bonding and intimacy?

Here is an example of how this set of questions may be helpful during counseling sessions. The client, Rollie, is an assistant professor of sociology at a local university. He suffered a traumatic attachment loss early in life. In particular, his mother died in an automobile accident when he was nine years old. This loss was seldom discussed within his family. Rather, Rollie was expected to get on with life. Developing a dismissive approach to life, Rollie subsequently poured his energy into academics where his intellectual successes were rewarded. He also gradually became dependent upon marijuana, starting with an occasional smoke in his late teens and increasing to daily use in his late twenties. His marijuana dependence affected his motivational level as well as his abstraction abilities, limiting his achievements in early adulthood. He mostly smoked marijuana alone, sometimes with his wife Amy who did not appreciate the full extent of his dependence.

Here are a few (summarized) answers to the questions noted previously:

a. Q: How did you handle situations in which people left you (specifically, your mother's death)?
   A: I mostly read books and tried not to feel anything at all.
b. Q: How do you think growing up that way has affected your adult relationships?
   A: I've stayed more distant from Amy than I had to. She often wants more closeness and connection than I feel comfortable giving. Part of me wants to get close but part of me just keeps staying away.
c. Q: In terms of parenting styles, how are you like your parents?
   A: I've been told by relatives that my mother was a wonderful parent until she got sick. She let us kids jump on the sofa all the time. I try to be more like her than my Dad. He did his best but he couldn't handle the job after Mom died.
d. Q: How have your traumatic experiences affected your behavior with regards to alcohol and drug use and other addictive behaviors?

A: Smoking weed is a way of getting away from everybody. I mostly smoke alone. I'm most likely to want to get high when something goes wrong in my life.

e. Q: To what extent do you rely upon your addictive experiences to provide you with feelings of safety and security? To what extent do you use your addiction as a substitute for human interactions?
A: I feel mellow. Calm. Safe. I feel less anxious. I know I could go to Amy when I feel bad, but I don't. I go to weed instead.

f. Q: If you were to quit using addictive substances and processes how would you meet your basic needs for friendship, closeness to others, bonding and intimacy?
A: I guess I would start talking more with Amy. Maybe I'd try out those N.A. [Narcotics Anonymous] meetings you told me about, but I don't think I'd like them much.

Rollie did make and keep a commitment to abstain from marijuana. His academic performance improved considerably, which for him was perhaps the single most important reason not to relapse. He also gradually developed greater empathy for others and for himself, relinquishing his "just don't feel anything" dismissive approach and replacing it over a several year period with the ability to more deeply connect with others and himself at an emotional level.

SPECIFIC APPROACHES TO TAKE
WITH DISMISSIVELY ATTACHED TRAUMATIZED CLIENTS

Addictive clients who have developed a dismissive attachment style partly as a result of traumatization can be especially difficult to work with in group therapy settings. This is because they have pulled away from others in their attempts to maintain boundaries and personal safety. One result is a lack of empathy: "I don't like A.A. They're all a bunch of losers. Why should I have to listen to all their pathetic stories?" Additionally, dismissive persons often take a stance of superiority over others. They don't need others. They don't want to be bothered with anyone else's needs. They just want to be left alone. But these clients are often anxious and insecure beneath their dismissive cover. They have turned to addictions in an attempt to alleviate their stress without having to rely on fundamentally unreliable human beings.

Addiction counselors can assist these clients in the following ways:

a. Help clients distinguish between really not having needs for intimacy, dependency, and human relationships vs. defending against those needs with a veneer of self-sufficiency and addictive processes;
b. Maintaining a focus upon feelings during discussions, since these clients tend to utilize addictions to avoid affect;
c. Suggesting specific and concrete ways in which the client could move closer to others;
d. Empathy training to enhance involvement with and curiosity about others;
e. Suggesting the concept of "interdependence" to help dismissers realize they can maintain independence while developing their capacity for intimacy;
f. Helping the client specifically understand the linkages between his or her traumatic experiences and pulling away from emotional vulnerability;
g. Helping the client understand how his or her dismissive attachment style has contributed to addiction as a risk-free alternative source for attachment ("My best friend "Al").

SPECIFIC APPROACHES
TO TAKE WITH PREOCCUPIED CLIENTS
WHO HAVE BEEN TRAUMATIZED

Anxiety attending the dread of abandonment is the disaster that drives preoccupied clients toward such unfortunate behaviors as continually seeking contact with their objects of affection, jealous accusations of infidelity and a constant need for reassurance. Traumatic experiences frequently heighten these fears, especially if beatings or other abuses were perpetrated by caregivers and accompanied by the threat of abandonment ("I should just take you to the orphanage and get rid of you once and for all! And it will be all your fault because you are such a bad child."). Addictive processes may be discovered and utilized by preoccupied clients to assuage their otherwise intolerable feelings of anxiety centered on a working attachment model that predicts inevitable loss.

Addiction counselors can assist these clients in the following ways:

a. Help them recognize and discuss their fears of aloneness and abandonment that are based upon the belief that they are less worthy or lovable than their partners;
b. Encourage a movement toward autonomy, for instance by giving them assignments to do things alone that they would normally do with others;
c. Discourage desperation efforts by the preoccupied client to force others to demonstrate their love, caring and interest in them (but get them to discuss how their repeated efforts do occasionally pay off for them since they have developed a powerful reward system based upon random and irregular rewards);
d. Encourage self-esteem and shame work to gradually raise the client's self-worth and self-respect;
e. Help preoccupied clients understand how their traumatic experiences encouraged both a movement toward preoccupation and toward addiction.

SPECIFIC APPROACHES TO TAKE WITH FEARFUL CLIENTS WHO HAVE BEEN TRAUMATIZED

Clients with fearful attachment style share the problems of both dismissive and preoccupied persons. On the one hand, like dismissers, they shy away from developing deep relationships in the first place. On the other hand they tend to become anxious and fear abandonment and betrayal when they do allow themselves to attach. This combination leads to a severe lack of trust in others. This leads to a continuing doubt about the reliability and level of commitment of their relationship partners even when those individuals have done nothing to warrant suspicion. Traumatic experiences create, increase and maintain this sense of distrust in the world, although not all fearful individuals have experienced trauma.

Addiction counselors can assist these clients in the following ways:

a. Help fearful clients set goals both for autonomy and closeness since they are deficient in both areas;

b. Providing self-esteem and shame readings, discussions and exercises in order to gradually raise the client's self-worth and self-respect;

c. Focusing on the theme of trust: how trust has been broken in the past, negative belief systems ("Nobody can be trusted, especially . . . "), the possibility of developing trust in the present, and challenging negative belief systems about current or future relationships;

d. Encouraging opening up to others, especially in close relationships, since it is impossible to learn to trust without occasional vulnerability; discuss fears of being seen by others;

e. Getting clients to understand how their traumatic experiences may have increased their fearfulness and led them toward addictive processes.

CONCLUSION

The relationships between addiction, trauma and attachment styles are complex and unique for each individual. Nevertheless, these linkages can sabotage effective addiction treatment if left unaddressed. Addiction counselors who are aware of the connections noted above can help their clients understand the effects of trauma on their attachment beliefs and how these beliefs in turn have contributed to their addictive tendencies.

REFERENCES

Bartholomew, Kim, Henderson, Antonia and Dutton, Donald (2001). Insecure Attachment and Insecure Intimate Relationships. In Christopher Clulow (Ed.), *Adult Attachment and Couple Psychotherapy*. London: Brunner-Rutledge, 43-62.

Berman, William and Sperling, Michael (1994). The Structure and Function of Adult Attachment. In M. Sperling and W. Berman (Eds.), *Attachment in Adults*. New York: Guilford Press, 1-30.

Bowlby, John (1969). *Attachment and Loss: Vol. One. Attachment*. New York: Basic Books.

Bowlby, John (1973). *Attachment and Loss: Vol. Two. Separation: Anxiety and Anger*. New York: Basic Books.

Bowlby, John (1980). *Attachment and Loss: Vol. Three. Loss: Sadness and Depression*. New York: Basic Books.

Clulow, Christopher (2001). Insecure Attachment and Abusive Intimate Relationships. In Christopher Clulow (Ed.), *Adult Attachment and Couple Psychotherapy*. London: Brunner-Rutledge, 85-104.

Diamond, Diana and Blatt, Sidney (1994). Internal Working Models and the Representational World in Attachment and Psychoanalytic Theories. In M. Sperling and W. Berman (Eds.), *Attachment in Adults*. New York: Guilford Press, 72-97.

Dutton, Donald (1998). *The Abusive Personality*. New York: Guilford Press.

Fraley, R. Chris, Davis, Keith and Shaver, Phillip (1998). Dismissing-Avoidance and the Defensive Organization of Emotion, Cognition and Behavior. In Jeffry Simson and W.S. Rholes (Eds.), *Attachment Theory and Close Relationships*, New York: Guilford Press, 249-279.

Karen, Robert (1994). *Becoming Attached*. New York: Oxford University Press.

LeDoux, J. (1996). *The Emotional Brain*. New York: Touchstone.

Levy, Terry and Orlans, Michael (2000). Attachment Disorder as an Antecedent to Violence and Antisocial Patterns in Children. In Terry Levy (Ed.), *Handbook of Attachment Interventions*. San Diego: Academic Press, 1-25.

Nakken, C. (1996). *The Addictive Personality*, 2nd Edition. Center City, MN: Hazelden Publications.

Slade, Arietta (1999). Attachment Theory and Research: Implications for the Theory and Practice of Individual Psychotherapy with Adults. In Jude Cassidy and Phillip Shaver (Eds.), *Handbook of Attachment*. New York: Guilford Press, 575-594.

Wilson, Samantha (2001). Attachment Disorders: Review and Current Status. In *Journal of Psychology*, 135 (1), 37-52.

Affect Centered Therapy
for Substance Abuse of Traumatic Origin

John Omaha, PhD

SUMMARY. Affect Centered Therapy holds the promise of providing lasting treatment for many forms of substance abuse disorder because it appears to effectively address the true causes of the disorder. ACT is derived from a developmental model that accurately describes the etiology of addictive behaviors. The developmental model is supported by a large body of empirical evidence (Sroufe, 1997). ACT itself is supported by clinical impressions and limited single case design studies (Omaha, 1998, July 11; 1999, June 19; 2000, September 10). *[Article copies available for a fee from The Haworth Document Delivery Service: 1-800-HAWORTH. E-mail address: <docdelivery@haworthpress.com> Website: <http://www.HaworthPress.com> © 2006 by The Haworth Press, Inc. All rights reserved.]*

KEYWORDS. Adversity and trauma, attachment, substance abuse

INTRODUCTION:
SUBSTANCE ABUSE TREATMENT BASED
ON A DEVELOPMENTAL MODEL

Affect Centered Therapy (ACT) translates recent advances in several areas of psychotherapy into effective treatment for substance abuse. Six

[Haworth co-indexing entry note]: "Affect Centered Therapy for Substance Abuse of Traumatic Origin." Omaha, John. Co-published simultaneously in *Journal of Chemical Dependency Treatment* (The Haworth Press, Inc.) Vol. 8, No. 2, 2006, pp. 89-113; and: *Psychological Trauma and Addiction Treatment* (ed: Bruce Carruth) The Haworth Press, Inc., 2006, pp. 89-113. Single or multiple copies of this article are available for a fee from The Haworth Document Delivery Service [1-800-HAWORTH, 9:00 a.m. - 5:00 p.m. (EST). E-mail address: docdelivery@haworthpress.com].

Available online at http://www.haworthpress.com/web/JCDT
© 2006 by The Haworth Press, Inc. All rights reserved.
doi:10.1300/J034v08n02_05

advances are: understanding the fundamental role of emotion in all dimensions of human functioning (Omaha, 2004); attachment (Cassidy, 1999); socioemotional development of the central nervous system (Schore, 1994); the central role of adversity and trauma in conditioning subsequent psychopathology (Kessler, Davis, & Kendler, 1997); a theory of personality based on ego states (Watkins & Watkins, 1997); and the emergence of personality according to principles of dynamical systems theory (Lewis & Granic, 2000). One consequence of these advances has been the appearance of a developmental model for psychopathology in general (Sroufe, 1997) and substance abuse and other ingestive disorders in particular (Omaha, 2004). The developmental model challenges the medical or disease model for substance abuse disorders that has dominated the field of addictions treatment since it was first formulated (Jellinek, 1960). The developmental model is more robust than the disease model, because it can clarify substance abuse disorders as well as most of the Axis I and II disorders. The developmental model is more comprehensive than the disease model because it describes the emergence of both adaptive and maladaptive personalities.

The developmental model entails a substantially divergent treatment approach from that derived from a disease model. The present chapter introduces an overview of a psychotherapeutic orientation, ACT, for treatment of substance abuse disorders where childhood deficit and trauma were etiologic factors. To date, ACT derived from this developmental model has been applied to treatment of the full spectrum of substance abuse disorders, the range of eating disorders, compulsive sexual acting out including Internet pornography, generalized anxiety disorder among the mood disorders, obsessive compulsive disorder, and gambling addiction. The success of ACT has been determined by a limited number of single case design studies, clinical impressions, and client self-report.

The case of Dan, a research participant whose confidentiality has been protected and who has given permission for his case to be described, illustrates principles of the developmental model and ACT treatment. Dan is a male in his mid-forties who reports a long history of alcohol abuse. He has been in and out of AA over a number of years. His longest period of sobriety since he began drinking in adolescence is 18 months. His drinking entailed many consequences including several serious car accidents. Dan was the third boy born to upper middle class parents. He has one younger sibling, a sister.

Dan's history includes the types of deficit and trauma often seen in alcoholics of his severity level. Deficit characterizes Dan's relationship with his mother. He describes his mother as distant, authoritarian, so-phisticated, selfish, and organizing. Dan wrote in his history that his mother didn't want to hear anything that would upset her. He recalls that he was punished for making his own decisions. He felt his mother aban-doned him, and this loss contributed to the traumatic origins of his alco-holism. Dan's father supplied physical abuse trauma. Dan describes his father as distant, impatient, and intolerant. Dan's father slapped Dan's face on numerous occasions. He wrote that his father always made him feel worse about himself on those times he did try to talk to his father. Throughout his history, Dan writes that he felt confused and lost grow-ing up in his family. At the inception of therapy, Dan said he was feeling urges to drink. He reported he had not had a drink for one month and had supported his abstinence by attending AA meetings although he feels he does not fit in.

TRIPARTITE MODEL

Adoption of a developmental model for psychopathology allows for accurate identification of etiological factors contributing to the emer-gence of the disordered personality. As with most psychopathology, the causal influences in substance abuse disorders can be grouped into three broad categories: the genetic component, the early childhood compo-nent (the attachment component), and the component of adversity and trauma in the period from around age three through adolescence.

The Attachment Component

The attachment period begins at birth and extends through the third year of life. If the maternal caregiver is primarily preoccupied with her child, if she is attuned, sensitive, and responsive, then the child will de-velop a secure attachment (Cassidy, 1999). When caregiving is not "good enough," an insecure attachment develops. Attachment disorder-ing characterizes the substance abuse (SA) disorders. Apparently, the preponderance of substance abusers endorse an insecure attachment style during childhood (Potter-Efron, chapter 4 of this book). In adoles-cence, some substance abusers begin to form an attachment to the abused substance, and this attachment mirrors the attachment style man-ifested in childhood toward the primary attachment objects, the mater-nal and paternal caregivers. Dan's history is replete with indicators of less than adequate caregiving. His mother had three boys to care for before Dan was born, so her ability to devote primary attention to his bids for emotion regulation was compromised (Schore, 1994). Dan describes his mother as distant, authoritarian, selfish, and abandoning. In these circumstances, an avoidant attachment often develops, as suggested for Dan by his dismissive and deactivating style in regard to attachment-related matters. Dan's dismissive adult attachment style extends to his relationship to AA and to his AA sponsors. The essence of the dismissive style is seen in Dan's diverting attention from AA and his sponsors to minimize the importance of early attachment relationships.

Trauma and Adversity

Adversity consists of the negative events of a child's life such as divorce, being raised by a single parent, parental substance abuse, parental incarceration, witnessing spousal abuse, and mental illness in the home (Anda, Croft, Gelitti, Nordenberg, Giles, Williams et al., 1999). Trauma consists of physical, mental, emotional, psychological, or sexual abuse. The prevalence of childhood adversity and trauma in the histories of substance abusers is well documented (Omaha, 2001, 2004). Significantly, studies have demonstrated a direct correlation between the severity of childhood abuse and the severity of subsequent substance abuse (Anda et al., 1999; Paone, Chavkin, Willets, Friedmann, & Des Jarlais, 1992; Triffleman, Marmar, Delucchi, & Ronfeldt, 1995). Dan's history demonstrates physical abuse as evidenced by his father slapping his face on many occasions.

The Genetic Component

Thresholds for the affects humans are hard-wired to experience are apparently genetically determined (Omaha, 2004). The human genome has been probed to determine the presence of regulatory alleles for the affects fear, anger, and sadness. Genetic data suggest that Type 1 alcoholism appears to be characterized by a low threshold for distress-anguish (sadness) affect (Tiihonen, Hallikainen, Lachman, Saito, Volavka, Kauhanen et al., 1999). Type 2 alcoholism, the early onset form characterized by severe antisocial behavior, may be associated with a low threshold for anger. It appears that lower thresholds for anger and sadness may constitute in part the inherited element of alcoholism, while alcoholism itself is not genetically determined. We do not have the capability to test Dan's genetic make up. However, Dan does appear to endorse the highly sensitive emotional type that may be in part determined by a low threshold for distress-anguish (sadness) affect.

ACT's Developmental Pathway to Substance Abuse

From ACT's developmental perspective, substance abuse constitutes the behavioral manifestation of a self that is dysfunctionally organized and lacks the inherent resources necessary to regulate current and unresolved archaic emotions. Facing the threat of disorganization of self that results from its lack of coherent structure and inability to regulate emotion, the individual turns to external, or secondary, means to stabilize itself. The drug of abuse becomes the external means providing the stability that the self is incapable of providing on its own.

Substance abusing behavior is the endpoint of a developmental trajectory that originates in the first months of life. At each stage of the trajectory, prior conditioning interacts with current circumstances. Deficiencies at an earlier stage make it more difficult for the individual to negotiate subsequent stages. Genetic liabilities, which apparently consist of lowered thresholds for anger-rage, distress-anguish (sadness), and probably other affects, create a sensitivity to the deleterious effects of the other two factors. Genetic liabilities are not predeterminative of substance abuse disorder in and of themselves, and these genetic liabilities can be overcome by "good enough" caregiving. However, inadequate caregiving will compound the genetic risk factor. Dan apparently endorsed a low threshold for distress affect, and his subsequent caregiving by both parents exacerbated this vulnerability. An example of the interaction of these two factors is provided by Dan's statement that he always felt worse about himself on occasions when he did attempt to talk to his father about matters of concern.

Deficiencies during the attachment phase of development from birth to age 36 months initiate the trajectory that if followed may lead to the onset of substance abuse in adolescence. These deficiencies include lack of sensitivity, impaired caring, misattuned responsiveness, and poor socialization of emotions. The child of deficit experience lacks skills to recognize, tolerate, and regulate emotions. Empirical studies demonstrate that this child is less likable and less prosocial and will be at risk for poor academic and social performance. The child of deficit experience is vulnerable to the emotional consequences of subsequent adversity or trauma. Dan's maternal caregiver was distant and abandoning. Already by age 3 Dan had enjoined a pathway to substance abuse. The events of his preschool and latency years would further solidify his engagement of that trajectory.

Adversity burdens the already vulnerable child of deficit experience with emotional loads that child has limited resources to manage. Adversity may arise from divorce or from being raised by a single parent, among other causes, and it burdens an insecurely attached child with fears of abandonment or annihilation. A secure attachment confers protection on the child faced with adversity, and a securely attached child is less likely to enjoin a pathway to substance abuse subsequent to divorce or other adversity than an insecurely attached child.

Trauma, whether emotional, physical, or sexual, further burdens the vulnerable child. Emotional trauma, especially socialization with anger or disgust broadcast by a caregiver, burdens the child with unresolved and unresolvable fear when socialized with anger. It burdens the child with unresolvable shame when he or she is socialized with broadcast disgust. Like many substance abusers, Dan was socialized with both rage and disgust emanating from both parents. Also like many substance abusers, Dan was physically abused in childhood. Dan's father slapped him on many occasions. The trauma of physical abuse burdens the vulnerable child with fear-terror affect and anger that dare not be expressed. The trauma of sexual abuse engenders disgust and shame that the vulnerable child must repress in order to survive. Unresolved shame, disgust, fear, anger or other trauma coded emotions express themselves from the unconscious position through substance abusing behaviors often beginning in adolescence.

Development of Substance Abuse Behavior

Substance abuse disorder of traumatic origin emerges in adolescence, conditioned by the three etiological factors described above. In adolescence the brain undergoes profound neurophysiological alterations (Spear, 2000). Unable to stabilize itself on the basis of its own resources, the self of deficit, adversity and trauma turns to substances for that stability. Over the course of adolescence the substance abusing personality emerges. This personality is characterized by impairments of self structure and impairments of affect regulation. Impairments of self structure manifest in a fragmentation of the self into dystonic ego states (Watkins & Watkins, 1997). Ego states emerge to manage emotions and memories that would otherwise create chaos in the personality system. These ego states express the symptoms of substance abuse. Over his adolescence, Dan developed an alcoholic ego state that became an integral structural component of his self. Dan's personality also contained a professional self that functioned competently in business. To use Federn's (1952) language, the energy of self could cycle between the professional ego state and the alcoholic ego state as Dan alternated between working and alcoholic drinking. These ego states represent the fragmentation of Dan's and any substance abuser's self structure. Fragmentation stabilizes the self system, preventing a descent into greater disorganization and psychotic chaos.

From ACT's perspective, which is one perspective on a continuum of theoretical models, substance abuse of traumatic origin is a disorder of emotion regulation. With the onset of adolescence, the impaired affect regulation that characterizes substance abuse disorders begins to threaten the personality system's stability. A secure attachment confers protection against this threat. The insecurely attached adolescent emerging from a history of deficit, adversity, and perhaps trauma will lack the tools to regulate the overwhelming affects originating from both the internal and external environments during this period. From ACT's developmental perspective the abused substance provides stability to the self-system. The abused substance accomplishes this by assisting the system to manage emotions that the system has limited tools to manage by itself.

Emotion regulation emerges in the context of the attachment, and so substance abuse is a disorder of attachment as well as of emotion regulation. The substance abuser forms an attachment bond with the abused substance, seeking physical proximity to the substance, just as he or she once sought physical proximity to the primary caregivers. In childhood, the caregiver was meant to function in the attachment dyad as an affect regulating external resource. When caregivers fail to provide this function, the child has no regulatory representation to internalize, and the deficiency becomes apparent in adolescence when the teenager turns to the external agency of substances for regulation of overwhelming affect. The abused substance functions as a secure base from which to venture out into the world and a secure haven to return to when the world is threatening. The abused substance provides for the three Rs of emotion management: regulation of current emotions that would otherwise overwhelm the system, reenactment of unresolved childhood adversity and trauma, and reexperiencing of unprocessed emotions assembled with the archaic adversity or trauma.

AFFECT CENTERED THERAPY FOR SUBSTANCE ABUSE

ACT formulates substance abuse as the current expression of a dysfunctionally structured self lacking emotion regulation skills and burdened with emotional loads from childhood adversity and trauma. Unlike cognitive-behavioral treatment models that seek to change a person's thinking and consequential behavior, ACT seeks to strengthen the self through teaching adaptive emotion regulation skills and resolving adversity and trauma. From an affect perspective, thinking and behavior are primarily driven by affect. When the self has acquired the skills to regulate its affects, when it has developed the intrinsic resources to stabilize itself under environmental stress, then it will demonstrate adaptive and positively functioning thinking and behaviors.

Affect dysregulation arising from deficit and trauma is the central deficiency in many substance abuse disorders. ACT begins by remediating the deficits of emotion regulation through the Affect Management Skills Training (AMST) protocol in phase I of treatment (Omaha, 2004). The self will not readily surrender the substances it has been using to regulate affects unless it is first provided with alternative skills. With the provision of effective affect regulation skills, therapy can be directed toward transformation of unresolved archaic adversities and traumas in phase II. With the resolution of these adversities and traumas, the impulses to abuse substances dissipate. Throughout phases I and II, the self is facilitated in reorganizing to a more coherent, more adaptively and positively functioning state. The final phase of ACT consists of integration of these skills into the newly emerging clean and sober personality through a process of relapse prevention.

ACT PHASE I: AFFECT MANAGEMENT SKILLS TRAINING

The function of AMST is to remediate deficits in the client's ability to recognize, tolerate, and regulate a range of affects. Clients often lack internal resources for qualities like trust, and the protocol uncovers and repairs these deficiencies. Another deficiency the protocol can remediate is the absence of internal representations of helpful, supportive persons. The protocol also assists the clinician in uncovering and restructuring covert protector ego states. Working through the protocol with a clinician will begin to remediate deficits in the client's attachment as well as begin the process of development of a more integrated, cohesive self structure. The protocol has been manualized (Omaha, 2004) and consists of 7 skills. Ethical issues of competency require that clinicians considering adopting these tools and skills obtain adequate training and supervision.

Skill I: Containment

Physical abuse, sexual abuse, psychological abuse, and emotional abuse as well as the range of adversity are prevalent in the socioemotional histories of many substance abusers. These unresolved adverse and traumatic experiences are stored in emotional memory where they affect current behavior. Emotional memory holds the unresolved emotions assembled with disturbing experiences in an excitatory state where they are more likely to be elicited in the present and motivate current thinking and behavior. For example, fear-terror affect will be trauma coded in a child experiencing physical or sexual abuse, and years later that individual will experience fear in a variety of contexts that would be innocuous for non-traumatized individuals. Because the original causes will be buried in the unconscious, the adult will be unaware of the motivations for his or her behavior.

Traumatized clients need to be taught how to "wall off" traumatic material so that it does not interfere with skills acquisition in the AMST protocol and so that the motivational effects of the trauma on current behaviors are diminished. The AMST protocol accomplishes this objective using the client-generated image of a container specified to be "sufficient to contain every disturbing thing." The client's acquisition of the AMST skills is facilitated by tactile alternating bilateral stimulation (TABS) provided by a battery powered device that delivers a gentle vibrating sensation through hand-held probes. The device is marketed under the trade name, TheraTapper™. TABS appears to facilitate skills acquisition by relieving the left hemisphere's rigid domination of right hemisphere function.

Dan's therapy illustrates skill I of the AMST protocol. Dan visualized a huge galvanized trash can when asked for an image of a container sufficient to hold every disturbing thing. He estimated its capacity at 50 gallons. The clinician turned on the TheraTapper™ and asked Dan to visualize the trash can and to form the intention that every disturbing thing would begin to flow into the container. He suggested that Dan would see a collective image and cautioned him not to look at any individual disturbing thing. Dan was asked to raise his left index finger when as much had gone into the container as would go in at this time.

After 20 seconds, Dan raised his finger, and the clinician helped Dan to visualize welding the lid on the can and then installing a special valve in the side of the can that Dan could use to take material out to work on or to add material if necessary. Also, a sign reading To Be Opened Only When It Serves My Healing was placed on the container. TABS was turned off, and Dan was asked to take a deep breath, let it out, and to report anything that had come up for him. Dan said, "It feels like I got rid of some junk. I saw a bunch of papers going in with writing on them." He also said he felt afraid to let go of all this stuff. When asked for an estimate, Dan said that 40 percent of every disturbing thing had moved into the container.

The theory informing ACT suggests that a client's inability to accomplish a skill indicates the client may be lacking a quality resource. Following the protocol, Dan was asked what quality he would need to be able to transfer more disturbing material to the container, and he volunteered "trust." The clinician then asked for an image that embodied the quality of trust, and Dan suggested the image of Jesus, "a being who was non-abusive and who was at peace with himself." With TABS facilitation provided by the TheraTapper™, the image of Jesus was developed, and then Dan was asked to hold the image of Jesus and to form the intention that more disturbing material would flow into the container through the valve. This second filling attempt resulted in the transfer of 80% of every disturbing thing into the container, and Dan stated he was comfortable with that level of containment.

Dan's case illustrates how the AMST protocol uncovers deficits in the resources available in the client's personality structure. Erikson's first stage of psychosocial development is trust versus mistrust (Erikson, 1963). This stage begins at birth and continues to 18 months. Infants who do not receive "good enough" care-giving from an attuned, sensitive, appropriately responsive care giver often endorse the mistrust end of the spectrum as does Dan. Like many others, Dan views the world as harsh and unfriendly. Also like others endorsing mistrust, Dan has difficulty forming close bonds with others. He does not feel hope, and since he never internalized the image of a trustworthy caregiver, he never came to believe he could fulfill his needs successfully on his own. AMST uncovers Dan's missing resource of trust and remediates it through installation of an image of a trustworthy person, in this case the image of Jesus.

Skill II: Safe Place

Substance abusers' childhoods were often characterized by deficit, adversity, and trauma, and as a result, these individuals may not presently possess an internal image of safety and security. The client needs to be provided with an internal image of safety and security so that he or she can feel safe while participating in ACT's phases. Clients can also use the Safe Place skill to improve their functioning in a variety of current emotionally stressful contexts, e.g., applying for a job, appearing in court, dealing with relationship difficulties, etc. The objective of skill II is to help the client develop and elaborate an internal image of a safe place.

Dan was asked to think of a place from adulthood where he believed he had been safe and secure. He identified a stream in the Sierra Mountains of California. With TABS facilitation, Dan was helped to elaborate what he could see, hear, smell, and feel as he visualized himself in the scene beside the stream. Dan saw himself in an open spot beside the stream. There were deer grazing in the meadow across from the stream with trees beyond the meadow and cliffs in the distance. He could hear the sounds of the slow running brook and could smell the fresh mountain air. Dan was also able to identify the tactile sensations of the sun warming him and the slight breeze on his skin.

Having developed the safe place image, Dan was now asked to recall the whole image, and with TABS facilitation he was asked to repeat the words, "I am safe." This appraisal is referred to as a positive cognition. Dan repeated the words. When an image is assembled with a cognition using TABS facilitation, the process is termed an installation. Following the installation, Dan was asked to assess how true the appraisal was using a 7-point scale in which 1 is completely false and 7 completely true. The scale is referred to as Validity of Cognition (VoC; Shapiro, 2001). One of the essential features of the AMST protocol is that it provides an outcome measure of success at each stage by means of client self-evaluation. Dan stated that the VoC for the appraisal "I am safe" was 4-5. The installation was repeated, but this time Dan was asked to recall the image of Jesus who provided the quality of trust. When assessed now, Dan reported a VoC of 7. Dan's experience illustrates how the quality resource of trust, once it has been established, can be used again and again throughout the work to facilitate the successful development of additional skills.

With TABS facilitation, Dan was now asked to recall the image of the Sierra stream and this time to repeat the affect-oriented appraisal, "I feel safe." Dan repeated the words, and when the TheraTapper™ was turned off, the clinician asked, "What comes up now, Dan?" Dan reported, "I feel better, safer. This is interesting. I can see myself making progress." Dan assessed the VoC for his statement "I feel safe" at 7. Dan's spontaneous comment that he was able to see himself making progress demonstrates how the AMST protocol builds structure in the self system. Dan's acquisition of the AMST skills promotes structuralization of his self system, and his self-reflective observation demonstrates that process.

In the final piece of the second skill, Dan was asked to hold the image of the stream, recall that he knows with certainty that he is safe and that he feels safe, and with TABS facilitation he was asked to notice where in his body he experienced sensations accompanying the statement "I feel safe." Dan identified sensations of "excitement in my upper chest" accompanying the emotion of safety. With TABS facilitation, the clinician asked Dan to now repeat the positive cognition, "The excitement in my upper chest tells me I am feeling safe." Dan did so, and he endorsed a VoC of 7 for this appraisal. Here we see how Dan was facilitated in cognizing, that is raising to conscious awareness, the sensations accompanying the emotion of safety.

Skills III-VII: Emotion Recognition, Tolerance, and Regulation

Skills III-VII transmit to the client the capability to recognize emotions by their physiological signals, to tolerate the experience of emotions, and to down-regulate distressing emotions or up-regulate comfortable ones. These skills are transmitted for a series of index emotions beginning with fear. Once the client has learned the basic protocol, he or she is taught to apply the skills to most of the remaining affects that humans appear genetically programmed to experience. AMST targets anger, sadness, yearning, startle, excitement, joy, disgust, and shame.

In Skill III, Dan was helped to recognize fear affect by the physiological signals associated with fear. Dan was asked to recall a recent time he felt fear at a relatively low level, a level 3 or 4 on an 11-point scale from 0 (neutral) to 10. He recalled a time he'd run his car off the road and was briefly trapped. As he held this visualization, TABS was applied, and he was asked to notice sensations accompanying the remembered images. Dan quickly identified a sharp pang in his chest. With TABS facilitation, Dan was asked to repeat the verbalization, "The sharp pang in my chest tells me I'm feeling fear." In order to check the validity of this verbalization, Dan was asked to rate how true it was on the VoC scale, and he assigned it a value of 7. Dan had now cognized fear affect, meaning that he had created pathways involving the emotion response system and the cortex. He could now proceed to learn to tolerate the experience of fear.

Tolerating fear was difficult for Dan because in childhood he had felt overwhelming fear when his father slapped him. Dan's unresolved and unmanageable childhood fear would surface in AA meetings and motivate him to leave. Tolerating fear or other affects depends upon developing an image called a grounding resource that enables the client to stay grounded and present while experiencing the index emotion. Dan chose to employ an image of cords emerging from the soles of his feet that anchored him to the ground. With TABS facilitation, Dan held the image of the cords emerging from his feet and anchoring him to the ground while noticing sensations that accompanied the image. Dan reported he felt "connectedness in his whole body." Again using TABS, Dan was asked to hold the image of the cords and verbalize, "The connectedness in my whole body tells me I'm grounded and present." The grounding resource could now be used to help Dan tolerate the experience of fear. Like many substance abusers, Dan lacked the imagistic tools to ground himself and stay in the present moment. Acquisition of this skill helped Dan, as it has helped many substance abusers, to avoid the acting out that often ensues when a strong emotion surfaces that the self has impaired abilities to tolerate.

The next two skills develop affect tolerance. Skill IV links deployment of Dan's grounding resource to the sensations accompanying fear. The purpose is to expedite deployment of the grounding resource. Dan was asked to visualize being trapped in his car, to notice the sharp pang in his chest, and to repeat with TABS facilitation the instruction, "The sharp pang in my chest signals me to put down my grounding cords." Dan was coached to visualize the cords emerging from his feet and then to become aware of the connectedness in his whole body. Skill V was immediately installed, again with TABS facilitation. Dan was asked to notice the connectedness in his whole body that told him he was grounded and present and then to notice the sharp pang in his chest. As he held both sensations, he was asked to repeat the positive cognition, "I can stay grounded and present while I'm feeling fear." Dan had now acquired the ability to stay grounded and present while feeling fear, and since he often drank when fearful, he was beginning to develop skills he would learn to use to stay sober.

Self-reflection is the ability to observe oneself from a detached per-spective as one is experiencing an emotion and its associated sensations. Skill VI, which is termed "Noticing," develops the skill of self-reflec-tion. People who can "just notice" themselves having an emotion do not *become* the emotion, that is, they do not identify or fuse with the emo-tion. Substance abusers tend to identify with their emotions as well as with the symptoms of their disorder. Skill VI trains the mind to detach. The abuser will learn he is not his symptoms, just as he is not his emo-tions. He is the one experiencing his emotions. Skill VI will generalize throughout the abuser's mind and facilitate his shedding the symptoms as he forsakes his substance abuse.

To learn skill VI, Dan was asked to visualize again the car accident and skills III through V were recapitulated. After reminding Dan he could stay grounded and present while feeling fear, the therapist guided him in noticing thoughts, images, sensations, and memories he had dis-closed relating to the accident. With TABS facilitation, Dan was asked to repeat the Skill VI positive cognition, "I can just notice myself feeling fear." The AMST protocol constructs a skill string, a linkage of apprais-als, images, memories, cognitions, affects, and sensations, and Skill VI develops the client's ability to reflect on the process and to become thereby aware of his or her expanding self.

The last skill in the protocol teaches the client emotion regulation. Emotion regulation means changing the intensity of emotions. The cli-ent learns to decrease or down-regulate distressing emotion and to in-crease or up-regulate syntonic emotion. Down-regulation requires an image for disposing of excess emotion. Dan chose to use a sink disposal. Dan and the therapist discussed what percent of his fear Dan would like to dispose of, and he opted for 90%. The therapist coached Dan to revisualize the car accident and to recapitulate each skill of the entire protocol with TABS facilitation. After reminding him he could just no-tice himself feeling fear, the therapist asked Dan to visualize the sink disposal, to turn on the water and the motor, and then to "form the inten-tion that 90% of the fear will begin to flow toward the disposal." Dan was coached to breathe into the place in his chest where the pang was leav-ing. He was asked to watch the process as the fear was washed down the disposal and ground up, and he was instructed to raise his left index fin-ger when all 90% had gone down. After about 10 seconds, Dan raised his finger, and the therapist asked him to repeat the Skill VII positive cognition, "I am learning to decrease my fear." Dan was asked to ap-praise the truth of that statement on the VoC scale, and he rated the statement completely true. Dan had now acquired the skills to recognize, tolerate, notice, and regulate fear.

In two subsequent sessions, Dan learned to apply the same protocol and resources to the other affects. Table 1 presents each of these affects and the sensations by which Dan recognized them. As Dan acquired the AMST skills he was given homework assignments to notice times he felt the emotions he'd learned to recognize and to chart what triggered them and to report his use of the AMST protocol. Dan's ability to use the skills improved with regular practice.

PHASE II:
AFFECT CENTERED THERAPY
FOR SUBSTANCE ABUSE DISORDERS

The second phase of ACT uncovers and resolves the client's unresolved childhood adversities and traumas that he or she has reenacted and reexperienced through substance abuse. Mastery of the AMST skills is a necessary precursor for moving to phase II. ACT employs the client's mental image of the abused substance as a key to unlock the neural network containing both the substance abuse and the unresolved adversity and trauma. Once uncovered, these adversities and traumas are resolved employing a pair of interventions that facilitate the client in discharging bound emotion and achieving cognitive meaning. Once resolved, the trauma or adversity moves from emotion memory to narrative memory where it no longer will influence current behavior.

TABLE 1

AFFECT	SENSATION	BODY
Safety	Excitement	Upper chest
Fear	Pang	Chest
Grounded	Connectedness	Whole body
Anger	Overwhelming tension	Moving from gut to chest
Sadness	Lowering of energy	Chest, gut, & legs
Excitement	Tension	Whole body
Disgust	Nauseated	Stomach
Shame	Hanging & shaking	Head

Uncovering Trauma and Adversity

ACT has adapted a Gestalt communication technique to the task for uncovering archaic trauma and adversity. In a diagnostic use of the "empty chair" technique, ACT asks the client to visualize his or her substance of abuse in an empty chair. The abused substance is referred to as a traumaphor, a neologism that calls attention to the fact that the client's use of the abused substance is a metaphor for trauma occurring during the attachment or childhood socioemotional history phases. The therapist asks the client a series of questions that uncover the client's relationship to the abused substance. These are termed traumaphor associations. Dan's traumaphor associations to alcohol illustrate this component of the process.

The therapist began by asking Dan if it would serve his healing to remove "alcohol and everything related to it" from the container he had visualized in the AMST skill I. Dan agreed that it would, and with TABS facilitation, Dan visualized alcohol and everything related to it coming out of the valve in the 50-gallon galvanized trash can. The therapist then asked Dan to place alcohol in an empty chair set facing Dan and to describe what he saw. Dan described a clear quart bottle of vodka and another of gin. He also visualized two six packs of beer and assorted empty bottles and glasses. Dan was asked what the alcohol was doing, and he responded, "It is swirling around, appearing and reappearing." In response to a question about what it was saying, he reported, "I want you to drink me and shut your brain off. You can get comfort out of me and turn your life off."

Now the therapist asked Dan what the alcohol was thinking about him. Dan said, "You're no good anyway. I'll get power over you." The therapist wondered what the alcohol was thinking itself. To this, Dan replied, "I get power out of getting you, Dan. I have no power on my own, but I get power by making you drink me. I have no life of my own. I have to dominate others." Shifting from the cognitive to the affective dimension, the therapist inquired what the alcohol was feeling towards Dan, and he answered, "I need you, Dan."

"What is the alcohol feeling itself, Dan?" the therapist asked.

"Weak," he replied.

The therapist now directed the same set of questions at Dan. "As you look at the alcohol, Dan, what are you thinking?"

Dan replied, "You've always pulled me down from what I wanted to achieve. You can consume me, alcohol. You can take me out of the picture."

The therapist inquired what Dan was thinking himself as he looked at the alcohol, and he stated, "I have a part that alcohol has power over." Continuing, the therapist asked what Dan was feeling toward the alcohol, and he replied, "Animosity and anger and need." When asked, Dan stated he himself felt "helpless" as he looked at the alcohol.

"What is the gender of the alcohol, Dan?" asked the therapist.

"Male," he replied without hesitation.

The therapist next recapitulated responses Dan had provided for alcohol and for himself, pointing out to Dan that these responses defined the relationship between Dan and alcohol. He finished by asking, "Dan, as you hold this relationship with alcohol as a pattern, I'd like you to go back in time through all your relationships to the earliest relationship that is like your relationship to alcohol. When you get it, tell me what it is."

"My father," Dan said almost immediately. "He had to be right all the time. He liked to see people squirm, because it gave him power."

This exercise accomplished the goal of identifying Dan's intrapsychic transactions energizing his alcoholism. The exercise also uncovered the affect fueling Dan's drinking: anger. Dan's mind contains a neural network comprised of images of his father getting power over him in order to acquire power for himself, because otherwise he felt weak. Dan felt anger in childhood when his father made him squirm, but it is the nature of childhood's essential helplessness that Dan could do nothing to resolve his anger. Because Dan could not resolve or even acknowledge his anger, it became trauma coded. In adolescence, Dan's anger threatened to overwhelm and disorganize him, and he found that through alcohol he could manage the anger. With the anger managed, Dan could feel comfort. The clinician's next task was to uncover and help Dan resolve the actual experiences, stored in emotion memory, that were assembled in this neural network. This part of the protocol is termed traumaphor focused processing.

Traumaphor Focused Processing

Traumaphor focused processing (TFP) helps the client uncover the specific memories from childhood that are assembled in a neural network that includes current addictive behaviors. TFP begins immediately upon completion of the traumaphor associations component. Holding the same image of alcohol in the empty chair, the clinician asked Dan for a negative thought about himself as he looked at the alcohol. Shapiro (2001) has named this a negative cognition (NC). Dan's NC was "I am unworthy." Next the clinician asked Dan to state how he would like to think about himself as he looked at the alcohol when the therapy was completed, and he stated, "I am worthy."

"Looking at the alcohol in the empty chair, Dan, how true right now is the statement 'I am worthy' on the 7-point VoC scale?"

"It's a one," Dan replied.

With therapist help, Dan identified disgust, resignation, and shame as the emotions he felt looking at the alcohol. He reported sensations of "a collapsing feeling in my chest" accompanying the emotions. Using Shapiro's (2001) Subjective Units of Disturbance (SUD) scale, Dan reported he felt a level 10 disturbance looking at the alcohol and holding the NC, emotions, and sensations.

Dan was next asked to focus on the image of the alcohol, to hold the NC, "I am unworthy," to recall the emotions of disgust, resignation, and shame, and feel the collapsing sensation in his chest. TABS was applied using the TheraTapper™ and continued for approximately 30 cycles. A cycle consists of a single stimulus burst, one from each hand-held probe. TABS was turned off, and the therapist asked Dan to take a deep breath, let it out, and report any thoughts, memories, emotions, or images that had surfaced. Dan said, "I can't stand feeling that kind of pain, disgust, and anger." ACT hypothesizes that Dan's neural network containing his alcoholism is constituted from the trauma coded affects Dan identified as well as the memories of events that originally generated those affects. The goal is to find a scene from Dan's early life in which the affects were coded by trauma. To accomplish this, the therapist used the affect bridge technique (Watkins & Watkins, 1997).

The therapist asked Dan to hold the pain, disgust, and anger he was experiencing, and with TABS facilitation, he was asked to "float back" on those emotions to "an early time, perhaps the first time you felt that same pain, disgust, and anger." Dan was asked to indicate when he'd accessed the scene by raising his left index finger. After a brief period of TABS, Dan raised his finger, the clinician turned off the device and asked Dan, "Tell me what you're seeing."

Dan described what ACT refers to as the trauma coded, or affect laden, scene. The scene Dan described lies at the inception of the developmental trajectory that led to Dan's alcoholism. In this scene, Dan was 6 years old. He had asked his father for help with his homework. His father attempted to help, but when Dan struggled to understand his father's explanation, his father stood up and walked away from Dan, saying, "It bothers me when you can't get it the first time." Commenting on this scene, Dan said, "Dad hurt me bad. I can see how petty he was, how he needed to get into arguments. I needed him, and he intimidated me. I was his son and he should have cared more." Dan was now prepared for the abreactive intervention of ACT.

Clinical research suggests that an affect laden or trauma coded scene figures in the etiology of many disorders (Scarf, 2004; Siegel, 2003). Research on substance abuse indicates that each addict and alcoholic also has a trauma coded scene that contributed to the development of his or her disorder (Omaha, 2001). For some substance abusers this scene can be one of horrific sexual abuse. The trauma coded scene may be a memory of physical abuse, or like Dan, a scene of emotional abuse. Trauma and adversity can set in motion a pathway towards other disorders besides substance abuse. The childhood socioemotional histories of many Axis I and Axis II disordered clients contain a trauma coded scene of one kind or another. Circumstances will determine in part the exact nature of the psychopathology that emerges. Some emotionally abused children will grow up to be substance abusers, and others may become eating disordered. One day, we may understand the developmental process of these disorders well enough to understand their etiology even more precisely.

Once a trauma coded scene has been identified, the therapist helps the client to resolve the scene through a pair of interventions: the abreactive intervention and the redemptive intervention. A client may have many affect coded scenes stored in emotion memory. Not all of them have to be uncovered and resolved. The therapist attempts to find the first scene, the worst scene, and the most recent scene and to resolve these. The effects of resolving these scenes generalize through the personality system.

Abreactive Intervention

Having identified Dan's trauma coded scene, the therapist next facilitated a resolution of the trauma, in part through the abreactive intervention. The abreactive intervention promotes (a) expressing the emotion bound with the scene (b) developing awareness of what happened and what the consequences were (c) expressing forbidden thoughts (d) achievement of cognitive meaning (Chu, 1998; Watkins & Watkins, 1997). The intervention is considered complete when the client has constructed a coherent narrative of events. At completion of the intervention, the SUD for the target scene will be 0 or 1, suggesting that the memories are moving out of emotion memory and into narrative memory. Let's pick up Dan's case again at the point where he had accessed the trauma coded scene.

Turning on the TABS again, the therapist asked Dan to freeze the scene where his father had walked away from Little Dan saying "It bothers me when you can't get it the first time." Then he asked Dan to see himself as an adult entering the scene and placing his hand on Little Dan's shoulder. One purpose of this instruction is to begin the process of improving communication and cooperation between the adult self, Dan, and the child part, Little Dan. The long-term goal of this therapy is to help adult Dan become the parent that Little Dan never had. Another purpose of having adult Dan affiliate with Little Dan is to let the child part know that the events are not a purposeless reenactment or revictimization. The outcome will be different this time.

The therapist asked Dan if Little Dan was emotionally safe in the trauma coded scene, and he responded he was not. The therapist asked Dan to say who was responsible for Little Dan's lack of emotional safety, and he identified his father. "What is Little Dan feeling?" the therapist asked.

"He's feeling abandoned. He's feeling dumb, like a piece of shit. He feels like he had no father really."

The therapist asked Dan to place his father in the empty chair. He guided Dan in reporting his developing awareness to his father. Dan was helped to verbalize, "Dad, I am aware I was not emotionally safe when you walked away from me. I'm aware that I felt abandoned and stupid." The therapist then asked Dan to see if he could decode what his father was feeling in this scene. "I think he envied Little Dan. I could sing, and I think he wanted to be able to sing like me and he couldn't. I think he felt inadequate. His own mother crushed the creativity out of him, and I think he hated my creativity." Dan was helped to verbalize this cognitive meaning to his father seated in the empty chair using the format, "Dad, I am aware that you envied my creativity."

Next, Dan was helped to identify the consequences of what happened in the scene and to state these to his father. Dan said, "Dad, I am aware that one consequence of what you did when you walked away from me and shamed me was that I became an alcoholic. I'm aware that I internalized my toxic relationship with you. Alcohol is just you in disguise. You destroyed a part of me. You took away my belief in myself. You never gave me credit for anything. I hated you for what you did to me." Dan accessed his long held anger and sadness as he stated these consequences to his father, spitting out the words through clenched teeth with tears welling up in his eyes. When he appeared to have completed his abreaction, the therapist asked if he was done, and Dan said he was. The therapist asked Dan to say to his father, "I've put you in that chair, and I'm not letting you back in me again." Having done so, the therapist suggested Dan send his imaginal father to a treatment center where he would receive daily psychotherapy for his own mental health problems. The imaginal father was visualized going to therapy (Dan's actual father had been dead for 15 years at the time of this work), and the focus of therapy turned to Little Dan.

Redemptive Intervention

One purpose of the redemptive intervention is to alleviate some of the burden of trauma coded emotion from the child part. Little Dan had been carrying a load of disgust broadcast in part by his father. Trauma coded disgust affect forms the basis for Dan's NC, 'I am unworthy.' The therapist asked Dan to invite Little Dan to sit in his lap. With TABS accompaniment, he facilitated an affiliation between them by asking Dan to feel Little Dan snuggling against him. He asked Dan to look into Little Dan's eyes and to feel how much he yearned for what only Dan could provide, which was redemption. *To redeem* means to rescue or deliver from bondage. Little Dan had been held in bondage to his father's shaming behavior, and adult Dan could rescue him. The therapist asked Dan to speak to Little Dan, repeating these affirmations one at a time: You are good. You are pure. You are innocent. You are deserving. Dan added some affirmations of his own. He told Little Dan, "You are creative and artistic." He also added, "I love you." The therapist asked Dan for permission to speak to Little Dan, and when it was given, he introduced himself and then asked Little Dan to repeat what he had been told by adult Dan. When he had done so, the therapist checked on the progress of the therapy to this point by asking how disturbing the original target was as Dan looked at it now in the empty chair. Dan responded that it was a 0, that it was not disturbing at all. Readers will note that through the ACT process, Dan's emotional reactivity to the initial target, alcohol, decreased from 10, the top of the scale, to 0, the bottom. The therapist could now proceed to install the positive cognition.

Installing the Positive Cognition

The purpose of the positive cognition installation is to install an adaptive view of the self into the neural network that originally contained the now resolved dysfunctional thoughts and trauma coded memories and emotions (Shapiro, 2001). With TABS facilitation, Dan was asked to recall the original target in the empty chair, and then he was asked to verbalize aloud the positive cognition (PC), "I am worthy." TABS was continued for another 20 cycles, then turned off, and Dan was asked, "What comes up now?"

Dan replied, "I feel fairly worthy right now." The therapist instructed Dan to "just go with that" and turned on the TABS again for about 20 cycles. Again Dan was asked, "What comes up now?" Dan reported, "I feel a little more comfortable in my own skin than I have for a long time." At this point the therapist asked Dan to assess the validity of the statement 'I am worthy' on the 7-point VoC scale. Dan rated it at a 6. Readers will note that the statement was completely untrue (VoC = 1) at the beginning of the work. The therapist asked Dan if he could identify what prevented the VoC from going to a 7, and he said it had to do with his belief that he could never heal, that he would always be an alcoholic. The therapist explained the difference between a disease model for alcoholism and ACT's developmental model. He explained to Dan that from a developmental perspective, healing is possible. He also assured Dan that resolving the childhood antecedents of his alcoholism did not imply that he could now drink. ACT suggests that once a person has used a substance obsessively and compulsively, it is probably not possible to have a healthy relationship with that substance, even after resolution of the childhood traumas. The installation of the PC was repeated, and Dan was now able to assign complete validity to the statement "I am worthy."

I want to offer a few observations on the ACT therapy now that we've seen how the developmental model expresses in the actual therapy. Dan's case clearly illustrates the connection between his current problem with alcohol and the etiological antecedents in his father's emotional traumatization. ACT's traumaphor associations and traumaphor focused processing began with Dan visualizing an image of vodka, gin, and beer in an empty chair and quickly uncovered the childhood shaming, broadcast disgust, and unresolved anger that initiated Dan's developmental trajectory toward alcoholism. The trajectory began with Little Dan at age 6 and culminated with Dan's alcoholic drinking that began in adolescence.

Dan's case also demonstrates the central role played by affect in alcoholism and in development. Dan emerged from the attachment phase with developmental vulnerabilities, because his mother apparently failed to transmit affect regulation skills to him due to her avoidant parenting style. When, subsequently, Dan's father shamed him and broadcast disgust at him and Dan felt anger bordering on rage, he did not have the tools and skills to manage these emotions, and they exceeded his system's capacity for accommodation and became trauma coded.

Dan's work also highlights how ego states operate in the personality system. Dan's mind contained a paternal introject or ego state that continued to broadcast disgust at him currently. His self system contained an alcoholic ego state tasked with managing the trauma coded anger, shame, and disgust. Buried deeply in his self system was an child ego state, Little Dan, that held the system's unworthiness. ACT can resolve the introjects. One purpose of placing Dan's father, his emotional perpetrator, in the empty chair is to promote separation, individuation, and disidentification from this paternal ego state. The function of sending Dan's imaginal father to treatment is to begin an intrapsychic process of healing that paternal introject. The eventual objective of the intervention is that Dan will develop an ambivalent appreciation of his father in which he can hold both the negative and positive qualities of the man in one image. Dan's case also illustrates how ACT moves the self towards greater cohesion, towards improved vitality, and towards more intrapsychic order.

Relapse Prevention

The objective of ACT's final piece is integration of the client's new skills and more adaptively organized self structure with new, more positive ways of functioning. ACT accomplishes this by expanding on elements of traditional relapse prevention. Clients are asked to identify five situations in which impulses to use may be expected in the future. The client describes the situation and identifies triggers, images, cognitions, emotions, and sensations (TICES) accompanying each situation. The client also identifies his new recovery skills some of which will be his AMST skills and some of which will be more traditional resources like AA, NA, or after-care. With TABS facilitation, the client will be helped to assemble the target situation, the TICES elements, and the recovery skills with a positive cognition such as "I am learning to use my recovery skills to recognize and avoid a potential relapse situation." The validity of the cognition is appraised using the VoC scale. If the VoC does not equal 7, then the therapist works with the client to uncover the causes and these are resolved.

CONCLUSION

Affect Centered Therapy holds the promise of providing lasting treatment for many forms of substance abuse disorder because it appears to effectively address the true causes of the disorder. ACT is derived from a developmental model that accurately describes the etiology of addictive behaviors. The developmental model is supported by a large body of empirical evidence (Sroufe, 1997). ACT itself is supported by clinical impressions and limited single case design studies (Omaha, 1998, July 11; 1999, June 19; 2000, September 10). The next stage in development of the ACT protocol will consist in undertaking to provide empirical support for ACT. ACT is an accessible protocol. A narrative description of AMST, ACT's phase I, along with an extensive explication of the developmental model is available (Omaha, 2004). A DVD and CD presentation, *Introduction to Affect Centered Therapy*, is available through www.johnomahaenterprises.com where announcements of training opportunities can also be found. A non-profit, the Institute for Affect Centered Therapy, is being established in California where students, interns and fellows can acquire training under supervision. The Institute will provide sliding scale services to the community and will also conduct research programs.

REFERENCES

Anda, R. F., Croft, J. B., Gelitti, V. J., Nordenberg, D., Giles, W. H., Williams, D. F., & Giovina, G. A. (1999). Adverse childhood experiences and smoking during adolescence and adulthood. *Journal of the American Medical Association, 282*, 1652-1658.

Cassidy, J. (1999). The nature of the child's ties. In J. Cassidy & P. R. Shaver (Eds.) *Handbook of attachment: Theory, research, and clinical applications* (pp. 3-20). New York: The Guilford Press.

Chu, J. A. (1998). *Rebuilding shattered lives: The responsible treatment of complex post-traumatic and dissociative disorders.* New York: John Wiley & Sons.

Erikson, E. H. (1963). *Childhood and society.* New York: Norton.

Federn, P. (1952). *Ego psychology and the psychoses.* New York: Basic.

Jellinek, E. M. (1960). *The disease concept of alcoholism.* New Haven: College & University Press.

Kessler, R. C., Davis, C. G., & Kendler, K. S. (1997). Childhood adversity and adult psychiatric disorder in the U.S. National Comorbidity Survey. *Psychological Medicine, 27*, 1101-1119.

Lewis, M. D., & Granic, I. (2000). A new approach to the study of emotional development. In M. D. Lewis & I. Granic (Eds.) *Emotion, development, and self-organ-*

ization: Dynamic systems approaches to emotional development (pp. 1-12). Cambridge: Cambridge University Press.

Omaha, J. (1998, July 11). *Chemotion and EMDR: An EMDR treatment protocol based upon a psychodynamic model for chemical dependency.* Paper presented at the meeting of the EMDR International Association, Baltimore, MD. Retrieved July 15, 2005 from http://www.johnomahaenterprises.com/Omaha_1998_Chemotion_ EMDR.pdf

Omaha, J. (1999, June 19). *Treating nicotine dependency: An application of the Chemotion/EMDR protocol.* Paper presented at the meeting of the EMDR International Association, Las Vegas, NV. Retrieved July 15, 2005 from http://www. johnomahaenterprises.com/Omaha_1999_Nicotine.pdf

Omaha, J. (2000, September 10). *Treatment of bulimia and binge eating disorder using the Chemotion/EMDR protocol.* Paper presented at the meeting of the EMDR International Association, Toronto, Ontario, Canada. Retrieved July 15, 2005 from http://www.johnomahaenterprises.com/Omaha_ 2000_Eating_Disorder.pdf

Omaha, J. (2001). *The psychodynamic basis of chemical dependency.* Unpublished doctoral dissertation, International University of Professional Studies, Maui, HI.

Omaha, J. (2004). *Psychotherapeutic interventions for emotion regulation: EMDR and bilateral stimulation for affect management.* New York: W. W. Norton.

Paone, D., Chavkin, W., Willets, I., Friedmann, P., & Des Jarlais, D. (1992). The impact of sexual abuse: Implications for drug treatment. *Journal of Women's Health, 1,* 149-153.

Scarf, M. (2004). *Secrets, lies, betrayals: How the body holds the secrets of a life and how to unlock them.* New York: Random House.

Schore, A. N. (1994). *Affect regulation and the origin of the self: The neurobiology of emotional development.* Hillsdale, NJ: Lawrence Erlbaum Associates, Inc.

Shapiro, F. (2001). *Eye movement desensitization and reprocessing: Basic principles, protocols, and procedures.* New York: Guilford Press.

Siegel, D. J. (2003). An interpersonal neurobiology of psychotherapy: The developing mind and the resolution of trauma. In D. J. Siegel and M. F. Solomon (Eds.) *Healing trauma: Attachment, mind, body, and brain* (pp. 1-56). New York: W. W. Norton.

Spear, L. P. (2000). The adolescent brain and age-related behavioral manifestations. *Neuroscience and Biobehavioral Reviews, 24,* 417-463.

Sroufe, L. A. (1997). Psychopathology as an outcome of development. *Development and Psychopathology, 9,* 251-168.

Tiihonen, J., Hallikainen, T., Lachman, H., Saito, T., Volavka, J., Kauhanen, J., Salonen, J. T., Ryynanen, O. P., Koulu, M., Karvonen, M. K., Pohjalainen, T., Syvalahti, E., & Hietala, J. (1999). Association between the functional variant of the catechol-O-methyltransferase (COMT) gene and type 1 alcoholism. *Molecular Psychiatry, 4,* 286-289.

Triffleman, E. G., Marmar, C. R., Delucchi, K. L., & Ronfeldt, H. (1995). Childhood trauma and posttraumatic stress disorder in substance abuse inpatients. *Journal of Nervous & Mental Disease, 183,* 172-176.

Watkins, J. G. & Watkins, H. H. (1997). *Ego states: Theory and therapy.* New York: W.W. Norton and Co.

EMDR in the Treatment of Addiction

Joan Zweben, PhD
Jody Yeary, PhD

SUMMARY. EMDR offers so much promise and great challenges to addiction treatment providers. It is a powerful tool for trauma resolution, but it must be carefully integrated into addiction treatment. Organizational as well as individual safety structures must be in place so that vulnerable indivduals may be offered this opportunity under conditions which maximize their chances for success. Efforts are underway to obtain funding for controlled trials, and it is hoped that these will clarify safety and efficacy questions, as well as many clinical issues that arise as more clinicians work with this method. *[Article copies available for a fee from The Haworth Document Delivery Service: 1-800-HAWORTH. E-mail address: <docdelivery@haworthpress.com> Website: <http://www.HaworthPress.com> © 2006 by The Haworth Press, Inc. All rights reserved.]*

KEYWORDS. EMDR, childhood trauma, recovery from addiction

INTRODUCTION

It has long been recognized that a significant number of people seeking substance abuse treatment have a history of trauma in childhood, adulthood or both (Najavits, Weiss, & Shaw, 1997; Zweben & Clark, 1994). For many, this results in enduring symptoms of Post Traumatic Stress Disorder (PTSD) that both makes it difficult to achieve extended periods of abstinence and reduces the quality of recovery. These symp-

[Haworth co-indexing entry note]: "EMDR in the Treatment of Addiction." Zweben, Joan, and Jody Yeary. Co-published simultaneously in *Journal of Chemical Dependency Treatment* (The Haworth Press, Inc.) Vol. 8, No. 2, 2006, pp. 115-127; and: *Psychological Trauma and Addiction Treatment* (ed: Bruce Carruth) The Haworth Press, Inc., 2006, pp. 115-127. Single or multiple copies of this article are available for a fee from The Haworth Document Delivery Service [1-800-HAWORTH, 9:00 a.m. - 5:00 p.m. (EST). E-mail address: docdelivery@haworthpress.com].

toms include nightmares, flashbacks, heightened vigilance and reactivity, irritability and a tendency to numb out that may affect everything from interpersonal relationships to intellectual achievement. Many clinicians view PTSD as a major factor influencing addiction treatment outcomes. Developing more effective interventions for this condition therefore becomes the key to improvement. Symptoms of PTSD affect the ability to get clean and sober, stay that way, and create a satisfying life without the use of alcohol and other drugs. Clinicians have also noted that even subthreshold symptoms that do not meet criteria for PTSD can nonetheless interfere with mastering recovery tasks.

Systematic work is underway to develop treatments that can be used in residential, inpatient, and outpatient community-based settings. Lisa Najavits (Najavits, 2001) has been studying and developing her *Seeking Safety* model, a cognitive behavioral approach designed to stabilize clients and give them psychoeducation and other tools for coping with their PTSD symptoms. Elise Triffleman has developed an integrated cognitive-behavioral model combining relapse prevention and coping skills training with psychoeducation, stress inoculation training, and in vivo exposure for PTSD (Triffleman, Carroll, & Kellogg, 1999). Exposure therapy has been combined with an empirically supported treatment for substance use disorders, modified for use with an inner city population (Coffey, Schumacher, Brimo, & Brady, 2005). Although these models are promising, experienced clinicians are also drawing on developments outside the field of substance abuse in an effort to find effective interventions for reprocessing trauma. Eye Movement Desensitization and Reprocessing (EMDR) (Shapiro, 1995, 2001, 2002) has attracted considerable attention because of the large number of clinicians using it and reporting positive results, and because of the growing body of research evidence documenting its effectiveness in a variety of populations. Although descriptive articles and a small pilot have appeared in the literature on addictions (Henry, 1996; Lazrove, Triffleman, Kite, McGlashan, & Rounsaville, 1998; Shapiro, Vogelmann-Sine, & Sine, 1994), controlled studies of substance abusers have not been published. There is, however, considerable interest in investigating this potentially powerful tool for reprocessing trauma.

EMDR: Process and Procedures

Although EMDR is the name by which this therapy is widely recognized, it is actually an integrative therapy that encompasses a range of clinical interventions based on the treatment plan formulated from a comprehensive assessment. It is conceptualized as an information-processing model of trauma resolution, in which the standardized procedures and bilateral brain stimulation facilitates entry into an accelerated learning state in which traumatic experiences can be processed effectively and efficiently. Although the eye movements themselves have received an enormous amount of attention, it appears that bilateral and/or focused stimulation is the salient ingredient, and this is frequently achieved by sounds (using earphones) and taps (administered by therapist or a machine). Shapiro notes that she named the treatment EMDR in the early stages of its development, but it would have been more appropriately called "Reprocessing Therapy" (Shapiro, 2001).

The Adaptive Information Processing model (AIP) (Shapiro, 2001, 2002) that guides EMDR practice states that unprocessed experiential contributors are the basis of most pathology. In order to make sense of the present, a physical information processing system integrates perceptions into existing memory networks. Under circumstances of intense stress the processing system may be unable to function properly and disturbing events remain isolated in memory networks that are unable to link with anything more adaptive. These unprocessed memories essentially contain the emotions, thoughts, and physical sensations fundamentally unchanged since the time of the event. Current circumstances act as triggers and these aspects of memory arise to color current perceptions, and drive behaviors because of the emotions and physical sensations experienced by the client. Essentially, since the client is feeling the emotions and sensations of these unprocessed events: the past becomes present. The purpose of EMDR therapy is to identify and process the experiential contributors of dysfunction and health.

There are eight phases and specific protocols used to address the presenting complaints (Shapiro, 1995). A careful Client History is taken to evaluate the entire clinical picture. This includes identifying the experiences that will need to be processed in order to address the elements of the negative experiences (dysfunctional cognitive, emotional, somatic and behavioral elements) and incorporate a positive vision of the future. In the Preparation phase, the client is educated about the symptom picture, and given tools to facilitate stabilization and processing. The Assessment phase focuses on the disturbing target experiences and the attendant negative beliefs, emotion and physical sensations. The client specifies current rating of distress using the 0-10 Subjective Units of Disturbance (SUD) scale (Wolpe, 1958), and strength of the desired positive belief using the 1-7 (1 = completely false; 7 = completely true) Validity of Cognition (VOC) scale (Shapiro, 1989).

Once the client is considered ready, standardized procedures for Desensitization, Installation, and Body Scan Phases are used to process the target. The standardized procedures include the bilateral stimulation (e.g., eye movement, taps, tones) and an association procedure that are important elements to producing effective and efficient information processing that will ultimately lead to a reduction of symptoms. During the reprocessing phases clients experience insights and shifts in affective and somatic manifestations of the targeted events. In the Closure Phase the focus is on returning the client to equilibrium, with preparation for any distress between sessions. The Reevaluation Phase, which opens every subsequent session ensures that positive treatment effects have maintained, and guides the clinician to the next target. The standardized protocols for addressing PTSD and chronic distress both include the targeting of past events that set the groundwork for the pathology, present triggers that elicit disturbance, and positive templates for appropriate future action.

FROM RESEARCH TO PRACTICE

Eighteen randomized clinical trials have been conducted on EMDR with a wide range of trauma populations and comparison conditions. For comprehensive reviews see Bradley, Greene, Russ, Dutra, and Westen, 2005 (Bradley, Greene, Dutra, & Westen, 2005) (Department of Veterans Affairs & Department of Defense, 2004; Maxfield & Hyer, 2002). A variety of international guidelines have given EMDR the highest level of effectiveness ("A") rating as a first line treatment for PTSD (American Psychiatric Association, 2004; Bleich, Kotler, Kutz, & Shalev, 2002; Department of Veterans Affairs & Department of Defense, 2003). A comprehensive meta-analysis reported the more rigorous the study, the larger the effect (Maxfield & Hyer, 2002).

In addition to issues of efficacy, clinical efficiency and practicality should also be examined. As noted in an extensive meta-analyses (VanEtten & Taylor, 1998) while EMDR and behavior therapy were superior to psychotropic medication, EMDR was more efficient than behavior therapy, with results obtained in one-third the time. While it has been concluded in the above cited International Practice Guidelines that EMDR is at least equivalent to exposure and other cognitive behavioral therapies (CBT), it should be noted that exposure therapy uses one to two hours of daily homework and EMDR uses none (Perkins & Rouanzoin, 2002; Shapiro & Maxfield, 2002). In fact, the only randomized study to find some superiority for exposure therapy (on two of ten subscales) used an additional 48 hours of daily homework along with therapist assisted in vivo exposure (Taylor et al., 2003). In addition, EMDR may also be better suited to the dynamics inherent in a substance abuse population. As noted in the Department of Veterans Affairs/Department of Defense (2004) guidelines, EMDR may take only a few sessions, and unlike exposure therapies, can be used with clients experiencing guilt. Further, as noted in the American Psychiatric Association guidelines (American Psychiatric Association, 2004), EMDR does not demand a full narrative from the client, and therefore may be particularly useful for those troubled by disclosure and shame issues.

In short, more than enough research evidence has been amassed to warrant the study of EMDR in substance abusers in random assignment clinical trials.

Use of EMDR in Clients with Substance Abuse

EMDR can be useful in a variety of ways during the recovery process. The recovery process encompasses a number of tasks: enhancing motivation, becoming abstinent, addressing and preventing relapse, and enhancing the quality of recovery. If tailored appropriately for the individual, EMDR can help facilitate all aspects of recovery, including abstinence. Although many substance abusers enter addiction treatment in too fragile a state to permit reprocessing major traumas, there are a number of other ways to begin using EMDR. As noted previously, EMDR engenders a "processing" or "learning" state that targets the experiential contributors of dysfunction and health. Negative imagery, emotions and thoughts are targeted during trauma processing and transform to a positive state. Likewise, EMDR can be used to accentuate and increase the client's access to positive affective states. A standard preparation phase in EMDR includes the utilization of a Safe Place exercise that uses imagery to evoke a positive affect (see Shapiro, 2001). Extensions of this protocol called EMDR Resource Development and Installation have been evaluated in a case series (Korn & Leeds, 2002) and found to increase stabilization.

The therapist can use the resource development process to help the client build the support system, emotional stability, and self-soothing capacity to begin to address the traumatic experiences. For example, clients have a variety of reasons to avoid self-help participation. A process for increasing a sense of security can be used to assist clients to overcome important resistance:

Marie began having serious addiction problems as an adolescent and was hospitalized. She always had a difficult time using the 12-step system because she felt so unable to socialize. She would go to meetings, feel bewildered and preoccupied with what others were thinking, hypervigilant for evidence they were judging her harshly. She achieved sobriety for a period of time, but relapsed in college and returned home and entered outpatient treatment. The therapist explored her feelings in social situations, and she shared that she had felt painful awkwardness most acutely on the playground in elementary school.

The therapist asked her to think of her favorite color and imagine being surrounded by it. She replied that her favorite color was pink, and described a bubble. The therapist asked her to picture being in the pink bubble, using the bilateral stimulation. After she was comfortable and relaxed in her body, the therapist suggested that she picture herself in the pink bubble while at a 12-step meeting, and notice how her body felt. She was then able to use this image when she went to meetings to create a sense of safety and develop more internal resources. The anxiety she felt diminished, and over time, she realized that she was able to be more comfortable at meetings.

Although Marie's anxiety originated in childhood, it was not necessary to address those images directly in order to strengthen her confidence. In this case, the therapist felt that much work was required before other kinds of processing of the painful experiences could be undertaken, but that resource installation (Shapiro, 2001) could be beneficial in moving the patient forward.

It should also be noted that at times, the apparent affect dysregulation may actually be the product of insufficiently processed traumata. For instance, a recent study (Brown & Shapiro, in press) of a client with Borderline Personality Disorder/Complex PTSD indicated that a client who had been seen for a number of years using CBT and psychodynamic therapy presented again for treatment because of on-going difficulties. The clinician, now trained in EMDR, inaugurated treatment. Once the client had been taught the Safe Place exercise, standard EMDR trauma processing brought all scales on the Inventory of Altered Self Capacities (Briere, 2004) into the subclinical range. These included scales initially indicating a high level of dysfunction related to affect control (Affect Dysregulation, Affect Instability, Affect Skills Deficits, and Tension Reduction Activities). One should discriminate between affect dysregulation caused by organic deficits, and those caused by experiential contributors.

EMDR can also be used to target traumatic experiences that trigger cravings (Saladin et al., 2003; Vogelmann-Sine, Sine, Smyth, & Popky, 1998). Although most clinicians agree that stability is necessary to do significant trauma work, many clients may never get clean and sober unless some of the emotional charge is taken out of their traumatic past. As noted by Shapiro (2001) the use of EMDR to assist in establishing abstinence is different from its use to address relapse after a significant period of abstinence. Clients are encouraged to become good detectives, discover their triggers, work on them in sessions, and use EMDR between sessions to neutralize urges until the desire fades. They are also asked to remind themselves of their positive goals, and to monitor urges between sessions.

For those further along in recovery, processing of painful experiences can be part of addressing relapse:

> Judy began drinking at age 10, and her alcoholism progressed steadily for ten years. She got sober in her 20's and was very involved with 12-step recovery activities, but avoided dealing with her painful childhood with highly neglectful parents. After 14 years of sobriety, unexpected events brought back her childhood difficulties, and she began drinking again and became suicidal. Her outpatient therapist referred her to an inpatient program and recommended that they utilize EMDR to assist her in reprocessing her early family trauma. She entered an inpatient trauma program that offered EMDR sessions, which she found to be most helpful.
>
> When she returned to her own community, she agreed to continue the EMDR sessions on an outpatient basis. Her therapist typically used EMDR processing in about one out of four sessions, with the sessions in between used for discussion of the material that had emerged. She uses 2-3 sessions to continue integrating the information in discussions with her therapist following each EMDR session.

Judy's recovery tools were strong, but her recovery collapsed because her PTSD interfered with maintaining ongoing recovery. Although she had a strong 12-step support system with a sponsor, a supportive family and years of recovery, her traumatic history prevented her from being comfortable in the world. Given the right circumstances, it was inevitable that she would become triggered and lose the resources necessary to maintain sobriety. The pain was too overwhelming and she regressed. EMDR assisted her in reprocessing the early memories so they would be less potent as a trigger to use. This will hopefully reduce her vulnerability to further relapse. If the client has not returned to extended periods of alcohol and other drug use, and has not deteriorated too greatly in functioning, targeting the trauma in an outpatient setting may help re-establish abstinence as well as address previously unfinished business. Additional cases of EMDR trauma treatment (Shapiro & Forrest, 1997) indicate that the need for the self-medication caused by the earlier traumata may be the cause of chronic relapsing and can be addressed through appropriate processing. As noted earlier, the AIP model indicates that the stored perceptions color present reactions. Those clients that have feelings of helplessness and hopelessness emerge from the stored experiences may not be able to resist self-medication. Once the earlier events are processed, the client is able to make healthier choices.

The overall treatment for addictions includes using EMDR protocols to address the past experiences that set the groundwork for the dysfunctional behavior. These are generally experiences that give the client the sense that s/he is defective, unsafe, or not in control (Shapiro, 2001). The current triggers including people, places, or things that elicit the desire to use (Shapiro & Forrest, 1997). These are processed along with new skills and behaviors for the future. Finally, EMDR is a valuable tool to enhance quality of recovery in clients who are stable in their abstinence and working on a variety of issues in their psychotherapy.

INTEGRATING EMDR INTO OUTPATIENT AND RESIDENTIAL TREATMENT

Currently, it is much more likely for patients to have access to EMDR if they are in treatment funded by private insurance or they can pay themselves. However, the high prevalence of trauma history among clients in the indigent care system has stimulated interest in bringing it there. How EMDR can be used depends on the level of the client's functioning and presence or absence of a strong support system. Programs can incorporate EMDR by hiring trained therapists to work with clients on a consultant basis, by bringing them onto their regular staff, or by training existing staff. It is important to remember that the addiction field is very diverse, with strong subcultures, in the sense of beliefs, norms and practices, in particular modalities. Therapists brought in from the outside may have some understanding of addictive disorders, but it will still be necessary to orient them carefully to the program's philosophy and approaches, and provide mechanisms for ongoing communication about clinical issues. When outside clinicians become too isolated from the program, problems inevitably result. Inasmuch as EMDR involves working with intense feelings, it is especially important that clinical care coordination does not become lost in the demands of busy schedules or fracture from the schism of differing clinical philosophies.

Residential treatment represents a highly desirable setting for EMDR, because the safety structures are more extensive for unstable clients. Nonetheless, these programs vary widely in structure, with therapeutic communities offering the highest level of structure, coordination of clinical activities, and duration of stay (DeLeon, 1995). These programs may represent an optimal setting for clients who are fairly impaired in their functioning. The inpatient treatment system largely funded by insurance or managed care often serves higher functioning clients who can utilize EMDR sessions despite the relatively shorter length of stay. Explicit procedures for outside therapists to report to the regular staff after each EMDR session are crucial. Staff must have clear plans for what to do if the client appears to become more upset, dissociated or unstable in the hours or days following an EMDR session. The EMDR therapist must be able to add special sessions in acute situations. This is particularly important in less structured residential settings, such as alcohol recovery homes, which aim to provide a protected setting rather than intensive clinical intervention.

Outpatient treatment represents a much greater challenge. It is more difficult to gauge the quality of the support structure outside the program itself. Although it is preferable to begin such work when the client has achieved stable abstinence, many with trauma histories are unable to stop drinking and using for long periods of time. Some clinicians have described success in using EMDR early in treatment, resulting in progress in achieving abstinence. The risks of using such a powerful approach with an unstable client must be weighed against the frustration of a motivated client who seems unable to progress beyond brief periods of abstinence. In order to increase resilience and stability, this population is ideally suited for the EMDR resource work previously described.

Outpatient treatment requires that the clinician set a standard of safety and assess the degree of stability of the client, as this determines how EMDR can be used. In the early stages of addiction recovery, it is critical that the client develops resources for maintaining abstinence, and tolerating feelings without drinking or using. The EMDR protocol for resource development is a wonderful tool to teach self-soothing skills in order to facilitate abstinence. However, Shapiro has emphasized that "preparation is not processing." As demonstrated by Korn and Leeds (2002), increase in stabilization does not decrease the symptoms caused by the underlying trauma. The affects that cause the desire for self-medication and relapse potential are inherent within the unprocessed memories and should be dealt with the standard EMDR protocols that address the past experiences, current triggers, and templates for appropriate future action.

An addiction specialist who is proficient in EMDR offers an ideal skill set for working with clients with a trauma history. However, this is currently a rare combination. At present, it is more likely that this resource can be brought into addiction treatment by collaboration. It is necessary for the therapist doing EMDR to work closely with other outpatient staff to maximize attentiveness and support for the client during the period when sessions are taking place. As in residential treatment, it is important for the EMDR therapist to understand as much as possible about the resources and limits of the addiction program, and to have clear communication protocols established from the outset. If an acute reaction occurs, the collaborating therapist should be willing to provide support and consultation to the staff.

TRAINING AND ONGOING SUPERVISION

EMDR is a complex treatment approach that requires significant training. In order to understand the principles, procedures and protocols of EMDR, the mental health professional is required to undertake 18 didactic hours and 13 supervised practicum experience hours with a trained EMDR clinician. This training is designed to insure safety, and maximize the treatment outcome. After therapists have completed the formal training, it is recommended that they continue with on-going case consultation from an EMDR trained supervisor when they first begin using EMDR in their practice to insure a broad understanding of the process. It can also be helpful to have other colleagues to talk with on an informal basis about how EMDR is utilized in their practices.

EMDR training is open to mental health professionals who are licensed, certified or registered for independent practice. The training is also open to advanced graduate students, interns and other mental health professionals on a licensure track, with a letter of support from their supervisor. As with any other therapeutic approach, the more the therapist uses EMDR, the greater the understanding of its use and application. Information about training can be obtained by contacting the EMDR International Association (www.emdria.org). The EMDR Humanitarian Assistance Programs (www.emdrhap.org) is a non-profit organization that provides low cost trainings for mental health agencies and can facilitate such integration and supervision. More information and relevant updates on research can be obtained through a website devoted to such functions (www.emdrnetwork.org).

CONCLUSION

EMDR offers much promise and great challenges to addiction treatment providers. It is a powerful tool for trauma resolution, but it must be carefully integrated into addiction treatment. Organizational as well as individual safety structures must be in place so that vulnerable individuals may be offered this opportunity under conditions which maximize their chances for success. Efforts are underway to obtain funding for controlled trials, and it is hoped that these will clarify safety and efficacy questions, as well as many clinical issues that arise as more clinicians work with this method.

REFERENCES

American Psychiatric Association. (2004). *Practice Guideline for the Treatment of Patients with Acute Stress Disorder and Posttraumatic Stress Disorder.* Arlington, Virginia: American Psychiatric Association Practice Guidelines.

Bradley, R., Greene, J., Dutra, E., & Westen, D. (2005). A multidimensional meta-analysis of psychotherapy for PTSD. *American Journal of Psychiatry, 162*, 214-227.

Briere, J. (2004). *Inventory of Altered Self-Capacities.* Florida: Psychological Assessment Resources.

Brown, S., & Shapiro, F. (in press). EMDR in the treatment of borderline personality disorder. *Clinical Case Studies.*

Coffey, S. F., Schumacher, J. A., Brimo, M. L., & Brady, K. T. (2005). Exposure therapy for substance abusers with PTSD: Translating research to practice. *Behav Modif, 29*(1), 10-38.

DeLeon, G. (1995). Residential therapeutic communities in the mainstream: Diversity and issues. *Journal of Psychoactive Drugs, 27*(13-15).

Department of Veterans Affairs & Department of Defense. (2003). *The VA/DoD Clinical Practice Guideline for the Management of Post-Traumatic Stress.* Retrieved

April 11, 2005, from the World Wide Web: http://www.oqp.med.va.gov/cpg/PTSD/ PTSD_Base.htm

Henry, S. L. (1996). Pathological gambling: Etiological considerations and treatment efficacy of eye movement desensitization/reprocessing. *Journal of Gambling Studies, 12,* 395-405.

Korn, D. L., & Leeds, A. M. (2002). Preliminary evidence of efficacy for EMDR resource development and installation in the stabilization phase of treatment of complex posttraumatic stress disorder. *J Clin Psychol, 58*(12), 1465-1487.

Lazrove, S., Triffleman, E., Kite, L., McGlashan, T., & Rounsaville, B. (1998). An open trial of EMDR as treatment for chronic PTSD. *Am J Orthopsychiatry, 68*(4), 601-608.

Maxfield, L., & Hyer, L. (2002). The relationship between efficacy and methodology in studies investigating EMDR treatment of PTSD. *Journal of Clinical Psychology, 58*(1), 23-41.

Najavits, L. M. (2001). *Seeking Safety: A Treatment Manual for PTSD and Substance Abuse.* New York: Guilford.

Najavits, L. M., Weiss, R. D., & Shaw, S. R. (1997). The link between substance abuse and posttraumatic stress disorder in women. A research review. *Am J Addict, 6*(4), 273-283.

Perkins, B. R., & Rouanzoin, C. C. (2002). A critical evaluation of current views regarding eye movement desensitization and reprocessing (EMDR): Clarifying points of confusion. *Journal of Clinical Psychology, 58,* 77-97.

Saladin, M. E., Drobes, D. J., Coffey, S. F., Dansky, B. S., Brady, K. T., & Kilpatrick, D. G. (2003). PTSD symptom severity as a predictor of cue-elicited drug craving in victims of violent crime. *Addict Behav, 28*(9), 1611-1629.

Shapiro, F. (1989). Efficacy of the eye movement desensitization procedure in the treatment of traumatic memories. *Journal of Traumatic Stress Studies, 2,* 199-223.

Shapiro, F. (1995). *Eye Movement Desensitization and Reprocessing: Basic Principles, Protocols, and Procedures.* New York: The Guilford Press.

Shapiro, F. (2001). *Eye Movement Desensitization and Reprocessing (EMDR), Second Edition: Basic Principles, Protocols, and Procedures.* New York: Guilford Press.

Shapiro, F. (Ed.). (2002). *EMDR as an Integrative Psychotherapy Approach: Experts of Diverse Orientations Explore the Paradigm Prism.* Washington D.C.: American Psychological Association.

Shapiro, F., & Forrest, M. S. (1997). *EMDR.* New York: Basic Books.

Shapiro, F., & Maxfield, L. L. (2002). EMDR: Information processing in the treatment of trauma. *Journal of Clinical Psychology, 58* (Special Issue: Treatment of PTSD.), 933-946.

Shapiro, F., Vogelmann-Sine, S., & Sine, L. (1994). Eye movement desensitization and reprocessing: Treating trauma and substance abuse. *Journal of Psychoactive Drugs, 26*(4), 379-391.

Taylor, S., Thordarson, D. S., Maxfield, L., Fedoroff, I. C., Lovell, K., & Ogrodniczuk, J. (2003). Comparative efficacy, speed and adverse events of three PTSD treatments: Exposure therapy, EMDR, and relaxation training. *Journal of Consulting and Clinical Psychology, 71*(2), 330-338.

Triffleman, E., Carroll, K., & Kellogg, S. (1999). Substance dependence posttraumatic stress disorder therapy: An integrated cognitive-behavioral approach. *Journal of Substance Abuse Treatment, 17*(1-2), 3-14.

VanEtten, M., & Taylor, S. (1998). Comparative efficacy of treatments for post-traumatic stress disorder: A meta-analysis. *Clinical Psychology and Psychotherapy, 5*, 126-144.

Vogelmann-Sine, S., Sine, L. F., Smyth, N. J., & Popky, A. J. (1998). *EMDR Chemical Dependency Treatment Manual.* Honolulu, Hawaii.

Wolpe, J. (1958). *Psychotherapy by reciprocal inhibition.* Stanford, California: Stanford University Press.

Zweben, J. E., & Clark, H. W. (Eds.). (1994). *Traumatic Experiences and Substance Abuse* (Vol. 26 (4)). San Francisco, CA: *Journal of Psychoactive Drugs.*

Psychoneurobiology
of Co-Occurring Trauma and Addictions

Joyce Fowler, PhD

SUMMARY. The primary goals of this chapter are threefold. First, a general overview of psychoneurobiology and the stress response will be given to help the clinician gain a basic understanding of normative and pathological stress responses. This information will not only provide clinicians with a basic understanding but could be useful for psycho-educational purposes in treatment settings. Secondly, reviews of some recent research findings are provided to further facilitate understanding of the implications of co-morbid trauma and addictions. Finally, suggestions for conducting in integrative assessment to facilitate treatment planning will be discussed. *[Article copies available for a fee from The Haworth Document Delivery Service: 1-800-HAWORTH. E-mail address: <docdelivery@haworthpress.com> Website: <http://www.HaworthPress.com> © 2006 by The Haworth Press, Inc. All rights reserved.]*

KEYWORDS. Trauma resolution, responses to stress, co-occurring addictions

INTRODUCTION

The need to address co-occurring trauma and addiction has been well established (Heather & Gilvary, 1998; SAMHSA, 2002). Recently,

[Haworth co-indexing entry note]: "Psychoneurobiology of Co-Occurring Trauma and Addictions." Fowler, Joyce. Co-published simultaneously in *Journal of Chemical Dependency Treatment* (The Haworth Press, Inc.) Vol. 8, No. 2, 2006, pp. 129-152; and: *Psychological Trauma and Addiction Treatment* (ed: Bruce Carruth) The Haworth Press, Inc., 2006, pp. 129-152. Single or multiple copies of this article are available for a fee from The Haworth Document Delivery Service [1-800-HAWORTH, 9:00 a.m. - 5:00 p.m. (EST). E-mail address: docdelivery@haworthpress.com].

Available online at http://www.haworthpress.com/web/JCDT
© 2006 by The Haworth Press, Inc. All rights reserved.
doi:10.1300/J034v08n02_07

trauma experiences involving large numbers of people that are associated with terrorism, war and natural disasters have heightened awareness and concern of the residual effects of trauma events. However, individual trauma experiences related to physical and/or psychological trauma such as relational trauma (e.g., physical, sexual or emotional abuse), social disruptions (i.e., neglect, abandonment, separation, divorce, illness, and grief/complicated bereavement), violence (e.g., stalking, rape, assault and battery), or accidents (e.g., motor vehicle accidents) make up a large portion of those with co-morbid trauma and addiction problems. A multiplicity of risk factors (e.g., genetics, personality, socio-economic status, cognitive functioning, dysphoria, supersensitivity and kindling) has been associated with co-morbidity across addictions (Mueser, Drake, & Wallace, 1998). Functional difficulties associated with co-occurring trauma and addictions include cognitive problems, attentional difficulties, memory problems, impulse control problems, and affective/behavioral dysregulation. Contemporary practice calls for integrated treatment of co-occurring disorders (SAMHSA, 2002; U.S. DHHS, 1999) to maximize treatment effectiveness and facilitate recovery. Co-occurring trauma and addiction represents a unique challenge to clinicians in assessing and planning for treatment. The primary goals of this chapter are threefold. First, a general overview of psychoneurobiology and the stress response will be given to help the clinician gain a basic understanding of normative and pathological stress responses. This information will not only provide clinicians with a basic understanding but could be useful for psychoeducational purposes in treatment settings. Secondly, reviews of some recent research findings are provided to further facilitate understanding of the implications of co-morbid trauma and addictions. Finally, suggestions for conducting an integrative assessment to facilitate treatment planning will be discussed.

PSYCHONEUROBIOLOGY AND THE STRESS RESPONSE

Significant advances in the understanding of the stress response system have been made since the seminal research findings from early stress researchers like Walter Cannon and Hans Selye. Cannon identified the fight/flight response or emergency reaction in response to acute stress and proposed the homeostatic model and the wisdom of the body (Cannon, 1929, 1932, & 1953). Fighting or fleeing is the behavioral analogue to the physiological stress response. Hans Selye proposed the general adaptation syndrome with three distinct stages (i.e., alarm, resistance and exhaustion) and also emphasized homeostasis (Selye, 1974). The theory of homeostasis refers to the body's tendency to maintain a steady state despite external changes, i.e., the body operates independently of the brain, emphasizes internal milieu constancy, and local, negative feedback mechanisms. A homeostatic mechanism is called a negative feedback control mechanism because it reverses a change. In the strictest sense, homeostasis is limited to a number of systems related to survival such as pH, body temperature and oxygen tension (McEwen, 2000). Sterling and Eyer (1988) proposed the allostasis model of adaptation to explain arousal pathology, which indicates the CNS has pre-eminent regulatory influence on somatic physiology:

> Allostasis emphasizes that the internal milieu varies to meet perceived and anticipated demand. This variation is achieved by multiple, mutually reinforcing neural and neuroendocrine mechanisms that override the homeostatic mechanisms. The allostatic model, in emphasizing the subordination of local feedbacks to control by the brain provides a strong conceptual framework to explain social and psychological modulation of physiology and pathology.

Extending the allostatic model, McEwen (1998, 2000) emphasized the cost of allostasis (i.e., allostatic load). In contrast to an overemphasis on the damaging effect of classic stress hormones, McEwen underscores the protective and adaptive role of hormones and other physiological agents. In the short term, hormones and other physiological agents have protective and adaptive effects for brain and the immune system. Acute stress enhances immune function and even repeated stress over weeks has been associated with adaptive plasticity of the brain. However, the adaptive processes of allostastis have a potential cost to the body, which can accelerate pathophysiology when allostasis is either called upon too often (e.g., chronic stress suppresses immune function) or is inefficiently managed (McEwen, 2000). In McEwen's model, the brain's perception of stressors and/or anticipation of demands (e.g., perceived threat, experience of helplessness, and/or vigilance in anticipation of threat) are influenced by multiple factors, which converge to influence physiologic responses. These factors include:

- external factors (e.g., environmental stressors, major life events, and trauma/abuse)
- individual differences (e.g., genes, development, and experience)
- behavioral responses (e.g., fight/flight, personal behaviors such as diet, smoking, alcohol/drug use, exercise)

The central allostatic response to stressors is activation of the hypothalamic-pituitary-adrenal (HPA) axis, the sympathetic nervous system and the adrenal gland (particularly the sympathetic adrenal medulla and the sympathetic adrenal cortex). Activation results in a cascading release of neuroendocrine hormones, which facilitates adaptation followed by inactivation of these systems and a return baseline.

There are two major divisions of the nervous system, the Peripheral Nervous System (PNS) and the Central Nervous System (CNS). The autonomic nervous system, a subdivision of the PNS, is involved in the regulation of a number of organs that are central to survival and homeostasis, the so-called vegetative functions. These include the body's automatic, involuntary functions such as heartbeat rate, control of smooth muscles, and a number of glands. There are two parts of the autonomic nervous system, the sympathetic nervous system and the parasympathetic nervous system both of which enervate many of the same organs with opposing influences. For example, activation of the sympathetic nervous system accelerates heartbeat and activation of the parasympathetic nervous system slows the heartbeat. There is a natural diurnal fluctuation of the sympathetic and parasympathetic nervous system that facilitates a balance between restorative states and expenditure of energy, i.e., rest and activity. The second subdivision of the PNS is the somatic system, which controls movement of skeletal muscles and transmits somatosensory information to the CNS contributing to perception of threats/stressors or anticipation of threats/stressors. Before turning to an overview of neuroendocrine responses to stress, a brief overview of the CNS is warranted.

Anatomically, the CNS (Central Nervous System) has six major regions: telencephalon, diencephalon, mes-encephalon, metencephalon, myelencephalon, and spinal cord (see Table 1 for delineation of specific brain structures by region). Functionally, there are three primary systems: the sensory system, the motor system and the motivational system. The *sensory system* consists of pathways that regulate visual, auditory, somatic sensory, gustatory (i.e., taste), and olfaction (i.e., smell) functions. The *motor system* consists of pathways that regulate muscle functions. Finally, the *motivational* system consists of pathways that influence voluntary behavior. Each of the three primary functional systems is composed of several distinct pathways with complex interconnecting neural network inputs and/or outputs (i.e., synaptic relays via local interneurons and projections interneurons) in the brain and spinal cord. Furthermore, inputs and outputs are also influenced by neuroendocrine/humoral inputs and/or outputs. Neural pathways mostly cross over

TABLE 1. Six Regions of the Central Nervous System

REGION	STRUCTURES	PRIMARY FUNCTIONS
Telencephalon	Cerebral Cortex • Frontal lobe (primary motor cortex & prefrontal association cortex) • Parietal lobe (primary somatic sensory cortex & parietal-temporal-occipital association cortex) • Temporal lobe (primary auditory cortex) • Occipital lobe (primary visual cortex) Basal Ganglia Hippocampal Formation (hippocampus & dentate gyrus) Amygdala Olfactory Bulb	Regulating motor performance Memory storage Autonomic & endocrine responses Emotional states
Diencephalon	Thalamus Hypothalamus Sub-thalamus Epithalamus Retinae Optic nerves & tracts	Processing most information reaching the cerebral cortex Regulating autonomic, endocrine & visceral function
Mes-encephalon	Midbrain	Controls many sensory & motor functions
Metencephalon	Pons Cerebellum	Pons conveys information about movement from cerebral hemisphere to cerebellum; Cerebellum modulates force & range of movement and involved in learning of motor skills
Myelencephalon	Medulla	Control of vital autonomic functions (e.g., digestion, breathing & control of heart rate)
Spinal cord	Spinal cord	Controls movement of limbs & trunk; receives & process sensory information from the skin, joint, & muscles of limbs & trunk

Adapted from Kandel, Schwartz & Jessell, 1991; Thibodeau & Patton, 1997; and Scanlon & Sanders, 1995 within the spinal cord or in different parts of the brain resulting in contralateral (opposite side) representation. For example, motor pathways for right side body movements cross over and are processed in the left side of the brain. Commissures (fibers/bundles of axons) in the brain connect functionally related areas in each half of the brain. The largest commissure in the brain is the corpus callosum, which connects the right and left hemispheres providing right/left integration. However, some connections are ipsalateral (same side). For example, the visual neural map has both ipsalateral and contralateral connections.

All in all, involuntary and voluntary behaviors result from the very complex, interactional nature of the brain. Of particular importance to the upcoming discussion of the stress response is to understand that there are complex interconnections between the limbic system and the hypothalamus. In turn, the hypothalamus significantly influences neuroendocrine and autonomic nervous system regulation. The limbic system consists of brain structures and interconnecting fiber bundles primarily in the teleencephalon and diencephalon including: pre-prefrontal association cortex (inclusive of the prefrontal association cortex proper and orbitofrontal cortex), cingulate gyrus, hippocampal formation (including the hippocampus proper and dentate gyrus), fornix, amygdala, parts of the hypothalamus, mammilary bodies, thalamus (anterior thalamic nuclei, mammillothalamic tract), septal area, and nucleus accumbens. The limbic system influences all three functional systems (i.e., sensory, motor and motivation) and is involved in learning, memory, motivation and emotion. A normative response to traumatic events is an orchestrated activation of these key brain structures, which facilitates survival and adaptation. Non-normative responses and/or chronic stress have been associated with disruptions in limbic system functioning and dysregulation of the sympathetic and parasympathetic nervous system.

Stressors, whether immediate or anticipated, trigger limbic system interconnections resulting in a cascade of neuroendocrine responses via the HPA (hypothalamic pituitary adrenal) Axis. These neuroendocrine responses are integral to activation of the ANS (Autonomic Nervous System). The ANS is comprised of two branches, the sympathetic and parasympathetic. The sympathetic nervous system is associated with expenditure of energy/activity and the parasympathetic nervous system is associated with conservation of energy/restoration/relaxation. The hypothalamic control of the autonomic nervous system and endocrine system is related to a number of survival behaviors including fighting, fleeing (so called fight or flight response), feeding, drinking, mating, and sleeping. The hypothalamus generates several releasing and stimulating hormones that function to both stimulate the pituitary to release hormones and inhibit the pituitary's secretion of hormones. The pituitary gland is connected to the hypothalamus via the pituitary stalk. The hormone most relevant to the activation of the sympathetic nervous systems is corticotrophin releasing hormone (CRH), which is produced when stressors occur. Hypothalamic neurosecretory cell terminals release CRH in capillaries connected to the anterior pituitary gland, which stimulates secretion of adrenocorticotropic hormone (ACTH). Circulating ACTH stimulates the sympathetic nerves that enervate the adrenal cortex and adrenal medulla, which in turn produces cortisol (via adrenal cortex) and epinephrine and norepinephrine (via adrenal medulla). Cortisol promotes gluconeogenis (increased use of fats and excess amino acids for energy), which spares glucose for use by the brain. Cortisol also has an anti-inflammatory and anti-histamine effect and influences the immune response. Epinephrine and norepinephrine prolong and intensify the sympathetic nervous system response during stress. Therefore, as indicated by Sterling and Eyer (1988), the internal local homeostatic negative feedback loops are subordinated to these CNS control mechanisms.

The parasympathetic nervous system is also important relative to the stress response system first for its inhibitory influence on the HPA axis. Secondly, the parasympathetic system becomes activated to facilitate an immobilization response during extreme stress/terror situations. Self-regulation strategies that focus on relaxation training are predicated on activation of the parasympathetic nervous system to facilitate relaxation and restoration. However, the parasympathetic system is also associated with dissociation and conservation-withdrawal. Dissociation and conservation-withdrawal is a functional expression of heightened dorsal vagal complex (i.e., dorsal vagal and nucleus ambiguous) activity (Shore, 2002; Porges, 1997, 2001, 2003) during extreme stress/terror. Physiological manifestations of conservation-withdrawal include slowed heart rate and breathing. Behavioral manifestations include a confused/dazed state, staring into space with a glazed look, behavioral stilling/freezing, death feigning and hiding behaviors (Schore, 2002; Porges, 1997, 2001, 2003). Unsuccessful massive sympathetic activation can result in a sudden, rapid transition to this metabolically conservative state (Porges, 1997, 2001, 2003).

Thus, trauma events may activate both the sympathetic and parasympathetic nervous system with alternating hyper-hypo activation with manifest physiological and behavioral states indicative of mobilization and immobilization. These alternate responses may explain the mixed symptom presentation in Post Traumatic Stress Disorder. Hypersympathetic activation is consistent with PTSD symptoms such as hyperarousal and reexperiencing (e.g., intrusive recollections, distressing dreams, flashbacks). Heightened activation of the dorsal vagal complex is consistent with symptoms of avoidance and numbing. Figure 1 provides a general overview of the primary influences of the sympathetic and parasympathetic nervous system activation on different organs in the body.

A normal stress response system facilitates survival and adaptation. However, repeated stress or non-normative stress responses can contribute to allostatic load and can have medical, psychological or behavioral consequences. McEwen (1998) delineated four types of situations associated with allostatic load:

1. repeated "hits"
2. lack of adaptation
3. prolonged response
4. inadequate response

Repeated "hits" refers to experiencing multiple stressors, repeated over time, with each triggering a normal stress response. While the response is normal, repetitive stress responses may cause wear and tear. Examples of repeated hits are people living in environments with chronic exposure to potential life threatening or psychologically threatening events (e.g., living in a prison system, living in a country during wartime) or working in high risk environments (e.g., police officers, emergency personnel). Normal adaptation to a repeated experience would be the development of adequate coping skills (e.g., understanding the culture, how to stay safe) and habituation (i.e., decreased responsiveness to stimuli). Therefore, activation of the stress response system upon re-exposure relative to initial exposure should result in decreased activation across time. *Lack of adaptation* refers to exposure to a repeated stressor of the same type with no adaptation. When there is no adaptation, individuals respond in a similar manner to their initial exposure, i.e., no learning or habituation occurs. For example, a prisoner experiences the same stress response every day as if it's the first day. *Prolonged response* refers to the inability to shut off allostatic responses after stress is terminated. In this instance, an individual has an extended reaction to a traumatic event. For example, an adopted child runs and hides in the closet every time someone knocks on their door for fear of

FIGURE 1. Relationship between the stress response and the autonomic nervous system: Anatomically related structures to the stress response and the sympathetic and parasympathetic target organs.

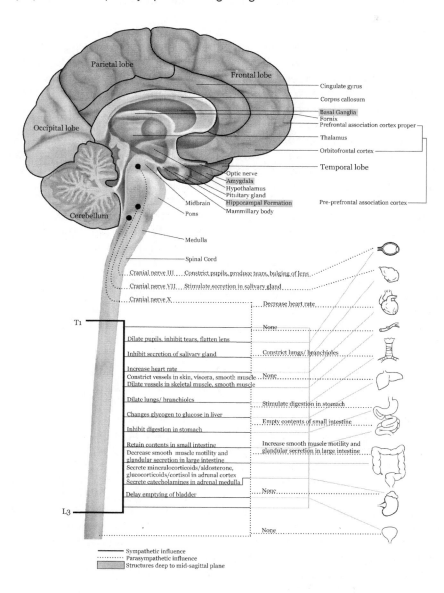

being taken back to foster care despite assurances from his parents. *Inadequate response* refers to initial hypoactivity of the stress response. In other words, there is no initial activation of the stress response system as would be expected to a traumatic event. For example, being extremely calm after being in a car wreck or assaulted may result in not taking necessary actions for an adequate adaptation to the event (e.g., getting to safety, seeking help, attending to wounds). This hypoactivity can cause hyperactivity of other mediators (hormonal or behavioral) and has been associated with increased risk for subsequent development of PTSD (Grossman, Buchsbaum, & Yehuda, 2002; McEwen, 2002; Yehuda, 2002).

Hypoactivity or hyperactivity of the autonomic nervous system, HPA Axis, adrenal cortex, adrenal medulla, cardiovascular, metabolic and immune systems can lead to multiple consequences. Cardiovascular disease, immune dysfunction, brain damage/dysfunction, and substance abuse/addiction are among the primary medical, behavioral, and neuropsychological consequences frequently cited in the stress literature. Substance abuse/addiction (i.e., a hyperactive behavioral response) can further contribute to allostatic load due to CNS effects, particularly when use is chronic. Likewise, chronic effects of trauma have been linked with damaging effects on the brain, particularly the hippocampus and amygdala but also to Broca's area and the prefrontal cortex. These effects have been highlighted in a number of contemporary studies and reviews (Hull, 2002; Salposky, 2002, 2000, 1996; Herbert, 1997).

CONTEMPORARY FINDINGS RELATIVE TO TRAUMA/STRESS RESPONSE

Neuroimaging studies are advancing our knowledge relative to structure and function of the brain. While neuroimaging studies are in their infancy, they are contributing to our knowledge regarding the plasticity of the brain. There are a small but growing number of neuroimaging findings in human subjects with PTSD. Most studies are primarily of homogeneous populations, use differing methodologies, and lack of control or comparison groups. Notwithstanding these limitations, Hull's (2002) review of 30 published reports indicates the brain may be damaged by psychological trauma. The primary findings are related to hippocampal damage, amygdala hyperactivation, underactivity of Broca's area, and possible right-hemispheric lateralization. These findings in conjunction with findings from other research methodologies using both human and animal models are further advancing our understanding of the potential effects of traumatic exposure.

Trauma Related Hippocampal Damage/Dysfunction

Although findings are mixed, the most replicated structural finding is smaller hippocampal volume in individuals with PTSD compared to controls (Hull, 2002; Grossman, Buschsbaum, & Yehuda, 2002). It is unclear whether this is an outcome of PTSD or a preexisting risk factor. While human research is still sparse with mixed findings and methodological challenges yet to be met, animal research is more compelling regarding stress-induced hippocampal atrophy (Salposky, 2002, 2000, 1996, 1992; McEwen, 2002). Exposure to glucocorticoids/cortisol has been correlated with hippocampal atrophy in combat veterans, adults with PTSD associated with childhood abuse, and combat veterans with PTSD versus no-PTSD (Salposky, 1996). Overall, hippocampal atrophy is correlated with chronic/prolonged exposure or repeated bursts of glucocorticoids/cortisol. Damage to the hippocampus has several implications. The hippocampus serves a regulatory function by inhibiting (i.e., a negative feedback brake) adrenal cortex secretion of glucocorticoids/cortisol (Sapolsky, 1992). Glucocorticoids in conjunction with other neurochemicals influence the remodeling of hippocampal dendrites and neurogenesis. Therefore, hippocampal damage can result in hypersecretion of glucocorticoids/cortisol thus compounding the problem of neuronal degeneration and interfering with neuronal remodeling and neurogenesis. In addition to problems with inhibition of the regulatory function of the hippocampus, hippocampal damage also contributes to episodic, declarative, contextual, and spatial learning and memory deficits. Decreased hippocampal function has been postulated to impair the process of habituation or extinction of the fearful response, contribute to a tendency for stimulus generalization secondary to decreased awareness of contextual constraints (Grossman, Buchsbaum, & Yehuda, 2002) and limit proper evaluation and categorization of experience (Hull, 2002).

In addition to the effects of chronic or repeated exposure to stress, recent findings relative to acute stress reactions are providing important insights. Short term, reversible acute effects of adrenal steroids on selective attention, memory consolidation, long-term potentiation and primed-burst potentiation have been found (McEwen, 2002). Such acute effects of elevated glucocorticoid levels are the result of direct impairment in the biochemical process of long-term potentiation (Grossman,

Buchsbaum, & Yehuda, 2002). Alternately, adequate levels of stress hormones (glucocorticoids and catecholamines) in the short term actually have protective/adaptive benefits, e.g., helping to form memories of events associated with strong emotions (McEwen, 2002) and facilitating adaptive coping. Recent findings indicate that some individuals who develop PTSD have a deficiency in HPA Axis their response (i.e., low cortisol levels) in the aftermath of traumatic events (Grossman, Buchsbaum, & Yehuda, 2002; McEwen, 2002). These findings suggest there may be different subtypes of PTSD (for an in depth review of the current status of cortisol finding in PTSD see Yehuda, 2002). Findings are hopeful that some hippocampal dysfunction can be prevented or reversed as we further our understanding of the protective, adaptive, and damaging effects of the mediator of stress and allostasis (McEwen, 2002). In the final analysis, current findings indicate that chronic or repeated exposure to stress is associated with hippocampal dysfunction and is directly relevant to individuals with trauma exposure regardless of whether they go on to develop PTSD or not.

Trauma Related Amygdala Hyperactivation

The amygdala, part of the limbic system, is centrally related to emotional response, both primitive emotion and higher order emotional awareness/consciousness. The amygdala has been implicated in the emotion of fear, fear learning, and control of the accompanying behavioral, autonomic, and neuroendocrine correlates (Grossman, Buchsbaum, & Yehuda, 2002). The amygdala has direct connections to the orbitofrontal cortex, hippocampus, hypothalamus, thalamus and serves as a relay center to connect the olfactory cortex with the hypothalamus and the tegmentum of the midbrain (Kandel, Schwartz, & Jessell, 1991). The amygdala typically has a high density of receptor sites for GABA (an inhibitory neurotransmitter typically associated with calming effects), barbiturates, and benzodiazepines. However, exposure to early stress has been associated with lower density of these receptor sites (Teicher, Anderson, Polcari, Anderson, & Navalta, 2002). Furthermore, amygdaloid neurons have been reported as among the most sensitive structures in the brain for the emergence of kindling. Kindling is an important phenomenon related to neuronal excitability. Initially kindling was identified through experimental repeated mild intermittent electrical stimulation of the amygdala, which produced greater and greater alteration in neuronal excitability and even leads to seizures (Gilbert, 1994; Kalichman, 1982). However, limbic kindling is also associated with affective/behavioral dyscontrol. Exposure to trauma early in life or multiple/repeated traumas across time may influence amygdaloidal neurons resulting in limbic kindling. Limbic system irritability may produce hyperarousal, enhanced fear/startle responsive, augment fight/flight responses, and lead to intrusive memories (Teicher, Anderson, Polcari, Anderson, & Navalta, 2002). Hyperperfusion of the amygdala has been seen in neuroimaging studies showing increased activation (i.e., greater emotional responsiveness) to personalized provocation paradigms (i.e., exposure to personally relevant trauma cues) versus generalized provocation paradigms (Hull, 2002).

Overall, hyperactivation of the amygdala and associated limbic structures are related to heightened fear-conditioning, fearful response, and emotional learning (Grossman, Buchsbaum, & Yehuda, 2002). Connections between the hippocampus and amygdala have reciprocal influences on the formation and recollection of emotionally laden memory. The hippocampus provides contextual information for events and the amygdala provides information regarding emotional valence/salience both of which influence declarative memory. Hippocampal dysfunction has been speculated to impair the process of habituation or extinction of the fearful response and an increase in the tendency for stimulus generalization secondary to a decrease in contextual constraints that the hippocampus usually may supply (Grossman, Buchsbaum, & Yehuda, 2002). Low density of inhibitory receptors sites and neuronal excitability/kindling of the amygdala along with hippocampal dysfunction represent important correlates of trauma exposure.

Trauma Related Hypoactivation of Broca's Area

In regard to neuroimaging findings of underactivity of Broca's area, Hull (2002) concluded that deactivation (hypoperfusion) of Broca's area during trauma-related memories likely interferes with ability to label and understand intense emotions. The clinical implications are that during episodes of accessing trauma-related memories there is a need to go beyond talking therapies that focus primarily on semantic representations to interventions that target all sensory modalities. Alternate sensory integration strategies may help facilitate reactivation of language centers and help with integration of one's experience. These findings lend support to treatment approaches such as exposure treatment and EMDR (eye movement desensitization and reprocessing) that target differing sensory modalities. These findings also support psychoeducational/ preteaching strategies for individuals with PTSD in the early phases of treatment to help facilitate labeling and understanding. However, findings regarding possible right hemispheric lateralization may also provide insight into these findings as described below.

Possible Right-Hemispheric Lateralization

Findings relative to proposed right-hemisphere lateralization are mixed. However, right-hemispheric lateralization may explain the "timeless" quality of traumatic memories (Hull, 2000) and warrants further investigation.

Schore (2002) emphasizes problems with right hemisphere development in prefrontal lobe (i.e., right orbitofrontal cortex) as a predisposing factor for PTSD. His explanatory model focuses on the correlation of early attachment experiences (i.e., a socio-emotional, environmental influence) and development of the right orbitofrontal cortex. Early developmental influences impact the development of a cognitive working model relative to situational threat assessment, coping strategies and attendant distress levels. As cited earlier, this part of the limbic system represents higher cortical functions that facilitate regulation of affect and behavior. Schore argues that the right orbitofrontal cortex is the center for CNS control over the ANS and thus central to affect regulation and stress modulation.

Tiecher et al. (2002) has also emphasized the development neurobiology of childhood stress and trauma with more expansive implications and fit well with the overall information presented previously relative to the psychoneurobiology of stress . The following is an outline of the premises of Tiecher et al.'s proposed cascade model:

1. Exposure to stress early in life activates stress-response systems and alters molecular organization to modify their sensitivity
2. Exposure of the developing brain to stress hormones affects myelination, neural morphology, neurogensises, and synaptogenesis
3. Different brain regions differ in their sensitivity, which depends, in part upon genetics, gender, timing, rate of development and density of glucocorticoid receptors
4. Enduring functional consequences that include attenuated left hemisphere development, decreased right/left hemisphere integration, increased electrical irritability within limbic system circuits and diminished functional activity of the cerebellar vermis

5. Associated neuropsychiatric consequences and vulnerabilities lead to enhanced risk for development of PTSD, depression, borderline personality disorder, dissociative identity disorder and substance abuse

Schore's emphasis on right hemisphere lateralization as a risk factor for PTSD (i.e., the role of higher cortical functions adaptation and stress modulation) is supported by Teicher et al.'s model. Schore's model lends support to psychoeducational, cognitive and psychodynamic interventions that target development and change in the cognitive working model associated with this part of the brain. Teicher et al.'s more expansive cascade model highlights some of the implications of stress on the developing brain, both right and left hemispheres. For example, identification of decreased right/left hemispheric integration problems is in line with imaging studies showing decreased left brain activity in language centers (i.e., hypoactivation of Broca's area) during recall of trauma. As cited previously, this has implications for treatment due to the role of interference in "talking therapies" during trauma activation (i.e., language centers not engaged). Furthermore, Tiecher et al. proposed limbic irritability (kindling) and inadequate cerebellar vermis development as enhancing risk for later substance abuse. Connections between the cerebellar vermis and ventral tegmental area and locus coeruleus, exerts strong effect on the turnover of dopamine and norepinephrine in the caudate and nucleus acumens (Teicher et al., 2002). These parts of the brain have also been identified as part of the limbic-motor reinforcement circuit associated with the rewarding effects of drugs (Gardner, 2005; Trujillo et al., 1993; Watson, 1989).

In summary, there is significant overlap in relevant brain circuitry associated with stress/trauma responses and addictions. These findings also may explain in part individual differences in normative and non-normative stress responses (e.g., repeated hits, lack of adaptation, prolonged stress response, and inadequate response).

FINDINGS RELATIVE
TO CO-OCCURRING ADDICTIONS AND TRAUMA

While limbic system dysfunction is of primary concern relative to trauma exposure, these same brain structures have been identified as targets for disruptive and even toxic effects following both acute and chronic exposure to drugs of abuse with functional disruptions of neural circuitry affecting both cognitive and emotional processing (Rogers & Robbins, 2003). For example, findings of neurotoxic effects MDMA ("ecstasy") are associated with hippocampal dysfunction and cognitive impairments (Jacobsen, Menel, Pugh, Skudlarski, & Krystal, 2003). Likewise, preliminary evidence suggests that methamphetamine dependence may cause long-term neural damage and concomitant cognitive deficits (Nordahl, 2004). Widespread hypoperfusion in periventricular areas has been found in acute use of cocaine and long-term users have exhibited cerebral hypoperfusion of frontal, temporoparietal, or perventiricular regions (Allen & Landis, 1998). Physiological and behavioral hyperarousal symptoms are common in cocaine intoxication with concommittant euphoria often followed by dysphoria. Moderate-heavy cocaine abuse has been associated with impairment in mental flexibility and control, attention and concentration, visuomotor ability, verbal and visual learning and memory (Allen & Landis, 1998; O'Malley, Adams, Heaton, & Gawin, 1992; Strickland Mena, Villanueva-Meyer, Miller, Cummings, Mehringer, Satz, & Myers, 1993). Alcohol addiction is associated with a wide range of acute, short-term, and long-term cognitive deficits. Acute cognitive deficits include impaired intellectual functioning, memory, and visual motor problems. Short-term cognitive deficits (i.e., 2-5 weeks abstinent) include impairment in abstraction ability and problem solving, perceptual-motor ability, and short and long-term memory impairment. Long-term cognitive deficits include impairment in problem solving, perceptual-motor abilities, learning and memory as well as risk of Wernicke-Korsakoff syndrome, alcohol-induced persisting dementia, and hepatic encephalopathy (Allen & Landis, 1998).

Therefore, the psychophysiological correlates of neurocognitive and socio-emotional activity of the brain are particularly relevant to both trauma and addictions. Implications relative to these psychoneurobiological dynamics include:

- Cognitive and memory impairments in areas such as attention, impulse control, problem solving, cognitive/mental flexibility, learning difficulties, and short term or long-term memory problems
- Affective dysregulation problems such as hyperarousal, hypersensitivity to stimuli, heightened fear response, anxiety sensitivity, dysphoria, anger/irritability, numbing, and dissociation
- Hemispheric integration problems, deactivation of language centers (i.e., difficulty with articulation or speechlessness) during trauma processing

- Behavioral and socio-emotional problems such as avoidant coping, interpersonal difficulties, intimacy problems such as hypersensitivity or trust problems

Thus, co-occurrence of trauma and addiction represents complicating factors for treatment and recovery. An integrative approach that addresses both is imperative. Evaluation and treatment of both disorders should take into account unique individual differences in clinical presentation. Some individuals have normative stress response systems but suffer from wear and tear due to cumulative effects of multiple/repeated stressors (i.e., "repeated hits"). Others have non-normative stress response systems (i.e., lack of adaptation, prolonged response, inadequate response).

Another area to assess is the temporal relationship between trauma and addictions. Pre-existing trauma exposure is a risk factor for addiction. Early trauma exposure, especially during early infant development has been cited as a primary risk factor for PTSD due to the developmental influences on brain development, particularly limbic system structures (Schore, 2002). Also, a high incidence of sexual abuse has been cited as a risk factor for addiction (Janikowski & Glover-Graf, 2003). Alternately, in some cases addiction is a preexisting condition to trauma exposure and subsequent trauma related difficulties. Epidemiological evidence shows traumatic events associated with at-risk drinking were involvement in life threatening accident, witnessing severe injury, rape and being the victim of serious physical assault with a high incidence of post traumatic stress sequalae (McFarlane, 1998). On the other hand, findings relative to the development of alcohol abuse post trauma suggest that other risk factors (e.g., genetic, environmental, developmental influences, relational trauma, sexual abuse, and behavioral responses) are necessary to predict alcohol abuse following exposure to traumatic events. These findings may extend to other substances of abuse.

Explanatory models such as biological supersensitivity and self-medication have been proposed relative to the development of substance abuse/addictions post trauma (McFarlane, Yehuda, & Clark, 2002). A review of research emphasizing studies of the HPA axis and the noradrenergic system suggest a functional relationship between PTSD and substance use disorders with PTSD preceding substance abuse or dependence (Jacobsen, Southwich, & Kosten, 2001). In line with the self-medication model as an etiology of substance abuse/dependence Jacobsen et al. (2001) suggests sedatives, hypnotics, or alcohol are often used in an attempt to interrupt the stress response. Likewise, the biological supersensitivity model purports a psychobiological vulnerability that is determined by a combination of genetic and early environmental events (Meuser, Drake, & Wallach, 1998). Meuser et al. suggest a biological sensitivity to stress also applies to sensitivity to the effects of alcohol and other drugs. In other words, smaller amounts of alcohol or drugs may have greater negative consequences for those with biological sensitivity. Early empirical studies in support of these findings are mostly limited to studies of schizophrenic and bi-polar patients. More recent elaborations of the supersensitivity model focus on anxiety sensitivity and addictive behaviors with limited support (DeHass, Calamir, Bair, & Martin, 2001; Forsyth, Parker, & Finlay, 2001). Further research is needed to explore developmental contributions and specific anxiety components such as trauma.

In addition to etiology, PTSD has been identified as a risk factor for relapse (Read, Brown, & Kahler, 2004). Individuals with alcohol use disorders reported greater numbers of reexperincing symptoms (Read, Brown, & Kahler, 2004). Also, there is a greater correlation of alcohol dependency in those with greater levels of arousal symptoms (Saladin, Brady, Dansky & Kilpatrick, 1995). Intuitively, the self-medication model makes sense relative to the proposed attempt to interrupt the stress response (Jacobsen et al. 2001) or limited risk for abusing arousal-dampening drugs such as alcohol or benzodiazepines (McNally, 1996). However, rebound effects such as anxiety and exacerbation of sleep disturbance can compound the problem. Furthermore, there is a high incidence of trauma exposure in cocaine dependent individuals as well, which is counterintuitive to these assertions. Evaluations of trauma history in groups of cocaine dependent individuals revealed a high number of lifetime traumatic events (Najavits, Runkel, Neuner, Frank, Thase, Crits-Christoph, & Blaine, 2003; Najavits, Gastfriend, Barber, Reif, Muenz, Blain, Crits-Christoph, Thase, & Weiss, 1998). Among those diagnosed with PTSD, the most prominent symptom cluster was arousal. Avoidance was found to the most prominent in individuals with subthreshold symptoms. Even though cocaine use may exacerbate arousal symptoms other explanations suggest the positive reinforcement of the drug (i.e., euphoria) may be more salient (McFarlane, 1998; Volpicelli, 1987). Other factors such as drug expectancies (i.e., what an individual thinks a drug will do) may influence drugs of choice. Also, different alcohol craving profiles in alcohol addictions (i.e., reward craving, relief craving, and obsessive craving) have been identified (Addolorato, Leggio, Abenaivolvila, & Gasbarrini, 2005) indicative of very complex constitutional and environmental factors. Addolorato et al. conclude the need for personalized therapy to address different types of craving neuromechanisms These findings may extend to other addictions and further explain problems with intuitively limited explanations of self-medication model.

Beyond these most prominent findings, there is emerging research on the importance of other neurochemical processes such as those related to the body's opioid system, the role of excitatory amino acids, and temporal lobe neuron loss as related to not only stress/trauma but also addictions. While these findings are beyond the scope of this chapter, the reader is referred to Lowinson, Ruiz, Millman, and Langrod, 2005; McEwen, 2002, 2000; Yehuda, 2002 for further elaboration.

In conclusion, the primary importance of findings relative to co-occurring addictions and trauma is to gain an understanding of the general nature of the stress response system and relevant brain structures along with an understanding of the importance of recognizing individual differences in the manifestation of co-morbid trauma and addiction. Conducting an integrated assessment inclusive of individual differences is important to the development of appropriate treatment planning.

INTEGRATIVE ASSESSMENT

Current knowledge suggests an integrated assessment would include assessment of four domains to facilitate appropriate treatment planning:

1. Substance exposure/abuse/dependency
2. Trauma history
3. Normative/Non-normative stress response
4. Functional deficit assessment

First, gathering a thorough individualized history of the onset and progression of addiction is paramount in an addiction setting. Alcohol and drugs influence the central nervous system and have implications for structural and functional change in the brain. While acute effects of substances are often an initial priority, gathering historical information is also important. As with trauma exposure, alcohol and drugs can impact both prenatal and postnatal brain development (e.g., fetal alcohol syndrome, attention deficits, etc.). Therefore, a developmental approach to assessment (e.g., use of a timeline approach of documenting alcohol/drug use) to check for exposure at critical periods of development is indicated. Also, influences in socio-emotional and personality development may occur when substances are abused during formative years. Thus age of onset of substance abuse/dependence (e.g., early adolescence versus middle age) differentially influences outcome. While acute effects and mental status changes may wane as alcohol/drugs are metabolized, the risk for acquired deficits due to neurotoxic injury is also a concern. Furthermore, chronic abuse of alcohol/drugs likewise has implications for structural and functional changes in the brain (e.g., brain atrophy, Korsakoff's syndrome, alcohol induced dementia). Thus, gathering a timeline of age(s) of exposure(s), type of exposure (alcohol, drug, or polysubstances), timeframe (i.e., single episode versus repeated, chronic abuse), and amount/dosage should be included.

Secondly, an individualized assessment of trauma needs to identify type(s) of trauma experiences, severity of trauma, number of traumas (i.e., single versus multiple trauma experiences), and the temporal relationship of trauma and addiction. Types of trauma include physical trauma (e.g., assaults, rape, accidents) and/or psychological trauma (e.g., terrorism, relational trauma, social disruptions). Gauging the severity of trauma is important, as severity is associated with increased trauma sequelae. Furthermore, delineating whether a person has experienced a single or multiple traumas also is relevant due to cumulative effects. Finally, the temporal relationship of trauma to addictions (i.e., pre-existing trauma versus pre-existing addictions) is likewise important to the understanding of individual differences. Furthermore, attending to early stress exposure (as suggested by Schore, 2002 and Teicher, 2002) may shed light on socio-emotional and psychoneurological development problems that will need to be incorporated into treatment planning to help facilitate cognitive, behavioral and socio-emotional changes to facilitate overall recovery. For example, a middle age female client who presents with a history of repeated early childhood incest, subsequent rape during adolescence and rapid onset of substance dependence following a divorce at age 38 presents a different clinical challenge than a young single adult who grew up with alcoholic parents, developed a polysubstance abuse problem during adolescence, and PTSD following a motor vehicle accident at age 21.

Next, inclusion of an assessment of individual differences in psychoneurobiologic responses to stressors is also indicated. As stated above, a number of advances in psychoneurobiology are contributing to our understanding of normative stress responses and pathologies related to the wear and tear of chronic stress and non-normative stress responses. Increasingly, attention to structural and functional brain changes have become an important focus in stress research, particularly in regard to trauma experiences. Neuroendocrine influences that impact brain development (particularly during prenatal and early childhood development) and that are associated with acquired changes throughout the lifespan have been associated with trauma experiences (McEwen, 2000, 1998; Schore, 2002). McEwen's model of normative and non-normative stress responses can be applied to analyze differential stress responses to trauma exposure relative to the above recommended trauma assessment. These responses include:

- repeated hits
- lack of adaptation
- prolonged response
- inadequate response

Finally, an assessment of current functional deficits should be included in an integrated assessment. At a minimum a mental status exam and current emotional status should be included. More formalized assessment may include a neuropsychological assessment to evaluate brain/behavior relationships with an emphasis on functional status. Neuropsychological assessment can be conceptualized as offering a continuum of assessment strategies that are selected relative to the presenting problem or area of concern. Assessments range from mental status evaluations or neurocognitive screenings on one end of the continuum to selected or full neuropsychological batteries at the other end of the continuum. Such assessment can augment evaluations and treatment planning by identifying current functional status, predicting ability to benefit from differing levels/types, and provide information about recovery and residual deficits across time.

CONCLUSIONS

Findings relative to the psychoneurobiology of trauma and addictions support the need for developing clinical interventions to facilitate resolution of trauma related sequelae and facilitate addictions recovery. The first step for treatment providers is to conduct an integrated assessment that includes a thorough history of substance exposure, trauma history, identification of individualized stress responses, and assessment of functional deficits. Such an integrated assessment will help guide the clinician in developing an individualized treatment plan to facilitate recovery from co-occurring trauma and addictions. Coordinated treatment to address both disorders will also minimize risks for relapse.

REFERENCES

Addolorato, G., Abenaivolvila, L., Leggio, L., & Gasbarrini, G. (2005). How many cravings? Pharmacological aspects of craving treatment in alcohol addiction: A review. *Neuropsychobiology.* 51(2):59-66.

Allen, D. N. & Landis, R. K. B. (1998). Neuropsychological correlates of substance use disorders. *Clinical neuropsychology: A pocket for assessment.* Washington, DC: American Psychological Association. pp. 591-612.

Cannon, W. B. (1929). *Bodily changes in pain, hunger, fear and rage.* New York: Appleton-Century.

Cannon, W. B. (1932). *The wisdom of the body.* New York: Norton.

Cannon, W. B. (1953). *Bodily changes in pain, hunger, fear, and rage.* Boston: Charles T. Branford Co.

DeHass, R. A., Calamir, J. E., Blair, J. P. & Martin, E. D. (2001). Anxiety sensitivity and drug or alcohol use in individuals with anxiety and substance use disorders. *Addictive Behaviors*, 26, pp. 787-801.

Fishers, Reason J. (Eds.). *Handbook of life stress, cognition, and health.* New York: John Wiley, pp. 629-649.

Forsyth, J. P., Parker, J. D., & Finlay, C. G. (2001). Anxiety sensitivity, controllability, and experiential avoidance and their relation to drug of choice and addiction severity in a residential sample of substance-abuse veterans. *Addictive Behaviors*, 28, pp. 851-870.

Gardner, E. (2005). Brain reward mechanisms. In Lowinson, R., Ruiz, P., Millman, R., & Langrod, J. (Eds.), *Substance abuse: A comprehensive textbook* (4th ed.). Philadelphia, PA: Lippincott Williams & Wilkins.

Gilbert, M. (1994). The phenomenology of limbic kindling. *Toxicology & Industrial Health*, 10(4-5), pp. 343-58.

Grossman, R., Buschsbaum, M. S., & Yehuda, R. (2002). Neuroimaging studies in post-traumatic stress disorder. *Psychiatric Clinics of North America*, pp. 317-340.

Heather, N. & Gilvary, E. (1998) Introduction to a special issue of *Addictive Behaviors*. *Addictive Behaviors*, Vol 23, 6, pp. 715-716.

Herbert, J. (1997). Fortnightly review: Stress, the brain, and mental illness. *British Medical Journal*, 315(7107), pp. 530-535.

Hull, Alistair M. (2002). Neuroimaging findings in post-traumatic stress disorder: Systematic review. *The British Journal of Psychiatry*, 081, pp. 102-110.

Jacobsen, L. K., Menel, W. E., Pugh, K. R., Skudlarski, P., & Krystal, J. H. (2003). Preliminary evidence of hippocampal dysfunction in adolescent MDMA ("ecstasy") users: Possible relationship to neurotoxic effects. *Psychopharmacology*, 173, pp. 383-390.

Jacobsen, L., Southwick, S., & Kosten, T. (2001). Substance use disorders in patients with posttraumatic stress disorder: A review of the literature. *American Journal of Psychiatry*, Vol 158(8), Aug 2001. pp. 1184-1190.

Janikowski, T. & Glover-Graf, N. (2003). Qualifications, training, and perceptions of substance abuse counselors who work with victims of incest. *Addictive Behaviors*, 28, pp. 1193-1201.

Kalichman, M. (1982). Neurochemical correlates of the kindling model of epilepsy. *Neuroscience & Biobehavioral Reviews*, 6(2), pp. 165-181.

Kandel, E. R., Schwartz, J. H., & Jessell, T. M. (1991). *Principles of Neural Science*, 3rd Ed. Prentice Hall: Englewood Cliffs, NJ.

Lowinson, J., Ruiz, P., Millman, R., & Langrod, J. (Eds.) (2005). *Substance abuse: A comprehensive textbook* (4th ed.). Philadelphia, PA: Lippincott Williams & Wilkins.

McEwen, B. (1998). Seminars in medicine of the Beth Israel Deaconess Medical Center: Protective and damaging effects of stress mediators. *The New England Journal of Medicine*, 338, pp. 171-179.

McEwen, B. (2000). The neurobiology of stress: From serendipity to clinical relevance. *Brain Research Interactive*, 886, pp. 172-183.

McEwen, B. (2002). The neurobiology and neuroendocrinology of stress implications for post-traumatic stress disorder from a basic science perspective. *Psychiatric Clinics of North America*, 25, pp. 469-494.

McFarlane, A. C. (1998). Epidemiological evidence about the relationship between PTSD and alcohol abuse: The nature of the association. *Addictive Behaviors*, 23, pp. 813-825.

McFarlane, A. C., Yehuda, R., & Clark, C. R. (2002). Biological models of traumatic memories and post-traumatic stress disorder: The role of neural networks. *Psychiatric Clinics of North America*, 25, pp. 253-270.

McNally, R. J. (1996). Anxiety sensitivity is distinct from trait anxiety. In: Rapee, R.M., Editor, 1996. *Current controversies in the anxiety disorders*. Guilford: New York, pp. 214-227.

Mueser, K. T., Drake, R. E., & Wallace, M. A. (1998). Dual diagnosis: A review of etiological theories. *Addictive Behaviors*, 23, pp. 717-734.

Najavits, L., Gastfriend, D., Barber, J., Reif, S., Muenz, L., Blaine, J., Frank, A., Crits-Christoph, P., Thase, M., & Weiss, R. (1998). Cocaine dependence with and without PTSD among subjects in the National Institute on Drug Abuse Collaborative Cocaine Treatment Study. *American Journal of Psychiatry*, 155(2), pp. 213-219.

Najavits, L. M., Runkel, R., Neuner, C., Frank, A. F., Thase, M. E., Crits-Christoph, P., & Blaine, J. (2003). Rates and symptoms of PTSD among cocaine-dependent patients. *Journal of Studies on Alcohol*, 64, pp. 601-606.

Nordahl, T. E., Salo, R., & Leamon, M. (2004). Neuropsychological effects of chronic methamphetamine use on neurotransmitters and cognition: A review. *Journal of Neuropsychiatry & Clinical Neurosciences*, 15, pp. 317-325.

O'Malley, S., Adams, M., Heaton, R. K., & Gawin, F. H. (1992). Neuropsychological impairment in chronic cocaine abusers. *American Journal of Drug and Alcohol Abuse*, 18, pp. 131-144.

Porges, S. W. (1997). Emotion: An evolutionary by-product of the neural regulation of the autonomic nervous system. *Analysis of the New York Academy of Sciences*. 807, pp. 62-77.

Porges, S.W. (2001). The polyvagal theory: Phylogenetic substrates of a social nervous system. *International Journal of Psychophysiology*. 42(2):123-46.

Porges, S. W. (2003). The polyvagal theory: Phylogenetic contributions to social behavior. *Psychology & Behavior*, vol. 79, issue 3. pp. 503-513.

Read, J. P., Brown, P. J. & Kahler, C.W. (2004). Substance abuse and posttraumatic stress disorders: Symptom interplay and effects on outcome. *Addictive Behaviors*, 29, pp. 1665-1672.

Rogers, R., & Robbins, T. (2003). The neuropsychology of chronic drug abuse. In Ron, M. & Robbins, T. (Eds.). *Disorders of brain and mind 2*. New York: Cambridge University Press.

Saladin, M., Brady, K., Dansky, B., & Kilpatrick, D. (1995). Understanding comorbidity between PTSD and substance use disorder: Two preliminary investigations. *Addictive Behaviors*, 20(5), pp. 643-655.

Sapolsky, R. (1992). Stress: The aging brain and the mechanisms of neuron death. Cambridge, MA: MIT Press.

Sapolsky, R. (1996). Why stress is bad for your brain. *Science*, 273, pp. 749-750.

Sapolsky, R. (2000). Glucocortucoids and hippocampal atrophy in neuropsychiatric disorders. *Archives of General Psychiatry*, 57, pp. 925-935.

Sapolsky, R. (2002). *Stress, the aging brain and the mechanisms of neuron death.* Cambridge, MA: MIT Press.

Scanlon, V. C. & Sanders, T. (1995). *Essentials of Anatomy and Physiology*, 3rd. Ed. F.A. Davis Company: Philadelphia.

Selye, H. (1974). *Stress without distress.* Philadelphia: Lippincott.

Sterling, P. & Eyer, J. (1988). Allostasis: A new paradigm to explain arousal pathology. In Fisher, S., & Reason, J. (Eds.), *Handbook of life stress, cognition and health*, pp. 629-649. New York: John Wiley.

Strickland, T. L., Mena, I., Villanueve-Meyer, J., Miller, B. L., Cummings, J., Mehringer, C. M., Satz, P., & Myers, H. (1993). Cerebral perfusion and neuropsychological consequences of chronic cocaine use. *Journal of Neuropsychiatry and Clinical Neurosciences*, 5, pp. 419-427.

Substance Abuse and Mental Health Service, Administration, 2002. *Report to Congress on the Prevention and Treatment of Co-occurring substance abuse disorders and mental disorders.* Rockville, MD: SAMHSA.

Teicher, M. H., Anderson, S. L., Polcari, A., Anderson, C. M., & Navalta, C. P. (2002). Developmental neurobiology of childhood stress and trauma. *Psychiatric Clinics of North America*, 25, pp. 397-426.

Thibodeau, G. A., & Patton, K. T. (1997). *Structure and function of the body.* 10th Ed. Mosby-Year Book, Inc: St. Louis.

Trujillo, K., Herman, J., Schafer, M., Mansour, A., Meador-Woodruff, J., Watson, S., & Akil, H. (1993). Drug reward and brain circuitry: Recent advances and future directions. In Korenman, S. & Barchas, J. (Eds.), *Biological basis of substance abuse*, pp. 119-142. New York: Oxford University Press, Inc.

Volpicelli, J. (1987). Uncontrollable events and alcohol drinking. *British Journal of Addiction*, 82(4), pp. 381-392.

Watson, S., Trujillo, K., Herman, J., & Akil, H. (1989). Neuroanatomical and neurochemical substrates of drug-seeking behavior: Overview and future directions. In A. Goldstein (Ed.), *Molecular and cellular aspects of the drug addictions*, pp. 29-91. New York: Springer-Verlag.

Yehuda, R. (2002). Current status of cortisol findings in post-traumatic stress disorder. *Psychiatric Clinics of North America*, 25, pp. 341-368.

Managing Trauma Reactions in Intensive Addiction Treatment Environments

Lisa M. Najavits, PhD

SUMMARY. Intensive addiction treatment environments present an outstanding opportunity to help trauma survivors with substance use disorder (SUD). Typically, such environments provide an array of group therapies, close monitoring by staff, and peers with whom to connect. However, only relatively recently has trauma become more accepted as a legitimate focus for work in addiction treatment. *[Article copies available for a fee from The Haworth Document Delivery Service: 1-800-HAWORTH. E-mail address: <docdelivery@haworthpress.com> Website: <http://www.Haworth Press.com> © 2006 by The Haworth Press, Inc. All rights reserved.]*

KEYWORDS. Intensive addiction treatment, boundaries, multiple trauma

Intensive addiction treatment environments present an outstanding opportunity to help trauma survivors with substance use disorder (SUD). Typically, such environments provide an array of group therapies, close monitoring by staff, and peers with whom to connect. However, only relatively recently has trauma become more accepted as a legitimate focus for work in addiction treatment. The old message was, "Get clean and sober first, and then we'll help you with co-occurring issues such as trauma." In some places, this message is still heard. The

[Haworth co-indexing entry note]: "Managing Trauma Reactions in Intensive Addiction Treatment Environments." Najavits, Lisa M. Co-published simultaneously in *Journal of Chemical Dependency Treatment* (The Haworth Press, Inc.) Vol. 8, No. 2, 2006, pp. 153-161; and: *Psychological Trauma and Addiction Treatment* (ed: Bruce Carruth) The Haworth Press, Inc., 2006, pp. 153-161. Single or multiple copies of this article are available for a fee from The Haworth Document Delivery Service [1-800-HAWORTH, 9:00 a.m. - 5:00 p.m. (EST). E-mail address: docdelivery@haworthpress.com].

Available online at http://www.haworthpress.com/web/JCDT
© 2006 by The Haworth Press, Inc. All rights reserved.
doi:10.1300/J034v08n02_08

new message, widely recommended at this point (K. T. Brady, 2001; Donovan, Padin-Rivera, & Kowaliw, 2001; Evans & Sullivan, 1995; Miller & Guidry, 2001; L. M. Najavits, 2002a; Ouimette & Brown, 2002; Triffleman, 1998) is, "Let's help you with trauma-related problems as well as SUD." This *integrated approach* (treating SUD and co-occurring mental illness at the same time), is believed to be more helpful both for the SUD and for mental illness. Moreover, a handful of studies thus far have evaluated outcomes for psychosocial treatments that were designed to treat both trauma problems and SUD at the same time. The bottom line? In all of them, clients overall were helped, not harmed (e.g., K. Brady, Dansky, Back, Foa, & Caroll, 2001; Donovan et al., 2001; Morrissey et al., under review; L. M. Najavits, Schmitz, Gotthardt, & Weiss, in press; L. M. Najavits, Weiss, Shaw, & Muenz, 1998; Triffleman, Wong, Monnette, & Bostrum, 2002; Zlotnick, Najavits, & Rohsenow, 2003). Also, the few studies that compared manual-based treatment to addiction "treatment as usual" showed the former to be significantly more helpful (Hien, Cohen, Miele, Litt, & Capstick, 2004; L. M. Najavits, Gallop, & Weiss, under review).

Yet there are notable challenges to help addicted survivors of trauma. Both for clients and for staff, a variety of dilemmas may emerge. In this paper, several broad themes will be identified.

CLIENT DILEMMAS

Clients who suffer from both trauma-related problems and SUD are as unique as their stories. Yet several common dilemmas can be named that appear especially prominent in these clients (and more than in other clients).

Splitting. Both trauma and SUD are characterized by splitting–that is, the tendency for parts of the self to be fragmented or disavowed. Examples of splitting include the following.

- "I want to feel; I don't want to feel."
- "My trauma is everything; my trauma doesn't matter."
- "I want to be heard; I'm afraid of being heard."
- "I want to use substances; I don't want to use."
- "I'm always angry; I never get angry."

In each of these, clients flip from one state to the other, often without conscious control. Indeed, dangerous behavior–such as substance use and self-harm–may occur when states of mind change without the client's awareness. The client may say, "I was committed to staying abstinent, but then before I knew it, I was sitting at the bar with a drink." Also, clients may have parts of the self that they give names to: the young side, the vulnerable side, the angry side, the adolescent. In severe cases of splitting (as in dissociative identity disorder), the sides of the self may have their own gender, personality, and age, and may not know each other. Why does splitting arise in trauma and SUD? There is no one answer. But clients often describe a family environment in which they were not allowed to have their own thoughts and feelings. They may have been punished or rejected if they tried to express aspects of themselves that parents or others did not want to see. For example, they may have been told never to cry, never to get angry, that their feelings didn't matter, or that the trauma did not really occur. The mind's adaptation to such messages, particularly in children, may be to defensively wall off the unacceptable sides, even to themselves.

Triggering. Both trauma-related problems and SUD are beset by triggering– that is, intense reactivity. Clients may describe their feelings and impulses going from "zero to a hundred in a heartbeat." There is ample physiological research at this point demonstrating that trauma survivors, as well as those with SUD, may have altered reactivity to normal stimuli (Childress, McLellan, Ehrman, & O'Brien, 1987; Yehuda, 2002, 2004). Even once they have achieved improved functioning (and in some cases, no longer meet criteria for actual disorders), the reactivity may continue to occur life-long. For trauma survivors, they may feel as though they are back in a dangerous traumatic situation; they may lose a sense of being in the present. They may have diminished ability to control impulses (to use a substance, to engage in unsafe sex, to hurt themselves such as by self-cutting).

Boundaries. Boundaries are an area of particular difficulty for the addicted survivor of trauma. Particularly if they grew up in a home where addiction, trauma, or both were present, there may be little understanding of how normal boundaries are set and maintained in healthy relationships. They may enact relationships that are too close or too distant. Too-close relationships may be marked by domestic violence, excessive care-taking of others at the cost of self-care, or repeated entry into abusive relationships. Too-distant relationships may be characterized by isolation, inability to open up to anyone, fear of intimacy, and excessive hostility. Clients may also switch between these boundary extremes, either at the same time or different times in their lives. In clinical settings, the client may "pull" for boundary violations, sometimes without being aware of it. The clinician may feel drawn to extend the standard treatment session, to reveal personal information that they would ordinarily not give, to be overly harsh or overly indulgent, or to engage in sexual activity. For both client and clinician, boundary issues may or may not be fully conscious. When not fully conscious, there is often a feeling of watching oneself behave in ways that one does not want, yet unable to stop it.

Demoralization. Clients with both trauma and SUD may struggle with intense feelings of personal failure. They may be the "revolving door" clients who cannot achieve sustained SUD recovery. Or, they may feel overwhelmed by emotion or trauma memories, even if they are able to consistently sustain abstinence from substances. They may be unclear of who they are, what they like, or whether they are "good" people. Some clients will describe feeling empty or false. They may express confusion, child-like dependency or, the opposite, alienation and inability to connect. However, many factors can influence the degree of demoralization. Clients who experienced a single trauma in adulthood may appear temporarily demoralized but soon may be able to return to the higher functioning they displayed before the event. Clients who experienced multiple traumas (the pattern of most SUD clients with PTSD) (L. M. Najavits et al., 2003) may present with deeper and chronic demoralization features.

Suggestions for Clinicians

Several guidelines may be helpful in addiction treatment settings.

1. *Keep trauma details to a minimum.* Some very caring clinicians may unwittingly "do harm" by asking clients too many trauma details too soon. This may occur as part of assessment, in which generally more information is considered better. Or it may occur as part of treatment where, in trying to truly listen to the client, the clinician may either encourage or allow the client to relate graphic trauma narratives. In general, the safest approach in early recovery is to identify the client's trauma experiences, but to limit this to a phrase or sentence and not more (e.g., "I was raped," "I was physically beaten as a child"). The same holds true for group therapy sessions, in which clients should be able to reveal what their trauma was in a short phrase, if they choose to, but not reveal additional details that can so easily trigger other clients (and even may be too much for the client him/herself). Although it is true that at

some point, the client may benefit from the opportunity to work through memories of trauma, early stage addiction treatment is generally not the time for this due to the client's fragility, their likelihood of leaving the treatment program (i.e., there may not be enough time to fully process trauma memories), and the general lack of individual therapy by skilled trauma specialists. Processing trauma memories is an important method of treatment for some clients, but can potentially induce clinical worsening if done poorly (Keane, 1995; Solomon, Gerrity, & Muff, 1992). Also, there now exists evidence-based trauma-focused treatment specifically designed for early SUD recovery that does not require the client to explore trauma memories. For example, the treatment model Seeking Safety (L. M. Najavits, 2002b) focuses on psycho-education and coping skills. Such integrated treatment validates trauma, diagnoses and teaches the client about trauma-related disorders (such as PTSD), and teaches a wide range of coping skills that can be applied to both trauma and SUD. Yet it does not require the client to delve into trauma details.

2. *Focus on empowerment.* Twelve-step groups historically focused on males and on SUD without co-occurring trauma. Such models sometimes evolved to a strongly confrontational stance and even in some therapeutic community models, to "bringing the client down a peg" from arrogance to humility. Such methods may work for some clients, but for the addicted survivor of trauma, they may be experienced as overly harsh, judgmental, and even emotionally abusive. In general, an empowerment stance–while still holding the client accountable–is key. Empowerment includes empathy for their trauma, a collaborative stance, a high degree of support, asking the client's permission when possible before intervening (e.g., "Would you like some feedback on that, or not?"), and offering a menu of choices rather than an inflexible treatment program. Yet it is just as important that such empowerment methods not be misinterpreted either by staff or clients as license to just do anything they want, to violate basic program rules, or to harm self or others. The truest empowerment is not blind tolerance, but rather, like a good parent, a balance of support and accountability (L. M. Najavits, 2002b). The clinician can still challenge a client, but does it in a kind and supportive tone. For example, if the client has relapsed the clinician may say, "I'm concerned about you; can we talk about what happened? It is common for trauma survivors to have a hard time staying abstinent, but nonetheless it can be done.

I hope I can help you with that." This type of communication conveys that relapse is not inevitable, is not healthy, and is important to address. The clinician builds rapport non-judgmentally so that the client can freely open up about what happened.

3. *Learn about trauma and related areas.* No matter how skilled the clinician, knowledge of the impact of trauma is key. This means learning the criteria for trauma-related disorders such as PTSD, acute stress disorder, and dissociative identity disorder. It means staying up-to-date on current trauma literature by reading reputable journals and websites. It means being able to respond accurately (based on research) when clients ask questions such as "What is trauma?" "Can I ever recover from PTSD?" and "How common is trauma among people with addiction?" In a recent study (L. M. Najavits & Kanukollu, in press) of trauma training to addiction and mental health treatment programs, clinicians improved significantly in their knowledge of trauma topics. Yet, they also still evidenced substantial gaps in knowledge on such basic questions. Some recommended websites to learn more about trauma include the following.

- www.ncptsd.org
- www.ptsdalliance.org
- www.nimh.nih.gov/HealthInformation/ptsdmenu.cfm
- www.sidran.org
- http://coce.samhsa.gov/ (for co-occurring disorders)

4. *Distinguish trauma-informed versus trauma-competent treatment.* Trauma-informed treatment means offering basic trauma education to all staff, from secretaries and security guards through high-level administrators. Trauma-competent treatment means educating fewer, carefully selected staff (generally clinicians) to conduct actual treatment for PTSD and trauma-related problems (Fallot & Harris, 2001; Morrissey et al., under review). Clinicians who seek to become trauma-competent need to become educated about manual-based treatments for trauma/PTSD and may need supervision and formal training (especially if they plan to conduct treatments that focus on exploring trauma memories). It is important to remember that not all clinicians are a good fit for trauma-focused treatment. Sometimes clinicians' own trauma history may make them particularly good at the work or particularly ill-suited for it. For example, some clinicians bring great empathy

to the work informed by their own direct experience of trauma. Other clinicians may not yet have worked through their trauma-related problems and may enact negative countertransference dynamics such as blaming the victim, scapegoating, boundary problems, or excessive caretaking. It may be helpful to obtain clients' feedback about particular clinicians before having them engage in trauma-focused work. Generally clients have a good sense of whether clinicians are sympathetic, helpful, and knowledgeable—or not. Other strategies include supervision in which the clinicians' work is directly observed and peer supervision that allows staff to hear each other's conceptualization of clients.

In sum, intensive addiction treatment provides an excellent opportunity to help clients work on both SUD and trauma at the same time (integrated treatment). Manual-based models that focus on coping skills and psychoeducation are generally the safest approach. The exploration of trauma details is not generally recommended in early stage addiction recovery, except under specific conditions (e.g., clinicians who are trained and supervised in trauma processing models; clients who are able to do the work without become destabilized; and usually individual rather than group modality (L. M. Najavits, 2002b; L. M. Najavits et al., in press)). All addiction treatment staff should be trained in basic trauma education ("trauma informed treatment"), with some clinicians then conducting actual trauma counseling ("trauma-competent treatment"). Principles for working with the addicted survivor of trauma include *keeping trauma details to a minimum, empowerment, learning about trauma*, and *distinguishing trauma-informed versus trauma-competent treatment*. Clients with trauma and SUD problems tend to display problems in a variety of areas, including quite prominently, *splitting, triggering, boundaries*, and *demoralization*. The good news is that such clients can improve (particularly when given evidence-based treatments). Yet, more clinical innovation and research are needed to continue to develop best-practice methods for this population.

REFERENCES

Brady, K., Dansky, B., Back, S., Foa, E., & Caroll, K. (2001). Exposure therapy in the treatment of PTSD among cocaine-dependent individuals: Preliminary findings. *Journal of Substance Abuse Treatment, 21*, 47-54.

Brady, K. T. (2001). Comorbid posttraumatic stress disorder and substance use disorders. *Psychiatric Annals, 31*, 313-319.

Childress, A., McLellan, A., Ehrman, R., & O'Brien, C. (1987). Extinction of conditioned responses in abstinent cocaine or opioid users. *NIDA Research Monograph, 76*, 189-195.

Donovan, B., Padin-Rivera, E., & Kowaliw, S. (2001). Transcend: Initial outcomes from a posttraumatic stress disorder/substance abuse treatment study. *Journal of Traumatic Stress, 14*, 757-772.

Evans, K., & Sullivan, J. M. (1995). *Treating Addicted Survivors of Trauma.* New York: Guilford.

Fallot, R. D., & Harris, M. (Eds.). (2001). *Using Trauma Theory to Design Service Systems.* New Directions for Mental Health Services. San Francisco: Jossey-Bass.

Hien, D. A., Cohen, L. R., Miele, G. M., Litt, L. C., & Capstick, C. (2004). Promising treatments for women with comorbid PTSD and substance use disorders. *American Journal of Psychiatry, 161*(8), 1426-1432.

Keane, T. M. (1995). The role of exposure therapy in the psychological treatment of PTSD. *Clinical Quarterly (National Center for Posttraumatic Stress Disorder), 5*, 1, 3-6.

Miller, D., & Guidry, L. (2001). *Addictions and Trauma Recovery.* New York: Norton.

Morrissey, J. P., Jackson, E. W., Ellis, A. R., Amaro, H., Brown, V. B., & Najavits, L. M. (under review). 12-month outcomes of trauma-informed interventions for women with co-occurring disorders.

Najavits, L. M. (2002a). Seeking Safety: A new psychotherapy for posttraumatic stress disorder and substance use disorder. In P. Ouimette & P. J. Brown (Eds.), *Trauma and Substance Abuse: Causes, Consequences, and Treatment of Comorbid Disorders* (pp. 147-170). Washington, DC: American Psychological Association Press.

Najavits, L. M. (2002b). *Seeking Safety: A Treatment Manual for PTSD and Substance Abuse.* New York, NY: Guilford.

Najavits, L. M., Gallop, R. J., & Weiss, R. D. (under review). Seeking Safety therapy for adolescent girls with PTSD and substance use disorder: A randomized controlled trial.

Najavits, L. M., & Kanukollu, S. (in press). It can be learned, but can it be taught? Results from a state-wide training initiative on PTSD and substance abuse. *Journal of Dual Diagnosis.*

Najavits, L. M., Runkel, R., Neuner, C., Frank, A., Thase, M., Crits-Christoph, P. et al. (2003). Rates and symptoms of PTSD among cocaine-dependent patients. *Journal of Studies on Alcohol, 64*, 601-606.

Najavits, L. M., Schmitz, M., Gotthardt, S., & Weiss, R. D. (in press). Seeking Safety plus Exposure Therapy-Revised: An outcome study in men with PTSD and substance dependence. *Journal of Psychoactive Drugs.*

Najavits, L. M., Weiss, R. D., Shaw, S. R., & Muenz, L. R. (1998). "Seeking Safety": Outcome of a new cognitive-behavioral psychotherapy for women with posttraumatic stress disorder and substance dependence. *Journal of Traumatic Stress, 11*, 437-456.

Ouimette, P., & Brown, P. J. (2002). *Trauma and Substance Abuse: Causes, Consequences, and Treatment of Comorbid Disorders.* Washington, DC: American Psychological Association Press.

Solomon, S. D., Gerrity, E. T., & Muff, A. M. (1992). Efficacy of treatments for posttraumatic stress disorder. *Journal of the American Medical Association, 268,* 633-638.

Triffleman, E. (1998). An overview of trauma exposure, posttraumatic stress disorder, and addictions. In H. R. Kranzler & B. J. Rounsaville (Eds.), *Dual Diagnosis and Treatment: Substance Abuse and Comorbid Medical and Psychiatric Disorders* (pp. 263-316). New York: Marcel Dekker.

Triffleman, E., Wong, P., Monnette, C., & Bostrum, A. (2002). *A pilot trial of treatments for PTSD-substance use disorders among the opioid addicted.* Paper presented at the International Society for Traumatic Stress Studies, Baltimore, MD.

Yehuda, R. (2002). Clinical relevance of biologic findings in PTSD. *Psychiatr Q, 73*(2), 123-133.

Yehuda, R. (2004). Risk and resilience in posttraumatic stress disorder. *J Clin Psychiatry, 65 Suppl 1,* 29-36.

Zlotnick, C., Najavits, L. M., & Rohsenow, D. J. (2003). A cognitive-behavioral treatment for incarcerated women with substance use disorder and posttraumatic stress disorder: Findings from a pilot study. *Journal of Substance Abuse Treatment, 25,* 99-105.

Trauma and 12-Step Recovery

Steven V. Schneider, PhD, CADClll

SUMMARY. Self-help groups are part of a larger mutual aid movement. Found in many forms, the concept of peer-to-peer help is an effective, worldwide phenomenon. This chapter is concerned with single disorder 12-Step groups for chemical dependency, which have the largest participation of any other kind. There is evidence supporting the utility of 12-Step groups for alcohol and other drug dependence. Based on the principles of Alcoholics Anonymous (AA), there are now 12-Step groups for a wide range of addictions and other conditions. 12-Step groups best serve the chemically dependent as opposed to those with a diagnosis of clinical abuse. However, concerns have been raised about their appropriateness for chemically dependent people who have experienced trauma. In this chapter, 12-Step groups are discussed as to their conceptual and practical utility for chemically dependent victims of trauma. *[Article copies available for a fee from The Haworth Document Delivery Service: 1-800-HAWORTH. E-mail address: <docdelivery@haworthpress.com> Website: <http://www.HaworthPress.com> © 2006 by The Haworth Press, Inc. All rights reserved.]*

KEYWORDS. 12-step recovery, dual diagnosis, abstinence

[Haworth co-indexing entry note]: "Trauma and 12-Step Recovery." Schneider, Steven V. Co-published simultaneously in *Journal of Chemical Dependency Treatment* (The Haworth Press, Inc.) Vol. 8, No. 2, 2006, pp. 163-186; and: *Psychological Trauma and Addiction Treatment* (ed: Bruce Carruth) The Haworth Press, Inc., 2006, pp. 163-186. Single or multiple copies of this article are available for a fee from The Haworth Document Delivery Service [1-800-HAWORTH, 9:00 a.m. - 5:00 p.m. (EST). E-mail address: docdelivery@haworthpress.com].

Available online at http://www.haworthpress.com/web/JCDT
doi:10.1300/J034v08n02_09

INTRODUCTION

The relationship between trauma, mental illness and substance use disorders (SUD) is well documented (Stewart, 1996; Drake & Osher, 1998). Coping style, social support and other factors will affect response to trauma (Bonanno, 2004). Trauma can stunt emotional development along with appropriate means of dealing with uncomfortable feelings (Hughes, Johnson, & Wilsnack, 2001). This is especially true if the trauma occurred in childhood (Wadsworth, Stampneto, & Halbrook, 1995). Research has also shown that the abuse of alcohol and other drugs often lead to traumatic experiences. Experimentation for quick relief can progress to substance abuse and dependence (McNeece & DiNitto, 2005). Alcohol and other drugs can become a coping mechanism that allows a person to deal with the effects of trauma and creates a cycle of physical and emotional problems that is difficult to break. This is even more difficult when substance abuse leads to dependence. Both trauma and chemical dependency can result in relational, occupational and internal instability (Drake, Mercer-McFadden, Mueser, McHugo, & Bond, 1998).

The literature describes those who suffer from two related but independent disorders as dually diagnosed. Although estimates of comorbidity vary, approximately 50% of those with severe mental illness develop a substance use disorder (Drake, Mueser, Brunette, & McHugo, 2004). Between 41% and 66% of those treated for substance use disorder admit to a history of trauma (McNeece & DiNitto, 2005) with post traumatic stress disorder (PTSD) being the most common related disability (Najavits, 2004). The addiction and trauma need to be diagnosed and treated (Fortney, Booth, Zhang, Humphrey, & Wiseman, 1998). Application of research findings may not generalize to all dual diagnoses. The most prevalent populations studied include those with severe mental illness, which influences research recommendations. An additional caution relates to the use of the terms abstinence, sobriety and recovery. The terms are often used synonymously but are very different conceptually. Abstinence refers to stopping the use of mood-altering substances. Abstinence is needed for sobriety, which is a state of stability that is achieved by improving life conditions. Finally, recovery is the process of living a sober life. While this has received little attention, White (2002) has discussed its importance. In a practical sense, it can affect the interpretation of outcome studies.

Self-Help and the 12 Steps

Modern self-help groups are part of a larger movement that began over 150 years ago. The major impetus for the current self-help movement occurred in 1935 with the creation of Alcoholics Anonymous (AA) and the 12-Step recovery program (White, 1998). The majority of self-help groups are for substance use disorders but can differ in form and intent. Most self-help groups today were started because of or in response to the 12-steps of AA. Since World War II, groups specific to a wide range of other mental health problems have been active (Hatzidimitriadou, 2002). Self-help groups have been created for many physical illnesses and psychological disorders. Attendance at some groups (support for heart problems, cancer and diabetes) is time limited. Others (addictions) are life-long and AA makes up 87% of all self-help groups (Davidson, Pennebaker, & Dickerson, 2000). Self-help groups provide a safe place to practice socialization and improve functioning (Yalom, 1995).

Inspired by AA, additional groups have formed that are addiction specific. Narcotics Anonymous, Cocaine Anonymous, Overeaters Anonymous, and Gamblers Anonymous are just a few. All of these groups see their addictions as a lifelong disease, managed by regular attendance at meetings and "working" the original (or sometimes modified) 12-steps of AA (White, 1998). Individually and collectively, the steps encompass a program for living, not just abstaining from chemicals (AA, 1998). Although the steps are sequential, each member can develop their own method of implementation with the help of peers and a sponsor who acts as a mentor. 12-Step groups provide a service that is adjunctive to traditional treatment. Each group is comprised of others who have experienced the same or similar problems. Inherent in the 12-Step philosophy is that each person can learn to change his or her thinking and behavior. Abstinence from all mood-altering chemicals is a basic requirement for recovery. Riessman (1997) discussed ten principles, which help to explain the popularity and utility of 12-Step groups. They stress the fact that groups are comprised of peers who have experienced the same or similar problems and function as a non-professional support network. In 12-Step groups, there is a shift from the traditional patient-professional role in that spirituality and peer-to-peer support are key change agents.

Recent years have seen the advent of self-help groups, which provide an alternative to the 12-Step model. Although it is not within the scope of this chapter to provide a detailed discussion, a basic understanding is warranted. Like 12-Step groups, the alternatives provide a support network for a variety of addictions; however, their philosophical approach is very different. Many of the groups were formed in response to some of the concepts characteristic of the 12 steps, including abstinence (Moderation Management) and spirituality (Secular Organizations for Sobriety). Others are based on an evolving program based on scientific literature (Smart Recovery) and self-recovery without a group approach (Rational Recovery).

The foundation of 12-Step philosophy is based on core beliefs which can both attract and detract members. The first belief is that alcoholics and drug addicts are powerless over their addiction and other people. Alcoholics and drug addicts learn that powerlessness refers to the inability to control their chemical use and the behavior of other people; they are not powerless to change themselves. Past attempts to control substance use were not successful, generally evidenced by negative consequences. The second belief promotes spirituality and reliance on a Higher Power. Since group members are powerless over their addiction and other people, they come to rely on their Higher Power for guidance in their daily life. Finally, alcoholics and drug addicts have character defects (maladaptive character traits) that affect relationships with others and their own psychological well-being (AA, 2001). By admitting powerlessness and relying on a Higher Power, intra and interpersonal changes occur. According to AA, acceptance of these core beliefs is necessary for sobriety. Through active participation in the program and turning to their higher power, defects begin to resolve as cognitive and behavioral changes take place. In 12-Step programs, addiction is considered to be a disease that can be controlled but not cured. Given the chronic nature of chemical dependency, the program is life-long and flexible. The 12 steps are intended to be a guide for living. The book (Alcoholics Anonymous), which contains the 12-Step working model (A.A., 2001), states that the steps are suggestions, which can be followed in whole or in part. Group members are encouraged to use any or all of the steps as they see fit. It is up to each individual to interpret how they are implemented based on their own belief system. Below, the 12 steps are operationally defined to help illustrate their role in the recovery process.

EXPECTED OUTCOMES OF THE 12 STEPS

Step 1: Becoming honest: admitting there is a problem with alcohol and the role it played in our life.

Step 2: Changing attitudes: being willing to believe in a Higher Power who guides us and gives us hope.

Step 3: Faith: Belief and reliance on a Higher Power for strength and guidance.

Step 4: Self-reflection: understanding strengths, weaknesses and character defects; how they affect thoughts and actions.

Step 5: Humbleness: admitting our mistakes and character defects in order to improve our lives.

Step 6: Willingness: readiness to ask our Higher Power to remove our shortcomings and improve our life.

Step 7: Action and humility: asking our Higher Power to help us remove any barriers to self-improvement.

Step 8: Understanding: making a list of those we have harmed and become willing to ask for forgiveness.

Step 9: Atonement: asking for forgiveness from those we have harmed.

Step 10: Gaining insight: daily self-reflection of character defects.

Step 11: Strengthening faith: improving our relationship with our Higher Power and asking for guidance.

Step 12: Being of Service to others: helping peers and using the program in all areas of our life.[1]

Utility of 12-Step Groups

The current body of literature on the effectiveness of 12-Step group participation is becoming more prevalent and methodologically sound. The diverse structure of the groups, in addition to the need to protect anonymity, often prevented researchers from attempting empirical studies. Early research was not well designed (Miller & Hester, 1980); studies were specific to AA and used participants in both 12-Step groups and formal treatment (Vaillant, 1983). Self-help groups continue to attract members with past or concurrent treatment. Generalizing results is affected by the large percentage of treatment centers using a 12-step based approach (Kelly, 2003). This was discussed by Roman and Blum (1998) who reported that 90% of the private SUD programs in the United States were based on 12-Step principles and most studies are still limited to alcohol and AA.

Empirical studies show that both single and dual disorder populations derive benefits from 12-Step meetings (Dayton, 2000; Brown, Read & Kahler, 2003); however, results can be confounded by many variables (Kownacki & Shadish, 1999). Fortney, Booth, Zhang, Humphreys and Wiseman (1998) have discussed the variability of 12-Step groups as a major factor in selection bias. The structure of each group and meeting is determined by its members causing variations in procedure (A.A., 2001). Finally, individual group members can differ in how the steps are interpreted and in their activity level such as number of meetings and following the program (Tonigan, Miller & Conners, 2000). Recent studies have been able to minimize some of these variables (Kyrouz, Humphreys & Loomis, 2002).

Mechanisms of Change

Having empirical evidence that 12-Step groups can be effective gives validity to the large number of referrals made by mental health professionals, treatment centers and court systems. However, we need to ask what is meant by the word effective as it relates to the benefits and outcomes of group participation. Further, what are the mechanisms that allow one to become not just abstinent but sober? Sobriety was described by AA to be a function of program principles (A.A., 2001). Affiliation with AA after treatment, acceptance of powerlessness and reliance on a higher power were the mechanisms associated with positive outcomes (Bateson, 1971). The outcomes expected by AA are called the Twelve Promises (see Appendix B) (AA, 1998). The promises, in a general sense, refer to positive cognitive, behavioral and spiritual transformations in all areas of life. By following the 12-Step philosophy and their Higher Power, members find strength to accept life events without the use of chemicals. Similar to the 12 steps, interpretation of the promises is left to each person and is not easily empirically validated. Current studies have looked at the psychological constructs by which change takes place. Collectively, the studies point to behavior, cognitive and social factors to explain why the 12-Step programs are effective.

Laudet (2003) asked people in treatment for substance use disorders about their attitudes towards 12-Step meetings. Support from peers and having an opportunity for life improvement were given most frequently as positive aspects. The major obstacles reported were not specific to

12-step philosophy but related to motivation. However, Kelly (2003) questions the role of intrinsic motivation. He describes motivation relative to perceived consequences as something that fluctuates. Group involvement might maintain or enhance motivation. The literature did not mention the spiritual emphasis of 12-Step groups as a major obstacle. This was somewhat surprising given the criticism of some authors (Bufe, 1991). In comparison to professional help, the strengths of group involvement are the experience and commitment of recovering members and overall focus of the group (Gartner, 1997). In a study of mental health self-help groups, Hatzidimitriadou (2002) found that group members felt more empowered and optimistic due to self-disclosure and sharing of feelings.

Attendance at meetings (Tonigan, Miller & Conners, 2000), motivation, coping skills and self-efficacy (Morgenstern, Labouvie, McCrady, Kahler & Frey, 1997) have been discussed as variables that can affect 12-Step outcome. Attendance at meetings aids in developing and maintaining self-efficacy, motivation and active coping (Magura et al., 2003). Fiorentine and Hillhouse (2003) report abstinence is related to believing that loss of control and need for abstinence is permanent.

12-Step groups can provide a network of friends who are invested in recovery. Humphreys, Mankowski, Moos and Finney (1999) found that the social network provides a base of recovering friends who model appropriate, recovery-based behavior that can mediate positive changes. Clinicians and treatment programs are in a unique position to influence patient attendance (Humphreys, 1999). By understanding why 12-Step groups work, skills associated with the change process can be developed.

Chemically dependent individuals choose to attend meetings based upon numerous factors and these reasons may influence help seeking behavior. In a dually diagnosed population, Laudet, Magura, Vogel and Knight (2002) found that when using mood-altering substances, symptoms became worse in 69% of the participants with16% reporting their symptoms improved. Forty-four percent of those who were asked stated that their mental health symptoms acted as triggers for substance use. Motivation to stop chemical use was related to wanting to improve life in general as well as the negative consequences of using (Laudet, Savage, & Mahmood, 2002). However, negative consequences seem to be associated with initial attendance only and are not long lasting (Drake & Wallach, 2000). These authors explained that the consequences of substance abuse are often not readily recognized by the dually diagnosed. Over time, they can become a greater factor.

Relapse is common in both single and dual populations. In their study of the relationship between trauma history and relapse, Farley, Golding, Young, Mulligan and Minkoff (2004) found that of those reporting at least one traumatic event, 33% had relapsed with interpersonal trauma being the most common predictor of relapse. The relapse rate also varies based on other factors, including gender (DiNitto, Webb & Rubin, 2002), ethnicity (Brems & Namyniuk, 2002), age (Hughes et al., 2001) and sexual orientation (Eliason, 2000). Establishing self-help group membership within the first year of abstinence seems to help with growth and long-term remission (Ouimette et al., 2001).

Trauma and 12-Step Group Attendance

The traumatized individual in recovery is often caught in a double bind. If abstinence is achieved, intrusive symptoms of their traumatic stress can appear. Cravings and other triggers of their addiction may lead to relapse (Evans & Sullivan, 1995). It is important for those with dual disorders to understand the relationship between substance abuse and co-occurring disorders. This population often uses multiple service agencies. Psychotherapy and psychiatric medication are two key services. However, help is often needed in areas such as housing, finances, education and legal issues. Compliance with provider recommendations is an important factor in their treatment. Segal, Hodges and Hardiman (2002) evaluated the perception of service delivery between community mental health agencies and self-help groups using non-substance using mental health clients already in treatment. Ability to socialization and the fact they can just drop in were reasons given for attending self-help meetings. However, due to fear of treatment and perceived coercion in community agencies, self-help groups were sometimes used as an alternative to formal treatment. Although both services were utilized, formal treatment supplied their need for counseling and medication. However, the study points out the need for greater collaboration between treatment providers and self-help groups.

The process by which changes take place is a critical factor to the traumatized person in recovery. Perceived social rejection (Maercker, Andreas & Muller, 2004), impaired social functioning (Polcin & Zenmore, 2004), shame and self-blame (Ouimette, Brown, & Najavits, 1998), are some of the common barriers faced by individuals with a history of trauma.

Many studies on trauma and substance use looked at dually diagnosed populations without specifying the co-existing disorder. The term special populations, used to describe a wide range of homogeneous groups (i.e., developmentally disabled, homeless, women, ethnicity as well as the traumatized) who also present with substance use disorders, was the topic of a 2001 panel discussion (Hegamin, Anglin, & Casanova, 2002). Grouping like people together allows research and treatment to be more specific, addressing the unique needs each group presents. Misperceptions, stereotypes and limited utility were seen as common outcomes when a single descriptor is used. Unmet treatment needs was seen as a disadvantage due to the likelihood of multiple problems. The need to integrate the many systems these populations already use was seen as an important step in order to isolate the effects of comorbidity (Hegamin et al., 2002).

However, when identified, PTSD was the most common symptom of trauma studied and often, the terms PTSD and trauma were used to mean the same thing. This is important because comorbid diagnosis might affect participation and beneficial effects of 12-step groups (Kelly, 2003). Substance abusers with a psychotic disorder attended traditional meetings less often and did not get beneficial effects (Tomasson & Vaglum, 1998). Kelly, McKellar and Moos (2003) found that major depression was a factor in deriving progressively fewer benefits and socializing less while attending 12-Step meetings. However, overall psychiatric severity did not seem to affect abstinence (Polcin & Zenmore, 2004). Using participants with PTSD and substance use disorders Ouimette et al. (1998) found specific fears that were barriers to seeking help. Fear that talking about their trauma and others finding out was endorsed by 40% as barriers. The same study identified inadequate diagnosis as a reason for not receiving care. Additionally, Ouimette et al. showed substance related 12-Step group attendance rate and beneficial effects to be similar between comorbid (PTSD) and substance use only populations. A similar result was found by Borgenschutz and Akins (2000). However, having a dual diagnosis resulted in more difficulties related to their comorbidity.

Gender does not appear to be a factor in the long-term treatment outcomes for those with co-occurring SUD and PTSD. However, the risk for exposure to trauma and development of PTSD is greater for women (van der Walde, Urgenson, Welz, & Hanna, 2002). While questions remain about the need for gender specific trauma and substance use treatment, Herndon (1998) interpreted many of the steps as being male oriented. This has the effect of revictimization due to stereotyped sex roles (i.e., God as He). A history of childhood sexual abuse is a reliable predictor of later substance use disorders (Wadsworth et al., 1995). The clinical presentations of sexual trauma and substance use disorders are remarkably similar. Relationship and intimacy problems, anxiety, feelings of loneliness, guilt and compromised emotional development have been reported in both populations (McBride & Emerson, 1989; Yablonsky, 1989). The importance of abstaining from mood altering drugs was discussed by Wadsworth et al. (1995) as a reason for making alcohol and drug treatment the primary goal. An early study on sexual trauma reported that, if untreated, a variety of seemingly unrelated symptoms could emerge due to insufficient ego strength. However, they can also lead the victim to seek treatment (Gelinas, 1983).

Some AA literature refers to a singleness of purpose. This means that only alcoholics should attend AA and only drug addicts should attend NA. It allows members to concentrate on their drug of choice without the distraction of other issues (Bean-Bayog, 1993). Recently, the 12-Step principles have been adopted by individuals who suffer from a variety of addictive and emotional disorders. Social and emotional support is given and received in meetings that are focused on the member's specific issues. Even with the formation of single focused programs, many groups are becoming more inclusive. The high percentage of mentally ill individuals who are chemically dependent make it likely that any given 12-Step meeting will be attended by many who are dually diagnosed. However, real and perceived barriers can keep some people from attending.

The co-founders of AA recognized the fact that some people may not fully benefit from the program (A.A., 2001). Some who are dually diagnosed might not be prepared to be open with others who do not share their same problems. Concerns of being stigmatized can cause denial or minimization of feelings. Those can cause denial or minimization of feelings. Those with dual disorders have also cited the need for safety, group focus and group identity as being important elements for group support (Vogel, 1993). For these reasons, dual disorder 12-Step groups have become an alternative that allows members to realize the benefits of traditional meetings as well as having the full support they need. Two of the largest groups are Dual Recovery Anonymous and Double Trouble in Recovery. In these 12-Step settings, members can be open and honest without fear or shame. Instead of being discouraged from taking prescribed medication, they are taught about side effects, how drugs of abuse and medication interact and how sobriety can be affected. In the group meetings, the difference between taking medication and the addictive use of mood-altering substances is emphasized (Vogel, 1993). The dual focus of the groups makes them an attractive alternative. However, limited availability of meetings as well as location and transportation problems can often make traditional single focus groups the only option.

Factors That Can Limit 12-Step Group Attendance

It has been long understood that prolonged reactions to stressful events adversely affect overall health (Baum, 1990). Disclosing severe trauma can improve physical and psychological functioning to a greater degree than those with trauma deemed less severe (Esterling, Antoni, Fletcher, Margules, & Schneiderman, 1994). Inhibition of feelings places stress on the body of traumatized individuals. This often leads to emotional and physical distress (Greenberg, Wortman, & Stone, 1996). Research suggests that the regulation of affect is a major component of trauma therapy (Fairbanks, Hansen, & Fitterling, 1991). Successful psychological adjustment appears to rely on being able to confront and reframe thoughts and feelings about traumatic events.

An abreaction has been used in the literature to describe awareness of an emotional insight, and the emotional recall of traumatic events. Often used synonymously with the term catharsis, it allows the expression of past or present emotions and has been shown to produce changes in attitude and behaviors (Bemak & Young, 1998). Yalom (1995) discussed catharsis as an interpersonal process. Emotions need to be both expressed and acknowledged. This suggests that 12-Step groups can provide the interpersonal component as thoughts and emotions are expressed and discussed on a regular basis at meetings. In appropriate therapeutic settings, abreactive work helps to assimilate the traumatic event through arousal techniques (van der Hart & Brown, 1992). While 12-Step groups are therapeutic, they are not formal treatment settings where abreactive work can be completed. However, recalled memories of traumatic events vary in intensity. In the case of PTSD and other conditions, 12-Step groups can be very appropriate settings (Ouimette, Moos, & Brown, 2003).

Frank and Frank (1991) identified curative factors that are shared by many therapeutic approaches. These include providing new learning experiences, providing opportunities to practice new behaviors and enhancing self-efficacy. These are all applied in 12-Step meetings. Group members help by pointing out discrepancies between verbalizations and actions, how the victim mentality is impeding improvements and differences between verbal and non-verbal behavior. Hammond, Hepworth and Smith (1977) see these as being more of a corrective effort rather than confrontational. However, it is possible that recalling traumatic memories can cause further repression and decompensate those with PTSD (Peebles, 1989). This indicates the need for psychological assessment at a minimum and concurrent psychotherapy for those in need.

Participation in most 12-Step work requires the use of cognitive and psychological resources. Eliminating alcohol and other drugs will help to increase overall functioning. Barriers to successful participation are both individual and group related. Rychtarik, Connors, Dermen and Staslewicz (2000) point to a survey that showed 86% of the AA members polled were against the use of psychotropic medication. However, many trauma victims take medication to help control symptoms (i.e., anxiety, depression). In some 12-Step groups, they may receive mixed messages regarding medication use, which can be confusing. In the same survey, self-criticism, difficulty in self-examination and problems completing the 12 steps were barriers cited by dually diagnosed participants. The authors saw the barriers as limiting the acceptance of powerlessness, belief in a higher power, self-disclosure, introspection, admitting wrongs and asking for forgiveness. Although the objective of each step is conceptually concrete, they are open to interpretation. The 12 steps are guidelines, which can be implemented many ways. Symptoms of trauma are often first experienced when the use of mood-altering substances is discontinued. Symptom severity and coping ability will affect both the decision to attend and ability to maintain attendance at 12-step meetings. However, those who self-identify as an alcohol or addict have better 12-step outcomes (Morgenstern, Labouvie, McCrady, Kahler, & Frey, 1997).

Conceptual Issues in 12-Step Principles

The literature related to 12-step group attendance and trauma should be evaluated cautiously. Confounding variables can make between and within group comparisons difficult. Due to significant group and individual differences, it is difficult to generalize change and maintenance factors (Koski-Jannes & Turner, 1999: Tonigan, Miller & Conners, 2000). A second consideration relates to differences in coping with trauma. Many people have experienced some form of trauma. Much of the literature on the trauma and chemical dependency relate to individuals in treatment who are in great distress. However, response to trauma is variable and many victims are able to maintain psychological and physical stability. Bonanno (2004) reports that the ability for resilience is common, due in part, to a variety of coping styles. Many victims do not show chronic symptoms and this lack is not indicative of other pathology (Bonanno & Kaltman, 2001). The implication is that many of the barriers to 12-Step group attendance do not apply to all trauma victims. Problems in generalizing 12-Step research, differences in implementing the steps and the variability of responses to trauma all affect the utility of 12-Step programs.

The principles behind the 12 steps have remained constant but adaptable. The 12-Step literature has addressed this as a research variable but not in a practical sense. Conceptually, the 12 steps are constant but they are open to interpretation. There is flexibility in how the steps are practiced. The main text of AA calls the 12-Steps a "suggested program of recovery" allowing for individual differences and stages of readiness. AA teaches that dependency on a chemical is a symptom of character defects or maladaptive behavior. The majority of those with a substance use disorder are or have been dually diagnosed (depression, anxiety), (McNeece & DiNitto, 2005), yet they attend single disorder meetings. Although there are similarities in presentation, the dynamics of trauma-induced pathology are different. The implication is that trauma victims can benefit from single disorder 12-Step groups.

Eleven of the 12 steps are spiritual and behavioral approaches, which help in reconnecting internally and externally. Alcohol is mentioned only in the first step. There have been cautions and criticisms of 12-Step programs in the literature. The potential for abreactions was discussed in an earlier section. The literatures on alternatives to 12-Step groups discuss the spiritual nature of the steps and the belief it creates dependence. These cautions and criticisms are discussed below.

Powerlessness: Step 1

The goal of the first step is a realization of being powerless over alcohol and other drugs; that it has made life unmanageable. Attempts at controlling their own lives had not been successful. For the active alcoholic and addict, power and control are often a perception. In this context, group members begin to realize the futility of continuing their maladaptive thoughts and actions. Chemical dependency is seen as a disease. Members are in recovery but cannot be cured. Meeting attendance and following the 12 steps are considered necessary to remain sober. Bufe (1991) cautioned that members could develop a dependency on the program, which can be seen as another addiction. On a clinical level, there is some truth to this. However, levels of dependency change with the needs of each person. Initially, attendance at meetings is greater as members begin to learn and accept the program. With sobriety, alcoholics and addicts become stable and are able to do more by themselves.

The overwhelming nature of traumatic events often leaves victims feeling they have lost control over their lives. It might seem counterintuitive to stress the importance of being powerless to someone who has been victimized. However, there is a difference between having the control forcefully taken and giving it up voluntarily.

Admitting powerlessness is particularly difficult in the case of sexually abused women. Herndon and Eastland (1999) view powerlessness as a paradox since one purpose of the group is empowerment. They state that due to the stereotype that women are weak in a patriarchal society, this restriction places them in a subservient role. Wadsworth et al. (1995) found that males make up the majority who seek treatment for substance use disorders and that fear and mistrust of men is common in abused women. This can have a direct impact on the attendance and effectiveness of 12-step group attendance. Disruption of self-regulation is a key impact of trauma and admitting powerlessness can be seen as revictimization (Winhall & Falls, 2003).

The principle of powerlessness relates to the need for personal responsibility and developing insight into past and current problems (A.A., 2001). Denial, blame and dishonesty, to varying degrees, are common in the chemically dependent. Alcoholics and addicts have their own perception of control without clear insight as how it is best achieved. Since this can be problematic for some, it is important to stress that the concept of powerlessness is not the inability to make choices. The development of decision-making ability is important for reestablishing empowerment (Linhorst & Eckert, 2003). The implication is that those in 12-Step recovery programs learn to manage their own lives and they are powerless to change others. 12-Step recovery from addiction begins with the principle of powerlessness.

Spirituality: Steps 2 and 3

Tortorici (1993) wrote that for trauma victims, the focus on spirituality is to regain hope and to re-establish a connection to the self. Spirituality is the foundation of all 12-Steps programs. Belief and trust in a Higher Power develops the spiritual relationship. A Higher Power of each person's understanding can take any form. It provides an external source that is more powerful than each individual. Spirituality is often confused with but need not be contingent upon religion (Twerski, 2000). The process of developing and maintaining a relationship with a Higher Power is the cornerstone of all other steps.

Loss of faith has been called the essence of psychological trauma (van der Kolk, 1987). Order, continuity and meaning in life are no longer the same. Similar to admitting powerlessness in step 1, the spiritual foundation of the 12 steps can be difficult for trauma victims. However, interpretation is an important factor in accepting the need and determining the reality of a Higher Power. The mental representation of a Higher Power can affect the understanding and acceptance of spirituality (Rizzuto, 1979). In the 12-Step process, members seek to improve their contact and relationship with a Higher Power (A.A., 2001). This process generally begins early in life and is pervasive. Spirituality is due partly to psychological development and becomes part of the self (Spero, 1990).

Spirituality is an individual experience. The lack of an immediate and dramatic transformation as described in many AA stories (A.A., 2001) discourages some members. However, the ultimate acceptance of and relationship with a Higher Power, in recovery, is dependent on the current spiritual relationship and a belief that the Higher Power will provide whatever is needed (McDargh, 1986). Trauma can create doubts in an otherwise spiritual person and affect the development of spiritual acceptance in others. A traumatic experience often leads to doubts because victims feel angry they were not protected. Others begin to see a Higher Power as vengeful (Decker, 1995). Believing that the same Higher Power who allowed the trauma will help them to heal can be a slow process. Eliminating substance abuse, losing the desire to use and gaining inner peace are the results of a spiritual awakening. Presenting the spiritual experience in a concrete way can make it easier to understand (Forcehimes, 2004).

A review of the literature did not produce empirical evidence showing that spirituality is a factor in recovery; however, 12-step members with a strong spiritual foundation are convinced that without a Higher Power, they would not be sober. Spirituality often needs to be either introduced or reestablished. Waldfogel and Wolpe (1993) defined six dimensions of religious experience that can be used in reestablishing a spiritual connection. Related to the 12-Step program are the intellectual, experiential, supportive and consequential dimensions. Learning about the program is at first an intellectual process. It often begins by attending a meeting and reading AA or other 12-Step literature. New members are able to read and hear stories of what the program did for others. It is a non-threatening start to the process of spiritual development. Knowing that the program works for others leads to an understanding that these same principles can be applied to oneself. The experiential dimension begins with being in contact with other recovering people. Overcoming the difficulty some trauma victims have connecting with others may require time (Waldfogel & Wolpe). However, by following suggestions heard in meetings, the supportive dimension can develop. Socialization was seen as a factor in 12-Step attendance. Sharing thoughts with others in recovery that are non-judgmental provides safety to explore feelings and reestablish intimacy. Group members reinforce for each other how their Higher Power influences their lives. The consequential dimension of spiritual and religious beliefs is used to reinforce desired behaviors. Waldfogel and Wolpe point out that participation in 12-Step groups help in this aim. Van der Walde et al. (2002) recommend that spirituality in the context of treatment and 12-Step meetings can help empower rather than make one powerless. Developing spirituality is an individual experience and an ongoing process (DiLorenzo, Johnson, & Bussey, 2001). An introduction or re-introduction to spirituality should consider the type of spiritual assistance needed (Twerski, 2000). Step 2 asks that one become willing to believe. This is less threatening and allows for experimentation. When a 12-Step member reaches step 3, it creates a transformation where one turns their life over to the care of their Higher Power. For a trauma victim this is a significant step. Their Higher Power is now one who is loving, caring and can be trusted. Order, continuity and meaning in life are now possible.

Self-Reflection and Acknowledgement: Steps 4 and 5

The need to identify and correct maladaptive behavior is a core belief in 12-Step recovery. Referred to as character defects, they are considered impediments to intra and interpersonal functioning. Through self-reflection, members begin to gain insight into their core problems (A.A., 2001). 12-Step programs call this taking a searching and fearless moral inventory. Shame and self-blame, which are so cogent to trauma, can make this step difficult for some traumatized individuals (Ouimette et al., 1998). Self-reflection is difficult for many non-traumatized alcoholics and addicts. Introspection encourages the release of blocked emotions through insight (Prochaska, 1984). Discovering both their strengths and weaknesses members learn to accept themselves and others. Through prayer, meditation or other means, members rely on spiritual strength to remove the defects (A.A., 2001). The work in step 4 is generally but not always completed alone and is an ongoing process. Acknowledgement and verbalization of the inventory follows in step 5. However, deficits in coping skills can affect how this step is approached (Ouimette et al., 1998). The anger and resentment often associated with addictions and trauma can affect program participation and sobriety. Denial of these feelings can affect self-reflection and further progress.

The release of resentments is considered a necessary part of recovery (A.A., 2001). Through step 4, the alcoholic and addict have a clearer understanding of their inappropriate behavior and the people they harmed. Wei-Fen, Enright, Krahn, Mack and Baskin (2004) reported on their use of forgiveness therapy, which targets anger, anxiety and depression. Participants were taught the importance of and how to forgive. Forgiving others reduced anger, depression and raised self-esteem, all goals of 12-Step groups. Litz et al. (1997) discussed the role of emotional numbing (diminished interest in activities, feelings of detachment and restricted range of affect) in a group of people with PTSD. They hypothesized that due to hyperarousal and reactivity, cognitive, psychological and emotional resources are depleted. While emotional numbing can affect successful 12-Step involvement (Drake et al., 1998), program implementation can be adapted to fit specific needs. Krystal (1978) cautioned that recovery from trauma is affected, in part, by the ability to regulate affect. Prior or concurrent psychotherapy can aid in the release of blocked emotions (DeWald, 1994). Steps 4 and 5 do not have to be impediments to successful 12-Step group attendance.

This is the case for all 12-step members. While any one aspect can be perceived to be a barrier to attendance, it is important to understand the reasons given so adaptations can be made.

CONCLUSION

Traumatized individuals who suffer from substance use disorders have the burden of two separate but related conditions. The additive effect can compromise their ability to benefit from 12-Step group participation. Although the dually diagnosed can benefit from single focused 12-Step groups, factors have been identified that can deter attendance. Perceived social rejection, impaired social functioning, shame and self-blame are common barriers to attending. Fear of talking about their trauma and not wanting others to know affected not only attending 12-Step meetings but also therapy. These factors are not unique to trauma victims as they affect alcoholics and addicts as well.

The potential barriers discussed are important considerations for the dually diagnosed. However, research findings do not always give an accurate representation of how the 12-Step program works in a practical sense. Due to group and individual differences, there are variables in program implementation that are difficult to control. In addition, the effect of trauma is not consistent across all victims. Many lack the motivation or emotional stability to benefit from 12-Step programs. However, others seem to be unaffected or have non-chronic symptoms.

12-Step groups can provide the opportunity to learn and practice skills that will help improve intra and interpersonal functioning. The 12 steps can be followed in whole or in part. Difficulty with any part of the program does not preclude group membership. The 12-Step principles, practiced on a daily basis, are a process. For the traumatized person in recovery, this philosophy allows them access to the tools necessary for abstinence and sobriety. The steps have a transformative quality. The 12th step involves carrying the message to others with similar problems and practicing the steps in all areas of life. It allows for community integration and is healing for the traumatized individual in recovery.

NOTE

1. The Twelve Steps are reprinted with permission of Alcoholics Anonymous World Services, Inc. (A.A.W.S). Permission to reprint the Twelve Steps does not mean that A.A.W.S. has reviewed or approved the contents of this publication, or that A.A.W.S. necessarily agrees with the views expressed herein. A.A. is a program of recovery from alcoholism *only*–use of the Twelve Steps in connection with programs and activities which are patterned after A.A., but which address other problems, or in any other non-A.A. context, does not imply otherwise.

REFERENCES

Alcohol Anonymous World Services, Inc. (2001). *Alcoholics Anonymous* (4th). New York: Author. (Original work published 1939)

Alcoholics Anonymous World Services. (1998). *Twelve steps and twelve traditions*. New York: Author.

Alcoholics Anonymous World Services, Inc. (Ed.). (2001). How it works. *Alcoholics Anonymous* (pp. 58-71). New York: Alcoholics Anonymous World Services, Inc.

Baum, M. (1990). Stress, intrusive imagery and chronic stress. *Health Psychology, 9*, 653-675.

Bean-Bayog, M. (1993). AA processes and change: How does it work? In B. McCrady & R. Miller (Eds.), *Research on Alcoholics Anonymous: Opportunities and alternatives* (pp. 99-112). New Brunswick, NJ: Rutgers Center on Alcohol Studies.

Bemak, F., & Young, M. (1998). Role of catharsis in group psychotherapy. *International Journal of Action Methods, 50*(4).

Bonanno, G. A. (2004). Loss, trauma, and human resilience: Have we underestimated the human capacity to thrive after extremely aversive events? *American Psychologist, 59*(1), 20-28.

Bonanno, G. A., & Kaltman, S. (2001). The varieties of grief experience. *Clinical Psychology Review, 21*, 705-734.

Borgenschutz, M., & Akins, S. J. (2000). 12-step participation and attitudes towards 12-step meetings in dual diagnosis patients. *Alcoholism Treatment Quarterly, 18*, 31-45.

Brems, C., & Namyniuk, L. (2002). The relationship between childhood abuse history and substance use in an Alaskan sample. *Substance Use and Abuse, 37*, 473-494.

Brown, P. J., Read, J. P., & Kahler, C. W. (2003). Comorbid posttraumatic stress disorder and substance use disorders: Treatment outcomes and the role of coping. In Ouimette, P. and Brown, P. (Eds.) (Ed.), *Trauma and substance abuse: Causes, consequences and treatment of comorbid disorders.* Washington, DC: American Psychological Association.

Bufe, C. (1991). *Alcoholics Anonymous: Cult or cure.* San Francisco: See Sharp Press.

Davidson, K. P., Pennebaker, J. W., & Dickerson, S. (2000). Who talks? The social psychology of illness support groups. *American Psychologist, 55*(2).

Dayton, T. (2000). *Trauma and addiction: Ending the cycle of pain through emotional literacy.* Deerfield Beach, FL: Health Communications, Inc.

Decker, L. (1995). Including spirituality. *NCP Clinical Quarterly, 5*(1). Retrieved February 10, 2005, from http://www.ncptsd.org/publications/cq/v5/n1/decker.html

DeWald, P. A. (1994). Principles of supportive therapy. *American Journal of Psychotherapy, 48*(4), 505-520.

DiLorenzo, P., Johnson, R., & Bussey, M. (2001). The role of spirituality in the recovery process. *Child Welfare, 80*(2), 257-273.

Drake, R. E., & Osher, F. C. (1998). Treating substance abuse in patients with severe mental illness. *Innovative approaches for difficult-to-treat populations* (pp. 191-209). Washington, DC: American Psychiatric Press.

Drake, R. E., & Wallach, M. A. (2000). Dual diagnosis: 15 years of progress. *Psychiatric Services, 51*, 1126-1129.

Drake, R. E., Mercer-McFadden, C., Mueser, K. R., McHugo, G. J., & Bond, G. R. (1998). Review of integrated mental health and substance abuse treatment for patients with dual disorders. *Schizophrenia Bulletin, 24*(4), 589-608.

Drake, R. E., Mueser, K. T., Brunette, M. F., & McHugo, G. J. (2004). A review of treatments for people with severe mental illness and co-occurring substance use disorders. *Psychiatric Rehabilitation Journal, 27*(4), 360-374.

Eliason, M. J. (2000). Substance abuse counselors' attitudes regarding lesbian, gay, bisexual and transgender clients. *Journal of Substance Abuse, 12*, 311-328.

Esterling, B. A., Antoni, M. H., Fletcher, M. A., Margules, S., & Schneiderman, N. (1994). Emotional disclosure through writing or speaking modulates latent Epstein-Barr antibody titers. *Journal of Consulting and Clinical Psychology, 62,* 130-140.

Evans, K. & Sullivan, J.M. (1995). *Treating addicted survivors of trauma.* New York: The Guilford Press.

Fairbanks, J. A., Hansen, D. J., & Fitterling, J. M. (1991). Patterns of appraisal and coping across different stressor conditions among former prisoners of war with and without posttraumatic stress disorder. *Journal of Consulting and Clinical Psychology, 59,* 274-281.

Farley, Melissa, Golding, Jacqueline, M., Young, George, Mulligan, Marie & Minkoff, & Jerome, R. (2004). Trauma history and relapse probability among patients seeking substance abuse treatment. *Journal of Substance Abuse Treatment, 27,* 161-167.

Fiorentine, R., & Hillhouse, M. P. (2003). When low self-efficacy is efficacious: Toward an addicted self model of cessation of alcohol and drug dependent behavior. *American Journal on Addiction, 12*(1), 346-364.

Forcehimes, A. A. (2004). De profundis: Spiritual transformations in Alcoholics Anonymous. *JCLP/In Session, 60*(5), 503-517. Retrieved February 1, 2005, from http://www.interscience.wiley.com

Fortney, J., Booth, B., Zhang, M., Humphrey, J. & Wiseman, E. (1998). Controlling for selection bias in the evaluation of Alcoholics Anonymous. *Journal of Studies on Alcohol, 59*(6), 690-697.

Frank, J. D., & Frank, J. B. (1991). *Persuasion and healing* (3rd). Baltimore: Johns Hopkins University Press.

Gartner, A. (1997). Professionals and self-help: The uses of creative tension. *Social Policy, 27*(3), 47-52.

Gelinas, D. J. (1983). The persisting negative effects of incest. *Psychiatry, 46,* 313-332.

Greenberg, M. A., Wortman, C. B., & Stone, A. A. (1996). Emotional expression and physical health: Revisiting traumatic memories or fostering self-regulation? *Journal of Personality and Social Psychology, 71*(3), 22-35.

Hammond, D. C., Hepworth, D. H., & Smith, V. G. (1977). *Improving therapeutic communication.* San Francisco: Jossey-Bass.

Hatzidimitriadou, Eleni. (2002). Political ideology, helping mechanisms and empowerment of mental health self-help/mutual aid groups. *Journal of Community and Applied Social Psychology, 12,* 271-285.

Hegamin, A., Anglin, G. M., & Casanova, M. (2002). Deconstructing the concept of "special populations." *Journal of Drug Use Issues* (Summer), 825-836.

Herndon, S. L. (1998). The paradox of powerlessness: Gender, sex and power in 12-step groups. *Women and Language, 24*(2), 7-12.

Herndon, S. L., & Eastland, L. S. (1999). Introduction. In L. S. Eastland & S. L. Herndon (Eds.), *Communication in recovery: Perspectives on twelve-step groups* (pp. 1-10). Cresskill, NJ: Hampton Press.

Hughes, T. L., Johnson, T., & Wilsnack, S. C. (2001). Sexual assault and alcohol abuse: A comparison of lesbians and heterosexual women. *Journal of Substance Abuse, 13,* 515-532.

Humphreys, K., Mankowski, E. S., & Moos, R. H., & Finney, J. W. (1999). Do enhanced friendship networks and active coping mediate the effects of self-help groups on substance abuse? *Annals of Behavioral Medicine, 21,* 54-60.

Humphreys, Keith. (1999). Professional interventions that facilitate 12-step self-help group involvement. *Alcohol Research and Health, 23*(2), 93-108.

Kelly, J. F. (2003). Self-help for substance-use disorders: History, effectiveness, knowledge gaps, and research opportunities. *Clinical Psychology Review, 23*, 639-663.

Kelly, John, F., McKellar, John D. & Moos, Rudolf. (2003). Major depression in patients with substance use disorders: Relationship to 12-Step self-help involvement and substance use outcomes. *Addiction, 98*, 499-508.

Koski-Jannes, A., & Turner, N. (1999). Factors influencing recovery from different addictions. *Addiction Research, 7*(6), 469-492.

Kownacki, R.J. & Shadish, W.R. (1999). Does Alcoholics Anonymous work? The results from a meta-analysis of controlled experiments. *Substance Use and Misuse, 34*(13), 1897-1916.

Krystal, H. (1978). Trauma and affects. *Psychoanalytic Study of the Child, 33*, 81-117.

Kyrouz, Elaine, M., Humphreys, Keith & Loomis, Colleen. (2002). A review of research on the effectiveness of self-help mutual aid groups. In White, Barbara, J. and Madara, Edward J. (Eds.) (Ed.), *American self-help clearinghouse self-help sourcebook*. Palo Alto, CA: Department of Veterans Affairs Mental Health Strategic Health Group.

Laudet, A. (2003). Attitudes and beliefs about 12-step groups among addiction treatment clients and clinicians: Toward identifying obstacles to participation. *Substance Use and Misuse, 38*(14), 2017-2047.

Laudet, A. B., Magura, S., Vogel, H. S., & Knight, E. (2002). Recovery challenges among dually diagnosed individuals. *Journal of Substance Abuse Treatment, 18*(4), 321-329.

Laudet, A., Savage, R., & Mahmood, D. (2002). Pathways to long-term recovery: A preliminary investigation. *Journal of Psychoactive Drugs, 34*(3).

Linhorst, D. M., & Eckert, A. (2003). Conditions for empowering people with severe mental illness. *Social Services Review* (June), 281-305.

Litz, B. T., Schlenger, W. E., Weathers, F. W., Caddell, J. M., Fairbank, J. A., & LaVange, L. M. (1997). Predictors of emotional numbing in posttraumatic stress disorder. *Journal of Traumatic Stress, 10*(4), 607-620.

Maercker, Andreas & Muller, Julia. (2004). Social acknowledgement as a victim or survivor: A scale to measure a recovery factor of PTSD. *Journal of Traumatic Stress, 17*(4), 345-351.

Magura, S., Laudet, A., Mahmood, D., Rosenblum, A., Vogel, H., & Knight, E. (2003). Role of self-help processes in achieving abstinence among dually diagnosed persons. *Addictive Behaviors, 28*, 399-413.

McBride, M. C., & Emerson, S. (1989). Group work with women who were molested as children. *The Journal for Specialists in Group Work, 14*, 25-33.

McCrady, B. S. (1994). Alcoholics Anonymous and behavior therapy: Can habits be treated as diseases? Can diseases be treated as habits? *Journal of Consulting and Clinical Psychology, 62*(6), 1159-1166.

McDargh, J. (1986). God, mother and me: An object relational perspective on religious material. *Pastoral Psychology, 34*(4), 251-263.

McNeece, C. A., & DiNitto, D. M. (2005). *Chemical Dependency: A systems approach* (3rd). New York: Pearson.

Miller, W. R. (Ed.), & Hester, R. K. (1980). Treating the problem drinker: Modern approaches. *The addictive behaviors: Treatment of alcoholism, drug abuse, smoking, and obesity* (pp. 11-141). Oxford: Pergamon Press.

Morgenstern, J., Labouvie, E., McCrady, B. S., Kahler, C. W., & Frey, R. M. (1997). Affiliation with Alcoholics Anonymous after treatment: A study of its therapeutic effects and mechanisms of action. *Journal of Consulting and Clinical Psychology,* 65(5), 768-777.

Morgenstern, J., Labouvie, E., McCrady, B.S., Kahler, C.W. & Frey, R.M. (1997). Affiliation with Alcoholics Anonymous after treatment: A study of its therapeutic effects and mechanisms of action. *Consulting and Clinical Psychology,* 65(5), 768-777.

Najavits, Lisa M. (2004). Assessment of trauma, PTSD and substance use disorder: A practical guide. In Wilson, J.P. and Keane, T. (Eds.), *Assessing psychological trauma and PTSD* (2nd, pp. 466-491). New York: Guilford Press.

Noordsy, D.L., Schwab, B., Fox, L. & Drake, R.E. (1996). The role of self-help programs in the rehabilitation of persons with severe mental illness and substance use disorders. *Community Mental Health Journal,* 32(1), 71-81.

Ouimette, P. C., Humphreys, K., Moos, R. H., Finney, J. W., Cronkite, R., & Federman, B. (2001). Self-help group participation among substance use disorder patients with PTSD. *Journal of Substance Abuse Treatment, 20,* 25-32.

Ouimette, P., Brown, P. J., & Najavits, L. M. (1998). Course and treatment of patients with both substance use and posttraumatic stress disorder. *Addictive Behaviors,* 23(6), 785-795.

Ouimette, P., Moos, R. H., & Brown, P. J. (2003). Substance use disorder-posttraumatic stress disorder: A survey of treatments and proposed practice guidelines. In P. Ouimette & P. J. Brown (Eds.), *Trauma and substance abuse: Causes, consequences and treatment of comorbid disorders* (pp. 171-180). Washington, DC: American Psychological Association.

Peebles, M. J. (1989). Through a glass darkly: The psychoanalytic use of hypnosis with post-traumatic stress disorder. *International Journal of Clinical and Experimental Hypnosis, 37,* 192-206.

Polcin, D. L., & Zenmore, S. (2004). Psychiatric severity and spirituality, helping, and participation in Alcoholics Anonymous during recovery. *The American Journal of Drug and Alcohol Abuse, 30*(3), 577-592.

Prochaska, J. O., DiClemente, C. C., & Norcross, J. C. (1992). In search of how people change: Applications to addictive behaviors. *American Psychologist, 47,* 1002-1114.

Riessman, Frank. (1997). Ten self-help principles. *Social Policy, 27*(3), 6-11.

Rizzuto, A. M. (1979). *The birth of the living God: A psychoanalytic study.* Chicago: University of Chicago Press.

Roman, P. M., & Blum, T. C. (1998). *National treatment center study.* Athens, GA: University of Georgia.

Rychtarik, R. G., Connors, G. J., Dermen, K. H., & Staslewicz, P. R. (2000). Alcoholics Anonymous and the use of medications to prevent relapse: An anonymous survey of members attitudes. *Journal of Studies on Alcohol, 61,* 134-138.

Segal, S. P., Hodges, J. Q., & Hardiman, E. R. (2002). Factors in decisions to seek help from self-help and co-located community mental health agencies. *American Journal of Orthopsychiatry, 72*(2), 241-249.

Spero, S. (1990). Parallel dimensions of experience in psychoanalytic psychotherapy of the religious patient. *Psychotherapy, 27*(1), 53-71.

Stewart, S.H. (1996). Alcohol abuse in individuals exposed to trauma: A critical review. *Psychological Bulletin, 120,* 83-112.

Tomasson, K. & Vaglum, P. (1998). Psychiatric co-morbidity and aftercare among alcoholics: A prospective study of a nationwide representative sample. *Addiction, 93*(3), 423-431.

Tonigan, J.S., Miller, W.R. & Conners, G.J. (2000). Project Match client impressions about Alcoholics Anonymous: Measurement issues and relationship to treatment outcome. *Alcoholism Treatment Quarterly, 18,* 25-41.

Tortorici, J. (1993). *Multiple personality and other trauma-related disorders.* Paper presented at the meeting of the Menninger conference on Dissociative States.

Twerski, A. (2000). *The spiritual self: Reflections on recovery and God.* Center City, Minnesota: Hazelden.

Vaillant, G. E. (1983). *The natural history of alcoholism.* Cambridge: Harvard University Press.

van der Hart, O., & Brown, P. (1992). Abreaction re-evaluated. *Dissociation, 5*(3), 127-140.

van der Kolk, B. A. (1987). The separation cry and the trauma response. In B. A. van der Kolk (Ed.), *Psychological trauma* (pp. 31-61). Washington, DC: American Psychiatric Press.

van der Walde, H., Urgenson, F. T., Welz, S. H., & Hanna, F. J. (2002). Women and alcoholism: A biopsychosocial perspective and treatment approaches. *Journal of Counseling and Development, 80,* 9.

Vogel, H. (1993). *Double Trouble in Recovery.* Albany, NY: Mental Health Empowerment Project.

Wadsworth, R., Stampneto, A. M., & Halbrook, B. (1995). The role of sexual trauma in the treatment of chemically dependent women: Addressing the relapse issue. *Journal of Counseling and Development, 73,* 401-406.

Waldfogel, S., & Wolpe, P. R. (1993). Using awareness of religious factors to enhance interventions in consultation-liaison psychiatry. *Hospital and Community Psychiatry, 44*(5), 473-477.

Wei-Fen, L., Enright, R. O., Krahn, D., Mack, D., & Baskin, T. W. (2004). Effects of Forgiveness Therapy on anger, mood and vulnerability to substance use among inpatient substance-dependent clients. *Journal of Consulting and Clinical Psychology, 72*(6), 1114-1121.

White, W. (2002). *Toward a new recovery movement: Historical reflections on recovery, treatment and advocacy.* Manuscript submitted for publication.

White, William, L. (1998). *Slaying the dragon: The history of addiction treatment and recovery in America.* Bloomington, IL: Chestnut Health Systems/Lighthouse Institute.

Winhall, J., & Falls, N. (2003). Focusing oriented therapy and trauma–a brief outline. *Proceedings of the 15th International Focusing Conference, 2003, Pforzheim/Germany.*

Yablonsky, L. (1989). *The therapeutic community: A successful approach for treating substance abusers.* New York: Garden Press.

Yalom, I. D. (1995). *The Theory and Practice of Group Psychotherapy.* Basic Books.

Enhancing Hope and Resilience Through a Spiritually Sensitive Focus in the Treatment of Trauma and Addiction

Patricia A. Burke, MSW

SUMMARY. Recent research demonstrates a strong relationship between spirituality and the development of a resilient world view. This paper explores the meaning of spirituality, hope, and resilience as intervening factors in the treatment of and recovery from trauma and addictions and some distinctions between religion and spirituality. It provides a conceptual framework for understanding spirituality as a clinical resource for helping people expand and enliven their personal narratives of hope and resilience and a clinical method, influenced by narrative and transpersonal therapy, for engaging people in an exploration of a larger context within which universal meanings can transport them beyond survival of trauma to a richer, more meaning-filled experience of life. *[Article copies available for a fee from The Haworth Document Delivery Service: 1-800-HAWORTH. E-mail address: <docdelivery@haworthpress.com> Website: <http://www.HaworthPress.com> © 2006 by The Haworth Press, Inc. All rights reserved.]*

KEYWORDS. Enhancing hope and resilience, spiritually sensitive therapy

[Haworth co-indexing entry note]: "Enhancing Hope and Resilience Through a Spiritually Sensitive Focus in the Treatment of Trauma and Addiction." Burke, Patricia A. Co-published simultaneously in *Journal of Chemical Dependency Treatment* (The Haworth Press, Inc.) Vol. 8, No. 2, 2006, pp. 187-206; and: *Psychological Trauma and Addiction Treatment* (ed: Bruce Carruth) The Haworth Press, Inc., 2006, pp. 187-206. Single or multiple copies of this article are available for a fee from The Haworth Document Delivery Service [1-800-HAWORTH, 9:00 a.m. - 5:00 p.m. (EST). E-mail address: docdelivery@haworthpress.com].

INTRODUCTION

Religious beliefs and spiritual practices have traditionally been an avenue by which people develop a sense of what it means to be human including values, hopes, dreams, and purpose in life. These meanings are often shattered by the experience of trauma (Weaver et al., 2003). Much of the clinical literature on trauma makes reference to the concept that traumatic experiences often engender a kind of "crisis of faith" (Herman, 1992) and that spirituality and/or religion can help heal this shattering by "providing a sense of purpose in the face of terrifying realities by placing suffering in a larger context and by affirming the commonality of suffering across generations, time, and space" (McFarlane and van der Kolk, 1996, p. 25).

This paper explores the meaning of spirituality, hope, and resilience as intervening factors in the treatment of and recovery from trauma and addictions and some distinctions between religion and spirituality. It provides a conceptual framework for understanding spirituality as a clinical resource for helping people expand and enliven their personal narratives of hope and resilience and a clinical method for engaging people in an exploration of a larger context within which universal meanings can transport them beyond survival of trauma to a richer, more meaning-filled experience of life.

A PERSONAL NARRATIVE OF RESILIENCE

There are many ways to explore meaning, including the metaphor and imagery in personal narratives or stories. The following personal narrative is one that I have used in psychotherapy sessions, workshops, and seminars to offer clients and students a universal metaphor of the natural world as an expanded consciousness of spirituality within which individual meanings regarding trauma, resilience, and hope can be evoked and explored.

Trumpet Daffodils

Every year round about the middle of March I put on my garden gloves, grab the shovel from the shed, and head out to the south side of the house to my perennial garden. I live in an old cape style farm house circa 1868. It's a huge structure with a connecting shed and another shed that connects to a barn which we now use as a garage. The upper corner of the perennial bed is located just beneath the point where the metal roof of the house dovetails with the metal roof of the first shed into a smooth "V" where the heavy winter snow collects and crashes down like a landslide with great rumbling noises. My trumpet daffodils lay buried for weeks beneath this mound of snow and ice which can sometimes reach the height of four or five feet.

So every year when the garden begins to show brown around its edges I take my shovel and slice away at the mound, layer by layer, until there is only a thin sheath of ice left. Then I carefully break that into manageable chunks and lift them gently off the earth. Every year, without fail, beneath the oppressive weight of snow and brittle ice those trumpet daffodils have already poked their green heads up from the deep earth. Every year, I am astounded. Every year I turn over a chunk of ice to make sure—but there they are, without fail, small indentations where each daffodil has begun to chisel its way through the rock hard ice . . . That is resilience. I am certain that if daffodils could grow five feet tall they would push right through that mound of ice and snow; but since they don't grow five feet tall, I give them a little help. Every year. (Burke, 2002)

This story also offers a metaphor for the psychotherapist as a "spiritual gardener" who supports the daffodil by mindfully slicing off the oppressive layers of snow and ice until its green stem and bud (soon to flower) reveal themselves. But it is not the gardener that makes the flower grow. The resilience is in the very nature of the daffodil's desire to move toward the sun. In nature, life finds its own way. The gardener can only offer a shovel now and then.

Exploring the Landscape of Meaning

In order to build a framework for understanding the inter-relationships between resilience, hope and spirituality and their impact on recovery from trauma and addictions, it is necessary to explore the rich texture of the landscape of meanings these words and images evoke.

What Is Psychological Resilience?

In her long term work with adults who experienced trauma in childhood, Gina O'Connell Higgins (1994) suggests that resilience implies the ability "to negotiate significant challenges to development yet consistently 'snap back'. . ." She goes on to say that, "unlike the term *survivor, resilient* emphasizes that people do more than merely get through difficult emotional experiences, hanging on to inner equilibrium by a thread . . ." and that "resilience best captures the active process of self-righting and growth that characterizes some people. . ." (p. 1).

In accordance with this definition and the metaphor of the daffodil pushing its way through the ice and snow, psychological resilience can be viewed not merely as an inner state or intrinsic quality of the human psyche, but as a dynamic expression of the relationship between life's desire to move forward and the adversity it meets along the way. It is in this meeting with adversity that the meaning of resilience comes alive.

Relationship Between Hope and Resilience

Higgins (1994) also describes other qualities of resilience in people that illuminate the rich texture of this dynamic process of self-righting, including the ability to actively construct a positive vision of life and a fulfilling interpersonal world in spite of trauma. The key word is "vision." This word evokes a sense of imagining– but not simply a false hope for a different experience, but an active imagining of a new relationship to the experience of trauma, in which the memory of the trauma may still linger, but no longer dominates or controls one's life or sense of meaning, nor determines one's identity. This proactive imagination requires a sense of hope and faith in life.

Yahane and Miller (1999) offer a number of meanings of hope in the context of a spiritually sensitive clinical practice including "hope as way," which encompasses a sense of meaning and direction in life and a giving over to a "higher power" or transcendent experience. They also use the language of "hope as horizon," which they describe as "a vision that transcends the present" (p. 221). Again, there is the language of "vision." Returning to the Trumpet Daffodil story for a moment; the daffodil cannot see beyond the darkness of the oppressive weight of the snow, but still reaches out toward what is beyond its limited perspective ("hope as horizon") to what transcends it–the light of the sun ("hope as way"). In the context of this metaphor, one might say that hope is the driving force of the righting response which characterizes resilience.

In his seminal work, *Man's Search for Meaning*, Viktor Frankel (1984) describes the role of proactive imagination in the sense of "hope as horizon" in combating the horror of everyday life as a prisoner in Auschwitz and how it is distinguished from false hope. He tells a story in which he becomes disheartened with himself for being so consumed with everyday survival issues such as whether or not to trade his last cigarette for a bowl of soup. It is this mental obsession with what he describes as "trivial things" (p. 82) that is the foundation of his immense suffering.

In one illuminating moment Frankel purposefully engages his imagination and transports himself to a great lecture hall where there is an attentive audience in comfortable seats. He is lecturing on the psychology of concentration camps. In his words, "All that oppressed me at that moment became objective, seen and described from the remote viewpoint of science. By this method I succeeded somehow in rising above the situation, above the sufferings of the moment . . ." (p. 82). In this personal narrative Frankel is essentially describing that sense of "hope as horizon," in which he engages his imagination to reach beyond the oppression of his mental obsession and from the place of a greater perspective is able to enter into a different relationship with his suffering.

In contrast, Frankel (1984) tells a story of another prisoner who hears a voice in a dream that predicts the date the allied forces will liberate the camps. Initially the prisoner is quite hopeful that he will be released from his suffering in the near future, but as the date draws nearer and news of the war is grim, the prisoner loses faith. When the camps are not liberated on the predicted day the man loses consciousness, then dies from typhus. Frankel explains this phenomenon: "The ultimate cause of my friend's death was that the expected liberation did not come and he was severely disappointed. This suddenly lowered his body's resistance against the latent typhus infection. His faith in the future and his will to live had become paralyzed and his body fell victim to illness" (p. 84). Frankel is able to invoke his imagination and a sense of "hope as horizon" to transform his relationship to suffering. The other prisoner dies because all he has is a false hope for liberation from his suffering.

Relationship Between Spirituality and Religion

In order to develop a framework for a spiritually sensitive clinical focus, it is important to explore the diverse expressions and meanings of spirituality in both religious and non-religious contexts. This is no easy task given that there is a mysterious quality of spirituality in its universal meaning that is beyond language. "The tao that can be told is not the eternal Tao" (Lao-tzu, "n.d"/1991, p. 1). Nonetheless it may be clinically useful to make some distinctions between spirituality and religion and to further illuminate both individual and universal meanings of spirituality.

Canda and Furman (1999) offer the following definitions consistent with the framework developed here: "Spirituality relates to a universal and fundamental aspect of what it is to be human– to search for a sense of meaning, purpose, and moral frameworks for relating with self, others and the ultimate reality. In this sense, spirituality may express through religious forms, or it may be independent of them. Religion is an institutionalized pattern of beliefs, behaviors, and experiences oriented toward spiritual concerns, and shared by a community and transmitted over time in traditions" (p. 37).

Spirituality is primarily concerned with the personal search for meaning and a felt sense of connection with some ultimate or transcendent reality. In contrast, religion is primarily concerned with organized beliefs as expressed through the rituals and traditions of an institution. For some individuals spirituality and religion are intimately intertwined; for others they are very separate. It is essential for the therapist to listen for the language of both spirituality and religion when working with traumatized people and to help them unpack these meanings for themselves.

Importance of These Distinctions in Clinical Practice

The search for meaning is also an integral part of the traumatized person's efforts to cope with helplessness and vulnerability (Turner, McFarlane, & van der Kolk, 1996). If therapeutic conversations with people who have experienced trauma focus on personal meaning in the context of story, metaphor, and the imagination these conversations often move naturally toward the universal meanings of spirituality– just as the trumpet daffodil naturally moves toward the sun. In this sense, spirituality can be a source of "hope as way" for the traumatized person.

In contrast, because religion is primarily concerned with beliefs, conversations about religion can easily turn into debates about doctrine. Griffith and Griffith (2002) describe the difficulties that can arise when therapeutic conversations focus primarily on beliefs. "Beliefs are propositional statements asserting 'truth'–what is real or what matters. Beliefs differ from metaphors and stories in their abstractness and in the propositional form of their language. Beliefs operate differently in human affairs than do metaphors or stories. Most people can find a way to live alongside others even when their metaphors and stories differ. This is not always so with beliefs. When beliefs are discovered to differ, conflict often is near at hand" (p. 139).

While religious beliefs may be essential to some people for their identity development and a resource in helping them cope with trauma; for others beliefs are only one aspect of a rich, meaning-filled experience of spirituality. For example, a discussion about beliefs may be very important to a person who identifies as a Christian, but less valuable to a person who practices Judaism, Buddhism, or Hinduism (Griffith and Griffith, 2002) or has no particular religious affiliation. In addition, some people experience a negative relationship between the religious beliefs they were raised with and their current spiritual meanings and purposes.

In order to effectively navigate the landscape of spiritual and religious meanings in therapeutic encounters with people, as therapists, we must thoroughly explore our own beliefs and study their impact on our lives and relationships (Griffith & Griffith, 2002), have a working knowledge of the diversity of religious beliefs systems in the world (Canda & Furman, 1999, Richards & Bergin, 1997, Richards & Bergin, 2000), and be able to honor a client's beliefs, while maintaining a stance of respectful inquiry into the relationship of those beliefs, whether positive or negative, to a person's identity and recovery from trauma and addiction. Otherwise conversations about spirituality, hope, and meaning may turn into debates about assertions of truth.

Spirituality as One Dimension and as Essence of Human Experience

In addition to the meanings explored above, spirituality can be thought of both as one aspect of a person's life experience– equal to the biological, psychological, and social/cultural aspects of the individual–and as essence or the universal human experience that transcends the personal (Carroll, 1998). In this framework spirituality as one aspect of human experience can be a resource that supports traumatized people to meet and combat suffering through the exploration of meaning; whereas spirituality as essence enhances the person's experience of vitality, the realization of ultimate reality, and a sense of interconnectedness with all existence (Carroll, 1998); thus combating the pervasive sense of disconnection that traumatized people experience (Herman, 1992). For the purposes of the conceptual framework for the clinical approach developed here, the word spirituality will be used to describe an inclusive, multi-dimensional human experience, including both personal and transpersonal/universal meanings, which people may express from within or outside the context of religious institutions, practices, customs, and beliefs.

Spirituality and Resilience as Intervening Factors in Trauma and Addiction

While it is beyond the scope of this paper to offer a comprehensive review of the research on spirituality and resilience, a brief look at some recent results of quantitative and qualitative studies may help illuminate the relationship between spirituality and resilience and their ecological impact on trauma and addiction recovery.

Research on Spirituality and Resilience

Recent research suggests that resilience can function as an intervening variable buffering the stress response and helping traumatized people be less reactive to stressful experiences (Kass, 2000). By modulating stress reactions, resilience can help prevent psychological problems and health-risk behaviors such as smoking, drug/alcohol abuse, and overeating (Kass, 2000). A qualitative study of minority women revealed several factors that enhanced their resilience including well-defined faith lives (Bachay & Cingel, 1999). In another study 60% of a sample of inner-city, minority women who had been sexually abused indicated an increased role of spirituality in their lives, which was positively associated with the restoration of psychological and emotional well-being (Kennedy et al., 1998). In several studies spirituality has been positively associated with measures of resilience in both men and women and linked to increases in a positive sense of self, decreased intent to drink among recovering alcoholics, decreased dysphoria, decreased hostility, and increased levels of happiness (Kass, 2000).

In his research using several measures of both resilience and spirituality Kass (2000) found two elements of spirituality that contribute to the formation of a resilient world view: (1) an experiential aspect that enhances a felt sense of the existence of God or sacred aspect of life; and (2) a relational aspect that emphasizes the perception of a meaningful relationship with God or sacred aspect of life. This research suggests that it is not simply a belief in God, but a deeply felt experience of and relationship to that which is sacred that contribute to resilience.

RESEARCH ON THE INTERVENING EFFECTS OF SPIRITUALITY ON TRAUMA AND SUBSTANCE ABUSE

Recent studies on the impact of a variety of measures of spirituality and religious participation report a positive correlation between religious commitment and less severe symptoms of PTSD in battered women (Astin et al., 1993 as cited in Drescher & Foy, 1995), an association with low scores on religious orientation and a greater incidence of PTSD symptoms in Vietnam era combat veterans (Drescher & Foy, 1995), and hope for the future and a greater belief in God in Holocaust survivors (Carmil & Breznitz, 1991 as cited in Weaver et al., 2003).

Other research has shown that alcohol/drug use is associated with lack of meaning in life, and that active spiritual involvement can reduce the risk of alcohol or other drug abuse and enhance long-term recovery (Miller, W. R., 1998); that higher levels of religious faith and spirituality are associated with increased coping and greater resilience to stress among people recovering from substance abuse (Pardini & Plante, 2000); and that spirituality and religious participation by multicultural youth is a protective factor in preventing alcohol and drug abuse (Hodge et al., 2001).

These studies suggest that spirituality and religious involvement can not only enhance resilience, a sense of hope in the future, and long-term recovery from addictions, but can also be a protective factor and contribute to the prevention of PTSD and substance abuse.

A Spiritually Sensitive Clinical Focus

It has long been known in the addiction treatment field that spirituality is an essential part of the recovery process, but the spiritual component of addictions recovery and treatment has largely fallen under the auspices of Alcoholics Anonymous and treatment programs based on the Twelve Steps of AA. More recently, there has been a growing body of clinical literature emphasizing the integration of a spiritually sensitive focus into counselling (Richards & Bergin, 1997), social work practice (Canda & Furman, 1999), and psychotherapy (Miller, 1999; Griffith & Griffith, 2002). The spiritually sensitive clinical focus presented here is influenced by both narrative and transpersonal approaches and emphasizes the exploration and enhancement of individual and universal spiritual meanings through personal narrative and proactive imagination within the context of a mindful psychotherapeutic container.

Spirituality as One Dimension: A Narrative Approach

The narrative framework is a collaborative, non-pathologizing approach to therapy based on the idea that people's personal stories or narratives provide "a context for our experience, one that makes the attribution of meaning possible" (White, 1995, p. 13). Narrative therapy assumes that the person seeking consultation is the expert in his/her own life experience and that it is the job of the therapist to shape conversations through respectful inquiry that helps the person link the meaning of life events over time into a personal narrative consistent with that person's values, intentions, commitments, and purpose (Morgan, 2000). This narrative framework offers a culturally sensitive context within which people can explore their spiritual narratives and their relationship to hope and resilience as allies in combating the negative effects of trauma and addiction in their lives.

Circle of Meaning: A Narrative Tool

The Circle of Meaning was developed as part of a seminar on Spirituality and Addictions (Nakken & Burke, 2002) for the first World Health Organization China Institute on Substance Abuse. I envisioned the Circle as a respectful and culturally sensitive tool, in alignment with the narrative framework described above, that would help Chinese addiction treatment professionals explore their clients' spirituality and its relationship to recovery from substance abuse.

Circle as Symbol

The circle is a universal symbol of wholeness and spaciousness (Burke, 2005). In Taoism the circle, with its quality of inclusiveness, contains both light and dark (Yin and Yang) and offers a symbolic container within which suffering is transformed and where all values and concepts are deemed to be relative not absolute (Smith, 1991). The circle is also associated with sacred or consecrated space (Walker, 1988) and a symbol that embodies the Buddhist principle of mindfulness; thus reflecting the quality of sacred space of the psychotherapy container. The circle provides a metaphorical context within which the dominance of "assertions of truth" regarding spiritual and religious beliefs are diminished. "In the center of the circle, all beliefs, meanings, and experiences are welcomed, thus supporting an open and richly textured conversation that can embrace any individual, cultural, philosophical, or language differences that might arise" (Burke, 2005).

Seven Themes of Spiritual Narratives[1]

Within the context of the spaciousness of the Circle of Meaning, the narrative approach provides a way of shaping conversations about spirituality. In keeping with narrative therapy's emphasis on story (Morgan, 2000) I envisioned a focus on narrative themes as a way of helping people uncover and expand their own spiritual meanings. This idea of themes is different from the concept of religious/spiritual dimensions that is emphasized in the clinical literature on spiritual assessment (Canda & Furman, 1999; Richards & Bergin, 1997; Gorsuch & Miller, 1999). Working with themes shifts the emphasis from assessment and objective measures which are scientifically derived, to meaning and metaphor which are culturally and relationally derived (Burke, 2005). The following are universal themes that do not impose any particular images, beliefs, or meanings onto people and often arise spontaneously in therapeutic conversations (Burke, 2005):

1. *Spiritual Beliefs:* which may include concepts of God as supreme being or God as a non-personal Presence, ultimate reality, life after death, the meaning of suffering, reincarnation, etc.
2. *Spiritual Principles:* which may include values, ethical guidelines, and principles for living such as the Twelve Steps of Alcoholics Anonymous, the Ten Commandments, Buddhist precepts, etc.
3. *Spiritual Behaviors and Practices:* which may include rituals, ceremonies, and culturally derived customs, prayer and meditation, use of sacred objects, metaphor, symbols, and imagery, creative endeavors, and service.
4. *Spiritual Experiences:* which may include mystical, profound, or life changing experiences, moments of insight and awareness and/or realization of purpose and meaning in life.
5. *Spiritual Teachers or Guides:* which focuses on the nature of and meaning of relationships with teachers including spirits of ancestors, living teachers, real or mythical beings–human, animal, or plant, or symbolic/metaphoric representations.
6. *Spiritual Community:* membership in and a sense of belonging to a community which may include friendship circles, church, sangha, meditation group, AA or other twelve-step groups, etc.
7. *Spiritual Home:* the meaning of and relationship to sacred space or sanctuary including nature, church, synagogue, temple, mosque,

psychotherapy relationship, and/or a state of consciousness or place in the imagination.

Once these themes are placed inside the spaciousness of the Circle, meanings expand naturally and the richness of a person's spiritual narrative and the ways in which hope and resilience are expressed throughout that narrative become more apparent and present. For example, at the training institute in China, after describing the themes and drawing an empty circle on newsprint, I invited seminar participants to fill it with their own images, symbols, and meanings. One participant revealed that her spiritual teacher was grass because it is trampled on all the time, but in spite of this keeps growing toward the sun. Halfway across the world, in a cultural context that is very different from ours here in the West, a metaphor for resilience arose within the spaciousness of the Circle that is strikingly similar to the metaphor in the Trumpet Daffodil story.

The intention of the psychotherapist is to listen for these themes and welcome them into the Circle of Meaning either literally on paper or metaphorically into the sacred space of the psychotherapy container. It then becomes possible to engage in a collaborative, respectful and culturally/spiritually sensitive inquiry that helps people expand their own meanings (Burke, 2005) and actively envision a different relationship to trauma.

SPIRITUALITY AS ESSENCE: A TRANSPERSONAL APPROACH

Ferrer (as cited in Caplan et al., 2003) suggests that a transpersonal approach to psychotherapy is essentially concerned with understanding the wholeness of human nature and seeks to integrate psychology and the universal dimension of spirituality in an effort to "foster an integrative spiritual life that is fully embodied, socially engaged, and ecologically sensitive" (p. 147). An important focus of the transpersonal therapist is to help people regain a sense of fullness and vitality (Louchakova as cited in Caplan et al., 2003) through engagement with psychological processes that enhance self-awareness and spiritual practices that facilitate the realization of unified consciousness and a felt-sense of Presence in everyday life. Whereas narrative therapy explores the landscape of spiritual meanings in the personal and relational realm through story, transpersonal therapy explores universal spiritual meanings through a focus on the inner landscape via experiential processes such as mindfulness, sensate focusing, and spiritual inquiry.

Mindfulness: A Pathway to Expanded Awareness

Mindfulness is a concept and meditation practice borrowed from Buddhism and is essentially a practice of paying attention to moment-to-moment experience in a non-judgmental way (Kabat-Zinn, 1994). Mindfulness can also be described as "nonidentified witnessing" (Welwood, 2000, p. 127) and "a state of alert but relaxed consciousness" (Johanson & Kurtz, 1991, p. xiv). Mindfulness can aid in the development of a witnessing stance and enhance acceptance of and tolerance of intense affect, compassion for self and others, resilience, and relaxation (Perez-De-Albeniz & Holmes, 2000).

Mindfulness can also help people open to a felt sense of Presence. Returning to the Trumpet Daffodil story, the daffodil reaches upward toward the sun–a metaphor for the image or idea of God (Burke, 1999)–even though it cannot see or touch the sun. Yet there is something else that supports this movement. It is a felt sense of warmth. This visceral experience has been described as unconditional friendliness (Welwood, 2000), acceptance, and love.

In addition to opening to this felt sense of Presence, engaging in a practice of mindful awareness facilitates the expansion of consciousness within which traumatic events and the long-term after-effects of trauma such as depression, anxiety, addiction, etc., lose their power to dominate a person's life. Figure 1 illustrates the movement from a limited, reactive consciousness to an expansive, resilient consciousness within which trauma's scope and power are diminished.

Elaine, a survivor of childhood abuse, started meditating everyday after a conversation in a session focusing on the Circle of Meaning theme of spiritual practices and behaviors. She adopted a practice of consciously remembering at the first hint of the debilitating anxiety that had plagued her that she is made of the same energy that moves ocean waves. This gave rise to an experience of fullness in her chest and awakened a felt sense of Presence. The anxiety diminished and no longer had the power to dominate her mood, thinking, or behavior.

FIGURE 1. A Transpersonal Perspective on Trauma

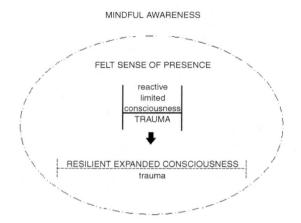

INTEGRATING NARRATIVE AND TRANSPERSONAL MEANING

The exploration of personal narratives of spirituality facilitated by the use of such tools as the Circle of Meaning can enhance a person's sense of hope, resilience, meaning, and fulfillment. When unpacked within a mindful therapeutic container, these stories can also open a doorway to a felt sense of vitality that is the antithesis of the pervasive numbness that so many traumatized people suffer. This numbness destroys the ability to imagine a future (van der Kolk et al., 1996) or "hope as horizon" and is linked to negative beliefs and conclusions about one's identity. The therapist's purpose is to facilitate the establishment of a mindful therapeutic context within which the themes of the Circle of Meaning can emerge, where hope flourishes, and a sense of vitality and connection to Presence expands so that hopelessness, despair, numbness, and anxiety no longer dominate the traumatized person's consciousness.

Creating a Mindful Container in Psychotherapy

In order to create such a spacious and inclusive therapeutic context the therapist must hold a focus of mindful awareness that includes these qualities: (1) open attention/non-judgmental awareness; (2) curiosity; (3) faith in the client's expertise, wisdom, intentions, purposes, meanings, and innate desire to grow; (4) a here-and-now-focus through the gateway of sensate focusing; and (5) inclusiveness, which is essentially an intention to not exclude anything from awareness (Burke, 2003).

Creating a mindful container is not a technique. It is a way of being present in the therapy relationship (Burke, 2003). The mindfulness of the therapist is the basis for any compassionate encounter with suffering and therefore must rest in the heart of the therapeutic relationship. Thus, mindfulness is not only a practice we can offer our clients, but it is also the foundation for our own practice as therapists engaged in this spiritually sensitive clinical focus.

Karen's Story

Karen was in the middle of her life when she first walked into my office after breaking off a longstanding friendship with a woman whom Karen described as critical and domineering. In spite of the deepening lines of despair on her face and a flatness in her voice, there was an unmistakable flicker in Karen's eyes. Karen's early childhood narrative included a "hypercritical" mother who suffered a serious postpartum depression and an alcoholic father whom she described as absent from her life. She talked a great deal about her early experience of trauma–the emotional abandonment by her depressed mother and absent father. She grew up in a family of Fundamentalist Christians and expressed difficulty with connecting to a felt sense of Presence due to the dissonance between the strict belief system she grew up with–including a "commitment to personal purity" (Richards & Bergin, 2000)–that dictated to her what a "good Christian" should be and her own meanings and purposes. In her mind, Karen's shamed-based identity was inextricably linked to the legacy of this religious idea of personal purity–that she must do everything right and be perfect.

Karen had attended AA meetings and maintained continuous sobriety for over fifteen years. She was fearful of abandonment and suffered from chronic feelings of worthlessness, anxiety and depression. The disconnection she experienced as a result of the abrupt ending of her friendship opened the door for hopelessness, fear, and a pervasive sense of numbness to dominate her waking life. She quit her job, left her husband to live with her mother because she was frightened to be alone in the house during the day, and was overcome at times with an impulse to drink. In spite of her relational world contracting and tumbling into chaos, she managed to find her way into therapy and reach out to some new women friends at AA. Like the daffodil, Karen was already pushing up through the oppressive weight of the legacy of trauma toward the sun. I simply needed to get out my gardening tools and mindfully slice away at it layer by layer.

It was clear that an important focus of our conversations would initially be on the Circle of Meaning theme of spiritual beliefs. I did not want to become embroiled in a debate, however, about "assertions of truth" with Karen regarding her early religious experience, so I became mindful by envisioning Karen in the center of the Circle of Meaning with her ambivalent relationship to the belief of "personal purity." I then invited her into a mindful state by asking her to focus briefly on her breathing. When her breathing relaxed I asked her to tell me her "story of God." This question opened up the possibility for her to engage in a richly textured, meaning-filled narrative about her relationship with God. To Karen, God was a masculine authority figure who punished her for not being perfect and would surely abandon her because she was not a "good Christian." She also revealed that she did not want to feel this way about God; that she hoped for a relationship with a loving being. I heard this longing as the seed of "hope as horizon" and became curious about the possibility of enlisting her new friends at AA into the ranks of "spiritual gardeners" who might be willing to till the ground and water this seed. I wondered aloud if she might be interested in sharing her hopes and dreams with some of her new friends.

At our next meeting, Karen revealed that she had, in fact, begun to tell her story of God to some of the women at her meeting and she felt more connected and less fearful. She then told me a deeply moving story of how she found a caterpillar in the middle of a desolate road on her way back from the meeting. With tears in her eyes, she talked about how lonely and vulnerable the caterpillar seemed. I hoped to bring the caterpillar into the here-and-now by engaging Karen's imagination with this question, "When you envision the caterpillar in your mind, right now, what do you notice inside?"

D: I love her.
P: Where do you notice the love in your body?
D: It's in my heart. It feels warm.
P: If the love had a voice and could speak, what would it say?
D: I want to protect her, take care of her, take her to safety.
P: Love wants to protect her.
D: Yes. *Her chest shudders deeply with sobs.* Now I see myself picking her up. I am cradling her in my hand. I take her to the side of the road and put her under a leaf in the woods.

P: Love picks her up and brings her to safety.

D: Yes. I want someone to take care of me that way. I want God to take care of me that way. *With a curious look on her face.* Is that possible? Could God love me like the caterpillar?

Her question was like a small pebble dropped into a still pool. I became curious about how it might ripple through Karen's life if, instead of presuming that I could answer it for her, we unpacked its meaning together. I encouraged her to take the nonidentified witness position characteristic of mindfulness and Frankel's "remote viewpoint" by inviting her to make up a fairy tale about the caterpillar. Karen began her story with *Once upon a time* . . . then described the experience of the caterpillar who had been rebuffed by its family and ended up alone in the road. *A silent Presence touched the caterpillar. She was both terrified and filled with a deep warmth. It must be God, she thought. Then the Presence lifted her and gently placed her on the other side of the highway in a soft pile of leaves. She felt a great sense of relief, then awe.*

By actively engaging her imagination within the mindful therapeutic container Karen had at once become the caterpillar, witnessed herself as the caterpillar, and answered her own question about God. Shortly after this experience, Karen revealed that she asked an older woman with thirty years of sobriety in AA to be her sponsor and they had developed a plan for Karen to work the Twelve Steps again, this time with a focus on engaging in a meaningful relationship with the God of her own understanding. Just as a caterpillar eventually turns into a butterfly, Karen's relationship with God was transformed from an ambivalent belief-based relationship with a punishing God to a deeply fulfilling felt sense of a loving Presence. Within a relatively short period of time not only had Karen re-engaged with her spiritual community of AA, but returned home and started doing some volunteer work. The hopelessness and anxiety did not disappear, but they faded into the background and no longer dominated her life.

CONCLUSION

Exploring personal narrative using the Circle of Meaning as a relational and cultural tool for enhancing resilience engages people in the domain of spirituality as one aspect. As Angell (2000) suggests in his narrative work with First Nation people of North America, spirituality ". . . is an aspect of self that, although transcending life, guides us in how to live and find meaning in the here-and-now. In essence, through guidance and by offering hope, spirituality enables us to cope with the harsh realities of existence, and connects us with culturally like-minded others" (n. p.).

As therapists, when we employ this narrative tool, with its rich focus on metaphor, imagery, and meaning, within the context of the mindful and sacred space of the psychotherapy container we offer ourselves and the people who consult us an opportunity to engage with the transcendent meanings of spirituality as essence. For so many it is this felt sense of Presence that rekindles hope, enhances resilience, and enables them to not only rebound from the debilitating effects of trauma and addiction in their lives, but like Karen, to experience a new sense of vitality and connection with all of existence that transports them beyond survival to a richer, more meaning-filled experience of life.

AUTHOR NOTE

I wish to thank the people whose stories I have shared here. Please note that identifying information and narrative details were omitted or changed in accordance with professional guidelines in order to protect those individuals' privacy. In addition, written permission was granted by those who consulted me for psychotherapy to share their personal anecdotes in my teaching, training, and professional writing.

NOTE

1. The original Circle of Meaning presented at the China Institute contained five themes and was later expanded to include two additional themes–spiritual community and spiritual home.

REFERENCES

Angell, G. B. (Spring, 2000). Cultural resilience in North American First Nations: The story of Little Turtle. *Critical Social Work*, 1(1). Retrieved March 25, 2005, from http://www.criticalsocialwork.com/units/socialwork/critical.nsf/982f0e5f06b5c9a 285256d6e006cff78/cd0c747aa6b2bf2b85256ea6004da0e4?OpenDocument
Astin, M. C., Lawrence, K. J., & Fooy, D. W. (1993). Posttraumatic stress disorder among battered women: Risk and resiliency factors. *Violence and Victims*, 8, 17-28.
Bachay, J. B. & Cingel, P. A. (1999). Restructuring resilience: Emerging voices. *Affilia: Journal of Women and Social Work*, 14(2), 162-176.

Burke, P. A. (1999). The Healing Power of the Imagination. *The International Journal of Children's Spirituality*, 4(1), 9-17.

Burke, P. A. (2002, April). Trumpet Daffodils. In *Building Resilience Through Spirituality*. Presentation at the National Association of Social Workers Maine Chapter Annual Conference, Rockport, ME.

Burke, P. A. (2003, August). *Building Resilience Through Spirituality*. Seminar at the New England Institute of Addiction Studies Advanced School, Waterville Valley, NH.

Burke, P. A. (2005, May/June). Circle of Meaning: A narrative tool for exploring the multi-dimensional nature of spirituality. *Counselor: The Magazine for Addiction Professionals*, 6(3), 22-28.

Canda, E. R. & Furman, L. D. (1999). *Spiritual Diversity in Social Work Practice: The Heart of Helping*. New York: The Free Press.

Caplan, M., Hartelius, G., & Rardin, M. A. (2003). Contemporary viewpoints on transpersonal psychology. *The Journal of Transpersonal Psychology*, 35(2), 143-162.

Carmil, D. & Breznitz, S. (1991). Personal trauma and world view–Are extremely stressful experiences related to political attitudes, religious beliefs, and future orientation? *Journal of Traumatic Stress*, 4(3), 393-404.

Carroll, M.M. (1998). Social Work's Conceptualization of Spirituality. *Social Thought: Journal of Religion in the Social Services*, 18(2), 1-13.

Drescher, K. D. & Foy, W. D. (Winter,1995). Spirituality and trauma treatment: Suggestions for including spirituality as a coping mechanism [Electronic version]. *NCP Clinical Quarterly*, 5(1), 4-5.

Frankel, V. E. (1984). *Man's Search for Meaning: An Introduction to Logotherapy* (Third Edition). New York: Simon and Schuster.

Gorsuch, R. L. & Miller, W. R. (1999). Assessing spirituality. In Miller, W. R. (Ed.). *Integrating Spirituality into Treatment: Resources for Practitioners*. Washington, DC: American Psychological Association.

Herman, J. L. (1992). *Trauma and Recovery*. New York: Basic Books.

Higgins, G. O. (1994). *Resilient Adults: Overcoming a Cruel Past*. San Francisco: Jossey-Bass.

Hodge, D. R., Cardenas, P., & Montoya, H. (2001). Substance use: Spirituality and religious participation as protective factors among rural youth. *Social Work Research*, 25(3), 153-162.

Kabat-Zinn, J. (1994). *Wherever You Go There You Are: Mindfulness Meditation in Everyday Life*. New York: Hyperion.

Kass, J. (2000). *Manual for the Spirituality and Resilience Packet (Version 4.2)*. Cambridge, MA: Behavioral Health Education Initiative. Retrieved February 28, 2005 from http://chppm-www.apgea.army.mil/dhpw/Readiness/spirit/SRA_OK.aspx?

Keister, J. (November, 2001). Substance abuse prevention in minorities: The role of religion and spirituality [Electronic version]. *Social Work Today*, 1(8).

Kennedy, J. E., Davis, R. C., & Taylor, B. G. (1998). Changes in spirituality and well-being among victims of sexual assault. *Journal for the Scientific Study of Religion*, 37(2), 322-329.

Lao Tzu (1991). Tao te ching. (S. Mitchell, Trans.). New York: HarperPerennial (Original work published n.d.).

McFarlene, A. C. & van der Kolk, B. A. (1996). Trauma and its challenge to society. In B. A. van der Kolk, A. C. McFarlane, & L. Weisaeth (Eds.), *Traumatic Stress: The Overwhelming Experience on Mind, Body, and Society* (pp. 24-46). New York: Guilford Press.

Miller, W. R. (1998). Researching the spiritual dimensions of alcohol and other drug problems. *Addiction*, 93(7), 979-991.

Miller, W. R. (Ed.). (1999). *Integrating Spirituality into Treatment: Resources for Practitioners*. Washington, DC: American Psychological Association.

Morgan, A. (2000). *What is Narrative Therapy: An easy-to-read introduction*. Adelaide, South Australia: Dulwich Entre Publications.

Nakken, C. M. & Burke, P. A. (2002). *Spirituality and Addictions*. Seminar conducted at the World Health Organization China Institute on Substance Abuse, Prevention, and Treatment. Beijing, China.

Perez-De-Albeniz, A. & Holmes, J. (2000). Meditation: Concepts, effects, and uses in therapy. *International Journal of Psychotherapy*, 5(1), 49-59.

Plante, T. G. & Pardini, D. A. (2000, August). *Religious denomination affiliation and psychological health: Results from a substance abuse population*. Paper presented at the Psychological Association's 108th Annual Convention, Washington, D.C.

Richards, P.S. & Bergin, A.E. (1997). *A Spiritual Strategy for Counseling and Psychotherapy*, Washington, DC: American Psychological Association.

Richards, P.S. & Bergin, A.E. (Eds.). (2000). *Handbook of Psychotherapy and Religious Diversity*, Washington, DC: American Psychological Association.

Smith, H. (1991). *The World's Religions (Revised and Updated)*. San Francisco: HarperSanFranciso.

Turner, S. W., McFarlene, A. C. & van der Kolk, B. A. (1996). The Therapeutic Environment and New Explorations in the Treatment of Posttraumatic Stress Disorder. In B. A. van der Kolk, A. C. McFarlane, & L. Weisaeth (Eds.), *Traumatic Stress: The Overwhelming Experience on Mind, Body, and Society* (pp. 537-558). New York: Guilford Press.

van der Kolk, B. A., McFarlene, A. C., & van der Hart, O. (1996). A General Approach to Treatment of Posttraumatic Stress Disorder. In B. A. van der Kolk, A. C. McFarlane & L. Weisaeth (Eds.), *Traumatic Stress: The Overwhelming Experience on Mind, Body, and Society* (pp. 417-440). New York: Guilford Press.

Walker, B. G. (1988). *The Woman's Dictionary of Symbols & Sacred Objects*. San Francisco: HarperSanFranciso.

Weaver, Andrew J., Flannelly, Laura T., Garbarino, James, Figley, Charles R., & Flannelly, Kevin J. (2003). A systematic review of research on religion and spirituality in the *Journal of Traumatic Stress*: 1990 -1999. *Mental Health, Religion & Culture*, 6(3), 215-228.

Welwood, J. (2000). *Toward a Psychology of Awakening: Buddhism, Psychotherapy, and the Path of Personal and Spiritual Transformation*. Boston: Shambhala Publications.

White, M. (1995). *Re-Authoring Lives: Interviews and Essays*. Adelaide, South Australia: Dulwich Center Press.

Yahane, C. E. & Miller, W. R. (1999). Evoking Hope. In Miller, W. R. (Ed.). *Integrating Spirituality into Treatment: Resources for Practitioners*. Washington, DC: American Psychological Association.

Integrating the Creative Arts into Trauma and Addiction Treatment: Eight Essential Processes

E. Hitchcock Scott, PhD, NCC, LISAC, ATR, REAT
Carol J. Ross, MA, CADAC, ICRC

SUMMARY. Weaving creative arts into the practice of trauma and addiction therapy provides rich ground for gaining insight, catharsis, and the integration of a compartmentalized self and lifestyle. In this chapter, the word art is used to include all creative arts: imagistic, dramatic, literary, dance, and music. Although the theoretical stance of expressive arts psychotherapy suggests an inter-modal or multi-modal approach, the terms creative arts and expressive arts will be used interchangeably. Eight essential processes of creative arts psychotherapy will be described and illustrated through a case study and photos of artwork. Creative arts specifically described in this chapter are life-sized silhouette (body map), timeline, and psychodrama. The power and beauty of creative arts enhances trauma and addiction therapy. *[Article copies available for a fee from The Haworth Document Delivery Service: 1-800-HAWORTH. E-mail address: <docdelivery@haworthpress.com> Website: <http://www.HaworthPress.com> © 2006 by The Haworth Press, Inc. All rights reserved.]*

KEYWORDS. Trauma, addiction, creative arts, expressive arts, psychodrama, body map, body tracing, life-sized silhouette, timeline

A special thank you to Johanna Czamanski, Adelaide Santana Pellicier, Gayle Prather, and Ann Vargas.

[Haworth co-indexing entry note]: "Integrating the Creative Arts into Trauma and Addiction Treatment: Eight Essential Processes." Scott, E. Hitchcock, and Carol J. Ross. Co-published simultaneously in *Journal of Chemical Dependency Treatment* (The Haworth Press, Inc.) Vol. 8, No. 2, 2006, pp. 207-226; and: *Psychological Trauma and Addiction Treatment* (ed: Bruce Carruth) The Haworth Press, Inc., 2006, pp. 207-226. Single or multiple copies of this article are available for a fee from The Haworth Document Delivery Service [1-800-HAWORTH, 9:00 a.m. - 5:00 p.m. (EST). E-mail address: docdelivery@haworthpress.com].

doi:10.1300/J034v08n02_11

INTRODUCTION

Prior to recovery, addicts and trauma survivors wander lost, much like the "Israelites initially futile wandering in the wilderness" (Ochs & Olitzky, 1997, p. 128). Though lost, many seek a more authentic connection to self and spirit. While the patient begins therapy in despair, ". . . it is followed by revelation–a whole new way of seeing. And after revelation comes the long process of integrating the new perception" (p. 129). Art, like manna, the mysterious food sent by God to the Israelites, sustains the lost and seeking. Art feeds us during times when we are parched, hungry, and tired. The act of creation, whether an art piece or a meaningful life, is one of faith just as the act of collecting food that fell from the sky was an act of faith for the Israelites. The act of faith it takes to draw, sculpt, dance, sing, or role-play may be the first step to "the breakdown of old ways of viewing things" (p. 128) and the start of a new life. Rogers (1993) writes,

> Part of the psychotherapeutic process is to awaken the creative life-force energy. Thus, creativity and therapy overlap. What is creative is frequently therapeutic. What is therapeutic is frequently a creative process. . . . Expressive arts therapy uses various arts . . . in a supportive setting to facilitate growth and healing. It is a process of discovering ourselves through any art form that comes from an emotional depth. (pp. 1-2)

The creative arts have a unique ability to help trauma survivors and addicts navigate through life experiences and defenses to the center of the soul.

THE BRAIN FUNCTION OF TRAUMA

Even today there is a mysterious component of how the creative arts access, reveal, and transform the unconscious. We have gained a better understanding of the science of how right-brain creative processes may help heal those who are suffering. Research using positron emission tomography (PET) has shown that both hemispheres of the brain are affected by trauma. Rauch's research revealed, when people with PTSD are exposed to stimuli reminiscent of their trauma, . . . there is a . . . decrease in oxygen utilization in Broca's area, the region in the left inferior frontal cortex responsible for generating words to attach to internal experience. These findings may account for the observation that trauma may lead to 'speechless terror,' which . . . interferes with the ability to put feelings into words, leaving emotion to be mutely expressed by dysfunction of the body. (Rauch et al., in van der Kolk, 1996, p. 193)

To complicate matters, "There are few words in our language that adequately express pain. To express emotional or physical pain to another human being we often rely on metaphor" (Scott, 1999b, p. 149). These limiting factors, coupled with the emotion of shame, make the experience of talking about trauma and the pain of addiction difficult.

Prone to action, and deficient in words, these patients can often express their internal states more articulately in physical movement or in pictures than in words. Utilizing drawings and psychodrama may help develop a language that is essential for effective communication and for the symbolic transformation that can occur in psychotherapy. (van der Kolk, 1996, p. 195)

In seeking a path of wholeness it is important to include preverbal, non-verbal, and metaphorical ways of communication.

THE BROAD APPLICATION OF CREATIVE ARTS THERAPY

The creative arts psychotherapies may be practiced within the theoretical construct of any major counseling theory. In addition, the creative arts may be used in a variety of clinical settings including indoors, outdoors, inpatient, outpatient, individual, and group settings. Since the creative arts are able to take patients quickly to a great intra-psychic depth, it is necessary for the clinician to assess the strengths and vulnerabilities of the patient and match them with the assets and limitations of the treatment setting, as well as the most suitable art form.

The authors work as co-therapists for an inpatient program treating sexual and trauma recovery. We find the highly structured and supportive environment of this setting allows for a rich mixture of modalities to transform trauma, addictions, and the destructive thought processes associated with both.

Aside from cognitive-based therapy, our patients are offered a wide range of modalities such as equine therapy, adventure therapy, Chi Kung, and EMDR, as well as creative arts therapies (such as blind contour self-portraits, sand play, integrative movement, psychodrama, and individualized assignments). In this chapter we present our clinical observations of a life-sized silhouette, a timeline assignment, and a psychodrama.

The authors find psychodrama (role plays, reconstructions, and empty-chair work) to be a powerful intervention for addicts and trauma survivors. Psychodrama provides cathartic release, increased objectivity, preparation for integration of ego-dystonic material and disparate aspects of self, as well as an understanding of the importance of community. Drawing a life-sized silhouette or timeline, then presenting it in group therapy has a multi-layered effect. This process supplies structure to disclosure, challenges cognitive distortions, reveals patterns/themes of behavior, develops a more congruent life narrative, addresses trauma and body shame, and encourages proactive relapse prevention (Orzack & Ross, 2000).

THE EIGHT ESSENTIAL PROCESSES

All of the creative arts or experiential therapies, with the guidance of a skilled therapist, help evoke the essential processes necessary for wellness. There is no all-encompassing theory that defines art therapy. Rubin (1987) has stated that such a theory will be born out of the practice of creative arts psychotherapy and will include aspects of different theoretical disciplines. In 2002, Scott proposed a very succinct, distilled, set of seven processes that are essential in the practice of art therapy. These processes, listed below, may be used to structure one session or a long-term treatment plan. Originally published as seven essential processes, Scott recently added the process of balancing locus of control.

Authenticity

Art is used to identify, explore, and express emotions with integrity. The arts provide a safe ground for processing painful affect with color, line, texture, form, tone, timbre, rhythm, flow, movement, and shape. As individuals develop integrity and congruency with their emotions and thoughts, they experience empowerment.

Catharsis

An art form can be used to find a symbol that closely represents the person's inner world. Finding and portraying this symbol provides relief. Catharsis includes the purging process of recapitulation as defined by shamanistic practice (Abelar, 1992). Recapitulation is a review of the person's history with attention to what is "me" or "not me." Autobiographical artwork often produces the assertion "I am" or "I exist."

Projection

The art piece is used as a mirror of self. The use of projection as a creative therapy technique helps people bypass cognitive distortions and gain insight. For example, a patient creates a painting that is very chaotic and is able to recognize how it is a reflection of his or her own chaotic life.

Sublimation

Kramer (in Rubin, 1987) states that to sublimate is "to give symbolic vent to . . . pain" (p. 31). A Freudian definition of sublimation would be to transform primitive urges. A way to use sublimation for trauma survivors and addicts is to provide a safe place and space for the patient to channel negative energies into a creative process instead of against the self or others. Redirection and reframing may occur. A concrete example would be to have a patient who self-mutilates use felt-tip markers to draw his or her core emotions on a piece of paper or the body, rather than cut or burn skin. While sublimation is not a curative process it does help provide a safer period of time for the person to engage in processes that are curative. It also models a creative, rather than a destructive, process for discharging negative energies.

Balancing Locus of Control

Martin Luther King, Jr. said that life was a combination of fate and choice and that "freedom is the act of deliberating, deciding, and responding within our destined nature" (King, 1969, p. 90). We have a choice in how we respond to our fate and thereby shape our destiny. Whether or not one believes in fate, attention to locus of control helps us determine what we are able to control and what we need to accept.

Locus of control (LOC), a psychological construct developed by Rotter (1966), refers to the manner in which an individual perceives reinforcements or rewards. Reinforcement is seen as contingent either upon one's own behaviors, actions, efforts and skills or upon the actions of powerful others, luck, fate and chance. A LOC continuum is thus formed with rewards being externally dependent at one end and internally dependent at the other end. (Rosal, 1993, p. 231)

Balancing LOC is a bi-directional process in that some may need to internalize and others, externalize more, thereby helping the individual modify his or her own level of accountability or actions. For example, one patient wanted to create a psychodrama of all her bad boyfriends. While no one disputed that her boyfriends had been abusive, the treatment team decided it would be fruitful for a double (patient peer) to play *her* role in each relationship, instead of the roles of the boyfriends. It was revealed that in each relationship she dressed differently, cooked a different cuisine, and studied a different foreign language, frenetically changing herself like a chameleon. She realized, "I don't think I am loveable as I am." She made a commitment not to abandon herself again.

Identify Developmental Ego-States

It is essential to identify and honor the normative ego-states within all of us. For whatever reason an adult enters therapy, especially if in a crisis, there is often a bridge to a younger self that experienced a similar precipitating event at an earlier age. Due to the nature of art therapy, this bridge is made and both dimensions of self have the opportunity to heal. These multiple selves are revealed in the variety of maturational stages of art produced by the person in therapy. During a disinhibiting stage, the patient's art may look very childlike. This experience of multiple selves (and roles or archetypes) and the linking bridge needs to be consciously identified and addressed by the therapist.

Integration

It is essential to identify disparate parts of self such as, young and old, hopeful or depressed, rigid or wild, and integrate them. Another way to describe this process would be to integrate polarized energies, which can be done symbolically through the use of color or other media. Accomplishing integration is an ultimate task in developing maturity, balance, and wholeness. Integration is one of the curative processes.

Transcendence

This is the ability to transform self, others, or situations through a spiritual connection to a higher source. It is well documented that while producing art, many experience altered states of consciousness or hypnotic states (May, 1975). In this state, the experience of intentionality (as described by phenomenologists) can be realized. This is the ability to investigate the full experience of things without preconceived notions or reductionistic models of mankind (Betensky, in Rubin, 1987). This trance state provides a threshold for crossing into realms of what can be referred to as the cosmos, the collective unconscious, the inner self, or God, depending upon the person's spiritual orientation. It is here that we transcend the limitations of humanness and embrace multiple possibilities and greater potentialities, i.e., miracles.

Finally, it is through the process of making art that the artist/patient, embraces the cyclic process of creation, preservation, dissolution, and recreation. May (1975) said, "every act of creation is first of all an act of destruction" (p. 63). This process helps the artist accept the world in non-dualistic terms and gain acceptance of even the most difficult situations.

Although The Eight Essential Processes might be considered a stage theory, it isn't strictly sequential. It is more like a multi-dimensional game of billiards. The cue ball, which best represents authenticity, must touch all other stages. The eight ball represents transcendence, in that it is the last ball to be pocketed in order to win the game. If transcendence is arrived at prematurely, it is diminished and may become just another cognitive defense in an effort to skip the processes that are more challenging to embrace. It is important to support each patient's need for time and depth. Rogerian and Socratic methods of inquiry and dialogue are best suited for this model of creative arts psychotherapy. It may be disputed which stages are more important, whether the stages are just supportive or curative. What is most important is that all stages work together.

It is also important to respect each person's understanding of symbol and metaphor. There are obvious symbols in our world for love and peace. Most Americans could, even visually impaired, draw a quick visual symbol for both. It is important for the therapist not to assume the meaning of what appears to be a commonly accepted cultural or universal symbol. Especially with patients who have experienced trauma, even the most benign symbols may be imbued with or over laden by the trauma survivors' personal experiences and meanings. In World War II, the swastika had different meanings for different people, even within the same country. For a person affiliated with the Nazi party, the meaning was most likely national pride and optimism. For the victims of the atrocities of the Holocaust, the swastika meant despair, horror, profound loss, and often death. The German swastika is reversed, as if a mirror image, of a symbol used by Native Americans. In Native American traditions the swastika-like symbol represents the four winds and connection to spirit. With patients who have a history of trauma and/or addiction, sometimes seemingly positive symbols may be associated with tragic loss and be a trigger for intense, overwhelming emotions. One of the advantages of the creative arts psychotherapies is that the symbolic meanings associated with trauma and addiction can be identified, processed, and transformed in a safe environment.

CASE STUDY AND OVERVIEW
OF CREATIVE ARTS PSYCHOTHERAPIES

This section provides an overview and history of the life-sized silhouette and timeline assignments, as well as instructions for the patient. These drawing assignments, shown in Figures 1 and 2, are analyzed largely from the perspective of the patient, his choice of symbols, and his chosen meanings. This is followed by an overview, description, and analysis of our case study's psychodrama. We believe this section illustrates the transformation possible when using these creative art forms.

Description of a Life-Sized Silhouette

Life-sized silhouettes, sometimes called body maps (see Figure 1) have been used in addiction treatment centers across the country as an intervention to address body perception distortion inherent in the experience of those with eating disorders. They have been used to map patients' internal and external worlds, as well as their histories of trauma, addiction, and sexuality. Scott, in her doctoral research (1999a) on self-mutilation, incorporated life-sized silhouettes as an art method of inquiry to gather data on how, when, and where research participants physically hurt their bodies. This method of inquiry was included in order to help access the non-declarative/implicit memory of the research participants who contributed to the phenomenological study.

Few publications mention, much less explore in depth, the vast possibilities of life-sized silhouettes as a creative arts therapy modality.

FIGURE 1. Life-size silhouette shows patient-defined symbols of depression as grass-green top-right-to-down-left slants, anger as a red tornado, anxiety as a lavender grid, trauma as a dark-green bulls-eye target, severe trauma as yellow highlighting, love as a red top-right-to-down-left slants, grief as an orange-red broken heart, fear as a blue X inside a circle, and happiness as a yellow happy face.

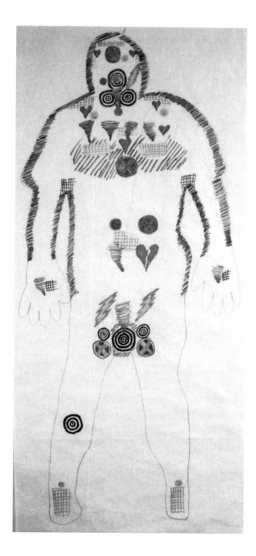

FIGURE 2. Timeline shows patient-defined symbols of grief as a navy blue spiral, fear and anxiety as a blue double cross with 8 prongs, general anxiety as a blue traditional 4-pronged equilateral cross, trauma as red top-right-to-down-left slants, additional trauma as red top-left-to-down-right slants, love addiction as a brown "X" inside a circle, sexual dysfunction and related anxiety as a blue circle, sexual experimentation as a pale lime-green "S," sexual compulsivity as a brown "X," periods of high volatility as a gentle wavy line and the words "high volatility" in purple, substance abuse as a wavy line in blue with navy-blue speckles, and workaholism-fitness extremist as a red spiked wavy squiggle.

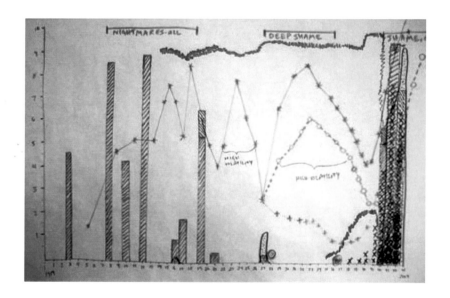

Liebmann (1993) makes a brief reference to it in her handbook of themes, games, and exercises. In 2001, Scott began to refer to the life-sized silhouette as a life-sized silhouette mandala due to the relationship between the two. "Mandala is a Hindu word derived from Sanskrit meaning circle or center" (Cox in Malchiodi, 2003, p. 428). According to Jung (1973), who brought the eastern practice to western psychology, a mandala represents a symbol of wholeness or the totality of self. "Unlike a diary, a linear account, the mandala acts in the manner of gestalt for retrospective reflection" (Kellogg, 1978, p. 3). This may also be said of the life-sized silhouette.

A tracing of the circumference of the whole body is a more concrete representation of the totality of self, than a drawing within a circle. This fact does not diminish the power of traditional mandalas as a therapeutic practice. It does point out the obvious similarities. What emerges from the creation of a mandala and a life-sized silhouette is often a surprisingly honest, complete, comprehensive exploration of self, traumatic history, and addictions. Patients describe having "ah-ha" moments while preparing, drawing, and later presenting their work to group members.

Description of a Timeline

The patient uses the timeline (see Figure 2) to tell his or her life story, from beginning to the present. Boriskin (2004) refers to a timeline as "an objective history tracking tool" (p. 86). Often the patient will develop insight when creating the timeline before the presentation. It is not uncommon, for example, for a person who is sexually addicted to notice that when he or she is not acting out sexually, his or her alcohol consumption increases. The relationship between multiple or cross addictions becomes clear. The link between trauma, grief, loss, and compulsivity usually becomes obvious even to the most defended person. It is interesting to note how creative and individualistic each timeline can be. More than a few patients have made up their own stages of maladaptive maturational development. Patients often portray geographical moves, historical events, or even changes in culture as impactful experiences.

How to Prepare the Client for Life-Sized Silhouette and Timeline Assignments

Before drawing the life-sized silhouette and/or timeline, the patient is asked to complete in writing all assigned first-step guides. These are based upon the principles of the twelve steps and include a biographical history of unmanageability and powerlessness as they relate to trauma and addictions. The majority of the questions in the guides are open-ended to encourage thoughtful reflection. Many patients have multiple addictions or co-morbidity, therefore, they may be given as many as 6 or 7 guides.

Next the patient is asked to list the following themes: core emotions, compulsivities/addictions, trauma, neglect, family dysfunction, self-harm, and illnesses/injury/accidents. Following the creation of themes, the patient is asked to create a legend. Each theme is to have its own patient chosen symbol. The symbol may be a color, a variety of lines, dots, arrows, dashes, or geometric shapes. Some patients use the same legend for both assignments and others choose different legends for the silhouette and the timeline.

Both assignments are completed on butcher-block paper, which is 3 feet wide. The patients are to use either felt tip pens or oil pastel crayons as the basic medium. They may also use cut out magazine pictures and words to add a collage effect. The use of sand, dirt, glitter, pipe cleaners, buttons, and objects of nature are also encouraged. Usually, these assignments are two-dimensional productions but sometimes they evolve into three-dimensional, sculptural-like pieces. To help with shame reduction patients are told that there is no wrong way to complete the assignments. They may scribble, cut, and tear if they want.

The life-sized silhouette drawing (see Figure 1) begins with a tracing of the outline of the patient's body on paper. Due to the fact that trauma survivors have difficulty with touch and boundaries, they are asked to choose a safe peer in treatment to trace the outline of his or her body. It is the one being traced who is to do the choosing, not the person doing the tracing. Both the tracer and the traced patient are encouraged to verbalize any fears or discomfort and to set boundaries accordingly.

The timeline drawing (see Figure 2) begins with a vertical and a horizontal axis. The horizontal axis plots chronological age. The vertical axis documents ratings of the intensity of an event or an addiction. The ratings of intensity are subjective units of disturbance (SUDS) determined by the patient on a scale of 1-10. The plot reveals the relationship between trauma symptomology and compulsivities.

Both life-sized silhouette and timeline illuminate the importance of the relational: the relation to self, others, addictions, and objects. It is the relational which is most undermined by trauma and addiction. This awareness is an important step in the reparative process.

Case Description

As a bright, creative, Caucasian, middle-aged man, the patient had built a successful business and a stable marriage with four beloved children. While some problems existed, the patient described life as "good." A few years prior to treatment the patient decided to have dental work to correct a relatively minor problem. The dental work evolved into a nightmare when he developed an infection. This resulted in numerous surgeries, excruciating pain for a year and a half, depression, and efforts to avoid and escape emotional and physical pain. Upon admission he described why he needed treatment, "alcoholism, smoking, and my wife thinks there might be sexual addiction and PTSD."

In spite of his struggle with addiction and trauma symptomology, he exhibited many resourceful coping skills throughout his lifetime, as well as a high motivation for recovery. After completing chemical dependency treatment, he elected to transfer to the program for sexual and trauma recovery for 3 weeks. His motivation for the transfer was to allow himself to feel more comfortable in his own skin, to heal the rift in his marriage, and to strengthen his capacity to achieve long-term sobriety. This was achieved through many modalities, including life-sized silhouette, timeline, and psychodrama. The patient presented all assignments in a primary group that met 3 times per week. He had a 3-hour psychodrama group once per week.

Case analysis of life-sized silhouette and timeline. The patient used both his life-sized silhouette and his timeline to present his biopsychosocial history in one group session. He used the assignments to describe his family of origin, his personality, his relationship to family members, the progression of his addiction(s), and significant early childhood traumas, including a gang rape by strangers. As he told his story with the support of the therapist, he was able to address cognitive distortions. For example, his problems in school were associated with the rape at age twelve, rather than low intelligence. As he processed the rape in more detail, it became clearer how and where he stored core emotions in his body. As he explored the link between the rape and his concerns with sexual dysfunction, experimentation, and romance addiction, he began to experience shame reduction. He began to understand how the unexpressed emotions resulting from the anal and oral rape had been triggered by problems with the infection in his jaw and the multiple surgeries.

Patients who are working on a very deep level not only tap into their own subconscious but also the collective unconscious, sometimes finding archetypal symbols within themselves, beyond their education or awareness. These archetypal symbols may clarify the trauma experience or foreshadow healing. The patient in our case study revealed an aspect of his rape that included racial victimization. He was in a foreign country at the time and his rapists called him "foreigner." Unbeknownst to the patient, he chose a Ku Klux Klan symbol as his symbol of fear. It is the "X" within the circle (see Figure 1). It is also interesting to note that his placement of three bulls-eye target symbols joined together at his mouth, suggesting 3 traumas, look very much like an ancient Celtic symbol representing divinity. It may have been too soon for him to be transmuting his experience, but perhaps a foreshadowing of healing was present.

Upon seeing the bulls-eye target symbols, the patient's symbol for trauma, located at the genitalia and mouth on his drawing, the therapist asked an open-ended question. "If the symbol located at your genitalia and mouth is a target, what would it mean?" This opened a dialogue about sexual orientation and identity. It is not uncommon for adult survivors of child rape to question their experiences of gender. It sometimes becomes confused. During his treatment our case study patient explored his questions about bisexuality and sexual addiction. After investigating these issues, it was not clear that he was either bisexual or sexually addicted. In discussing his life-sized silhouette and timeline, the patient reframed his questions about his sexuality within the context of his life experiences, thereby decreasing his shame.

Our patient chose another symbol of conflict, the juxtaposition of the complementary colors red and green, to outline the upper half of his body. In fact, the patient was conflicted about his height and weight, a contributing factor in his compulsive exercise.

He chose red top-right-to-down-left slashes shown on the drawing of his chest to represent love. He chose green top-right-to-down-left slashes shown on the drawing of his genitalia to represent depression.

The lavender grid, which he drew on his feet, hands, belly, chest, armpits, shoulders, and the top of his head all represented to him his physiological responses to anxiety. Anxiety and depression were components of his PTSD and ameliorated as his trauma was processed. The patient's Beck Depression Inventory score dropped from 20 upon admission to 6 upon discharge and his Beck Hopelessness score dropped from 11 to 3.

The timeline in Figure 2 reveals several isolated, profound traumas, most before adulthood. He portrayed these with bar graphs colored in with a red top-right-to-down-left slant to represent trauma (as opposed to representing it as love in the silhouette). All of his traumas were experienced outside of the home, except at age 8, when the family house burned down.

By age thirteen or fourteen the patient began to use sports and athleticism as a form of recognition and escape from his trauma symtomology. He described this as the early beginnings of his workaholism and "fitness extremist." The fitness extremist line on his timeline starts at a young age and continues across the top of his graph, suggesting a high level of intensity. Then it drops significantly, at which time it is replaced by symbols for grief, fear-anxiety, romance addiction, sexual compulsivity, alcoholism, and trauma related to his dental work and subsequent infection. It is interesting to note that the patient's increased sexual dysfunction correlates with his sexual compulsivity. As the patient began to make connections between his past history and his present symptomology, he began to describe what had previously been indescribable.

Description of Psychodrama

Psychodrama can be described as creating a multidimensional visual of the patient's presenting problem, trauma, addiction, or relational dynamic, using peers and props. Moreno, the creator of psychodrama as a psychotherapeutic intervention in 1921, said, "Psychodrama puts the patient on a stage where he can work out his problems with the aid of a few therapeutic actors" (Moreno in Dayton, 1994, p. 10). The protagonist patient (main character or leading role) is instructed to select peers to play various individuals or parts of self (auxiliaries). The therapists direct the psychodrama and encourage patients to expect, to experience, and to welcome feelings as the psychodrama unfolds. Skills such as breathing and grounding techniques to tolerate the feelings are described. For many, this becomes the first time they allow themselves to experience uncomfortable feelings, rather than literally or metaphorically running away from them. The purpose is to give the patient protagonist an opportunity to experience a missed developmental stage, to associate with his or her formerly dissociated self, or to begin to nurture child ego-states. Thus, psychodrama becomes a nurturing and corrective experience. Just as important as the psychodrama, is the feedback from group members about the feelings they experienced while participating in or observing the psychodrama. The emotional vulnerability of the protagonist allows peers the possibility of emotional vulnerability in kind. As directors, the therapists guide the patient to describe relational and emotional aspects of the scene and help create them visually in the room or on the stage. When the therapists are guided, however, by intuition, spontaneity, and intent listening to the words and actions of the protagonist and auxiliary roles, powerful, beautiful, and many times unexpected transformations materialize; thus, the sacredness of this creative art therapy.

Case analysis of a psychodrama. The patient in our case study first described the traumatic event as he set up the therapy room to represent the memory of his childhood home. The patient created a scene from age 8 when his house burned to the ground. Second, he chose patient peers to represent himself as a child and his family members (auxiliary roles).

Although only 8 years old at the time, the patient carried misappropriate feelings of guilt and shame from the event. He described himself as struggling, wiggling, and fussing while his mother tried to wash his hands. He thought his mother was frustrated with him for fidgeting. Somehow a candle was knocked over, setting the curtains on fire. The next thing he remembered was hearing his father yelling for them to get out of the house. He remembered seeing his father run through the smoke, pick up his mother, who was holding him in her arms, and carry both of them out over the flames. The patient saw his father as the hero and himself as the culprit or the guilty one. During the enactment by his peers, as he watched the scene played out before him, he regressed into terror. He hunched over, his toes pointed inward like a small boy, and he appeared frozen in shock. With direction from the therapist, he was able to ground himself. With this patient's permission the scene was replayed again; this time the patient was asked to rescue himself emotionally and spiritually from the event. He jumped into the flames (symbolically represented by whirling scarves), took his inner child by the hand, and led him to safety. He comforted the double (a peer representing his inner child-self), and explained to him that he was too little to have rescued his family, "Your legs were too small to carry anybody," and "It wasn't your fault that a fire was started in our home or that the house burned down." "It was Dad's job to help us; he was a grown up." As the patient continued his dialogue with his double (inner child-self), he was asked to switch roles back and forth until it was clear that the patient harbored no more false guilt. The patient then integrated his child ego-state into his heart for safety. Tearfully, the patient described how he felt more whole and complete. As the patient processed his experience of the psychodrama, he reiterated something he had always known, that his father had been a hero by rescuing their physical bodies from the fire. More importantly, he recognized that he, himself, was a hero for his inner child ego-state by rescuing him emotionally, physically, and spiritually from the flames of misappropriated guilt. At this point the patient began to weep deeply from relief.

CONCLUSION

"Human salvation lies in the hands of the creatively maladjusted" (King, 1969, p. 24).

Post treatment, the patient reported that reading The Eight Essential Processes "provided me with a strong foundation of understanding; this has allowed me to allocate that much more credibility to my treatment. I understand so much more, and consequently, feel more empowered in myself, and in my recovery." He went on to illuminate his experience of the processes.

In the following quote the patient described authenticity, "When I arrived at treatment, I had a very difficult time identifying my emotions. I couldn't understand what I felt, much less articulate my feelings. I knew there was sorrow and shame, and hope and happiness with the prospect of treatment. But I did not understand, and therefore could not explain, the longstanding pain in my loins, and the ache in the pit of my stomach." As treatment progressed the patient smiled less and became more congruent, for example, looking sad when he felt sadness. Another example of his development of authenticity occurred during psychodrama, when he allowed himself to regress into terror while patient peers played out the fire scene, then, wept with relief as he came to understand his innocence.

The expression of deep emotions, as described above, is also an example of catharsis. In speaking of catharsis related to the life-sized silhouette assignment and his rape at age 12, he said, "I felt very safe. The hard shell of composure was unnecessary, and I let my hands go to work. The best way I can describe it is that they were drawing of their own free will; my cognitive state was in low gear. Interestingly, athletics is the only other activity where I have experienced this. For the first time I can remember (other than sports), I didn't try to think my way through something." He went on to say, "My testicles felt like they were drawn up inside of my body as if in a too-tight corset. The pain in my belly was so strong that I recall I was almost doubling over. The dull aches had become acute, and then began to subside as we talked about the body map." As the patient found and processed symbols for his internal world, he felt relief.

One aspect of catharsis includes autobiographical review of a patient's history. Autobiographical review was a continuous thread that ran through the tapestry of this patient's total treatment.

The essential process of projection was also woven into every aspect of the patient's treatment in that aspects of his story and self were portrayed either onto a piece of paper or acted out in a psychodrama for him to observe.

Sublimation was achieved as the patient's self-destructive drives were channeled into creative modalities, such as life-sized silhouette mandala, timeline, psychodrama, and other experiential therapies.

Balancing locus of control (LOC) is referenced in the patient's commentary about how severely he was traumatized by the fire at age 8, "I sense the causality of the fire, and my wriggling may be significant in the level of trauma experienced." Here the patient begins to understand how his misperception of guilt for the fire exacerbated his deep experience of traumatization. As he correctly externalized LOC, the responsibility of the fire, into the hands of fate (as an accident), it helped him reduce his sense of shame and fear.

Regarding identifying and integrating developmental ego-states he said, "Art gave me the language to become emotionally literate, if only for a while. Art therapy helped me bridge my current state to the traumatic events; psychodrama, somatic therapy, and EMDR gave me an opportunity to heal the younger self, and liberate the older self." This can be said of psychodrama, whether in the role of protagonist, auxiliary, or observer. As he witnessed a peer's psychodrama he said, "Observing his (another peer's) psychodrama resulted in a very odd happening . . . I think that you call it dissociation. Never in my drunkest state did I separate from my body like that. I hadn't noticed any strong emotions during the psychodrama other than empathy; as we sat back down in the circle my mind flitted back to the image of a broken little ten-year old boy lying by the window. At that point, I felt I left the present world, and that image dissolved into one of me lying on a rock outcropping as a twelve-year-old boy. I was hovering over my younger self; feeling powerless to act. I don't know how long I had been watching . . . it could have been ten seconds, it could have been 60 seconds. As I was floating, I heard somebody address me; part of me realized that I was in the present, but I remained transfixed on the body of the small boy who is my daughter's age. I could not take my eyes off of him; I wanted to shoulder his pain; I knew I was being tugged back to the present, but I did not want to leave that spot hovering over the body. It wasn't until I made eye contact with you, that I realized it was safe to return. I understood that in the present with you, the little boy was going to find healing." In fact, the patient did practice integration when, on another occasion, he brought a younger aspect of himself into his heart. This is a process he may need to repeat in outpatient therapy, as various traumas or developmental ego-states surface to be healed. Each time this process is repeated he will feel stronger and more whole.

The trance state is one part of transcendence. The patient made reference to a trance phenomenon on several occasions, for example, while his hands "were drawing of their own free will," or "I was hovering over my younger self." It is noteworthy that transcendence is fluid and cyclical, hard to fully capture permanently without conscious effort and devoted attention. More than just a trance state, transcendence is included in the patient's comments about the fire in his home, "The psychodrama of my 8-year-old self was a powerful and moving experience for me. I'm not sure the term 'catharsis' is strong enough to describe the impact of my session. Liberating would be a term I would also use; the freedom from the deep wounds that were destroying me. The wounds are still there, but I feel empowered with the freedom to move on, and to rebuild my life."

The Eight Essential Processes, as a model for creative arts psychotherapy, may be used to structure one session, as well as short-term, or long-term treatment. Liberation isn't a quick fix, like a drug or an addiction. It is a beautiful, creative process of self-discovery that manifests throughout one's lifetime.

REFERENCES

Abelar, T. (1992). *The sorcerers' crossings: A woman's journey.* New York: Penguin Books USA Inc.

Boriskin, J. A. (2004). *PTSD and addictions: A practical guide for clinicians and counselors.* Center City, MN: Hazelden Foundation.

Dayton, T. (1994). *The drama within: Psychodrama and experiential therapy.* Deerfield Beach, FL: Health Communications, Inc.

Fincher, S. F. (1991). *Creating mandalas: For insight, healing and self-expression.* Boston: Shambhala Press.

Jung, C. G. (1973). *Jung extracts: Mandala symbolism.* Princeton, NJ: Princeton University Press.

Kellogg, J. (1984). *Mandala: Path of beauty.* Williamsburg, VA: ATMA, Inc.

King, M. L. (1963, 1969, 1977, 1986). Strength to love. Glasgow, Great Britain: William Collins Sons & Co.

Liebmann, M. (1986, 1993). *Art therapy for groups: A handbook of themes, games and exercises.* Cambridge, MA: Brookline Books.

Malchiodi, C. A. (Ed.). (2003). *Handbook of art therapy.* New York: Guildford Press.

May, R. (1975). *The courage to create.* New York: Bantam Books.

Ochs, C. & Olitzky, K. M. (1997). *Jewish spiritual guidance: Finding our way to God.* San Francisco: Jossey-Bass Publishers.

Orzack, M. H. & Ross, C. J. (2000). Should virtual sex be treated like other sex addictions? *Sexual Addiction & Compulsivity.* 7, 113-125.

Rogers, N. (1993). *The creative connection: Expressive arts as healing.* Palo Alto, CA: Science and Behavioral Books.

Rosal, M. L. (1993). Comparative group art therapy research to evaluate changes in locus of control in behavior disordered children. *The Arts in Psychotherapy,* 20, 231-241.

Rotter, J. B. (1966). Generalized expectancies for internal versus external control reinforcements. *Psychological Monographs: General and Applied.* 80 (1, Whole No. 609).

Rubin, J. A. (Ed.). (1987). *Approaches to art therapy: Theory and technique.* New York: Brunner/Mazel.

Scott, E. H. (1999a). The body as testament: A phenomenological study of chronic self-mutilation by women who are dissociative. (Doctoral dissertation, The Union Institute, 1999). *Dissertation Abstracts International,* 1999, 290. (UMI No: 921604).

Scott, E. H. (1999b). The body as testament: A phenomenological case study of an adult woman who self-mutilates. *The Arts in Psychotherapy,* 26 (3), 149-164.

Scott, E. H. (Speaker). (2002). *Expressive arts therapy: The seven essential processes.* (CD No. 2 of Mind-Body Conversations). Tucson: University of Arizona Associate Fellowship in Integrative Medicine.

Scott, E. H. (2004). *The seven essential processes.* Retrieved January 30, 2005, from http://www.artmanna.com

Van der Kolk, B. A. (1996). The complexity of adaptation to trauma self-deregulation, stimulus discrimination, and characterological development. In B. A. van der Kolk, A. C. McFarlane, & L. Weisaeth (Eds.). *Traumatic stress* (pp. 182-213). New York: Guilford Press.

Forgiveness Therapy
in Psychological Trauma
and Chemical Abuse Treatment

John M. Schibik, PhD, LPC, LCADC

SUMMARY. This chapter explores the role of forgiveness in treating comorbid psychological trauma and substance abuse disorders. Firstly, we will discuss the rationale for introducing forgiveness into treatment. Secondly, we will explore the neurological and psychological processes involved in the cross-contamination of trauma, substance abuse, and chronic unforgivness. Thirdly, we will describe the condition of unforgiveness, and the character strengths needed to resolve it. Fourthly, we will discuss the nature of forgiveness, the benefits of forgiveness, and the misconceptions about forgiveness. Finally, we will present eight phases of treatment for helping the traumatized substance abuser learn how to forgive self, to ask and receive forgiveness, and to forgive others. *[Article copies available for a fee from The Haworth Document Delivery Service: 1-800-HAWORTH. E-mail address: <docdelivery@haworthpress.com> Website: <http://www.HaworthPress.com> © 2006 by The Haworth Press, Inc. All rights reserved.]*

KEYWORDS. Forgiveness therapy, chemical abuse treatment, psychological trauma

[Haworth co-indexing entry note]: "Forgiveness Therapy in Psychological Trauma and Chemical Abuse Treatment." Schibik, John M. Co-published simultaneously in *Journal of Chemical Dependency Treatment* (The Haworth Press, Inc.) Vol. 8, No. 2, 2006, pp. 227-253; and: *Psychological Trauma and Addiction Treatment* (ed: Bruce Carruth) The Haworth Press, Inc., 2006, pp. 227-253. Single or multiple copies of this article are available for a fee from The Haworth Document Delivery Service [1-800-HAWORTH, 9:00 a.m. - 5:00 p.m. (EST). E-mail address: docdelivery@haworthpress.com].

INTRODUCTION:
WHY FORGIVENESS THERAPY?

Why focus on unforgiveness and forgiveness in healing traumatized substance abusers? Psychologists have demonstrated that forgiveness is effective for physical and mental health (Enright & Fitzgibbons, 2000; Plante & Sherman, 2001). Some social scientists argue that revenge is deeply ingrained in the biological, psychological, and cultural levels of human nature (McCullough & Witvliet, 2002). Some neurobiologist, suggests that the brain has evolved to specifically accommodate forgiveness that is necessary for our survival and our psycho-social-spiritual development. Newberg et al. (2002) discuss how forgiveness is a more evolved biological, psychological and cultural response to life-threat than revenge.

Specialists agree that psychological trauma and the negative consequences of substance abuse shatter the neurological and psychological strengths needed for psycho-social-spiritual development (Ouimette & Brown, 2003). Generally, therapy intends to restore these strengths. Forgiveness therapy, in particular, focuses on restoring the strengths needed to resolve conflicts within self, and to resolve the conflicted relationship between the offended and offender. Forgiveness is a preferred therapy in restoring the character strengths needed to overcome severe intrapersonal, interpersonal, and transpersonal damage (Affinito, 1999; Casarjian, 1992; Flanigan, 1992 & 1996; Janoff-Bulman, 1997; Miller, 2003; Rutledge, 1997). However, no research has been done to test the effects of resolving unforgiveness and applying forgiveness therapy in healing the comorbid disorders of trauma and substance abuse (Enright & Fitzgibbons, 2000). This chapter explores the parameters of how forgiveness can be helpful.

We need to be clear about the function of forgiveness in healing trauamtized substance abusers. Forgiveness is a process of internal growth that leads to a choice to surrender one's instinct to punish an offender, including self, when an offense causes serious damage to mind, body and spirit (McCullough, Pargament, & Thoresen, 2000). Immediately, we see that forgiveness has more to do with change in the offended person than in the offender. This understanding is critically important with persons who have experienced severe interpersonal trauma. In the context of this chapter, forgivenesss is a radical positive change in the offended person's perspective of psychological trauma and substance abuse. A positive perspective leads to a choice to extend empathy, compassion, and justice to an offender whether or not the offender assumes responsibility for the damage, and whether or not the offender changes (Enright & Fitzgibbons, 2000). Self-forgiveness, as well as asking and receiving forgiveness, is the foundation for forgiving serious transgressors. The choice to forgive is possible because the offended person changes and develops new attitudes, affects and actions toward self and transgressors (Worthington, 1998).

New breeds of research-practitioners have suggested that forgiveness can heal the mind, body, and spirit damaged by trauma and substance abuse (Enright & Fitzgibbons, 2000; McCullough, Pargament, & Thoresen, 2000). There is academic and anecdotal support for the role of forgiveness in treating traumatized substance abusers (Enright & Fitzgibbons, 2000). However, we need to understand the specific knowledge, attitudes and skills needed to help traumatized substance abusers forgive self and others (Enright & Fitzgibbons, 2000). We ask whether there can be posttraumatic growth without forgiveness (Tedeschi & Calhoun, 2004).

Therapists know that healing traumatized substance abusers takes place across the intrapersonal, interpersonal, and transpersonal self (Copeland & Harris, 2000; Miller, 2003; Najavits, 2002; Williams & Poijula, 2002). Trauma and substance abuse severely damages psychological strengths at all three levels. Forgiveness operates at all three personal levels. It requires the *cultivation of character strengths* needed to enhance personal dignity, integrity, identity, and efficacy. This therapeutic focus on cultivating character strengths is not unlike Najavits (2002) approach to "restore ideals that have been lost" (p. 8). Her intention is to help clients "aim for what they can be" and restore the beliefs that were destroyed, including the values of honesty, commitment, respect, integration, self-protection, and self-nurturing. We agree that these character strengths are linked to healing PTSD-SUD. In this chapter, we seek to more clearly explore the nature and purpose of specific character strengths in unraveling the comorbidity of symptoms. Specifically, we seek to understand the effects of treating unforgiveness, and to enhance the effects of forgiveness in dismantling the interactive symptoms of PTSD-SUD.

This chapter proposes a set of character strengths that heal the common neurological and psychological damage done by trauma, unforgiveness, and substance abuse. We seek to identify the essential character strengths needed to resolve this comorbid condition. We focus on the character strengths needed to heal unforgiveness, and to facilitate the process of self-forgiveness, asking and receiving forgiveness, and extending forgiveness to transgressors.

WHEN FORGIVENESS THERAPY?

When to integrate forgiveness therapy into trauma and chemical abuse treatment has not been clearly examined. Before we focus on healing the neurological and psychological wounds, the client must be physically, psychologically, and spiritually safe. Najavits (2002) offers the only empirically grounded integrative (i.e., treating PTSD-SUD simultaneously) program to restore client safety. Once the client is anchored in safety the work of healing the loss of self and relationships can begin. There are precedence in addressing unforgiveness and forgiveness in the process of healing substance abuse and psychological trauma.

The Twelve Step Model of chemical dependency recovery offers a program aimed at healing damage done to mind, body, and spirit (Kurtz & Ketcham, 1996). This recovery program is saturated with principles and practices of forgiveness and reconciliation relative to chemical abuse. Twelve step sponsors cautiously guide a person in "making amends" after the person is stabilized and anchored in relapse prevention attitudes and actions (B. Hamilton, 1996). Anecdotal evidence reports success. Step 10, in the Twelve Step Model of Recovery, calls for living a life of daily forgiveness and reconciliation. However, no empirical study demonstrates the effects of forgiveness on sobriety within the AA/NA model.

Trauma treatment specialists have cautioned about when, how and if forgiveness should be fostered in clients (Herman, 1997; Linn, Linn, and Linn, 1997; Miller, 2003). Other trauma specialists cultivate the principles of forgiveness while not using the language of forgiveness (Najavits, 2002). Recently, some trauma specialists have fostered forgiveness as an integral part of treatment (Miller, 2003). Indirectly, trauma models and substance abuse models support an approach which focuses on the *cultivation of new character strengths*, such as empathy, tolerance, courage, honesty, surrender, perspective, self-control, gratitude, prudence, etc. Each of these character strengths are created and supported by a set of life management skills (Miller, 2003; Miller & Guidry, 2001; Najavits, 2002; Schraldi, 2000; Williams & Poijula, 2002). Forgiveness is part of a matrix of 24 character strengths proposed by positive psychology that contribute to personal happiness (Seligman, 2002). Just as unforgiveness fosters misery, forgiveness fosters wellness.

In summary, forgiveness may be an effective therapy for traumatized substance abusers precisely because it facilitates a new experience of self, a new experience of people who hurt people, and a new experience of how we heal our hurts. Processing these new experiences in therapy, the person develops a specific set of character strengths that can help restore the natural process of psycho-social-spiritual development.

Sean is an example of a person who learned the character strengths needed to resolve unforgiveness and practice forgiveness. This therapy helped in healing the intrapersonal, interpersonal, and transpersonal wounds of psychological trauma and substance abuse.

> Sean, a 30 year old son of an alcoholic father and mother, was referred to counseling by his AA sponsor after he had relapsed for a 6 month period. Over 5 years Sean experienced abstinence from alcohol and an uneasy sobriety. His relapse to drinking was precipitated by a crisis at work and at home, and was linked to his chronic aggression, anxiety and sadness. These moods were exacerbated by the death of his active alcoholic father. Sean suggested that the current crises made him aware of how much he ruminated with anger, sadness, anxiety over the hurts he had experienced from his parents and siblings. He ruminated with shame and guilt over the painful consequences of his drinking. He felt powerless and overwhelmed by memories of past wounds. Ordinary coping skills helped him stabilize in recovery, but did not resolve the damage done to his self and relationships. His sponsor suggested that Sean engage counseling to resolve the crises, tragedy, and trauma of his life. During several interviews Sean became aware of the 'constant background noise' of unforgiveness that dominated his life. Years ago, he had superficially made amends to his wife and children, but never undertook a full forgiveness process.
>
> In order to curb his drinking he was referred to a residential program for detoxification, stabilization, and relapse education. As part of an aftercare program, we addressed being stuck in unforgiveness, and his inability to forgive himself, to ask-receive forgiveness, and to forgive transgressors.

AN INTEGRATED PROBLEM

The literature provides no theoretical link between the psychological and neurological damage done to traumatized substance abusers, the development of the state of unforgiveness, the process of forgiveness, and specific changes needed to restore the person to intrapersonal, interpersonal, and transpersonal development. The following discussion seeks to pinpoint the disabling features of comorbid PTSD-SUD in the mesolimbic system of the brain. We will discuss how creating specific character strengths, in the context of an environment of care, competence and challenge, can heal the specific neurological and psychological damage of trauma, unforgiveness, and substance abuse.

Tedeschi and Calhoun (2004) raise the question whether there can be posttraumatic growth without forgiveness. The damage done by trauma and substance abuse is an interconnected neurological and psychological process. Psychological processes include sensing, perceiving, imagining, feeling, thinking, deciding, acting, relating, and planning. As these processes are healed the damage to key brain processes is healed. The healing process requires more than new life management skills. It requires the reconstruction of personal traits through the cultivation of character strengths by engaging and resolving current crises (Tedeschi & Calhoun, 2004). Essential to this new way of being and behaving is resolving unforgiveness and practicing forgiveness. Had the client forgiven self and others as part of managing trauma and/or substance abuse, s(he) may not have developed the symptoms of trauma, substance abuse, and the state of unforgiveness. To heal the entrenched state of unforgiveness we need to understand the neuro-psychological connection among all three conditions.

Researchers of psychological disorders seek to understand the neurological processes behind the disorders in the DSM IV TR classification system. The symptoms of PTSD, SUD, and unforgiveness are associated with the mesolimbic system of the brain (Brick & Erickson, 1998; Newberg et al., 2001; Ouimette & Brown, 2003). The three conditions of trauma, substance abuse, and unforgiveness are linked in the same survival-reward pathway of the brain. This pathway integrates memory, meaning-making, emotion, motivation, and imagination (hence forward called "5Ms"). These five brain processes are impaired by trauma, substance abuse, and unforgiveness. Therapy for unforgiveness and forgiveness involves the cultivation of specific character strengths needed to release the mesolimbic system from a defensive focus caused by chronic trauma and substance abuse (Ouimette & Brown, 2003; Newberg et al., 2000). Once released the 5Ms can function on behalf of psycho-social development.

The mesolimbic system functions to evaluate environment and to protect and direct our activity toward our best interests in keeping with our core beliefs about self, others, and life. When healthy, the pathway generates experiences of safety, reward, relief, and control that support psycho-social development. When the mesolimbic system is healthy it differentiates and integrates positive and negative life experiences into development. Distress and crises are sorted out and resolved. Natural resolution of distress and crises creates character strengths (e.g., the internalized strengths of trust, tolerance, and temperance) that empower us to manage future adversity (Bradshaw, 1990; Erikson, 1964). Even tragedy is overcome in the course of most life challenges. However, trauma, by definition, is more radical than crises and tragedy. Trauma shatters more than the coping skills needed for physical, psychological and ontological survival. Psychological trauma shatters our trust in self and others, and our ability to continue our psycho-social-spiritual development (Janoff-Bulman,1997; Kauffman, 2002). Forgiveness aims to restore the innate capacities for psycho-social-spiritual development. Forgiveness is a self-corrective and self-creative learning process which cultivates the character strengths needed to resolve the devastating effects of trauma. These same character strengths have been shown to facilitate recovery from chemical abuse which is rooted in the reward-relief-control processes of the mesolimbic system, and which contaminates these processes in pursuit of survival (Bick & Erickson, 1998; Kurtz & Ketcham, 1996; Ouimette & Brown, 2003).

In traumatized substance abusers the 5Ms are impaired. A state of unforgiveness easily develops, but is not easily resolved. Unforgiveness seeks to rescue the person from the damage done to the differentiating and integrating processes of memory, meaning-making, emotion, motivation, and imagination (5Ms). These functions become separated from their integrative function, and become fix-focused on survival. Psycho-social-spiritual development is thwarted. Continual unresolved crises, plus increased negative consequences of chemical abuse, and increased unforgiveness creates more damage to the 5Ms. The neurological damage results in a deep psychological damage to personal safety, identity, efficacy, and relationships (Bremner, 2002). Healing traumatized substance abusers is not merely a matter of restoring coping skills. Wellness requires new character strengths based on the innate capacities of self-development. We know that positive psychological (i.e., sensing, perceiving, imagining, feeling, thinking, deciding, acting, relating, and planning) changes can heal damage to the brain. We need to create and direct specific psychological administrations to the mesolimbic region of the brain. These will refocus the reward-relief-control processes toward the whole self, and not merely toward survival. The forgiveness process can release the person from the negative influence of personal failure, vulnerability, and fallibility (through self-forgiveness), and from the negative influence of offense and offenders. Once released, the person can continue psycho-social-spiritual development through the standard practices of trauma and substance abuse therapy.

AN INTEGRATED CHANGE PROCESS

Researchers trace the neurophysiology of forgiveness to a distinct area of the brain responsible for physical, psychological, and ontological survival (Fincham & Kashdan, 2004). Somehow, in traumatized substance abusers, survival, reward, relief, and control become commingled and distorted. Under these conditions a state of unforgiveness toward self and other develops. Unforgiveness is not only a defense for physical survival. It provides temporary psychological and ontological safety. Survival is not only physical, but psycho-social and spiritual. Part of restoring the healthy functions of the 5Ms is to cultivate the specific character strengths/virtues needed to reduce unforgiveness by untangling the enmeshment of survival, reward, relief, and control. This process opens the way to learn the process of forgiveness. Newberg et al. (2000) strongly argues that forgiveness operates to restore the mesolimbic pathway (the 5Ms), which is necessary for intrapersonal, interpersonal, and transpersonal development (Newberg et al., 2000).

We have innate capacities for development grounded in our biology by an evolutionary process (Peterson & Seligman, 2004). These innate powers are turned into character strengths as we encounter and overcome the daily struggle of psycho-social development (Erikson, 1964). For example, to overcome the insidious power of the disease of chemical dependency a person needs to cultivate the character strengths of honesty, humility, surrender, gratitude, tolerance, empathy, compassion, and justice (Kurtz & Ketcham, 1996). As these character strengths are cultivated the person experiences a release from the restricted focus on survival of the mechanisms of reward, relief, and control. In the language of humanistic psychology the person's natural capacity for self-actualization is restored. The person experiences a restoration of the 5Ms to their natural functions on behalf of psycho-social development.

In summary, reducing the condition of unforgiveness helps untangle the focus of reward, relief and control mechanisms from the survival mode. Therapy for unforgiveness provides the character strengths needed to thrive again, and to move toward forgiveness. Positive sensing, thinking, feeling, acting, imagining, relating, and planning heals neurological damage and creates new psychological strengths. These strengths beget development, and development begets more character strength to continue the recovery process.

In this next section, we will identify the specific strengths needed to overcome unforgiveness, and to initiate healing the 5Ms of the meso-limbic system. These character strengths lay the foundation for learning self-forgiveness, to ask and receive forgiveness, and to forgive those who have seriously offended us.

UNFORGIVENESS DEFINED

Therapy for traumatized substance abusers involves the resolution of unfinished business. Unfinished business is defined as lingering negative feelings, repetitive negative thoughts, and self-defeating actions related to serious unresolved hurts (Malcolm & Greenberg, 2000). We focus on one aspect of unfinished business called 'unforgiveness.' We propose that chronic unforgiveness, whether conscious or unconscious, links the comorbid conditions of trauma and substance abuse. It keeps the person locked in a reactive posture toward unresolved conflict with self and offending others. Resolving unforgiveness means restoring a person to proactive mode. It opens the door to forgiveness work. Forgiveness therapy can clear the way to fruitful trauma and substance abuse treatment.

We examine the nature of unforgiveness as a primary defense system. Then we propose a specific set of character strengths that need to be developed in order to overcome unforgiveness.

The state of unforgiveness is a fixation of memory, emotion, meaning-making, imagination and motivation on survival. The natural flexibility of these five developmental processes becomes rigid. Worthington, Berry, and Parrott (2001) describe *unforgiveness* as:

> a complex of related emotions, consisting of resentment, bitterness, hatred, hostility, residual anger, and fear which are experienced after ruminating about a transgression. A transgression is perceived as a mixture of hurt and offense. To the extent that a transgression is perceived as hurt, the person responds immediately with fear. To the extent that a transgression is perceived as an offense, the person will respond immediately with anger. Fear and anger are not unforgiveness. Unforgiveness occurs when people ruminate about the event, its consequences, their own reactions to it, the transgressors' motives, and potential responses from the self

or the transgressor. Rumination can produce the emotions of resentment, bitterness, hatred, hostility, residual anger, and fear, which we call unforgiveness. (p. 108)

Tedeschi and Calhoun (1995) argue that rumination is the first defense against the impact of trauma. Ruminative thought arises in an effort to make sense out of the disarming impact of trauma. Whether trauma is accompanied by substance abuse or whether substance abuse follows upon trauma, the negative consequences of substance abuse can exacerbate ruminative thought. Trauma exceeds crisis in every way imaginable. Whereas crisis undermines coping skills, trauma undermines the person's beliefs about self and others (Kauffman, 2002). Rumination over traumatic events leads to the condition of unforgiveness. Unforgiveness artificially protects the fractured mind, body, and spirit from disintegration. As a defensive reaction, unforgiveness protects against additional hurt from an external aggressor or an internal accuser. Unforgiveness provides an artificial sense of power over powerlessness by focusing on survival rather than safety and development. By shifting the focus of the 5Ms toward survival, the natural differentiating and integrating functions of the mesolimbic system are restricted and contaminated. They become passive, reactive or aggressive. Their proactive, flexible, and creative movement is thwarted. The mesolimbic system becomes fixated on the wrong-done, the wrong-doing, and wrong-doer. It is not free to focus on differentiating and integrating hurts into total life development. Psychoactive chemicals along with other high risk behaviors provide a temporary experience of survival, reward, relief, or control. The person seeks to remove negative experiences by these self-defeating behaviors. However, the resolution of trauma and substance abuse requires new character strengths to overcome the defensive state of unforgiveness, and to restore healthy memory, imagination, emotion, motivation, and meaning to the process of development. If the key to restoration is the cultivation of specific character strengths, what symptoms of unforgiveness are these character strengths intended to overcome?

DYNAMICS OF UNFORGIVENESS

The core of unforgiveness has five possible components, namely, rumination, revenge, retaliation, resentment, and recrimination (Worthington, 1998; Worthington et al., 2001). We hypothesize these five dynamics (henceforward called: 5Rs) are resolved as the client creates specific character strengths. Cultivating specific character strengths can release the 5Ms to resume their natural function of providing safety, reward, relief, and control without the artificial help of substance use. The client can proceed toward self-forgiveness, asking and receiving forgiveness, and granting forgiveness to offenders. Having resolved the disposition of unforgiveness and attained a disposition of forgiveness, the client can proceed to resolve the complex symptoms of trauma and substance abuse.

Central to the dynamic of unforgiveness is the process of *rumination* over the physical, psychological, social, and spiritual devastation associated with trauma and substance abuse. Rumination is the recurrent and intrusive recollections of intrapersonal, interpersonal, and transpersonal losses. Trauma shatters a person across all areas of personality. The processes of sensing, perceiving, feeling, imagining, thinking, deciding, acting, planning, and relating are all disrupted. Therapy seeks to restore these to a healthy state of functioning. Intrapersonal losses involve doubt over one's ability to keep oneself safe. Interpersonal losses involve a breach of trust with others. Transpersonal losses involve shattered assumptions about the certainty and reliability of life itself. Ultimately, the resolution of *rumination* involves freeing memory and imagination. Remembrance no longer results in being overwhelmed by unresolved losses. Imagination is freed to *hope* in spite of vulnerability and fallibility. Rumination can resolve into the character strength of *integrity and self-control*. Calhoun and Tedeschi (1995) suggest that rumination can be resolved and set the conditions for posttraumatic growth if the person begins to make sense out of traumatic events, and to reshape their life assumptions relative to the trauma.

Unresolved rumination leads to revenge. *Revenge* makes one a prisoner of hate (Beck, 1999). Hate arises from extreme damage to self-identity and self-efficacy (Potter-Efron & Potter-Efron, 1991, 1995). Haters attack others or self with the intent to relieve their sense of extreme powerlessness. Hate is shame-based rage (Potter-Efron, 1999). A person who hates perceives offenses as unforgivable and demanding extreme punishment. There is no room for restitution, rehabilitation, or restoration (Beck, 1999; Flanigan, 1996). While intense anger is innate and spontaneous, aggression is a choice.

"Forgiveness is the classic antidote for hate" (Potter-Efron & Potter-Efron, 1995). The fastest way to temper hate is to recollect when and how the victim offended others. The victim recollects the times when he asked and received forgiveness for damage done to another's mind, body, and spirit. This process begins to create the character strengths of empathy, compassion, and justice. Each of these strengths involves a learnable set of intrapersonal, interpersonal and transpersonal skills (McKay, Rogers, & McKay, 1989). Together, they transcend the diminishing power of revenge, and enhance interpersonal and interpersonal strengths.

Retaliation is softer than revenge. Retaliation wants the offender to experience at least the same amount of pain. While the primary purpose of retaliation is punishment, the victim also wants the offender to change. The victim is willing to grow from punitive justice to rehabilitative and restorative justice (Enright & North, 1998). Once the debt is paid the offender is entitled to be reinstated to social grace. This reinstatement presumes that the offender accepts responsibility for the offense, and assumes accountability to change. Rehabilitative justice extends to the offender the resources to change. Restorative justice offers clemency to the offender as a way to challenge the offender to take responsibility. Restorative justice is a pure gift of mercy. Restorative justice does not mean restoration to the original state, prior to injury. Restorative justice overcomes injury by placing it in a more mature understanding of humanity's vulnerability, fallibility, and mortality. However, restoration is not reconciliation with the offender. The focus is not on the offender. Restorative justice means that the offended person takes responsibility to restore self to integrity and self-efficacy, and no longer links personal growth to change in the offender. Retaliation is resolved as the offended person cultivates a sense of justice, compassion, and mercy.

Resentment is a combination of anger toward the damage done and a distorted belief that the damage should not have happened. The focus is less on the offense or the offender than on the distorted shame-based-anger, and distorted belief of what should have been. Distorted shame-based-anger is rooted in an irrational idealism about the behavior of people, about self-competence, and/or the order of life. Flanigan (1996) points out four aspects of trauma that can lead to resentment. (1) Trauma shatters our assumption that other persons are predictable, consistent, and reliable. (2) Trauma fractures the belief in our personal ability to think, feel, act, and relate in your best interest. (3) Trauma contaminates intrapersonal safety, interpersonal safety, and transpersonal safety. (4) Trauma disrupts the belief that the universal and cosmic forces of life (including God) are fair, logical, good, providential, orderly, reliable and caring. Resentment fails to face the reality that bad things happen to good people, and that good people do bad things. The person feels powerless to resolve the chronic or acute hurts of life.

Resentment is resolved when the person moves from hardened anger to *regret.* Regret results from changed expectations. Regret balances what might have been with an understanding of why things were not as expected. "Regret is a more or less painful cognitive and emotional state of *feel sorry* for misfortunes, limitations, losses, transgressions, short-comings, or mistakes" (Landman, 1993). In moving from resentment to regret the person retains constructive anger, laced with sadness over the loss, plus the personal responsibility to heal oneself. Changing resent-ment into *regret* allows the victim to plan a new life to satisfy the very needs that were thwarted by the offense and offender. Ultimately, *resent-ment* can be resolved into regret by empathic understanding, rational thinking, wisdom, and hope.

Traumatized substance abusers engage in *self-recrimination* (Schraldi, 2000). This state of mind is fixed on the irrational demand that the client should have done something to stop the trauma or the process of addic-tion. Unhealthy shame and guilt often accompany the symptoms of trauma and substance abuse. The person judges self as not worthy of for-giveness, restoration or reconciliation (Potter-Efron & Potter-Efron, 1999). The resolution of self-recrimination is founded in overcoming in-ternalized shame and neurotic guilt, and working through the process of self-forgiveness. Self-forgiveness enables the person to accept and cor-rect the actual damage they did to themselves and others, and deciding to change. The change process involves the restoration of healthy guilt or healthy shame (Potter-Efron, 2002). When guilt is founded on real of-fense toward others, it is resolved by requesting, although not necessar-ily receiving, forgiveness. Healthy guilt challenges the person to change. Healthy shame is founded on the exposure of self as a wrong-doer, but not a bad person. Ultimately, *self-recrimination* is resolved by *the acceptance of self as fallible, vulnerable, responsible, and account-able.*

Resolving these 5Rs helps restore memory, motivation, emotions, meaning, and imagination on behalf of recovery. The person seeks safety and development rather than mere survival. Resolving the 5Rs opens the way to asking-receiving forgiveness as the way to self-for-giveness, and self-forgiveness as the foundation of forgiving devastating offenses.

Worthington et al. (2001) remind us that resolving unforgiveness is the first step in recognizing the need for self-forgiveness and asking-re-ceiving forgiveness. Healing unforgiveness can resolve the debilitating thoughts and feelings toward self and transgressors, but it does not automatically demand forgiveness of others. Treating unforgiveness is a necessary condition for forgiving others, but it is not an automatic process. As we shall see, to forgive serious offenses is a separate process and choice. Let us examine more closely the specific character strengths required to overcome unforgiveness. We will appreciate how this process lays the foundation for learning and practicing forgiveness.

HEALING UNFORGIVENESS

Worthington et al. (2001) suggests that the healthiest way to reduce the negative state of unforgiveness is to develop pro-social and pro-individual character strengths or virtues. This is not unlike the Twelve Step approach to building character strengths (Kurtz & Ketcham, 1996). In the earliest models of psychosocial development character strengths result from the resolution of psycho-social conflicts (Bradshaw, 1990; Erikson, 1964). Healthy environments facilitate the normal development of these strengths as we resolve developmental crises (Kegan, 1985). These strengths are the foundation of the resilience needed to overcome life crises, tragedy, and trauma (Reivich & Shatte, 2002). When the 5Ms are impaired the natural process of creating character strengths is also impaired. In therapy we 'jump start' the natural process by creating structured and strategic interventions aimed at restoring memory, imagination, motivation, emotion, and meaning-making to health.

Character strengths that enhance psycho-social development also decrease antisocial, destructive, and self-protective defenses. They increase self-efficacy and boundaries against interpersonal transgressions. This is the first phase of resolving unforgiveness. The second phase involves developing prosaically character strengths. Character strengths aimed at enhancing social harmony generate affinitive emotions. They motivate toward forgiveness and possible reconciliation (Worthington et al., 2001). In a therapeutic environment, the client is guided to create new character strengths out of the resolution of current psycho-social crises. In the process the 5Rs recede in prominence while the 5Ms advance in health. Resolving current crises with new resources provided by trauma therapy and twelve step programs can help the client create positive meaning, emotion, memory, motivation, and imagination. A new assumptive world is created out of the ashes of the old assumptive world (Kauffman, 2002).

Worthington et al. (2001) clarifies how seven particular character strengths or virtues resolve unforgiveness. *Self-Integrity* involves clarifying your principles, values, needs, wants, and preferences. Our primary needs are to be and to be safe. Trauma shatters the integrity of your assumptions about self and others, while substance abuse contaminates the mesolimbic system and its function to integrate hurts into self. A proactive response to devastation and disorder begins when you redefine who you are and who you will become in spite of the conditions of trauma and chemical disorder. These are conditions of life and do not define your whole self. This recognition opens the way to self-integrity. "Integrity involves the the pursuit of truth and the faithful sculpting of one's behavior in conformity to the way one perceives truth and goodness (p. 119). The person needs to understand the nature of the co-occurring disorders and his own fundamental goodness. The person needs to clarify personal rights, responsibilities, and boundaries vis á vis others. Self-integrity recognizes personal vulnerability, fallibility, and mortality. In Twelve Step language, self-integrity involves 'getting the first three steps': 'I have a problem'; 'My way has not worked'; 'I need and accept help.'

From self-integrity flows the second character strength of self-control or manageability. "*Self-control* may involve restraint of one's impulses to do harm to self or others, or it may involve delay of gratification" (p. 119). Therapy and Twelve Step programs can provide cognitive-behavioral strategies to enhance self-control. A *sense of justice* is the third character strength, which includes a restoration of balance after hurt has been done. Justice is rooted in responsibility and accountability, not in punishment. Demanding justice from another requires that we hold ourselves to the same standard of justice for the offenses we have committed, by omission or by commission, accidentally or deliberately. This is the function of steps 4 through 10 in the Twelve Step model of recovery.

A fourth strength is *peace or serenity*. Peace means the resolution of discordant events into harmony Cultivating peace involves using conflict, negotiation, and problem solving skills to create harmony out of tension; to create wholeness out of brokenness. These life management skills help activate the innate powers of self-efficacy, self-soothing, self-direction, self-correction, and self-fulfillment. When activated these innate powers provide a shelter in which safety, peace, and serenity can thrive. They not only provide enhanced coping skills, but they help recreate a new sense of self, and a new criteria for the choice of healthy relationships in recovery.

In summary these four character strengths restore the client's right to have rights, the responsibility to create a new life out of tragedy, and the powers to protect this new self from harm. The process, however, moves beyond the reestablishment of self in protective isolation.

Worthington et al. (2001) describe the power of warmth-based virtues/character strengths (empathy, humility, gratitude) for healing unforgiveness. *Empathy* facilitates altruistic behaviors. McCullough et al. (1997) demonstrated that empathy-based forgiveness mediates the interpersonal bridge that is broken by transgression. Empathy is learned by experiencing a non-judgmental helping relationship filled with active listening and unconditional regard. However, forgiveness is more than being validated by a disinterested other. It is more than social harmony. It involves the recognition that humans are bound to each other in survival in spite of our tendency to hurt each other. Compassion and mercy are two of the oldest virtues experienced and expressed by human beings (Peterson & Seligman, 2004). Newberg et al. (2000) argue that these strengths evolved as an essential way to protect our personal interests in society. *Humility*, a second affiliative virtue, facilitates forgiveness by acknowledging one's own real or potential transgressions and imperfections; a victim can experience empathy for the transgressor by experiencing and expressing a balanced sense of personal strengths and limits. *Gratitude* is a third affiliative virtue which acknowledges the fundamental social nature of our personal life and development. We are social beings, not isolated persons. In times of crisis, tragedy and trauma we need to recognize what others have done to help us survive and change our lives. These acts of benevolence can counteract acts of malevolence. Ultimately, gratitude is a psycho-social-spiritual ascent to the fact that our life is a gift given to us to cherish and cultivate in spite of crises, tragedy, and trauma. Our psycho-social-spiritual development is ultimately not destroyed by crises, tragedy and trauma. Gratitude is rooted in the intrapersonal, interpersonal, and transpersonal process of thriving beyond survival. This process, however, takes place in the healing environment of fellowship. In fellowship we find the care, competence, and challenge to sustain our efforts to resume natural psycho-social-spiritual development (Kegan, 1995). Recognizing that we thrive in social relationships opens the way to advocate for the rehabilitation, restoration and reconciliation of those who have offended us (Step 12). Kurtz and Ketcham (1996) outline the process of growing in these character strength by living the Twelve Step philosophy, principles and practices. Individuals learn these virtues by having the structured opportunity to practice them in structured therapeutic and fellowship relationships.

For Worthington et al. (2001) these seven strengths provide the character strengths to resolve unforgiveness. They lay the groundwork for learning how to forgive self, to ask-receive forgiveness, and to forgive grevious offenders. The process is developmental and incremental as we see in the case of Sean.

> For five years in recovery Sean had lived a life of unforgiveness and refused to make a 4th step inventory. He made amends only with his wife and children. He did not forgive himself, nor would he forgive those who had damaged him. Upon returning from in-patient treatment, Sean reported how much he learned about the connection between unresolved hurts and alcohol abuse. He was encouraged to address his unresolved crises, tragedies, and traumas in aftercare. The groundwork was set by the information he received in residential treatment about the nature of his comorbid illness. He appreciated his reluctance to investigate past hurts. He recognized that he was angry all the time and wanted to end the chronic 'background noise' of rumination, revenge, retaliation, resentment, and recrimination.
>
> Sean explored the character strengths he had developed over the years of recovery. He discovered psycho-social strengths that he had not developed, and we designed a plan to gain the strengths of integrity, control, justice, peace, empathy, humility, and gratitude. We examined the nature and process of unforgiveness and what attitudes, affects, and actions would be needed to overcome the 5Rs, to cultivate core virtues of recovery, and how these would help restore the 5Ms.
>
> The result, over many months, was a decrease in his focus on survival, and an increase in positive activities for safety, reward, relief, and control. He experienced a positive shift in memory, meaning, motivation, imagination, and emotions. This generated increased confidence and competence in his efforts to differentiate from negative life experiences and integrate them into his developmental processes. In the language of Stage of Change theory, Sean had moved out of the pre-contemplation and contemplation stage of change into the determination stage. He was ready to learn and practice the processes of forgiveness.

We contend that resolving unforgiveness is the logical first step. However, in clinical reality, addressing unforgiveness is integrated into self-forgiveness as well as asking-receiving forgiveness. These combined processes open the way to forgiving transgressors. The last step is the process and choice of resuming a reconciled relationship.

FORGIVENESS DEFINED

Therapy for unforgiveness and forgiveness therapy have continuous intentions. They seek to remove negative dispositions, and to instill positive dispositions toward offense and offender. Together, they intend to re-instate the natural positive processes of memory, emotion, meaning, imagination, and motivation toward healthy psycho-social development.

Forgiveness is commonly described as a process and a choice to surrender one's instinct and impulse to punish an offender. The forgiver acknowledges that his life was dramtically changed by the offense. Yet, he accepts responsibility for healing his own hurts. Additionally, he may offer resources to the offender to challenge the person to take responsibility and to change. Most importantly, forgiveness is about self, not about the transgressor. Integral to trauma symptoms is the fact that the traumatized person cannot shift focus away from the offender and offense. This fixed focus is contaminated by neurological damage done by chemical abuse. It is locked in place by the rumination of unforgiveness. Forgiveness therapy intends to shift the client's focus from the offense and offender to healing oneself (Enright & Fitzgibbons, 2000).

> Forgiveness is the accomplishment of mastery over a wound. It is the process in which the person first fights off, then embraces, then conquers a situation that has nearly destroyed them. Forgiving is also a gift given to the self (which releases) an injured person from the burdens and shackles of hate. Forgiveness is the ultimate liberator. It is not, however, easily accomplished. It is for those people who are willing to confront their pain, accept themselves as permanently changed, and make difficult choices. (Flanigan, 1994, p. 71)

There are four phases of the forgiveness process. Forgiveness of others begins with self-forgiveness (Enright & Fitzgibbons, 2000). *Self-forgiveness* involves the understanding, accepting and changing of the hurt one inflicts upon self and others. *Asking for forgiveness* (i.e., making amends) involves taking responsibility and accountability for hurts inflicted on others without excuse or blame. Requesting forgiveness allows another to understand and accept your fallibility and wrong-doing. *Forgiving others* involves the cultivation of empathy, humility, gratitude, integrity, self-control, justice, and serenity. Ultimately, forgiveness of self or others is a choice to not seek the destruction of the offender (or self). This restraint is rooted in self-integrity. Forgiveness reduces hate to justified anger and regret. Forgiveness of another involves being able to empathically understand how the offense happened. This empathy is rooted in the ability to humbly reflect on oneself as an offender. Gratitude and serenity are anchored in the recognition that personal safety and certainty of life is grounded in a larger context of fellowship of wounded healers. This experience is fostered by a much larger experience of a Higher Power who creates, sustains, and fulfills each human life.

Creating the character strength to forgive serious offenses requires practice and support. In standard recovery from chemical addiction the sponsor cautions a new twelve step member to attain mental and physical stability before attempting the forgiveness process outlined in Steps 4 through 10 (Hamilton B., 1996). Forgiveness research-practitioners also cautioned not to forgive and reconcile too soon (Linn, Linn, & Linn, 1997). In some cases reconciliation is counter therapeutic. In other cases reconciliation is dangerous. Therapists and sponsors need to help individuals discern when and how to forgive whom, and when and how to reconcile with those whom they forgive.

MISCONCEPTIONS ABOUT FORGIVENESS

We need to educate a client about the myths and misconceptions of forgiveness. Forgiveness is not denial or the unwillingness to accept damage done by others or self. Forgiveness is not condoning acts of transgression. It is not forgetting so as to remove hurt from awareness. Forgiveness is not pardoning, nor is it absolving or "letting an offender off the hook." It does not automatially lead to acts of reconciliation, restoration, or rehabilitation. All of these can be granted to the offender, but they are secondary to forgiveness of self, and asking-receiving forgiveness. Fundamentally, forgiveness of another is simply the choice to not retaliate and seek revenge, but to bestow mercy and compassion on a vulnerable, fallible, and mortal human who happened to be a transgressor.

Forgiveness holds interpersonal transgressors accountable and responsible (including self). Forgiveness is reasonable and logical. It looks toward personal and social long term best interests. Not all forgiveness ends in reconciliation and restoration of relationships. The empathy, humility, and gratitude, integrity, self-control, justice and peacemaking skills are focused on restoration of self. They are not primarily directed toward correcting or healing the offender.

Phases of Forgiveness Therapy

Forgiving self and requesting forgiveness is the learning process for forgiving others. This process can assist in healing memory, emotion, motivation, imagination, and meaning-making. Focusing on enhancing character strengths is a shorthand way of enhancing all aspects of a damaged personality. Forgiveness changes six basic personality components: sensing, feeling, imagining, thinking, acting, and relating. These components were distorted in their healthy function by trauma and substance abuse, and maintained in fixed focus on the past by the process of unforgiveness. Each new character strength requires a movement from negative (ineffective, unhealthy, irrational) to positive (effective, healthy, rational) in these six personality components. Accomplishing this change is an integrated process. All six areas must change in order to cultivate new character strengths, and to heal the 5Ms. For example, the development of compassion requires positive changes is all six areas of personality. A gradual introduction of healthy sensing, feeling, imagining, thinking, acting, and relating affects the damaged 5Ms. These positive experiences initiate shifts in the 5Ms so that they can be released from their fixed focus (5 Rs) on trauma and substance abuse experiences.

We propose eight phases for a forgiveness treatment plan. In the first phase, the client needs to understand (1) why and what forgiveness is (2) what forgiveness is not (3) the stages of forgiveness, (4) the process of forgiveness, (5) the costs and benefits of forgiving and not forgiving, (6) the readiness to forgive, (7) the reluctance to forgive, and (8) the integration of forgiveness into the recovery process.

> Sean demonstrated that he was stable in AA recovery and utilizing relapse therapy along with a strong sponsor relationship. Over several sessions we discussed what was forgiveness, what was not forgiveness. We discussed the cost and benefits of forgiveness, the problem of unforgiveness, the levels of forgiveness, and his readiness to forgive.

In the second phase, the client needs to recall who did what, when, where, how, how often, and to what outcome. In forgiveness therapy the person needs to recognize each offense, offender, and who is morally and legally responsible.

> Initially, we explored the damage Sean had done to himself throughout his psycho-social development, and how each event affected his subsequent development. We focused on (1) his chronic drinking from age 13 and how he refused treatment in high school when he knew he was alcoholic, (2) how he sabotaged his education and athletic potential, (3) how he undermined his military career, (4) how he jeopardized his marriage and relationships with his children, (5) how he neglected his family finances, and nearly ruined their financial future, (6) his chronic DWI behavior, and (7) his sexual promiscuity which created high risk for his wife. We discussed obstacles to forgiving himself, and ways to overcome these obstacles.
>
> We examined from whom he needed to receive forgiveness, and how to approach those whom he had offended. We set a time table for how and when to ask forgiveness of each individual. His primary focus was on the specific ways he had hurt his wife and children. His wife and four daughters participated in the process. His teenage son refused to accept amends or extend forgiveness to his father. Sean was able to understand this and respond with empathic understanding. Twelve step literature and practices were helpful in the 'amends' process.
>
> We explored the specific ways he was hurt by others. The list included (1) the impact of his father and mother's alcoholism on his development, (2) his father's physical and verbal abuse, (3) his mother's neglect and emotional distance, (4) his oldest sister for introducing him to marijuana when he was 13 years old, (5) a male neighbor drinking-friend of his parents for sexually abusing him from age 7 to 10, and (6) his business partner for having stolen 2/3 of his company money during Sean's active addiction.

In the third phase, the client needs (1) to understand the impact of trauma and substance abuse on psycho-social-spiritual development, and (2) to understand offenders in the context of the offense, and in the context of their own psycho-social-spiritual development.

We examined the close connection between his use of alcohol, other drugs, other compulsive behaviors (e.g., eating and exercise), the unresolved pain of trauma, and his contaminated thoughts and feelings. Sean applied his new understanding of what it meant to be a vulnerable, fallible, and mortal human living with other limited humans. He accepted a broader understanding of the first three steps of AA to include powerlessness over all permanent damage done by transgression. He accepted his responsibility to construct a meaningful and manageable daily life, and to rely on higher and healthier resources. He understood that he was one who had offended himself and others, and he was one who had received forgiveness. He was able to place those who had seriously transgressed and damaged him in a larger context of their fallible life. He understood that human beings who offend others have often been offended and need healing. Offenders were accepted as vulnerable humans. He understood that forgiveness did not mean letting the offender off the hook, including himself. Forgiveness was a challenge to reduce his demand for perfection toward others and himself.

Sean was able to distance himself from the power of the abuse he received from his parent, sister and neighbor. He was able to understand and confront these issues and persons using techniques of grief management. He addressed the neighbor, his mother, and his sister. He addressed his deceased father using creative grief therapy techniques. Anger and shame literature helped him understand the impact of these trauma on his development and his addictive behavior.

In the fourth phase, the client needs (1) to tolerate the frustrations of recovery, and (2) to increase daily practices of life-affirming behaviors (e.g., Step 10).

Sean's prior experience with AA and his longstanding relationship with a competent sponsor helped him construct a daily schedule of AA related activity involving daily fellowship, affirmation, confirmation, and reading. Combined with individual and group therapy Sean was able to systematically practice the primary attitudes and actions of recovery under the direction of a competent sponsor. He was able to shift his focus from wrongdoers and wrongs done to the positive task of creating a new set of virtues/strengths while resolving daily psycho-social conflicts.

In the tradition of the 10th step Sean maintained a daily inventory of forgiveness toward self and others. He realized how long he had carried the burden of unforgiveness. He experienced how satisfying was the process of forgiveness. He could share this experience with others in recovery meetings.

Sean experienced freedom in memory, emotions, motivation, meaning, and imagination. He practiced emotional regulation throughout the day with his family, friends, and strangers. Additionally, he learned to translate his needs into practical request. He learned to think and act with positive expectations and self-control in adverse situations.

In the fifth phase forgiveness therapy aims (1) to decrease exaggerated anger, anxiety, shame, fear, sadness, and guilt, (2) to increase the full range of positive emotions, and (3) to replace negative thinking with affirmative thinking regarding offenses and offenders.

Sean explored the connection of each hurtful event (1) to his chronically negative emotions, (2) to his negative attitudes, and (3) to his self-defeating behaviors. He learned to dispute his irrational thinking regarding himself and his past traumas. We created daily practices to increase his sense of self-worth, self-soothing, and self efficacy. He learned cognitive disputation, cognitive restructuring, and systematic desensitization over his irrational interpretations of offenders, offenses, and his role in past events.

In the sixth phase, the client needs (1) to acknowledge how trauma shattered the fundamental beliefs about himself and relationships, and (2) to recreate realistic beliefs about himself and relationships.

At this stage of the forgiveness process Sean was able to distance himself more from the pre-occupation with wrong-doing, wrong-done, and wrong-doers. His distorted feelings were reduced. His self-defeating behavior was reduced. He began to express realistic beliefs, expectations, and assumptions about living with fallible human beings who hurt and heal each other.

In the seventh phase, the client needs (1) to create specific plans to satisfy core psycho-social-spiritual needs, (2) to resolve recurrent daily conflict and crises, and (3) to have fun without chemicals.

Sean appreciated how trauma and chemical abuse stifled the way he took care of his basic bio-psycho-social-spiritual needs. Sean was able to construct a plan to satisfy his needs to be safe, to belong, to manage his life, to love and be loved, to have meaning and purpose, and to have fun. He learned to call upon the resources of recovery to resolve daily conflicts and family crises. He constructed reward, relief, and fun activities which were life-enhancing rather than self-defeating.

In the eighth phase, the client needs to cultivate relationships that support his resilience in recovery (Reivich & Shatte, 2002).

Sean joined a morning 12 step group which provided fellowship, empathic understanding, and hope for his recovery. He set a daily plan to practice the new attitudes/virtues he had learned. Utilizing the tools of 12 step recovery he was able to cultivate safe, reliable, and caring relationships. He learned to practice a "spirituality of imperfection." (Kurtz & Ketcham, 1996)

In summary these eight phases are conjoined. They do not proceed in lock-step order. They evolve as a matrix as the person learns the skills to activate innate capacities for development, and to create the character strengths needed to sustain that development.

CONCLUSION AND RESEARCH PROPOSAL

Our hypothesis is that forgiveness therapy can help heal the hurt of comorbid trauma and substance abuse by providing the character strengths needed to resolve the chronic conflict within self and with offenders. The process has two phases. The first is to resolve unforgiveness. The second is to enact forgiveness. Resolving unforgiveness and learning forgiveness can enhance the person's chances of success in standard therapy for traumatized substance abusers. Learning to resolve unforgiveness entails developing character strengths that release the person from the grasp of unresolved hurts. Learning how to forgive self, to ask and receive forgiveness, and to forgive others is part of reconstructing new attitudes, affects, and actions about self and others.

Outcome studies are needed to test the effects of *therapy for unforgiveness* in reducing the 5Rs: rumination, revenge, retaliation, resentment, and self-recrimination. Likewise, we need to test the effects of the four phases of *forgiveness therapy* in increasing the 5Ms: memory, meaning, imagination, emotion, and motivation. Finally, we need to test the effects of these two therapies on increasing PTSD-SUD treatment success.

REFERENCES

Affinito, M.G. (1999). *When to forgive.* Oakland, CA: New Harbinger.

Bastis, M.K. (2003). *Heart of forgiveness.* Boston, MA: Red Wheel.

Beck, A.T. (1999). *Prisoners of hate.* New York: Harper/Collins.

Bradshaw, J. (1990). *Homecoming.* New York: Bantam.

Bremner, J.D. (2002). *Does stress damage the brain?* New York: W.W. Norton.

Brick, J. & Erickson, C.K. (1998). *Drugs, the Brain, and Behavior.* New York: The Haworth Medical Press.

Calhoun, L.G. & Tedeschi, R.G. (1999). *Facilitating posttraumatic growth.* Mahwah, NJ: Lawrence-Erlbaum.

Casarjian, R. (1992). *Forgiveness.* New York: Bantam.

Copeland, M.E. & Harris, M. (2000). *Healing the trauma of abuse.* Oakland, CA: New Harbinger.

Enright, R.D. & Coyle, C.T. (1998). Researching the process model of forgiveness within psychological interventions. In Everett L. Worthington, Jr. *Dimensions of forgiveness: Psychological and theological perspectives* (pp.139-190). Radnor, PA: Templeton Foundation Press.

Enright, R.D. & Fitzgibbons, R.P. (2000). *Helping clients forgive: An empirical guide for resolving anger and restoring hope.* Washington, D.C: American Psychological Association.

Enright, R.D. & North, J. (1998). *Exploring forgiveness.* Madison, WI: University of Wisconsin Press.

Erikson, E. (1964). *Child and society.* New York: W.W. Norton.

Fincham, F.D. & Kashdan, T.B. (2004). Facilitating forgiveness: Developing group and community interventions. P.A. Linley and S. Joseph (Eds.), *Positive psychology in practice* (pp. 617-637). Hoboken, NJ: John Wiley & Sons.

Finley, J.R. (2004). *Integrating the 12 steps into addiction therapy.* Hoboken, NJ: John Wiley & Sons.

Flanigan, B. (1992). *Forgiving the unforgivable.* New York: Macmillan.

Flanigan, B. (1996). *Forgiving yourself.* New York: Macmillan.

Hamilton B., (1996). *Twelve step sponsorship.* Center City, MN: Hazelden.

Herman, J. (1997). *Trauma and recovery.* New York: Basic Books.

Janoff-Bulman, R. (1997). *Shattered assumptions: Toward a new psychology of trauma.* New York: Free Press.

Kauffman, J. (2002). *Loss of the assumptive world: A theory of traumatic loss.* New York: Brunner-Routledge.

Kegan, R. (1985). *The evolving self: Problem and process in human development.* Cambridge, MA: Harvard University Press.

Khantian, E.J., Halliday, K.S., & McAuliffe, W.E. (1990). *Addiction and the vulnerable self.* New York: Guilford.

Khantian, E.J. (1999). *Treating addiction as a human process.* Northvale, NJ: Jason Aronson Inc.

Kurtz, E. & Ketcham, K. (1992). *The spirituality of imperfection.* New York: Bantam.

Linn, D., Linn, S.F., & Linn, M. (1997). *Don't forgive too soon.* Mahwah, NJ: Paulist Press.

Mahoney, M.J. (2003). *Constructive psychotherapy.* New York: Guilford.

Malcolm, W.M. & Greenberg, L.S. (2000). Forgiveness as a process of change in individual psychotherapy. In M.E. McCullough, E.I. Pargament, K.I., and C.E. Thoresen, *Forgiveness: Theory, research, and practice* (pp. 179-202). New York: Guilford.

McCullough, M.E., Sandage, S.J., & Worthington, Jr. (1997). *To forgive is human.* Downers Grove, IL: InterVarsity Press.

McCullough, M.E., Pargament, K.I., & Thoresen, C.E. (2000). *Forgiveness: Theory, research, practice.* New York: Guilford.

McCullough, M.E. & Witvliet, C.V. (2002). The psychology of forgiveness. In C.R. Snyder & S.J. Lopez (Eds.), *Handbook of positive psychology* (pp. 446-458). New York: Oxford University Press.

McKay, M., Rogers, P.D., & McKay, J. (1989). *When anger hurts.* Oakland, CA: New Harbinger.

Miller, D. (2003). *Your surviving spirit: A spiritual workbook for coping with trauma.* Oakland, CA: New Harbinger.

Miller, D. & Guidry, L. (2001). *Addiction and trauma recovery.* New York: W.W. Norton.

Najavits, L.M. (2002). *Seeking safety: A treatment manual for PTSD and substance abuse.* New York: Guilford.

Newberg, A.B., d'Aquili, E.G., Newberg, S.K., & deMarici, V. (2000). The neuropsychological correlates of forgiveness. In M.E. McCullough, K.I. Pargament, C.E. Thoresen (Eds.), *Forgiveness: Theory, research, and practice* (pp. 91-110). New York: Guilford.

Nowinski, J. & Baker, S. (2003). *The twelve step facilitation handbook: A systematic approach to recovery from substance dependence.* Center City, MN: Hazelden.

Ouimettte, P. & Brown, P.J. (2003). *Trauma and substance abuse: Causes, consequences, and teaatment of comorbid disorders.* Washington, DC: American Psychological Association.

Peterson, C. & Seligman, M.E. (2004). *Character strengths and virtues.* New York: Oxford University Press.

Plante, T.G. & Sherman, A.C. (2001). *Faith and health: Psychological perspective.* New York: Guilford

Potter-Efron, R.T. & Potter-Efron, P.S. (1991). *Anger, alcoholism, and addiction.* New York: W.W. Norton.

Potter-Efron, R. & Potter-Efron, P. (1995). *Letting go of anger.* Oakland, CA: New Harbinger.

Potter-Efron, R. & Potter-Efron, P. (1999). *The secret message of shame.* Oakland, CA: New Harbinger.

Potter-Efron, R. (2002*). Shame, guilt, and alcoholism: Treatment issues in clinical practice.* New York: The Haworth Press.

Reivich, K.R. & Shatte, A. (2002). *The resilience factor.* New York: Random House.

Romig, C.A. & Veenstra, G. (1998). Forgiveness and psychosocial development. *Counseling and Values*, 2, 185-1999,

Rutledge, T. (1997). *The self-forgiveness handbook.* Oakland, CA: New Harbinger.

Schraldi, G.R. (2000). *The post-traumatic stress disorder sourcebook.* Lincolnwood, IL: Lowell House

Tedeschi, R.G., & Calhoun, L.G. (1995). *Trauma & Transformation.* Thousand Oaks, CA: Sage.

Tedeschi, R.G. & Calhoun, L.G. (2004). A clinical approach to posttraumatic growth. In P.A. Linley & S. Joseph (Eds.) *Positive psychology in practice* (pp. 405-419). Hoboken, NJ: John Wiley & Sons.

Williams, M.B. & Poijula, S. (2002). *The PTSD workbook.* Oakland, CA: New Harbinger.

Worthington, E.L. (1998). The Pyramid model of forgiveness: Some interdisciplinary speculations about unforgiveness and the promotion of forgiveness. In Everett L. Worthington, Jr. *Dimensions of forgiveness: Psychological and theological perspectives* (pp. 139-190). Radnor, PA: Templeton Foundation Press.

Worthington, E.L., Berry, J.W., & Parrott, III, L. (2001). Unforgiveness, forgiveness, religion and health. In Thomas G. Plante and Allen C. Sherman (Eds.) *Faith and health: Psychological perspective* (pp. 107-138). New York: Guilford.

Traumatized Addicted Women:
Treatment Issues

Chelly Sterman, LCSW, LCADC, NLP Level II, EMDR Level II

SUMMARY. Whereas in "natural" trauma the victim, for instance, often has a reference group and faces a by and large sympathizing world, victims of "intentional" traumas are most often isolated and unacknowledged by this same world. Also, relationship and intimacy issues in this population are generally very pronounced. Beliefs about betrayal, guilt, distrust, shame, and other emotions as well as coping skills and defenses are largely formed early in life and the traumatized woman in adulthood often replays her earlier experiences in some self-damaging form based on these early beliefs and defenses. This is examined further in this chapter. *[Article copies available for a fee from The Haworth Document Delivery Service: 1-800-HAWORTH. E-mail address: <docdelivery@haworthpress.com> Website: <http://www.HaworthPress.com> © 2006 by The Haworth Press, Inc. All rights reserved.]*

KEYWORDS. Women and addiction, domestic violence, sexual abuse and chemical dependency

"The problems we face today are not going to be corrected by the thinking that created them." –Albert Einstein

"The mind is its own place." –John Milton

[Haworth co-indexing entry note]: "Traumatized Addicted Women: Treatment Issues." Sterman, Chelly. Co-published simultaneously in *Journal of Chemical Dependency Treatment* (The Haworth Press, Inc.) Vol. 8, No. 2, 2006, pp. 255-282; and: *Psychological Trauma and Addiction Treatment* (ed: Bruce Carruth) The Haworth Press, Inc., 2006, pp. 255-282. Single or multiple copies of this article are available for a fee from The Haworth Document Delivery Service [1-800-HAWORTH, 9:00 a.m. - 5:00 p.m. (EST). E-mail address: docdelivery@haworthpress.com].

Available online at http://www.haworthpress.com/web/JCDT
© 2006 by The Haworth Press, Inc. All rights reserved.
doi:10.1300/J034v08n02_13

The trauma considered in this population in combination with drug abuse is generally sexual abuse, particularly incest or more formally, cumulative sexual trauma starting at some time in childhood, perpetuated by an abuser known to the girlchild and who is in some position of authority over her.

When considering incest, then, the picture is one of cumulative trauma, ongoing, not a particular event. Schiraldi (2000) distinguishes three forms of trauma, one of which is "intentional (man-made, malicious)" (p. 36), which sets this trauma apart from many other ones, but certainly not all. The relevance of separating "intentional" traumas from other forms of trauma, such as "natural" trauma, is the difference in approaches to treatment. Whereas in "natural" trauma the victim, for instance, often has a reference group and faces a by and large sympathizing world, victims of "intentional" traumas are most often isolated and unacknowledged by this same world. Also, relationship and intimacy issues in this population are generally very pronounced. Beliefs about betrayal, guilt, distrust, shame, and other emotions as well as coping skills and defenses are largely formed early in life and the traumatized woman in adulthood often replays her earlier experiences in some self-damaging form based on these early beliefs and defenses. This is examined further in this chapter.

HISTORICAL ACKNOWLEDGEMENTS

The trauma of sexual abuse came to the fore relatively late in the field of mental health though even Anna Freud (1967, as cited in Scharff & Scharff, 1994) already wrote that incest was more damaging than neglect, abandonment and physical abuse. Herman (1992) points out that it was not until the 1980s that the literature actually started to discuss incest traumas. It took more than 15 years until this field and society as a whole began to respect sexual abuse as an independent treatment issue. Viewing sexual abuse combined with addiction as co-occurring disorders is a quite recent development. In the mental health field, addiction was rarely a focus in the treatment of sexually abused women and this abuse was mostly neglected or kept separate in addiction recovery.

Societal reasons served as a cover for this underserved population. Kushner (1981) writes:

> Blaming the victim is a way of reassuring ourselves that the world is not as bad a place as it may seem and that there are good reasons

for people's suffering. It helps fortunate people believe that their good fortune is deserved rather than being a matter of luck. It makes everyone feel better–except the victim who now suffers double the abuse of social condemnation on top of original misfortune. (p. 39)

Societal reasons of a different kind, but equally forceful and judgmental, caused a lack of recognition for appropriate treatment of addiction. The combination of society's position toward victims of sexual abuse, particularly if it took place within the family, as well as addicts, created a large underserved population that only recently has begun to get its needed attention. Addiction and mental health professionals still have some distance to go, though, toward a cohesive treatment model.

The focus of this chapter will be on problems caused by interactions of elements of the original sexual abuse trauma with simultaneous or subsequent substance abuse. It will also address the process of effective treatment through cooperative efforts by the mental health profession and particularly twelve step programs.

THE WOUNDING FEEDBACK LOOP

There is a limited but increasing body of literature focused on the relationship between sexual trauma and chemical dependency. Statistics show high correlations in these areas: between sixty and eighty percent of incest appears to take place under the influence of alcohol. Herman (1992) states that studies show that between seventy and eighty percent of these traumatized women attempt to use alcohol or illegal drugs after sustaining trauma:

Although dissociative alterations in consciousness or even intoxication may be adaptive at the moment of total helplessness, they become maladaptive once the danger has passed. Because these altered states keep the traumatic experiences walled off from ordinary consciousness, they prevent the integration necessary for healing. (p. 46)

In *Healing the Incest Wound*, Courtois (1998) states: "The correlation between chemical dependence and (sexual) abuse has been noted repeatedly. That incest often occurs in the context of an alcoholic family or when the abuser has used alcohol or drugs is now well documented" (p. 312). A history of incest in the background of a sizable percentage of alcoholic women has also been identified. Courtois (1998) asserts further that:

> During assessment and treatment, the therapist must ask about alcohol and drug use as well as about the family history of chemical dependence. Two main patterns are in evidence. The first involves the survivor who had a family history of alcohol abuse and the second involves the survivor who began to abuse alcohol and drugs after the trauma to relieve stress and to self medicate. Different treatment is necessary for each. (p. 313)

Patrick Carnes, in *The Betrayal Bond* (1997), supports Courtois, stating that approximately fifty percent of abusers have a problem with alcohol and thirty-three percent with illicit drugs (p. 81). In *Don't Call It Love* he further explores this and writes: "Addiction is much bigger than any compulsive behavior, because it can manifest itself in any number of ways and still be the same problem" (p. 106). Flannery (1992) estimates that "eighty percent of prostitutes come from homes with abuse and or alcoholism" (as cited in Schiraldi, 2000). According to Miller and Guidry (2001) in *Addictions and Trauma Recovery*

> Studies further show that approximately fifty to seventy percent of women hospitalized for psychiatric reasons (Carmen, 1995), seventy percent of those seen in emergency rooms (Brier and Zardi, 1989) and between forty and sixty percent of those seen as psychiatric outpatients report having experienced physical or sexual abuse. More than seventy percent of women with drug or alcohol problems were victims of violence. Between seventy and eighty percent of women who experience domestic violence have also survived physical and or sexual abuse during childhood. (Nanley, 1999, p. 78)

Estimates for the general population are that one out of three to five women will be sexually abused in some way by age twenty, half of which by age twelve. Clearly, these numbers are much higher in addicted family systems with their diffused boundaries, impulse control limitations and crisis prone orientation. This highlights the vulnerability of this population and its lack of protection in our society.

DYNAMICS OF THE WOUNDING PROCESS

Sexual abuse covers a range from being inappropriately dressed around these female children to sexual abuse paired with physical abuse. One of my clients told me the many times she and her sister experienced horror as young children while they were in the room with their inebriated father who would only be wearing boxer shorts. Also, there is a distinct difference in the client's healing from sexual abuse by how the trauma was handled at the time of the trauma. Many studies demonstrate that children can heal from these traumatic experiences depending on how the event was managed at the time it occurred is well as in follow-up. Children often have far fewer residual symptomatology when a parental figure is available in a supportive, nurturing way and personal coping styles and self empowerment are encouraged. Many women describe the pain of not being believed or even removed from the household after they had entrusted the partner of the perpetrator with the information about the sexual abuse. In other words, the trauma is often severely compounded when the only person who was expected to protect the child rejects her in favor of the perpetrator. Almost universally, the addicted clients we see in our office received insufficient care to minimize their wounding, either within their family or their larger community.

CASE VIGNETTE

B.'s sexual abuse history was extremely serious and her addiction began at age nine. This was when her alcoholic father would get her and her younger sisters drunk so that they would be compliant with extensive multi-partnered sexual abuse. Story after story surfaced, with me in the role of steadfast witness to this young woman's tragic history. She was twenty four years old, but had a nearly fifteen year alcohol dependence history behind her. Her mother was also an alcoholic who overtly supported the father's frequent incestuous behavior to avoid personal intimacy with him. The sexual abuse did not end until B. at age sixteen, found herself drunk on the roof of her apartment building. She was holding a knife and her inebriated father was coming toward her. B. doesn't remember if she wanted to kill her father or protect her right to jump from the roof.

Discussion: In B.'s recollection, the sexual abuse began when she was about five or six years old. Both parents drank alcoholically by then and B. received no solace or support from the mother. All three daughters became addicted to alcohol, two moved on to other drugs. B. went through periods of sobriety but because of her abysmal financial situation she had virtually no access to mental health or addiction treatment professionals. During her periods of sobriety she began to dissociate and though she was well aware of the damage alcohol caused in her life, she was unable to give it up. Not only did her parents and society fail her in childhood, the pattern was repeated in adulthood and B. left before treatment was completed.

FINDING DIRECTION

Addicted victims of sexual abuse are under great internal and external stress. Individuals under stress cannot adequately process new information. Until they feel sufficiently safe and stabilized these women run new information, whether it comes to them through therapy, a twelve step program or other societal support systems, through their old perceptual filters. New information is distorted according to these filters. Change can begin to take place when these women feel safe with another human being. Here the clinician, who, through the therapeutic relationship, provides attunement, close pacing, this sense of true alignment. Then the beginning of a new, testable reality can form which eventually expands and encompasses a larger world view.

Sexual abuse permeates the female child's being quite literally, invades her core, erodes her self-esteem, her sense of self. The child who must defend herself does so with what is available to her at the time of the victimization and only later in life experiences that much of what she learned during the trauma to protect herself, now, in her adult life, turned against her. It is ironic that we call this protection "maladaptive defenses." In treatment it is essential to be aware that what appear as maladaptive defenses in the present, made sense in the context of the woman's reality when she first "designed" them, when she first formed coping skills, generally in a disempowered state. These were the defenses that were within her reach at the time of the abuse or after the traumatic experiences. As clinicians, we further need to keep in mind that these defenses initially worked quite well as coping skills and only after time passed did they become increasingly less effective. Conceptually, this context allows the clinician to validate the woman's strengths in protecting herself without judgment of the particular defense.

Drug abuse further erodes inner resources because the addict increasingly relies on external substances for survival. So once a victim of sexual abuse is addicted, the self continues to erode which makes it impossible for her to sufficiently process her trauma and lead a "good enough" life in the present. Important here is that sexually abused addicted women are at high risk for repeating the trauma, particularly under the influence of a drug, as well as for relapse. Again, this is not indicative only of this kind of trauma, but in its frequency and its severity it certainly puts this specific population at the high end of any continuum. A "good enough life" must mean then the woman's own views on the context of her life, her internal resources, her ability to continue to recover and to accept life on her own terms.

CASE VIGNETTE

K. was incested by her alcoholic father from an early age. The family was extremely religious, the father a pillar of the community and religious life. K. was very popular at school and tried to bridge the discrepancy between home and school life where she was validated and learned important life skills. At home, her mother was supportive but had no skills to earn a living, had a large number of children and a great fear of the self-absorbed husband. K. became addicted to alcohol in her late teens while going through her professional training. Though K. had several choices in marriage, she chose religious life for herself.

Discussion: K. had significant strengths and competently balanced her twelve step program and therapy, resorting to her spiritual commitment when she encountered conflict. She realized, though, that her world had been irreparably impoverished and that being intimate with a man and having children would never feel like an option to her. Though K. successfully avoided relapsing, any sense of entitlement was severely damaged by her narcissistic father.

THE EMOTIONAL HURDLES

In *Internal Family Systems*, Schwartz (1995) views an individual as "an entity whose parts relate to another in a pattern" (p. 17). Even if the clinician doesn't focus on all variables simultaneously "all parts of the person are in an intimate relationship with each other, somehow function as a whole." There is an intense synergy between trauma and chemical dependency and the woman's attempt to restore "internal balance and harmony" (p. 20). This pseudo balance, though, causes further internal and external disparity, eventually creating the decline of this internal system. Repetition compulsion plays an important role in these dynamics. It is fueled, on a less than conscious level, by the woman's desire to have her trauma experience result in a different outcome and therefore negate the original trauma experience. The very fact that she keeps repeating the trauma without being released from it naturally compounds it since she now finds evidence for her childhood experiences in the present.

> Example: T. came to see me after she was gangraped during a date with an older man with whom she had gotten drunk. When she had gone back to his apartment, she had found his friends waiting for her. T. and her younger sister, who had committed suicide at age seventeen, had been incested by their alcoholic father and older brother.

The danger of the repetition compulsion is greatly increased when the victim is under the influence of a drug since she cannot be in control of boundaries. Her judgment is impaired. Chemically dependent abused women have a far greater occurrence of rape and gangrape than other populations which accounts for the often repetitive nature in the treatment of this population. Co-morbid conditions such as depression and anxiety frequently exist and may become increasingly apparent once substance abuse is eliminated. Other, more severe states such as the emergence of a bi-polar or phobic disorder or active psychosis have been reported as well as cross addictions. These co-morbid conditions further decrease the likelihood of abuse victims successfully managing their internal conflicted states. It is essential to have reliable access to a female psychiatrist who has extensive knowledge of sexual and substance abuse. Though not all perpetrators are male, the majority of these clients will have experienced their direct trauma with a male. The indirect trauma, the lack of protection, support, nurturing that compounds the original trauma is generally seen as the female parent's domain. In my experience, it is useful, at least initially, to have a female clinician and psychiatrist work with addicted survivors of sexual abuse. This may avoid retriggering, regression and revictimization regarding the direct trauma and allows the woman to form a relationship she had needed after the trauma. This also maintains congruency with her twelve step program, which emphasizes same gender support. When the woman progresses and enters later phases of recovery such as mourning and reconnection, the client's relationship repertoire and its expansion certainly play a significant part in her healing.

In *Emotionally Focused Couple Therapy with Trauma Survivors* Johnson (2000) stresses that the primary effect of trauma " is a chronic inability to regulate one's emotional life" (p.11). When this is combined with drug abuse, the problem is compounded for the woman. The addictive substance temporarily becomes the victim's organizing life principle, until that life spirals out of control. This is echoed by Dayton (2000) in *Trauma and Addiction* when she discusses "emotional literacy" which she describes as the ability to convert feelings into words, to decode our inner world through the use of words: "Trauma and addiction interfere with emotional literacy by blocking access to our internal world" (p. 43). This complements M. Bowen's theories that wounded individuals have insufficient separation between emotion and intellect, which leads to a diminished observing self. The fusion between these functions results, among other things, in problems with impulse control which increase exponentially when a victim is drug affected. An important recovery goal in this population is to increase the "distance" between triggers, feeling and thinking on one hand, and actions on the other. The addicted survivors of sexual abuse generally don't have a "good enough" observing adult self, but rather a superimposed shaming, critical, sometimes angry and defiant substitute in its place. This naturally sets these women up for a high relapse rate. They also typically present with a high acuity level and are crisis prone. The clinician must be aware that this follows a lifetime of negating authentic feelings and suffering combined with distortion of feelings that occur in addiction. Only very strong expression of feelings appeared to get attention or created other responses that seem incongruous with their present lives. These highly charged emotional states diminish as they become increasingly grounded in an adult self who inhabits a safe environment. Keeping the focus on herself in treatment feels counter-intuitive to this population. The women were generally coerced to negate the sexual abuse along with their feelings. Once they became addicted, they were further out of touch with a genuine set of emotions and these clients often have to (re)learn a whole repertoire of feelings, feelings they were often taught not to recognize within themselves. In treatment, various issues are presented:

> As girls, these women were generally coerced to negate these painful experiences. In treatment, they are suggested to disengage from these taboos and begin to talk about the abuse. This virtually always creates significant internal conflicts.

> Bringing these experiences into the therapeutic process requires that the clinician maintain a delicate balance between the woman's fear of collusion in "the conspiracy of silence" of her childhood while keeping her relationship with the therapist safe. This implies attributing sufficient control over the therapeutic process to the client.

> Active addicts are naturally not inclined to be introspective, so the woman's "silence" will have continued longer and to a greater extent if she became chemically dependent.

> Clients must discover the connections between addiction and their sexual abuse issues, the meaning of these issues in their lives and their simultaneous or sequential appearance.

> Adult functioning is encouraged which increases the power of the observing self. In turn this helps in the client's ability to learn to timely recognize and modulate feelings, learn compassion for herself and take the risks to manage interrelated symptoms.

A compounding problem for these women in treatment is that they have learned to internally negate their emotions and generally do not have a vocabulary to express them. Until they are in the clinician's office they rarely have been asked or were allowed to express their feelings. Once they became addicted, they are further out of touch with their emotions. These clients may have to (re)learn the whole repertoire of feelings and often do not even recognize many of them. To identify these feelings in therapy has the advantage of making them more available for replication. These women need a larger repertoire of emotional choices as they learn to live more fully in their present reality.

The sexually traumatized woman may attempt to navigate a near impossible duality. When sober and abstinent, her emotional and intellectual radar may often function well to create awareness for external danger, but that does not imply that she has the capacity to move toward safety. She is often out of touch with her internal experience of an external harmful event so that her response to danger may frequently appear incongruous. She may seem frozen, immobilized, even drawn to it, but having this "radar" for danger under these circumstances in no way guarantees avoidance of it, which further increases the risk of revictimization and rewounding.

In *Secret Survivors* Blume (1990) poses that "the survivor has so much to struggle against that it is a surprise when she does not retreat into the illusion of control that addiction and compulsion provide" (p. 144) and she further states: "Even after becoming sober, a woman might relapse repeatedly or bounce from one addiction to the other." Again, Blume points to a most significant problem in the healing process of the addicted sexually abused woman: once the addiction appears managed, it may be transferred to another harmful defense unless the clinician has the client's alignment, time and knowledge to assist her in putting more helpful skills in place. These internalized skills and resources are discussed later in this chapter. These women often have not learned to delineate the "normal" parts of their histories versus distorted times. This coincides with the developmental issues so extensively explored by Evans and Sullivan (1995).

In the treatment of these vulnerable women, the clinician avoids flooding, overwhelming or even surprising experiences. These clients live an emotionally chaotic existence, often in a tumultuous world and the clinician must be very cautious not to sequence intense emotions closely. The therapist assists clients in reducing the intensity of these emotions as well as in shortening the emotional discharge itself to increase the women's sense of internal safety and control over themselves. When tension occurs, it is helpful if the women have learned to regulate discomfort rather than negate it. These women have lived in the eye of the storm and this is the place where the clinician connects with them. Cohesiveness in treatment–as opposed to their more customary chaos and turmoil–allows these clients to remain more easily in the therapeutic process and make gains toward recovery.

RECOVERY PHASES

Simultaneous recovery from sexual trauma and addiction is not linear although certain patterns have been identified by various authors. Herman (1992) identifies as the stages of healing: establishing safety, the mourning period and the reconnecting phase. A popular model (Courtois, 1998) consists of the burn-off phase, the evidence building phase and the mourning phase. In treatment, I find it useful to conceptualize the client's recovery in the context of a loosely sequenced structure that combines the components of both models. Establishing a safe therapeutic holding relationship is naturally a priority and this creates the space for the burn-off phase. During this time, the therapist remains a steadfast witness to the client's painful, conflicted history. Much doubt and despair often surfaces and the clinician must validate this while keeping the client process oriented to avoid discouragement. This phase can not be completed while the woman is active in an addiction. Addiction causes stories, thoughts and feelings to recycle and prevents her from moving toward resolution. In the evidence-building phase, the woman begins to emotionally put her past in her history. She now accumulates the skills to live in the present and begins to move toward the future. This is a most significant marker in recovery. Another difficult period follows, since skills the woman (re) gains in the evidence building phase allow her to begin to mourn her history. Martin Buber (1987) talks about grieving as the task of letting go of the trauma, not necessarily forgiving the perpetrator, and this is echoed by various authors such as Francine Shapiro (1995). Letting go means that the emotional charge is lifted to a large extent from the trauma and therefore no longer determines the woman's present. Forgiving often demands much additional energy and is almost paradoxically a form of revictimization. It is likely to be inauthentic when it does not occur naturally, even feels counter-intuitive and possibly like a loss of protection for the trauma victim. An important difference between this phase and the burn-off phase is that the survivor now takes ownership of her history, begins to take charge of it, rather than being overcome by guilt and shame. Here again is compatibility with the twelve step program–becoming responsible for one's history entitles the survivor of sexual abuse to decide how to hold her own history, an important transition in the move from victim to survivor. During this phase, a woman frequently begins to report a real sense of connection in her twelve step program. She learns to have compassion for herself in her history, allowing for an increasingly grounded adult self. Finally, the recovering woman will assemble the resources to connect with the world, within relationships and with a healing self. Herman (1992) describes the final phase of recovery as regaining "some capacity for appropriate trust." This is apparent in all areas of her life. The woman now has "the ability to feel autonomous while remaining connected to others" and this is reflected in the therapeutic relationship. Herman further states "As the trauma recedes into the past, it no longer represents a barrier to intimacy, which opens the way to reconnecting with a partner, children and the community" (p. 206). At every juncture, the recovering woman is taking great emotional risks and needs strength from the therapeutic relationship and the AA program. It is essential that the therapist remains aware of the fluidity of these phases, for instance, clients may temporarily regress before taking emotional risks. In any of these phases, additional defenses, skills and resources will be required in order to proceed in the healing process. These women are generally skill deficient, particularly early in treatment. The inclusive twelve step program and its important external structure frees these women to create internal space for work that needs to be done simultaneously on an intra-psychic level. The program does not immediately demand inner resources. It actually requires participants to "turn it over" to "a power greater than herself." When seen through a wrong lens, it may be terribly frightening for these women to see themselves as powerless again. If these first steps can be framed as providing safety and emotional space, congruency with the program will be maintained. Concurrently, the clinician must keep in mind that women referred for addiction often do not present their sexual abuse history and that this must be elicited directly. Frequently a woman in treatment for addiction continually repeats the same patterns, for instance, relapsing, involving herself in dangerous situations, remaining emotionally flat in therapy or conversely, becoming hyperemotional. It is often up to the therapist to carefully approach the topic of sexual abuse, since the woman may otherwise never know that she is entitled to be released from what often is her conspiracy of silence.

> Example: A female therapist I supervise spoke about a woman who relapsed frequently, who had been diagnosed by her psychiatrist as a borderline personality disorder and who had regrettably been over-medicated while in an active alcohol addiction. After a year of weekly therapy, the clinician began to probe into this woman's history and was presented almost immediately with an incest history of great severity and tales of a disturbed mother, who apparently once attempted to sell the girl. Naturally, the chance of progress in recovery is poor without access to this information and the diagnosis as well as the medication needed to be reviewed.

PACING PROGRESS

It is useful to visualize recovery of addicted survivors of sexual abuse as a perpetual staircase, rather than an uninterrupted line. The woman works in therapy and self help groups, emotionally rests, watches and evaluates the work and when ready, takes the next step. This allows the clinician a deepening of the therapeutic alignment, to pace the client and validate her for her accomplishments as well as keep her hope alive by supporting this process.

In other words, in treatment, these women frequently need "breaks" when their material is too overwhelming. It is important for clinicians to respect these breaks. This may take the form of the client actually leaving treatment (less desirable), continuing the sessions but feeling "flat" for some time while she regenerates or temporarily derailing sessions by producing "red herrings" (the client dangles an inviting topic before the clinician to get away from the overwhelming material). The clinician may acknowledge that the client is taking this break–it can be frightening for the client if she believes that she can so easily control the therapeutic relationship. She must show respect for the client's self knowledge in taking this break–a positive reframe is an important treatment intervention and strengthens the therapeutic relationship. At an appropriate time she can invite the client to bring her material back into the treatment process, so that she doesn't feel that the clinician, like other people in her experience, are in collusion with her remaining silent about her story.

Addiction counselors may have a tendency to prioritize substance abuse treatment, which initially may leave the sexually traumatized woman too defenseless. That is not to say that chemical dependence is a useful defense. However, untimely withdrawal–before better defenses are in place–may cause greater personality disintegration or lead to relapse. As it does with other trauma, the addictive substance allows the sexual abuse victim alternately to self soothe against overwhelming anxiety, sadness and rage. Among other functions, it allows her to act out without feeling responsible, temporarily not being conscious of the abuse and nurture the self without the risk of a real emotional connection. It provides temporary unconsciousness of the abuse or enables the client to nurture the self without the risk of a real emotional connection. The danger, of course, is that with the return of memory the woman's traumatic history is now compounded by the damage of the latest substance abuse episode.

Conversely, clinicians treating sexual abuse victims, in early addiction recovery, who ignore drug use, may find themselves constantly making short term progress but actually finding themselves after long hard work in a homeostasis. As explored earlier, no new thinking can be examined through old filters and as long as the old coping skill of substance abuse remains active, the human system remains largely static. In *Seeking Safety*, Najavits (2002) emphasizes the hazard of removing the addictive substance too soon when working with victims of sexual abuse, which means before the women have learned more appropriate ways of protecting themselves. She further states that because of the current approach to treatment this dually diagnosed population has generally had poorer treatment outcomes than others with a dual diagnosis.

This all emphasizes the paucity in systems of thinking about simultaneous treatment of chemical dependency and sexual abuse. Generally, the literature chooses one of the issues and then makes the other somewhat secondary or rather magically resolved. Regrettably, there is no magic. Both the clinician and the client work hard and long. A conscious, two prong approach to treatment is a necessity. It places high demands on the clinician and the literature provides limited guidance at this time. Najavits (2002) Evans and Sullivan (1995) and others consistently point out that for valid reasons only simultaneous treatment can be effective in the resolution of the duality of the sexual abuse trauma and chemical dependence.

In treatment, several demanding tasks need to be executed virtually simultaneously by the sexually abused recovering addict. Exploring and learning to express the range of emotions, acquiring life skills and strategies and executing life tasks requires much stamina. This is tightly interwoven with the trauma work itself as well as the addiction recovery process. The clinician in this process works with awareness of a near paradox: the client is likely to be close to exhaustion and quite fragile but is assumed to have great strengths, having survived her history of sexual abuse and addiction.

LIFE SKILLS

The sexually traumatized, chemically dependent woman generally has a severely fragmented timeline as noted earlier. Trauma victims in general have distorted timelines, but again, few have the extent of distortion this population deals with. The past severely intrudes into the present and determines actions into the future. The present with its frequent revictimizations as well as the effects of addiction and poor defenses bleeds into the past. The trauma victim's foreshortened sense of future may cause her timeline to stop in the present or hold unreachable goals for the future. Both of these dynamics are compatible with chemical addiction. The past needs to be experienced as containable, manageable, trustworthy, at best in a reframe that allows the woman to make her experiences useful to her in some way. Various studies show that trauma victims have a more complete healing sequence, an expanded sense of future, if they can make use of their tragic past in some way toward this future. Distorted timelines give rise to self limiting beliefs. These beliefs contain significant information about the superimposed self, the self the girlchild created to defend herself against external danger in combination with other life requirements. These beliefs were not reexamined, particularly during the period of addiction. In restoring timelines, these women begin to uncover a greater authentic self which had remained submerged until the safety of the therapeutic relationship and a twelve step program allowed it to surface. It is important to be mindful that reality is her experience, her model of the world and in restoring the woman's life continuum, her timeline, she expands her ability to recontextualize this reality.

When tracking the recovering process of these women, the clinician then sees a restored timeline which includes a past tied to but delineated from the present, a genuine and expanded life in the present and reachable goals, an accessible future. Restoring a timeline depends significantly on the life skills described in the following section. Without her competence in executing these strategies and tasks, feeling that she can sufficiently be in charge of herself and her life remains compromised. Competence in managing these life skills is essential in the woman's recovery. In addition to emotional disregulation, drug dependant sexual abuse victims are life skill deficient. Few trauma victims have experienced erosion of their world to the extent of those who grew up in chemically and sexually abusive systems. Imagine girlchildren who could never even find safety going to sleep, who were not allowed doors on their bedrooms or bathrooms.

CASE VIGNETTE

J. slept with her sneakers on and encouraged her younger siblings to do the same. On nights that her father would come home drunk, she knew she had to escape but always, responsibly, took the children. The mother was powerless and badly physically abused but unable to leave. J. was sexually abused from a young age, the younger siblings, boys, were physically abused. J. would run out the back door pulling her brothers along when she would hear her father enter at the front, drunk, knowing that her mother would then get beaten. She would either hide with her siblings behind cars in the street until morning or on occasion be taken in by a frightened neighbor. No one ever called the authorities. J. left home at a young age but had a severely disturbed sleeping pattern and became addicted to sleeping pills. When these failed her, she added downers. She then married, had a baby and became dependent on amphetamines during the day to stay awake. Her husband was an active alcoholic who was severely physically abused by both parents, particularly his mother.

Discussion: J. was truly gifted in many ways. Even in childhood she had obviously been resourceful, responsible, had excelled in sports and academics. She even excelled in treatment, started college, but hit the wall emotionally in her doctorate program. J.'s husband by then was in recovery, active in the twelve step program and therapy as well, but in many ways was not up to her high standards. J. felt that by getting her doctorate, she would lose the hard fought-for safety and security of the marriage and dropped out of school and therapy. She has become quite bitter, but her reality testing, value system and coping skills did not allow her a different choice.

TRIGGERS

Chemical dependency and the experience of sexual abuse are not static in the client's mind, but are always in flux. In therapy, therefore, the clinician must frequently check the client's perceptions of herself, therapy and the world at large, since these are, at least early on, incongruous with those of the clinician herself. This further solidifies the therapeutic alliance when the woman deals with her vulnerability, her fear of abandonment, hopelessness and painful memories of past rejection. By contrast, rigid thinking about their own roles and behavior is frequently observed in these women and this is naturally an outcome of, a defense against, a chaotic, dangerous external world and an internal self in turmoil. Adult roles may be truly unfamiliar, particularly if the sexual abuse as well as the addiction began at a young age. Large parts of adult functioning the clinician takes for granted are a mystery for these clients. The client must remain the expert on her history and at her pace, as she becomes safer to herself and in her relationship to the world, begins to unfreeze. As it were, unfreezing implies intense work with old triggers and in the past twenty years effective strategies have been developed in this area of treatment.

Working with trauma strategies implies decreasing energy from old triggers in order to reconstitute a continuous timeline. The client needs to be desensitized to triggers and develop control over them so that she may feel empowered and trust the healing process. "Leakage" of old triggers into the present must have safeguards. To accomplish this, she must learn a new referential index, a new way to interpret internal states and life experiences. Evans and Sullivan (1995) state: "Numerous research studies suggest that fear responses from conditioned stimuli are long lasting and never really disappear. However, if organisms have new and repeated experiences that a stimulus no longer 'means' pain, their fear responses gradually decrease" (p. 53).

> Example: R. was physically and sexually abused by a violent alcoholic father. She often protected her younger siblings by putting herself in danger with this man. Her mother was an abusive alcoholic as well. R. began drinking alcoholically in early adolescence, was sexually promiscuous, married several times and eventually married and had children with another alcoholic. For two years after R. attained sobriety and even after her husband got sober, R. would retreat, shaking, into a corner when the husband, who was not abusive, would raise his voice or even a stranger would appear aggressive. After about three years, R. began to recognize her fear triggers as they appeared. She was then able to initiate an overriding internal dialogue which most often prevented her regression and allowed her to remain in an adult state in the present with access to internal resources.

Research also indicates that chemical dependence inhibits this settling in of new responses so that new experiences have no or limited opportunities to assist in decreasing fear responses. Triggers may present as physical phenomena, as images and as internal dialogue they may or may not reach conscious awareness, but serve to mobilize the internal system against danger. Andreas (1987) wrote in *Change Your Mind and Keep the Change* that facets of the image (size, color), the internal dialogue (wording, tonality) and body experiences (location, dimensions of the distress) can be useful to explore in therapy. In various trauma strategies this forms the basis for corrective experiences. The issue is not the appearance of the trigger, but the loss of power over the self in the present. The able, resourceful female adult, when triggered is pre-empted as it were, by a sense of a younger, vulnerable self. This compounds earlier, negative self concepts and retards the recovering process. Triggers are hard wired, but new or rediscovered resources can be attached or "backed into" old triggers, so fully diminishing these that they barely remain emotionally charged. This shift in the strength of these triggers is a significant indicator of the move forward in the healing process and may be charted along lines of frequency, intensity and duration of their presence to measure this continued healing.

TO LIVE A LIFE

When these girlchildren then finally found solace in drug use, became adults and eventually entered treatment, there will have been precious little time for them to gather the skills and resources required for them to become competent and self sufficient enough adults.

There are several basic skills adults need to sufficiently master in order to live a life in a competent, drug free manner. Though these women come to a clinician in adult bodies, she must not assume that these life skills are present. Clinicians are generally aware of some of these absences, such as coping skills, but what about some of the others we learn almost automatically in childhood and generally don't discuss, quite as explicitly? Clients must master certain critical life skills as they begin to move from the burn-off phase to the evidence building phase. These skills are also essential with some different emphasis during mourning and again, with a stronger intellectual focus, during the reconnecting stage. At this point more of the woman clearly has become available.

Recovering women must defend themselves efficiently in the present, develop more coping skills and learn how to make their own life decisions. After a lifetime of initially being disempowered through sexual abuse and its aftermath, followed by drug dependence, many addicted victims lack decision making skills. They do not know how to make decisions based on a combination of external as well as internal cues, something adults are generally able to do naturally. They follow the advice of others or decide impulsively and frequently live with regrets. As an aside, "making suggestions" is a skillfully built in part of twelve step programs, giving these women the opportunity for reliable reality testing without disempowering them.

This provides safety and time for these women to move through the recovery stages and develop life skills. This lack of ability to make decisions may be open to misinterpretation unless the clinician has awareness of these skill deficiencies. Since we as clinicians generally take these life skills for granted, we must be cautious not to label their absence in these women's emotional repertoires as any kind of resistance. They frequently have to uncover, even design, an internal strategy that can assist them in decision making. Coping skills and decision making are interwoven with motivation skills. If the girlchild was habitually disempowered, it is unlikely that these skills developed sufficiently. They were then further stymied by the drug use, which inhibits planning, creating some form of vital future. For this reason, learning and memory skills are frequently poorly developed. There may have been little use for them in childhood. Their development was further hampered when these women moved into their addiction. It is no wonder then that these women don't trust their reality testing, another life skill. This leads to their limited ability to give meaning, particularly of a new, more helpful kind, to their experiences in balance with external validation. When a survivor of sexual and chemical abuse can trust her reality testing based on a grounded belief system, she has accomplished a great deal in her recovery.

Since sexual abuse, particularly incest, is generally cumulative, there is likely to be a substantial portion of the woman's childhood where her personal experiences were invalidated in favor of the perpetrator(s)' and possibly his enablers'. Since these individuals, generally adults, but always those with substantial power over the victim, imposed their reality onto the girlchild, the victim will have grown up with an unformed or negative image of self, the world and her relationship to it. If she then became submerged in an addiction process, she will have had little opportunity to further her reality testing skills in a positive way for reasons described earlier. Reality testing often needs to be demonstrated in various forms, either in therapy or other trustworthy situations. In the fund of the woman's experiences she for instance does not have appropriate models to show or respond to emotions such as fear, hurt, anger or sadness. She may be unfamiliar with her right to keep herself safe.

Example: H., a police woman, frequently got into dangerous situations with insufficient protection. She often got hurt, even shot once. She only shrugged when this came up in therapy. H. was severely sexually and physically abused as a child by an alcoholic father and she herself became addicted to alcohol and cocaine. Initially, and well into therapy, she was incapable of putting words to her feelings beyond "good" or "bad," getting frustrated if I attempted to get further descriptions. She could not formulate plans to physically protect herself either.

Discussion: Eventually H. understood that putting herself in danger not only repeated her childhood experience but also dealt with an overriding belief: it relieved her from the guilt over what she had assumed was her participation in the incest. Extreme fear had prohibited resistance and she also blamed herself for the autonomic physical responses at that time which she had felt substantiated her participation.

Generally, belief systems are functional when they are created originally. For instance, the child in an abusive home may decide that the world is a dangerous place. Once the belief system is entrenched, the rules guiding these beliefs make the world smaller. New information cannot enter, the woman continues to function out of her past belief system and her world becomes impoverished in the present, remaining a closed system. There is an old story about the difference between rats and humans. When, in a laboratory, cheese is put at the end of a tunnel, the rat will learn to go down that tunnel to find the cheese. Once you take the cheese away, after some tries the rat will stop going down that tunnel. The difference with people is that they keep going down that tunnel because they believe the cheese "ought" to be there. The story demonstrates both the trauma of sexual abuse victims caught in the repetition compulsion as well as the drug abuser who keeps hoping for the same effects and satisfaction from the drug.

Addicted adult survivors of sexual abuse generally have a paucity of internal markers for pain and hurt. They are disconnected from an authentic self in favor of a superimposed self who attempted, while mostly powerless, to help the girlchild survive. This survival mechanism, a defense system, continues, without being questioned sufficiently by these women in adulthood. They generally react automatically to triggers perceived through old filters. These are dysfunctional, incongruous in the present, but remain there until these women feel safe and ready to begin their work of recovery.

All these adult skills need to be mastered sufficiently so that the woman begins to feel that she is healing, moving from victim to survivor and beyond. The clinician's task is to place much emphasis on this client's testing out the world while experimenting with additional "filters" until she can feel competently grounded. The client can then actively participate in and have a relationship with her world. During this time, new values and beliefs are formed. The woman generally undergoes a series of belief changes about the self and the world, which naturally is the crux of therapy and a decisive time in the therapeutic relationship. This time has certainly been recognized in the literature in various forms, when the client clearly moves from victim to survivor and from survivor to the next phase where she perceives herself as sufficiently healed and separated from her history.

Evans and Sullivan (1995) find important commonalities in predicting positive treatment outcomes. They state that these women have a more positive self image as children and maintained a sense of hope through an active fantasy life. Also, they were more assertive, had a greater internal locus of control and had some consistent coping strategies. They were able to put the blame on the perpetrator(s) instead of themselves and performed well in other areas which contradicted negative messages.

CASE VIGNETTE

A. grew up with an alcoholic father who left the household when she was six years old. She and her younger brother remained with a severe borderline mother who was physically abusive on a daily basis. A.'s father began a new family and anytime A. went to him for comfort, she was met by incestuous behavior from him. He clearly only considered the daughters from his second marriage his real children. Both A. and her brother became drug addicts. The brother died of an overdose some years ago. A. regularly stabilized herself on medication and held a responsible job.

Discussion: A. saw me initially when she was with a severely addicted partner and was taking care of her brother and his addicted girlfriend simultaneously. A. left after some time because she couldn't handle the pain of her memories. She relapsed but when she returned to treatment she had been straight for eight months and only saw her boyfriend during periods when he would stop using. She had broken off the relationship with her mother and came to see me to deal with of her father's rejection now that she applied boundaries to him as well. She successfully worked through this, bought a house with a girlfriend and maintains a responsible job. Clearly, A. has restored a functional timeline, has acquired significant life skills but at times still has difficulties regulating her emotional life.

This coincides with Herman's (1992) criteria of trauma survival: a strong sense of being able to affect (one's) own history, a "capacity to preserve social connections" and "active coping strategies" (p. 58). A paucity of internal resources, the inability to execute basic life tasks and skills hinders progression through recovery phases. It arrests further development and gives rise to a cyclic way of living where hope continues to give way to despair, as is demonstrated by the following case.

CASE VIGNETTE

T. and her sister were physically and sexually abused, first by their alcoholic father, then their drug dependent step father. The mother was an alcoholic who was absent during her daughters' childhood. T. describes hunger, lack of clothing and other deprivation. Her sister suicided when she was seventeen. T. uses marijuana daily but wants to stop now that her own two children are becoming aware of this. T.'s husband has a job that keeps him away three out of four weeks and when home, he is emotionally abusive. T. has no friends and is a housewife. She alternately demonizes and elevates her drug as a saving grace and is in and out of therapy. She has been tried on a variety of medications without success.

Discussion: In reviewing Herman's (1992) as well as Evans and Sullivan's (1995) positive treatment prognosis, T. has virtually no access to personal resources. This is supported by Chu (1990) as well who writes in *Women Survivors of Sexual Abuse* that treatment is far more complicated when the sexual abuse began at a young age, when the women have had insufficient opportunity to protect themselves and when their defenses are generally passive in nature.

ROLE OF THE CLINICIAN

The clinician is most productive in an interactive relationship with these women. The sexual material is generally so threatening and painful, the loss of the drug so unbearable to accept, that especially early in treatment it is not realistic to expect the client to be forthcoming. The clinician must be cautious not to overpower this client. The literature suggests that even in case of sexual abuse alone, without the complication of chemical dependency, this may be the one exception to the rule that the clinician may wait for a client to present her material. Much of the time it needs to be carefully and gently elicited because of the tremendously painful energy attached to it. This is combined with a natural reluctance to give up a drug when it feels like this drug has been the woman's only "reliable" resource for her survival, regardless how much damage it has caused. So it is up to the clinician to be sufficiently active and participatory. She must pace appropriately, remain attuned, respectful and sustain safety during treatment.

It is essential that the clinician assists the addicted survivor of sexual abuse in ways to most fully make use of a twelve step program so that she can join a safe and structured world, larger than the therapeutic process and which makes its own contributions. The more safe spheres these clients enter and surround themselves with, the greater their chances are of achieving success in their recovery. Recovery, with its many facets, demands a plethora of modalities besides therapy.

Since these women have a high probability of being rewounded, rapid accumulation of reliable external resources such as twelve step program participation is again emphasized. Addicted victims of sexual abuse depend by definition on external resources which may create a double bind position in therapy. On one hand, dependency will be frightening to these women who have been harmed while they were powerless, on the other hand, drug dependence and erosion of a sense of self makes this dependence on the clinician almost unavoidable. The clinician finds herself navigating between the needs of the client to be dependant and her fear and resentment of this dependency. Issues of transference and counter transference are especially relevant then, but beyond the scope of this chapter. Clinicians are fortunate that in recent years more effective trauma approaches have been explored. Earlier in this book, EMDR is discussed at length and in my practice this technique in the various phases of recovery, and adjusted to these phases, has been of important and long lasting benefit. Other trauma strategies that go beyond the scope of this chapter from Neurolinguistic Programming and Milton Erikson's work (Dolan, 1991) are gentle and effective in dealing with trauma. They assist in restoring the client's timeline and grounding her in her adult self. The most important part of this process, though, is sustaining the therapeutic alliance, being attuned to this wounded woman who needs to know that the clinician is someone who will go shoulder to shoulder with her, ask nothing of her that is not on her behalf and remain trustworthy in her reality testing. Then ultimately, the woman who remains in the recovery process learns to honor her past, lead a full life in the present and allow for a path to the future. She will manage her addiction and drive toward revictimization to achieve optimal integration of parts of self, minimizing internal fragmentation.

FINAL COMMENTS

In Martin Buber's terms (1987), addicted victims of sexual abuse live in a "I it" relationship, a cyclic one, rather than a "I Thou" relationship, not in the world, but in a world of their own "surrounded by a multitude of content" which has "no present, only the past." They have "nothing but object." "But objects subsist in time that has been. True beings live in the present, the life of objects is in the past" (p. 13). However, I amend this with the words of Joan Dideon in "Slouching Toward Bethlehem" who writes:

> I think we are well advised to remain on nodding terms with the people we used to be, whether we find them attractive company or not. Otherwise they run up unannounced and surprise us, come hammering on the mind's door at four AM on a bad night and demand who deserted them, betrayed them, who is going to make amends. (p. 147)

Essentially all parts of self need to be connected since any part that remains left may continue to carry the wounded self and present behavior that can revictimize these women. Gilligan, in the *Courage to Love* (1997), states that to be whole is "to learn to dance with a broken heart" (p. 134), that the safest way to protect oneself is to open oneself further into the world. That this is very difficult for the addicted survivor of sexual abuse is a given. Real healing will come in the end when she truly knows that she will keep herself safe while continuing to become whole, expanding her world and her relationship with her world.

REFERENCES

Allison, D. (1992) Bastard Out of Carolina. New York: Harper and Row.

Andreas, S. and Andreas, C. (1987) Change Your Mind–And Keep The Change. Moab, UT: Real People Press.

Bass, E. and Kemper, K. (1994) Is Abuse During Childhood a Risk Factor for Developing Substance Abuse Problems as an Adult? Journal of Development and Behavioral Pediatrics.

Berstein, D. (2000) Childhood Trauma and Drug Addiction. Alcoholism Quarterly V.18(3).

Bloom, S. (1997) Creating Sanctuary. New York: Routledge Publications.

Blume, S. (1990) Secret Survivors. New York: Ballentine Books.

Bowen Center for the Study of the Family Symposium, 2001 and 2002. Papero, D. presenter.

Buber, M. (1987) I and Thou. New York: McMillan Publishing Co.

Carnes, P. (1997) The Betrayal Bond. Deerfield Beach, FL: Health Communications, Inc.

Chew, J. (1998) Women Survivors of Sexual Abuse. Binghamton, NY: The Haworth Press.

Chiavaroli, T. (1992) Rehabilitation from Substance Abuse in Individuals with a History of Sexual Abuse. Journal of Substance Abuse Treatment, V.10 (2).

Chu, J. (1990) Rebuilding Shattered Lives: The Responsible Treatment of Complex Post Traumatic and Dissociative Disorders. New York: John Wiley and Sons.

Clark, H. et al. (2001) Violent Traumatic Events and Drug Use Severity. Journal of Substance Abuse Treatment.

Courtois, C. (1998) Healing the Incest Wound. New York: W.W. Norton and Co.

Courtois, C. (1995) Therapeutic Approaches to Post Traumatic Stress Disorder and Incest. Cape Cod Summer Syposium, MA.

Dalenberg, C. (2000) Countertransference and the Treatment of Trauma. Washington, DC: American Psychological Association Press.

Dayton, T. (2000) Trauma and Addiction. Deerfield Beach, FL: Health Communication, Inc.

Dembo, R. et al. (1999) Physical Abuse, Sexual Victimization and Illicit Drug Use: Replication of a Structural Analysis Among a New Sample of High Risk Youth. Journal of Violence and Victims.

Didion, J. (1990) Slouching Toward Bethlehem. New York: Farrar, Straus and Giroux.

Dolan, Y. (1991) Resolving Sexual Abuse. New York: W.W Norton and Co.

Evans, K. and Sullivan, E. (1995) Treating Addicted Survivors of Trauma. New York: The Guilford Press.

Foa, E. et al. (2000) Effective Treatments for Post Traumatic Stress Disorder. New York: The Guilford Press.

Fullilove, M. et al. (1993) Violence, Trauma and Post Traumatic Stress Disorder Among Women Drug Users. Journal of Traumatic Stress, V.6 (4).

Gilligan, S. (1997) The Courage to Love. New York: W.W Norton and Co.

Harris, M. (1998) Trauma Recovery and Empowerment. New York, NY: The Free Press.

Herman, J. (1992) Trauma and Recovery. New York: Harper Collins.

Johnson, S. (2002) Emotionally Focused Couple Therapy with Trauma Survivors. New York: The Guilford Press.

Kroll, J. (1993) PTSD/Borderlines in Therapy–Finding the Balance. New York: W.W. Norton and Co.

Kushner, H. (1981) When Bad Things Happen to Good People. New York: Avon Books.

Linehan, M. (1993) Skill Training Manual for Treating Borderline Personality Disorders. New York: The Guilford Press.

Mastering Counseling Skills with the Masters (2002). Masterson, J. Symposium. Washington, D.C.

Meichenbaum, D. (1997) A Clinical Handbook/Practical Therapist Manual for Assessing and Treating Adults with Post Traumatic Stress Disorder. Ontario, Canada: Institute Press.

Miller, A. (1990) Banished Knowledge–Facing Childhood Injuries. New York: Double Day.

Miller, A. (1984) For Your Own Good–Hidden Cruelty in Child Rearing and Roots of Violence. New York: Farrar, Straus and Giroux.

Miller, B. et al. (1987) The Role of Childhood Sexual Abuse in the Development of Alcoholism in Women. Journal of Violence and Victims.

Miller, D. and Guidry, L. (2001) Addictions and Trauma Recovery: Healing the Body, Mind and Spirit, New York: W.W. Norton and Co.

Najavits, L. (2002) Seeking Safety. New York: The Guilford Press.

O'Hanlon, B. (1994) Even From a Broken Web: Respectful Solution Oriented Therapy for Sexual Abuse and Trauma. New York: W.W. Norton and Co.

Rothchild, B. (2000) The Body Remembers: The Psychophysiology of Trauma and Trauma Treatment. New York: W.W. Norton and Co.

Saakvitne, K. (1996) Intensive Psychotherapy with Survivors: Advanced Issues in Transference and Counter Transference Dynamics. Presentation, Fourth Annual Conference on Advances in Treating Survivors of Abuse and Trauma. Albuquerque, NM.

Sack, D. (1990) No More Secrets, No More Shame. Washington, D.C.: The Pia Press.

Scharff, J. and Scharff, D. (1994) Object Relations Therapy of Physical and Sexual Trauma. Northvale, NJ: Jason Aronson.

Schiraldi, G. (2000) The Post Traumatic Stress Disorder Source Book. Los Angeles: Lowell House.

Schwartz, R. (1995) Internal Family Systems Therapy. New York: The Guilford Press.

Shapiro, E. (1995) Eye Movement Densensitization and Reprocessing: Basic Principles, Protocols and Procedures. New York: The Guilford Press.

Van Der Kolk, B. (1996) Traumatic Stress: The Effects of Overwhelming Experiences on Mind, Body and Society. New York: The Guilford Press.

Vogelman-Sinne, S. et al. (1998) EMDR-Chemical Dependency Treatment Manual. Draft.

Volpicelli, J. et al. (1999) The Role of Uncontrollable Trauma in the Development of Post Traumatic Stress Disorder and Alcohol Addiction. Journal of Alcohol Research and Health.

Weis, R. (1996) Understanding Personality Problems and Addictions Workbook. Minnesota: Hazelton Publications.

Whitfield, C. (1989) Healing the Child Within. Deerfield Beach, FL: Health Communications.

Wilson, J., Friedman, M., and Lindy, J. (2001) Treating Psychological Trauma and Post Traumatic Stress Disorder. New York: The Guilford Press.

Zeig, J. (1985) Ericksonian Psychotherapy, Volume II. Clinical Applications. New York: Brunner Mazel.

Counselor Self-Care in Work
with Traumatized, Addicted People

Patricia A. Burke, MSW
Bruce Carruth, PhD, LCSW
David Prichard, PhD

SUMMARY. This chapter examines the impact on substance abuse professionals of working with traumatized, addicted clients in terms of secondary trauma, vicarious trauma, burnout, and countertransference. Each of these is examined in turn, and then individual, team, and organizational strategies and recommendations for counselor self-care are presented within a strengths-based framework. *[Article copies available for a fee from The Haworth Document Delivery Service: 1-800-HAWORTH. E-mail address: <docdelivery@haworthpress.com> Website: <http://www.HaworthPress. com> © 2006 by The Haworth Press, Inc. All rights reserved.]*

KEYWORDS. Secondary trauma, burnout, countertransference

The authors wish to express their appreciation to the staff of the Tri-County Mental Health Services and those individuals whose stories appear here. Identifying information was changed to protect people's privacy in accordance with professional and ethical guidelines.

[Haworth co-indexing entry note]: "Counselor Self-Care in Work with Traumatized, Addicted People." Burke, Patricia A., Bruce Carruth, and David Prichard. Co-published simultaneously in *Journal of Chemical Dependency Treatment* (The Haworth Press, Inc.) Vol. 8, No. 2, 2006, pp. 283-301; and: *Psychological Trauma and Addiction Treatment* (ed: Bruce Carruth) The Haworth Press, Inc., 2006, pp. 283-301. Single or multiple copies of this article are available for a fee from The Haworth Document Delivery Service [1-800-HAWORTH, 9:00 a.m. - 5:00 p.m. (EST). E-mail address: docdelivery@haworthpress.com].

doi:10.1300/J034v08n02_14

INTRODUCTION

This chapter examines the need for self-care among counselors who work with traumatized, addicted people. The impact on counselors of working with traumatized people is well-documented (Drake & Yadama, 1996; Farber & Hiefetz, 1982; Figley, 1995; Hesse, 2002; Kassam-Adams, 1995; McCann & Pearlman, 1990; Prichard, 2004; Regehr, Hemsworth, Leslie, Howe & Chau, 2004). What is missing in the literature is a body of research that examines the impact on counselors of working with co-existing trauma and addiction experiences. This is problematic because there is a body of research that clearly suggests comorbidity of PTSD and substance abuse (DiNitto et al., 2002; Hilarski, 2004; Khantzian, 1997; Schuckit & Hesselbrock, 1994).

This chapter examines the impact on substance abuse professionals of working with traumatized, addicted clients in terms of secondary trauma, vicarious trauma, burnout, and countertransference. Each of these is examined in turn, and then individual, team, and organizational strategies and recommendations for counselor self-care are presented within a strengths-based framework.

SECONDARY TRAUMA

Counselors who work with addicted, traumatized clients are at risk for developing secondary traumatic stress symptoms. Secondary trauma refers to the manifestation of posttraumatic stress symptoms in counselors, that are based on exposure to client narratives (Figley, 1983; Figley, 1995; Miller, Stiff & Ellis, 1988). Symptoms parallel those experienced by clients experiencing posttraumatic stress, and include re-experiencing the client's traumatic event through intrusive recollections, dreams, distressing reminders of the event; avoidance and numbing of feelings and reminders of the event; and persistent arousal including hypervigilance for the traumatized person (Figley, 1995). Secondary Traumatic Stress is "nearly identical to PTSD, except that exposure to knowledge about a traumatizing event experienced by a significant other is associated with the set of STSD symptoms, and PTSD symptoms are directly connected to the sufferer, the person experiencing primary traumatic stress" (p. 8).

JOHN'S STORY OF SECONDARY TRAUMA

John is a 42-year old addiction counselor in an outpatient mental health facility. He has been struggling the past 2 months with changes in his functioning. He states that he has been experiencing insomnia for the first time in his life, and that when he does sleep, has vivid nightmares about the war in Iraq, with a specific image of a young boy being shot in the chest and writhing on the ground in pain as he lay dying. John also talks about decreased concentration and intrusive thoughts of the boy dying in a pool of blood and the sounds of people yelling in a foreign language. John is not a combat veteran and has never been in war. These symptoms started shortly after John started working with Brian, a combat veteran of the war in Iraq who had been relating in great detail his combat experiences. John has been able to clearly identify the link between his intrusive re-experiencing of the traumatic event and the images that arose in his mind during the repeated telling of Brian's narrative of his war experiences.

VICARIOUS TRAUMA

Pearlman and Mac Ian (1995) define vicarious trauma as the cumulative effects on a therapist of engaging in therapeutic relationships with trauma victims. It is the counselor's traumatic reactions that are secondary to their exposure to clients' traumatic experiences (McCann & Pearlman, 1990). Similar to secondary trauma, vicarious trauma is a direct reaction to traumatic client material and is not a reaction to past personal life experiences (Figley, 1995). Whereas the cause of secondary trauma and vicarious trauma are the same (exposure to specific client traumatic experiences), the manifestations differ. While symptoms of secondary trauma often closely parallel those of PTSD (Figley, 1995), vicarious trauma is indicative of a deeper and more generalized transformation of the psychological functioning of counselors, including a shift in the cognitive schema in how they view themselves, others, and the world (Trippany, Kress & Wilcoxon, 2004). This transformation occurs by exposure of counselors to explicit and graphic details of clients' traumatic experiences during counseling sessions (Pearlman & Mac Ian, 1995). In addition to secondary trauma symptoms (such as intrusive imagery), vicarious trauma may manifest more broadly and generally by changes in trust, suspiciousness, feelings of control, issues of intimacy, esteem needs, safety concerns, cynicism, despair, emptiness, and pessimism (Pearlman & Saakvitne, 1995a; Rosenbloom, Pratt, & Pearlman, 1995; Steed & Downing, 1992).

JOANNE'S STORY OF VICARIOUS TRAUMA

Joanne is a 35-year old addiction counselor in an adolescent addiction treatment facility. She has been employed at the facility for 5 years and has emerged as a specialist for addicted teenage girls with sexual trauma histories, which includes most of the girls at the facility. She has also become aware of the fact that many teenage trauma survivors self-medicate with alcohol and other drugs. Joanne is familiar with secondary trauma and has learned to accept the intrusive thoughts and images from interviews with scores of abused and traumatized girls. Her most frequent images are those created by her work with 12-year old Abby who had been abused repeatedly over many years by several family members. Abby has been blind since birth, and therefore her narrative uses other sensory descriptions, which stand out for Joanne and trigger her own detailed visual images of the abuse Abby has endured and survived. More recently, Joanne has become aware of a general feeling of distrust of men, particularly those men who have any association with her children. She has repeated intrusive and graphic thoughts of her daughter as being the girl being abused in Abby's narrative. These experiences have caused Joanne to become extremely protective of her daughter to the point where her daughter is now beginning to feel suffocated. Joanne has also developed difficulty with emotional and sexual intimacy with her husband.

BURNOUT

Burnout refers to a generalized state of physical, emotional, and mental exhaustion that counselors experience by long-term involvement in emotionally demanding situations (Figley, 1999; Pearlman & Saakvitne, 1995a; Sexton, 1999; Pines & Aronson, 1988). Symptoms may include exhaustion, depersonalization, and a reduced feeling of accomplishment. While vicarious trauma is seen as a traumatic reaction to exposure to specific client narratives and experiences (Trippany, Kress & Wilcoxon, 2004), burnout is more the general psychological stress of working with difficult clients (Figley, 1995).

SUZANNE'S STORY OF BURNOUT

Suzanne is a 51-year old counselor who specializes in working with addicts in NYC. During her 11 years in corrections, Suzanne has come to realize that most of the women in the facility have a history of sexual abuse and many have used substances to numb out and to block the memories of their abuse. She is convinced that treatment for many of the women inmates should be trauma-focused with addictions treated as a co-existing disorder, or in many cases, a symptom of the trauma-related condition. Suzanne has become increasingly disillusioned with her job, and would have left the position years ago, if she was not concerned about her retirement benefits. Suzanne has been in the system long enough to have seen the recidivism among her inmate clients, and she has grown bitter at the lack of support of the corrections administration for providing adequate funding for trauma-focused practice with the women in the facility. She feels that addiction services are under-funded and that there needs to be a major clinical shift toward including trauma-based treatment for the inmates. She has little support for her concerns, and has grown increasingly bitter and frustrated by the placating attitude of the corrections administration. She feels that she is wasting her time and providing inadequate and misguided care for her clients.

COUNTERTRANSFERENCE

Countertransference has been an ongoing topic of interest to both addiction and trauma clinicians. Both substance abusers and trauma survivors have significant potential to evoke strong, and often unconscious, emotional, physical and interpersonal reactions from others and particularly, their counselors. When a client presents with a co-occurring trauma *and* addictive disorder, the potential for this countertransferential reaction becomes magnified.

Freud (1961/1910) first described countertransference as the analyst's blind spots, which became limitations or obstacles to the analysis of the patient. In this sense, the term has a negative connotation and is seen as a hindrance to therapy. Forrest (2002) has described the evolution of thinking about countertransference and notes that most contemporary discussions of this phenomenon make note of the potential negative impact on the therapeutic process, but also recognize that it is an inevitable aspect of therapy and can even foster growth and enhance the self-awareness of both the clinician and client.

More recently analytic writers, as well as writers from other schools of psychotherapy, have described countertransference in more generic terms; specifically, that countertransference embodies all emotional reactions of the counselor toward the client. In this sense, countertransference can be highly productive in the therapeutic environment, embodying the counselor's intuition, perceptions and impressions.

While not all schools of psychotherapy give great attention to countertransference, it is reasonable to assume that most therapy orientations acknowledge that the conscious and unconscious emotional, cognitive, physical and interpersonal reactions of the counselor to the client influence the conduct of therapy, and as such, should be monitored and discussed in clinical supervision. It also seems reasonable to assume that all counselors will experience certain clients that evoke more countertransferential reactions than other clients and that, through self-observation, supervision and the counselor's own therapy, these reactions can be mediated. It has been noted that addicts (Forrest, 2002) and trauma survivors (Pearlman & Saakvitne, 1995a) tend to produce strong countertransferential reactions among their counselors.

BOB'S COUNTERTRANSFERENCE REACTION

Bob acknowledges feeling "stuck" with an older, depressed female client. He finds himself being angry with her for her "impotence" and apparent unwillingness to change. He acknowledges that he "dreads" a particular afternoon of the week, knowing that she will be his two o'clock appointment. In part to cover his anger, he is solicitous of her and offers her helpful advice about combating her depression. He is also aware that other depressed clients don't tend to evoke the same response in him and he can remain present with them, in a more compassionate and objective position. During a supervision session, the supervisor asks, "Who does this woman remind you of?" Further exploration reveals that Bob's mother, a single parent, was cyclically depressed during his childhood and adolescence. During periods of her depression, Bob, the eldest child in a family of three, felt abandoned, rageful and helpless. He sublimated the rage by being the good son, taking care of his mom as best he could, and deferring his own needs. Later, in a therapy session, the client expressed concern that Bob was angry with her for not improving more quickly. As a result of the insight he achieved in supervision and his increased awareness of the link between his personal history and his current reactions to this client, Bob was able to share his sense of feeling helpless with her in the face of her depression.

COUNTERTRANSFERENCE DYNAMICS

Among traumatized, chemically dependent clients, certain dynamics tend to evoke strong emotional responses in many counselors. As Carruth (2002) noted, "Chemically dependent patients have a unique ability to provoke our own history. In early recovery, they excite our rescue fantasies by improving rapidly. Similarly, their relapses have the potential to activate our sense of impotence. We shift from therapist to parent offering well-intentioned advice and admonishments. The addicted client activates our past experience with addicted people in our own lives. Also, of course, in this field, where so many of the care providers are recovering addicts themselves, a counselor's experience with his or her own recovery cannot help but affect how the counselor relates to the recovery needs of the client."

Some of the more characteristic ego defenses of addicts lend themselves to countertransferential responses of counselors. For instance, addicted clients will deflect from their own internal processes, their pain, their low self-esteem and their emptiness by getting the counselor to describe their own recovery, or offer intellectualizations about the dynamics of addiction or explanations of how a twelve-step program works. In an effort to avoid confrontation, clients will intuitively "read" the needs of the counselor for validation, good intent, empathic connection or other needs, and will offer positive feedback to the counselor. Other clients will intuitively perceive content in the counseling session that makes the counselor uncomfortable and emphasize that content in the conversation, thereby gaining a power advantage in the relationship.

Similarly, clients with trauma disorders present unique countertransferential challenges. Pearlman and Saakvitne (1995a) cite responses to incest, work with dissociative processes, therapeutic boundary problems with trauma survivors and gender (sexual) issues as four significant factors that incite countertransferential reactions in clinicians treating trauma survivors. In addition, Dalenberg (2000) cites issues of client doubt, reality testing disturbance (e.g., "Does the therapist believe me when others haven't?"), issues of blame and shame, and counselor responses to repetition compulsion and client affect, particularly anger, as significant countertransferential issues. Herman (1992) discusses the clinician's defense to the helplessness experienced in working with trauma survivors and quotes Henry Krystal: "The impulse to play God is as ubiquitous as it is pathogenic."

The emerging pain, the pain of past event(s), the intensity of the therapeutic relationship, and the need for the clinician to serve as a container for the exposed content all significantly contribute to the potential for countertransference. For both trauma survivors and addicts, the projective defense, disowning self-deficits, deep wounds and self-perception of blame and shame invite the counselor to become a receptacle for unwarranted projections. Countertransferential content, left unexplored and unexpressed, has the potential to aggregate into characteristic negative patterns of reacting to traumatized, addicted clients. These patterns tend to limit the potential of the therapeutic process to heal and become an ongoing source of emotional and professional depletion for the counselor.

COUNSELOR SELF-CARE

A review of the literature on counselor self-care suggests individual, team and organizational strategies for mental health helpers and substance abuse counselors working with traumatized, addicted clients. Perhaps the single most important step in addressing the impact of secondary and vicarious trauma on clinicians is the recognition both personally and organizationally that these phenomena exist and are common, human responses of compassion and empathy that, without which, the counselor would not be particularly helpful. It is, after all, the empathetic response in the helping relationship that dissolves alienation and provides the client with a sense of being valued and accepted (Rogers, 1980). Unfortunately, in some contexts, there is little or no understanding or acceptance of the idea that reactions to traumatic material are not the result of personal weakness or inadequacy on the part of the clinician, but a normal response to the trauma itself (Astin, 1997). The key to self-care is finding a balance between being vulnerable so that the clinician can be present and available to clients' intense pain and taking reasonable steps toward protecting his/her own sense of integrity in the face of what can be an assault on that integrity, sense of faith, and worldview.

INDIVIDUAL STRATEGIES

While there may be tremendous diversity with respect to specific individual strategies to prevent and/or ameliorate secondary trauma reactions, vicarious trauma, and burn-out, it is clear that these strategies must encompass a holistic approach, including activities that address the counselor's mental/cognitive, emotional, psychological, relational, physical, creative, and spiritual needs both personally and professionally (Saakvitne & Pearlman, 1996). In recent studies, when mental health professionals were asked what activities helped them find balance and cope with the stress of trauma work, they responded with a wide range of activities including talking with colleagues about difficult clinical situations, attending workshops, social activities with family and friends, exercising, limiting client sessions, balancing caseloads with trauma and non-trauma clients, making sure to take vacations, taking breaks during the workday, listening to music, walking in nature, and seeking emotional support in both personal and professional arenas (Saakvitne & Pearlman, 1996). In addition, the literature suggests that personal psychotherapy may be a healthy positive coping strategy for mitigating the impact of working with traumatized addicted clients (Hesse, 2002; Pearlman & Saakvitne, 1995b; Yassen, 1995) and helping counselors enhance insight, self-awareness, and self-reflection needed for the investigation of countertransference issues.

The literature also suggests professional strategies such as supportive, relationally-based clinical supervision that addresses countertransference issues in a non-judgmental atmosphere and helps counselors untangle their personal histories from the issues that may arise in the current therapeutic relationship with the client (Etherington, 2000; Pearlman & Saakvitne, 1995a; Sexton, 1999; Walker, 2004) and specialized training in trauma theory which can not only provide the clinician with clinical methods and skills, but also "offers intellectual containment in the face of violence and the powerlessness/helplessness it can engender" (Yassen, 1995, p. 198).

SPIRITUAL SELF-CARE

Just as trauma can result in a loss of meaning, hope, connection, and a shattered world view for the client (Herman, 1992), secondary trauma and particularly the long-term impact of vicarious trauma can engender the same effects on the counselor (Pearlman & Saakvitne, 1995b; Saakvitne & Pearlman, 1996). Trauma counselors report fewer disruptions in their beliefs about the world when they engage in spiritually oriented activities (Schauben & Frazier, 1995) such as meditating, mindfulness practice, being in nature, journaling, volunteer work, church attendance, and finding a spiritual community (Saakvitne & Pearlman, 1996; Trippany, White Kress & Allen, 2004). While engaging in spiritual activities can be an important way to enhance a sense of spirituality, the clinical literature suggests that spirituality is a multi-dimensional human experience (Burke, 2005; Canda & Furman, 1999; Carroll, 1998). The thickening of meaning through the exploration of certain themes in people's spiritual narratives including beliefs, principles, practices, experiences, teachers, community, and sanctuary can enhance hope and resilience in traumatized addicted clients (Burke, 2006) and potentially ameliorates the impact of secondary and vicarious trauma on counselors.

COUNSELORS IN RECOVERY

Counselors who report positive personal coping strategies (e.g., physical exercise, spiritual practices, support from friends/family, psychotherapy) are less likely to report symptoms of secondary trauma, than counselors who use negative personal coping strategies (e.g., pornography, alcohol and illicit drug use) (Way, VanDeusen, Martin, Applegate & Jandle, 2004). This finding is particularly significant with regard to addiction professionals who are also in recovery from substance abuse. Clearly, a return to drinking or illicit drug use as a strategy for dealing with secondary trauma reactions would have profoundly detrimental effects on the recovering counselor. In addition to the personal and professional self-care strategies discussed here, it is essential for the recovering counselor (especially whose personal histories also include trauma) to develop a relapse prevention plan. A relapse prevention plan should include identifying high risk situations (which may include the appearance of intrusive memories and anxiety related to secondary trauma reactions) and learning or enhancing cognitive/behavioral skills to respond to those high risk triggers (Marlatt and Gordon, as cited in Lawson, Lawson, and Rivers, 2001).

LINDA'S PERSONAL SELF-CARE PLAN

Linda is a recovering alcoholic with a personal history of trauma who works as a substance abuse counselor in a mental health agency with an integrated substance abuse treatment program. Approximately eighty percent of the people she serves have a history of trauma. She is sometimes triggered by the intensity of the work and specific client narratives. One of her coping skills is to make sure she leaves her work at work. Prior to becoming a substance abuse counselor Linda was a nurse and tells a story about a creative cognitive tool and metaphor she has developed to help her establish a boundary between her work and personal life. Every night, at the end of her shift at the hospital, she would mindfully place her nurse's cap in her locker and make a mental note that she had taken her cap off, signaling the end of her work day. Today she puts a sticker on the steering wheel of her car that says, "cap off." This has become a kind of mindfulness bell, as she prepares to drive home, awakening her to remember herself and her boundaries and leave the intensity of her day at work.

Linda also describes herself as "a walker" and integrates a daily routine of exercise into her self-care plan. She makes sure to take a break at work by going outside, even if it is for a few minutes, to walk, take a few deep breaths and look around. She also makes sure she gets a good night's sleep and has lunch everyday at work with her colleagues. For Linda, the personal relationships she has developed at work and outside of work are deeply sustaining and help keep her from becoming isolated and alone with any trauma reactions that might arise. She also talks of her spiritual life as an extremely valuable resource for her in combating the impact of trauma in both her personal and professional life. She is very involved in her church and has stayed connected to her twelve step recovery network that includes a long-standing relationship with a sponsor. She also finds creative expression through gardening, painting and sculpting, and describes her home as a "sanctuary"– a safe and sacred place where the overwhelm from work cannot intrude and she feels free to take her "cap off."

TEAM STRATEGIES

Munroe et al. (1995) propose a team approach to preventing secondary trauma and vicarious traumatization. They suggest that a treatment team can prevent and/or ameliorate the impact of trauma reactions on clinicians by accepting and normalizing secondary trauma reactions, providing a community experience that absorbs an individual's traumatic reaction and diffuses it, providing a family-like support system in which the clinician feels cared for, and when necessary a safe container within which trauma reenactments, parallel process, and counter-transference can be raised into everyday consciousness and challenged.

In addition, peer supervision can offer individual counselors support and validation, an opportunity to debrief and share reactions to clients' trauma material, and a place to share positive coping strategies with colleagues (Trippany et al., 2004). Clinicians in private practice who engage in trauma work would benefit from attending a private supervision/professional development or peer supervision group that can provide the same functions as a treatment team.

SUPERVISION AND COUNTERTRANSFERENCE

Perhaps the single-most important resource in helping counselors manage the intense countertransferential affective responses to clients' trauma material previously described in this chapter is supportive, relationally-oriented clinical supervision. Pearlman and Saakvitne (1995a) recommend four components of trauma therapy supervision: (1) a solid theoretical grounding in trauma theory and trauma therapy; (2) a relational focus that emphasizes conscious and unconscious aspects of treatment; (3) a respectful and collaborative atmosphere that provides a safe, non-judgmental container within which countertransference and parallel process can be explored; (4) acknowledgment of the phenomenon of vicarious traumatization and education regarding its impact on the clinician. In addition, relationally-based clinical supervision that emphasizes exploration of transference and countertransference should focus on helping the counselor develop a witness stance so that he/she can be present with the client's pain, while remaining at a slight distance from the trauma material (Etherington, 2000); untangling the complexity of the client's transference reactions by reframing "these experiences as positive communications from the client that can lead to therapeutic change" (Etherington, 2000, p. 387); educating counselors about and modeling therapeutic boundary setting and healthy interpersonal interactions (Etherington, 2000; Pearlman & Saakvitne, 1995a; Walker, 2004); and assisting counselors to manage secondary trauma reactions, such as intrusive memories, by providing "not only affective holding and theoretical conceptualizations, but also information about vicarious traumatization and self-care" (Pearlman & Saakvitne, 1995a, p. 369).

In many addiction treatment contexts the focus of treatment is often cognitive-behavioral (which does not emphasize transference and countertransference effects in the therapeutic relationship). In addition, the pressures of managed care, cuts in state and federal funding, and constricting budgets force limits on supervision time for counselors. These factors create an environment in which supervision is often pressured and constricted in focus to behavioral treatment planning, case management, and administrative issues such as record-keeping in an effort to comply with funding and licensing requirements.

In this kind of environment the impact of vicarious trauma, secondary trauma, and countertransference responses of the clinician can be neglected and may eventually lead to burnout. It is not only essential for substance abuse counselors to be engaged in regular, frequent supervision that addresses countertransference, vicarious trauma, and secondary trauma reactions as part of a professional self-care plan, but it is also an ethical imperative (Pearlman & Saakvitne, 1995a). If this is not available at the organization, counselors would be well served to work collectively to advocate for trauma therapy supervision at work and engage in private supervision with a consultant who is trained in trauma theory. Pearlman and Saakvitne (1995a) suggest a minimum of an hour of weekly supervision for experienced clinicians and more for beginning counselors. This recommendation is consistent with recent research which suggests that clinicians new to trauma work are more likely to experience vicarious traumatization (Cunningham, 2003).

Linda's Professional Self-Care Plan

Linda describes three key elements of her professional self-care plan: (1) treatment team meetings; (2) a monthly peer support group at work; and (3) clinical supervision. She describes the multi-disciplinary treatment team as a group of "passionate people" who support her both personally and professionally. In addition to bi-weekly team meetings, the team is also committed to daily debriefings that provide an opportunity for Linda to deal with reactions to trauma material as they arise. The team also shares meals together at lunch, where there is an unspoken rule, "don't talk about clients." Breaking bread together suggests the quality of the family-like support system described by Monroe et al. (1995).

In addition to the treatment team, Linda is a core member of a monthly peer support group at work. She tells a story about how new clinicians at the agency are surprised when they first attend this group. She says that they think they are going to supervision, "but it is really a safe place where we can all feel free to talk about personal issues *and* our feelings about clients. It's a breath of fresh air." Linda also likens the group to twelve step meetings where old-timers offer their wisdom to newcomers about what has been helpful to them in coping with stress and managing secondary trauma reactions.

Finally, Linda's agency provides weekly clinical supervision for her, which she uses to its fullest. She states that "it sets the tone for the whole week." She describes her supervisor as supportive, knowledgeable, optimistic, and someone who "helps me get back on track." One of the most important aspects of the supervision for Linda is its relational focus, with only a secondary emphasis on paperwork and administrative issues.

ORGANIZATIONAL STRATEGIES

While individual and team strategies focused on preventing and reducing the impact of secondary trauma, vicarious traumatization, and burn-out are essential, most substance abuse counselors work in an organizational context where the efficacy of those individual and team strategies is linked to the organization's perspective on trauma and its approach to trauma work. It is the organization's mission and philosophy that shape the norms, values, and culture of the work environment. It is essential, therefore, for addiction treatment organizations to create a trauma-informed environment where trauma and addiction "are addressed within a single system and by a single model of care" (Harris & Fallot, 2001a, p. 57); secondary trauma and vicarious traumatization are accepted as normal aspects of trauma work (Arledge & Wolfson, 2001); where the organization views the problem as systemic and not the result of individual pathology or deficit on the part of the counselor (Sexton, 1999); and where the organization is fully invested in providing adequate financial resources for salaries, a comprehensive benefit package (including insurance for personal counseling), clinical supervision, and trauma therapy training (Trippany et al., 2004).

In addition, the literature suggests that an explicitly supportive, accepting and non-judging work culture may allow staff to share the shame and embarrassment they may feel for experiencing pain and being vulnerable to vicarious trauma (Neumann & Gamble, 1995), and limiting exposure to traumatized clients may prevent vicarious traumatization and burnout (Cerney, 1995; Chrestman, 1995; Yassen, 1995).

TRI-COUNTY MENTAL HEALTH SERVICES:
A TRAUMA-INFORMED APPROACH

Tri-County Mental Health Services (TCMHS) is a comprehensive community-based mental health agency with an integrated substance abuse treatment service that employs approximately four hundred staff across a wide geographic area in Maine (Tri-County Mental Health Services, 2003). In 2001 TCMHS instituted an agency-wide paradigm shift in its philosophy and approach to providing trauma services to its consumers based on a trauma-informed service delivery system (Community Connections, 2003). According to Harris and Fallot (2001b), "to be trauma-informed means to understand the role that violence and victimization play in the lives of most consumers of mental health and substance abuse services and to use that understanding to design service systems that accommodate the vulnerabilities of trauma survivors and allow services to be delivered in a way that will facilitate consumer participation in treatment" (p. 4). Adopting this model has changed the culture of service provision at the agency to one that values a collaborative and strengths-based/empowerment approach and recognizes that consumers' trauma impacts the entire staff. Counselor stress levels have decreased as a result of consumers becoming more empowered and responsible for their own recovery, the agency-wide recognition of secondary trauma and vicarious traumatization as normal aspects of trauma work, and administrative support for counselor self-care (C. Copeland, personal communication, May 10, 2005).

Integral to this shift to a trauma-informed approach at TCMHS has been the administration's commitment to giving clinicians specialized training in trauma theory and evidence-based approaches to working with trauma. This training has provided clinicians a sense of hope and specific skills that have enhanced their mastery of negotiating the intensity of working with consumers' trauma material (C. Copeland, personal communication, May 10, 2005). In addition, multi-disciplinary treatment teams now have a common philosophical focus based on a relational, collaborative model of working with consumers. This common focus empowers the clinical team and helps them feel more connected and aware (P. Newton, personal communication, May 10, 2005).

The clinicians at TCMHS report that they value this expansion of trauma awareness, the shift toward a more conscious focus on trauma, the non-judgmental culture where trauma is discussed openly, the skills-oriented clinical tools provided in the specialized training, and the formalization of team discussions on vicarious traumatization and clinician self-care (Community Connections, 2003). In addition to the integration of a trauma-informed model, TCMHS also addresses counselor self-care by offering its clinicians a comprehensive benefits package (including EAP services, coverage for personal counseling, and a wellness benefit), and on-going clinical supervision and trauma therapy training.

CONCLUSION

The concepts of secondary trauma, vicarious trauma, countertransference, and burn-out as discussed here are useful in understanding the impact on addiction treatment professionals in working with addicted, traumatized clients. Normalizing these experiences reduces the shame counselors may feel when faced with intense countertransference reactions to client narratives, their own experiences of anxiety, rage, depression, or intrusive memories, or the overwhelm of prolonged exposure to high stress levels which eventually results in burnout.

It is essential for substance abuse counselors and mental health clinicians to take responsibility for developing their own personal and professional self-care plans that include a relapse prevention plan for those in recovery from addiction. Personal self-care strategies should address the mental, emotional, psychological, physical, relational, creative, and spiritual needs of the individual and professional self-care plans must include relationally based trauma therapy supervision/consultation with a focus on resolving countertransference issues.

While personal responsibility is crucial, the clinical and research literature strongly suggests that a team approach can prevent and/or ameliorate the impact of trauma reactions on clinicians. The literature also suggests that mental health and addiction treatment organizations can support clinicians in their efforts by adopting a trauma-informed approach that normalizes secondary trauma reactions and vicarious traumatization, validates and encourages clinician self-care, minimizes the risk of burnout, and creates an atmosphere of empowerment and respect for both the client and the counselor (Arledge & Wolfson, 2001). In this kind of non-blaming and empowering environment counselors can bring their full unconditional presence to this challenging and rewarding work with addicted, traumatized clients *and* feel free to take their "caps off" at the end of each day.

REFERENCES

Arledge, E. & Wolfson, R. (2001). Care of the clinician. In M. Harris & R. D. Fallot (Eds.), *Using Trauma Theory to Design Service Systems* (pp. 91-98). New York: Jossey- Bass.

Astin, M. C. (1997). Traumatic therapy: How helping rape victims affects me as a therapist. *Women & Therapy*, 20(1), 101-109.

Burke, P.A. (2006). Enhancing hope and resilience through a spiritually sensitive focus in the treatment of trauma and addiction, In B. Carruth (Ed.). *Psychological Trauma and Addiction Treatment*, 185-204. New York: Haworth Press.

Burke, P. A. (2005, May/June). Circle of Meaning: A narrative tool for exploring the multi-dimensional nature of spirituality. *Counselor: The Magazine for Addiction Professionals*, 6(3), 22-28.

Canda, E. R. & Furman, L. D. (1999). *Spiritual Diversity in Social Work Practice: The Heart of Helping*. New York: The Free Press.

Carroll, M.M. (1998). Social Work's Conceptualization of Spirituality. *Social Thought: Journal of Religion in the Social Services*, 18(2), 1-13.

Carruth, B. (2002) Foreword. In G. Forrest, *Countertransference in Chemical Dependency Counseling*. New York: Haworth Press.

Cerney, M. (1995). Treating the heroic treater. In C. R. Figley, *Compassion Fatigue: Coping With Secondary Traumatic Stress Disorder in Those Who Treat the Traumatized*. New York: Brunner-Routledge.

Chrestman, K. (1995). Secondary exposure to trauma and self-reported distress among therapists. In B. H. Stamm (Ed.), *Secondary Traumatic Stress: Self-Care Issues for Clinicians, Researchers, and Educators*, Lutherville, MD: Sidran.

Community Connections. (2003, May). *Final report: Trauma informed pilot project at the Rumford Unit of Tri-County Mental Health Services*. Washington, DC: Roger D. Fallot & Maxine Harris.

Cunningham, M. (2003). Impact of trauma work on social work clinicians: Empirical findings. *Social Work*, 48(4), 451-459.

Dalenberg, C. (2000). *Countertransference and the Treatment of Trauma*. Washington, DC: American Psychological Assn. Press.

DiNitto, D., Webb, D., & Rubini, A. (2002). The effectiveness of an integrated treatment approach for clients with dual diagnosis. *Research on Social Work Practice*, 12(5), 621-641.

Drake, B., & Yadama, G. (1996). A structural equation model of burnout and job exiting among child protective service workers. *Social Work Research*, 20(3), 179-187.

Etherington, K. (2000). Supervising counsellors who work with survivors of childhood sexual abuse. *Counselling Psychology Quarterly*, 13(4), 337-389.

Farber, B. & Hiefetz, L. (1982). The process and dimensions of burnout in psychotherapists. *Professional Psychology*, 13, 293-301.

Figley, C. (1995). *Compassion Fatigue: Coping With Secondary Traumatic Stress Disorder in Those Who Treat the Traumatized*. New York: Brunner-Routledge.

Figley, C. (1983). Catastrophes: An overview of family reactions. In C. R. Figley & H. I. McCubbin (Eds.), *Stress and the Family Vol. II: Coping With Catastrophe*. New York: Brunner/Mazel, Inc.

Forrest, G. (2002). *Countertransference in Chemical Dependency Counseling.* New York: Haworth Press.

Freud, S. (1910-11). *Further Prospects for Psycho-analytic Therapy. The Standard Edition of the Complete Psychological Works of Sigmund Freud* (V. 11, p. 141-142). London: Hogarth Press.

Harris, M. & Fallot, R. D. (2001a). Designing trauma-informed addictions services. In M. Harris & R. D. Fallot (Eds.), *Using Trauma Theory to Design Service Systems* (pp. 57-73). New York: Jossey-Bass.

Harris, M. & Fallot, R. D. (2001b). Envisioning a trauma-informed service system: A vital paradigm shift. In M. Harris & R. D. Fallot (Eds.), *Using Trauma Theory to Design Service Systems* (pp. 91-98). New York: Jossey-Bass.

Herman, J. L. (1992). *Trauma and Recovery: The Aftermath of Violence – From Domestic Violence to Political Terror.* New York: Basic Books.

Hesse, A. (2002). Secondary trauma: How working with trauma survivors affects therapists, *Clinical Social Work Journal*, 30(3), 293-309.

Hilarski, C. (2004). The relationship between perceived secondary trauma and adolescent comorbid posttraumatic stress and alcohol abuse: A review. *Stress, Trauma, & Crisis*, 7, 119-132.

Kassam-Adams, N. (1995). The risks of treating sexual trauma: Stress & secondary trauma in psychotherapists. In B. H. Stamm (Ed.), *Secondary Traumatic Stress: Self-Care Issues for Clinicians, Researchers, and Educators*, Lutherville, MD: Sidran.

Khantizan, E. (1997). The self-medication hypothesis of substance use disorders: A reconsideration and recent applications. *Harvard Review Psychiatry*, 4(5), 231-244.

Lawson, G.W., Lawson, A. W. & Rivers, P. C. (2001). *Essentials of Chemical Dependency Counseling (Third Edition)*, Austin, Texas: Pro-Ed, Inc.

McCann, I. & Pearlman, L. (1990). Vicarious traumatization: A framework for understanding the psychological effects of working with victims. *Journal of Traumatic Stress*, 3, 131-149.

Miller, K., Stiff, J., & Ellis, B. (1988). Communication and empathy as precursors to burnout among human service workers. *Communication Monographs*, 55(9), 336-341.

Munroe, J. F., Shay, J., Fisher, L., Makary, C., Rapperport, & Simering, R. (1995). Preventing compassion fatigue: A team treatment model. In C. Figley (Ed.), *Compassion Fatigue: Coping with Secondary Traumatic Stress Disorder in Those Who Treat the Traumatized* (pp. 209-231). New York: Brunner-Routledge.

Neumann, D. & Gamble, S. (1995). Issues in the professional development of psychotherapists: Countertransference and vicarious traumatization in the new trauma therapist. *Psychotherapy*, 32, 341-347.

Pearlman, L. & Mac Ian, P. (1995). Vicarious trauma: An empirical study of the effects of trauma work on trauma therapists. *Professional Psychology: Research & Practice*, 26(6), 558-565.

Pearlman, L. A. & Saakvitne, K. W. (1995a). *Trauma and the Therapist: Countertransference and Vicarious Traumatization in Psychotherapy with Incest Survivors.* New York: W. W. Norton & Company.

Pearlman, L. A. & Saakvitne, K. W. (1995b). Treating therapists with vicarious traumatization and secondary traumatic stress disorders. In C. Figley (Ed), *Compassion Fatigue: Coping with Secondary Traumatic Stress Disorder in Those Who Treat the Traumatized* (pp. 150-177). New York: Brunner-Routledge.

Pines, A. & Aronson, E. (1988). *Career burnout: Causes & Cures.* New York: Free Press

Prichard, D. (2004). Critical Incident Stress and secondary trauma: An analysis of group process. *Groupwork: An Interdisciplinary Journal for Working with Groups,* 14(3), 44-62.

Regehr, C., Hemsworth, D., Leslie, B., Howe, P, & Chau, S. (2004). Predictors of posttraumatic distress in child welfare workers: A linear structural equation model. *Children & Youth Services Review,* 26(4), 331-346.

Rogers, C. (1980). *A Way of Being.* Boston: Houghton Mifflin Company.

Rosenbloom, D., Pratt, A., & Pearlman, L. (1995). Helpers' responses to trauma work: Understanding and intervening in an organization. In B. Stamm (Ed.), *Secondary Traumatic Stress: Self-Care Issues of Clinicians, Researchers, & Educators.* Luterville, MD: Sidran.

Saakvitne, K. W. & Pearlman, L. A. (1996). *Transforming the Pain: A Workbook on Vicarious Traumatization.* New York: W. W. Norton & Company.

Schauben, L. J. & Frazier, P. A. (1995). Vicarious Trauma: The effects on female counselors of working with sexual violence survivors. *Psychology of Women Quarterly,* 19, 49-64.

Schuckit, M. & Hesselbrock, V. (1994). Alcohol dependence and anxiety disorders: What is the relationship [see comments]. *American Journals of Psychiatry,* 151(12), 1723-1734.

Sexton, L. (1999). Vicarious traumatisation of counselors & effects on their workplaces, *British Journal of Guidance & Counseling,* 27(3).

Steed, L., & Downing, R. (1998). A phenomenological study of vicarious traumatisation amongst psychologists and professional counselors working in the field of sexual abuse/assault. *The Australasian Journal of Disaster and Trauma Studies,* 2.

Tri-County Mental Health Services. (2003, March). *Trauma-informed services: A self-assessment and planning protocol.* Rumford, ME: Peggy Newton.

Trippany, R. L., White Kress, V. E., & Wilcoxon, S. A. (2004). Preventing vicarious trauma: What counselors should know when working with trauma survivors. *Journal of Counseling & Development,* 82(Winter), 31-37.

Walker, M. (2004). Supervising practitioners working with survivors of childhood abuse: Countertransference; secondary traumatization and terror. *Psychodynamic Practice,* 10(2), 173-193.

Way, I., vanDeusen, K., Martin, G., Applegate, B., & Jandle, D. (2004). Vicarious trauma: A comparison of clinicians who treat survivors of sexual abuse and sexual offenders. *Journal of Interpersonal Violence,* 19(1), 49-71.

Yassen, J. (1995). Preventing secondary traumatic stress disorder. In C. R. Figley, *Compassion Fatigue: Coping With Secondary Traumatic Stress Disorder in Those Who Treat the Traumatized.* New York: Brunner-Routledge.

Index